For
Harry with...
a true seeker
of wisdom...

Gene Bammel

11/15/11

Everyday Philosophy: Practical Applications

Gene Bammel

authorHOUSE™

1663 LIBERTY DRIVE, SUITE 200
BLOOMINGTON, INDIANA 47403
(800) 839-8640
WWW.AUTHORHOUSE.COM

First published by AuthorHouse 02/21/05

ISBN: 1-4208-2971-8 (sc)

Library of Congress Control Number: 2005900825

Printed in the United States of America
Bloomington, Indiana

This book is printed on acid-free paper.

Table of Contents

Preface

Thinking philosophically involves progressively deepening insight into the same problems. Immanuel Kant proposed that doing philosophy was reflection on these three problems: What can I know? How should I act? What can I hope for? These essays are loosely organized along these lines. The author is not proposing definitive answers to any of these problems. My intention is both to provoke the reader to think about these and other issues, and to provide the reader with some of the materials necessary for this "progressively deepening" insight into the problems we all encounter as we go through life.

This book provides some everyday reflections. As the book develops, the same problems recur, but each time the problems are pursued in somewhat greater depth. Don't rush through this book. One or two reflections per day should be progress enough...

Chapter I.
Once, Over Lightly

1
Everyday Thoughts, Everyday Philosophy

Everyone thinks everyday thoughts, but some do it better than others. The most important "everyday thoughts" are part of a personal quest for wisdom, which we have come to call "philosophy." We all need some kind of "philosophy," just to get us through the day. Most of us acquired our philosophy without much reflection from some outside source, whether a parent, a teacher, a musical group, some character in a novel, or from some significant authority figure.

I became interested in reading the great philosophers while I was in high school, and it has been a life-long pursuit. My purpose in these essays is to encourage the reader to do some thinking, and to assume responsibility for the "philosophical" positions that the reader has. I want the reader to think about the things that are really important, and to see how some great thinkers have grappled with problems similar to your own. My expectation is that these "meditations" will help you understand your own thinking more clearly.

Most of the famous philosophers (Plato, Aristotle, Aquinas, Hume, Kant, Hegel, Whitehead, etc.) built some kind of "system," some coherent body of reflections relating to the nature of reality, the meaning of morality, and finding purpose in life. The critical issues of any philosophy are (1) the basic intuitions or assumptions, and (2) the logic that binds these various intuitions or assumptions together. If you want to criticize or disagree

1

with a philosophy, you either find fault with the basic assumptions the philosopher has made, or with the logic that binds them together into a coherent whole.

Philosophy is often confused with religion, with which it has much in common. But religion is a matter of belief, and relies on some kind of revelation, some kind of commitment of will, while philosophy begins and ends as rational reflection on experience. Both religion and philosophy talk about meaning and purpose, and about morality. Religion is generally a social experience, requiring a "community of faith." Philosophy requires feedback and criticism, and hence some kind of community, but it may also be a comparatively solitary adventure. No one, however, philosophizes in a vacuum: we are continually checking our big ideas up against what others say, and how well our philosophy works at getting us through the day.

What good does it do to philosophize? We all need philosophy at one time or another, we all practice it, perhaps unconsciously, and we all might benefit from responding to what philosophers have had to say. This may help us handle some of the life crises that are bound to come our way. Existential philosophers like Sartre have proposed that since there is no God, the only purpose in life is what you assign to it, and we are alone in the midst of a universe whose fundamental law appears to be entropy, an inclination to disorder. How different from the purposeful universe of Leibniz, created by a God determined to fashion this as the best of all possible worlds! That's an example of what philosophy does: present you with alternatives, and then asks: how do you respond to the basic intuitions presented, and the logic that binds them together? "Doing philosophy" demands that you check your basic intuitions, examine the logic that binds them together, and do some kind of "reality check," to see how your thinking agrees or not with the philosophical masters of yesterday and today. The goal is not just some abstract satisfaction, but improvement in everyday living. Philosophers are not just producers of empty and useless ideas, but the best philosophers are midwives, helping us give birth to our own ideas, and our own vision of how we can best live our lives.

2
History as Philosophy's Laboratory

We have established that all people philosophize, (ask questions about what really matters), and that the most important parts of any philosophy are the first principles or assumptions, and the logic that binds those assumptions together.

Philosophy began its life as a separate, identifiable discipline, thanks to the leisure that Greek civilization provided, about 26 centuries ago. These thinkers raised the big questions that have ever since been the basic issues of philosophy. What is the nature of reality? Can I attain the truth about anything, leave alone the nature of reality? Is reality just "atoms and the void," or is there some kind of Mind that imparts order to things? And, how should people behave towards each other? Is it just a matter of every man for himself, or do I have responsibilities to my fellow citizens? Do I have responsibilities to people in other parts of the world, or just to family, friends, and fellow-citizens? Do I die with my last mortal breath, or is there something within me that lives on?

Such were the questions raised by the earliest philosophers, usually lumped together and called "the pre-Socratics," on the conviction that with Socrates, philosophy took a new and much more mature turn. Indeed, with the life of Socrates, (470-399 B.C.E.) philosophy has a champion who will surrender his own life, rather than be unfaithful to his convictions. Plato and Aristotle are the clear disciples of Socrates, Plato putting some of Socrates' ideas into a more or less coherent system, and Aristotle taking some positions diametrically opposed to the basic "ideas" of that system. Plato wrote "Dialogues," suggesting that philosophy is a kind of endless conversation about the issues of great importance. This notion of philosophy as "dialogue," that is, a conversation that goes on until everybody gets tired and goes home, has persisted, and is kept alive not only in such formats as Oxford or Harvard seminars, but in coffee shops, Socratic cafes, and anywhere people gather to talk about the larger issues of human life, usually issues that admit of no simple solutions.

Aristotle is the first great system builder of philosophy. It is as if Aristotle said: to convince others of the logic of this system, I need to explain what logic is---and in several volumes, he did so. No one has systematically talked about nature, or what supports nature, so I will write a book, (now entitled "Physics,") to do that, and another book (now entitled "Metaphysics,") or "what is beyond nature." And to explain ethical and political behavior, I will write books on each of these, and he did. Much of what Aristotle wrote about nature simply reflects the learning of his time, and is no longer good "science." But what Aristotle wrote about the nature of human consciousness (the soul), about the Prime Mover (God), about ethical and political behavior, is as insightful, surprising, and helpful today, as when he wrote it centuries ago.

Scientists have their laboratories in which to work experiments, but philosophy has only its history for a laboratory, and only by seeing the consequences of a particular philosophy, can we really judge its usefulness. Aristotle has had a more profound impact on philosophical thinking, than all of the founders of modern scientific disciplines combined, have had on their followers. The Greek legacy lives on: a vision of endless questioning from Socrates, a vision of philosophy as dialogue from Plato, and a vision of philosophy as clear statements about reality from Aristotle.

The great issues of philosophy are as alive and vital today as when they were first raised by the great Greek thinkers of classical antiquity. They sought answers to the basic questions--what is real, how should I live my life, what really matters—questions that are as alive and pertinent for us today as they were then. We may need answers that are more contemporary, but their thinking can guide us along the way to producing answers that work for us, and that is the only issue that really matters.

3
History of Philosophy

Whenever I have taught history of philosophy classes, I have come away with renewed respect for the intellectual giants of the tradition, and with a sense of the spirit of what it is that the great philosophers were pursuing. Philosophy after all is an attempt to be wise about life, and from reading the great philosophers, one should get some greater sense of what life is all about. Thinking seriously about the great problems should help get one through the lesser problems of everyday life.

To the modern person who struggles just to make it through the day, and who wonders how the wide range of responsibilities can be handled adequately, the comment of Marcus Aurelius, a very busy Roman Emperor, may be pertinent: "For nowhere either with more quiet or more freedom from trouble does a man retire than into his own soul, particularly when he has within him such thoughts that by looking into them he is immediately in perfect tranquility." Philosophy may not always produce this tranquilizing effect, but it should be one of the benefits of a habit of thinking like a philosopher.

One might ask: why devote so much time to the doing of philosophy, when there are so many practical questions that need immediate answers, ranging from global political issues to issues of personal finance, and to very practical questions like how to unclog a plugged drain. No one has answered this question with greater clarity than Bertrand Russell who, in the course of his life, not only dealt with virtually every philosophical problem, but also attempted to apply his philosophy to problems of practical politics and to everyday moral considerations. Here is what Russell had to say about the spirit of philosophy:

"Philosophy is to be studied not for the sake of any definite answers to its questions, but rather for the sake of the questions themselves. Because these questions enlarge our conception of what is possible, enrich our intellectual imagination and diminish the dogmatic assurance which closes the mind against speculation; but above all because, through the greatness of the universe which philosophy contemplates, the mind also is rendered great, and becomes capable of that union with the universe which constitutes its highest good." That sets a rather high standard for the individual who would practice a little philosophy each day!

Reading the history of philosophy encourages one to reach up to the great minds of the past, and to benefit from the distilled wisdom gleaned after a lifetime of reflection. My hope is that these philosophical meditations impart to their readers some sense of the achievement of the great philosophers, and some ability to apply to everyday life the lessons of the masters. The spirit of philosophy is one of constant inquiry tempered by a degree of tranquility. The reader should come away with a sense that some degree of wisdom about life can be obtained, and the quality of everyday life can be improved upon.

It was something of the spirit of philosophy that enabled Wittgenstein on his deathbed to say: "Thanks. I have had a wonderful life." The major task of philosophy is to help us make some kind of sense of what it all means, and to be fully alert to the absolute wonder of being alive.

4
Mortality or Immortality

Philosophy responds to the need to ask the really big questions. One of the biggest of all is: What is the real duration of my life? The tombs of the Pharaohs are lasting monuments to a belief in a "second life," a life after physical death. The desire somehow to live forever, seems deep-seated in human nature. Even the nihilist philosopher Nietzsche wrote: "All joy wants eternity: deep, deep, deep eternity."

There are essentially three different philosophical positions with respect to immortality. Simple **Materialism** states that every thing that exists is matter, in one form or another. There is no life beyond the grave, because once the particular pattern of cells that forms your body disintegrates, there is no principle of life beyond the happy combination of cells that kept you breathing and moving. For some, this leads to an absolutizing of life here and now, a pursuit of pleasure, a "looking out for number one," or, as one sometimes hears in college bull sessions, "The purpose of life is to make money and have fun."

Enlightened Materialism is the second option. This is the position of Carl Sagan and Sherwin Nuland and a large number of modern scientists, but also of philosophers like Richard Rorty, theologians like Robert Funk, mythographers like Joseph Campbell, and a great many humanists. One of the theologians in this group wrote: "The entire notion of life after death has become difficult to affirm." As the scientific worldview predominated in the late Victorian age, the literature of the time seemed to reflect a certain sadness, that the hope for life everlasting had been banished. A characteristic of twentieth century philosophy has been the search for meaning and purpose in life, because what you have here and now is all that there is, and the challenge is to make the most of it. The hero and the saint, the philanthropist and all those who seek to make the most of human life, are clearly "nobler and better" as human beings, than the ego-centric, hedonistic, ardent consumer. Moralists working in this tradition might affirm that they are motivated to do the right thing because it is the right thing, and not from hope for reward or fear of punishment in an afterlife, and sometimes suggest that this is a more mature morality.

No less a philosopher than Kant affirmed that reason can neither prove, nor disprove, the postulate of immortality. And Blaise Pascal said the wager in favor of living your life as if there were a judgment to come, was well worth it, as there could be considerable reward in being found worthy, considerable loss if things went the other way. Plato first posed the philosophical postulate of immortality, defining man as "a soul using a body." Aristotle suggested that thinking, the act of knowing, was an "immaterial" act, and so the agent of knowing could not be a physical or material entity. (If Intel finally makes a chip that thinks, the debate about immortality will become much different.) Philosophers who affirm immortality usually follow in the footsteps of Plato and Aristotle.

For the religious believer, obviously God can do whatever He or She wants. Most of the religions of the world have some kind of provision for the everlastingness of human life, whether personal resurrection, reincarnation, or being subsumed into the Divine Breath. Contemporary physicists have done a great deal to explain the origin of the material universe, but we still understand very little about human nature, the awesome powers of thinking and loving, and the passion we have to insure that life will go on. Art, music and literature have become our modes of expressing the meaning of life. Philosophy has left us to our own intuitions about our make up: are we simply remarkable material bodies endowed with capacities for thought and love, or are we "be-souled" bodies, having a principle of life, and a reason for being, quite apart from our bodily existence? Your answer to this question determines a lot of what you do on a day-by-day basis, as well as your ethics, and your overall outlook on the meaning and purpose of life. The speaker at an international ethics symposium left the puzzle unsolved by asking: "The more I gaze out on the clear night sky, the more I ask: What is the point of the whole? Where is it going? Where am I going myself?"

5
Texts on Immortality

As regards the most important part of the soul, we must think this: that a god has given it as a spirit to each of us, that which we say dwells in the top part of the body, to lift us from the earth to its kindred in heaven, for we are not of earthly but of divine nature.

--Plato, *Timaeus*, 90a.

If we consider the majority of the emotions, there seems to be no case in which the soul can act or be acted upon without involving the body; e.g. anger, courage, appetite, and sensation generally. Thinking seems the most probable exception; but if this too proves to be a form of imagination, it too requires a body as a condition of its existence. If there is any way of acting or being acted upon proper to soul, soul will be capable of separate existence; if there is none, its separate existence is impossible.

--Aristotle, *On the Soul,* 403a5-12

Thus it is in old age the activity of mind or intellectual apprehension declines only through the decay of some other inward part; mind itself is impassable. Thinking, loving, and hating are affections not of mind, but of that which has mind, so far as it has it. That is why, when this vehicle decays, memory and love cease; they were activities not of mind, but of the composite, which has perished; mind is, no doubt, something more divine and impassable.

--Aristotle, *On the Soul,* 408b23-29

From this it indubitably follows that the soul is inseparable from its body...yet some parts may be separable because they are not the actuality of any body at all.... perhaps the soul is the actuator of its body as a sailor is the actuator of the ship....

--Aristotle, *On the Soul,* 413a3-8

It must necessarily be allowed that the principle of intellectual operation, which we call the soul, is a principle both incorporeal and subsistent...since it can know all material things, it must itself be non-material... It is also impossible for it to understand by means of a bodily organ, since the material nature of an organ would impede knowledge of all material things; (as when a given color is not only in the pupil of the eye, but also in a glass vase, the liquid in the vase seems to be of the same color.) Therefore the intellectual principle has essentially an operation in which the body does not share. We must conclude that the human soul is something incorporeal and subsistent.

--Thomas Aquinas, *Summa Theologiae,* Ia, Q. 5, a. 2

If we choose to let conjecture run wild, then animals, our fellow brethren in pain, disease, suffering, and famine--our slaves in the most laborious works, our companions in our amusements--they may partake of our origin in one common ancestor--we may be all melted together.

--Charles Darwin, *LLD,* Vol. 2, p. 6, 1837

Man in his arrogance thinks himself a great work, worthy of the interposition of a deity. More humble and, I believe, true to consider him created from animals.

--Charles Darwin, *Notebooks,* p. 300, 1838

The confronting of death gives the most positive reality to life itself. It makes the individual existence real, absolute, and concrete. Death is the one fact of my life which is not relative but absolute, and my awareness of this gives my existence and what I do each hour an absolute quality.

--Rollo May, *Existence*, p. 49

Egyptian Hieroglyphs at Abu Simbel

6
How Philosophy Became Psychology

The ambition of philosophy has always been to provide answers to the really big questions, to impart "wisdom about life." The Greek philosophers offered reasoned explanations for their convictions about the divine, about the nature of the universe, about how people should behave towards each other, and how governments should be organized. More than anything else, Greek philosophers offered people ideas about how they should live their lives, what the purpose of life was, and what constituted meaningful and acceptable behavior.

In the last two hundred years, with the rise of modern science, philosophy has been much less sure of itself. No one challenges a mathematical demonstration, and scientific experiments "prove" the assertions scientists make. In comparison, the uncertainties of philosophers, and the fact that every proof seemed subject to multiple challenges, caused philosophy to become much less ambitious. Philosophy became "analysis," a study of how language was used to make sense, or it became the study of logic, of how proofs in science were established. Philosophers turned to practical problems, and medical ethics, business ethics, environmental ethics, and other forms of "applied" philosophy became the bailiwick of the philosophers.

Who then to turn to, to ask the really big questions? Into the breach stepped the "science" of human behavior, Psychology. From the time of Freud, psychologists have become the purveyors of wisdom for the modern age, telling people what their behavior really meant, what they had to do to make their lives meaningful, and sometimes offering definitive declarations on the purpose of human existence. Dispensing wisdom about how to live your life, how to get along with people, how to impart meaning and purpose, has become very much the stock in trade of the talk-show psychologist.

In the late nineteenth century, Freud had suggested that understanding sexual motivation was the key to much of human behavior. Adler talked in terms of understanding human power struggles, and perhaps the greatest philosopher-psychologist of them all, C.G. Jung, proposed that powerful sub-conscious forces were the real explanatory roots of human behavior. No longer a matter of system building or mapping the universe, but understanding the hidden roots of human behavior, became the proper approach to providing "wisdom about life."

Pop psychology has become a major industry, and "self-help" is a large section of any bookstore. There is a superabundance of anecdotal reflection on what makes for the good life, and how to be well adjusted. Much of this is really well meaning, and some of it is very well done. But is it really philosophy? And can Philosophy do something to regain its heritage of offering wisdom about human existence? Can Psychology really be the highest wisdom available, about how to make sense of the human dilemma? Surely we deserve something more profound, more inspiring, more convincing, than what the world of "I'm OK, You're not so good," has to offer. Psychology turns out to be a valuable assistant on the path to the good life, but there is more to wisdom than what the talk show therapist has to offer. As we will say repeatedly throughout this book, every time philosophy has been mistaken for dead and gone, it comes back to life in some new and meaningful form. For good or ill, human beings just can't seem to get along without doing philosophy.

7
"Morals"

There are two very common formulations relating to ethical behavior. The first one is deceptively simple: "Do good things, don't do bad things." The difficulty lies in deciding what is truly good, and what is truly bad. The challenges lie in the elastic nature of goods and bads, of choosing goods that may conflict with other goods, and of not knowing beforehand the real consequences of your actions. "Thou shalt not kill" seems a fairly elementary moral principle, but whether you eat vegetables or meat, you are taking the life of something (probably not a good for it), to promote the "good" of your sustained life.

A second formulation is seductively simple: "Do anything you want, as long as it doesn't harm anybody." One of the persistent mottoes of the Counter-Culture of the Sixties was: "If it feels good, do it." These are both appealing formulas, because they seem to offer a convenient matrix for what is permissible, but the more you think about them the more deficient they appear. The biggest shortcoming is that they are minimalist: they only tell you what is permissible, they don't tell you what constitutes admirable, or desirable, behavior. How do you know what doesn't harm anyone? And why not talk in terms of what good you can do for another, instead of what harm you need to avoid? And, if the only morality were doing what feels good, there would not be much impetus to doing the truly worthwhile. Aristotle and his followers built an ethic based on "moral character," with some conviction that by your actions you both revealed what kind of character you had, and you added to that character by what you did.

Joseph Fletcher and others formulated a "Situation Ethics," in which moral choice was dominated by the simple principle: "Do whatever contributes to the total amount of love in the world." This was taken as justification, perhaps an encouragement, to sexual promiscuity, free love, and open sexual experimentation. It has become clear that sexual freedom does not necessarily contribute to the total amount of love in the world. It may increase sexually transmitted diseases, some of which are lethal, and may cause a great deal of emotional distress. The principle sounds nice, but it doesn't go very far in helping you make decisions about what to do. Clearly, greater specificity is needed.

Our society is said to be not necessarily immoral, but a-moral, without any strong convictions about right and wrong. And, being an experimental society bent on trying to test things out to see "what works," many people spend a good part of their lives trying to ascertain their most basic moral principles. By the time you use trial-and-error to formulate your morality, it may be too late, you may have made some irrevocable choices, and you may be unable to backtrack. Perhaps the greatest contribution of philosophy lies in preparing people to think about morals and how to make good moral choices. Perhaps we do not teach "philosophy" early enough in the school curricula, and our society might be much better off if philosophy enjoyed the same kind of commitment that mathematics and science education have.

By the time Plato wrote *The Republic,* and Aristotle *The Politics,* it was clear that if society was to survive and prosper, some agreement had to be reached as to what was acceptable behavior, and what could not be permitted. Both Plato and Aristotle based their ethics on an enumeration of the VIRTUES a "good" person should acquire. A virtuous person did not consume too much or too little, was neither cowardly nor foolhardy, gave everyone what was their due, but most of all, had a sense for doing what was right, and possessed a kind of super-virtue, simply called "prudence."

Contemporary moral discussion centers on what is not acceptable. Greek society sought to encourage EXCELLENCE, the pursuit of the best possible pattern of behavior. Morality should mean the encouragement to do what is admirable, what builds character, what builds society, what makes the person nobler, kinder, gentler, more in tune with the needs of self and others. In the Buddhist tradition, the person who was "enlightened" saw the hidden ultimate truth of what constituted perfect human behavior, and was tempted to leave society behind to contemplate the noble truths; but the Bodhisattva, the enlightened one, returned, to help bring others to the higher truths. This is the way society progresses: maturity means reaching some insight into right behavior, then passing it on to others, one's own children first of all, then to all with whom one comes in contact.

Whether we want to be or not, we are all moral educators, bringing others along the path we are traveling. By our conversation and by our actions, we influence how others will act. Perhaps Aristotle's suggestion that the "purpose" of life was "to become a virtuous person" is a view that needs to be resuscitated and given serious publicity. How different would society be, if it were composed of individuals determined to be on the path of becoming virtuous!

8
On Death and Dying

Mallarme wrote: "*La mort, c'est pour les autres.*" "Death is what happens to other people."

Death is an inescapable part of being a biological organism: one is born, matures, and eventually dies. But human beings do not easily accept death. We are willing to acknowledge that it happens to other people, but not to us. C.G. Jung wrote: "No young person believes they will ever die."

So is reflection on death just useless morbidity? Is it perhaps even psychologically unhealthy? Or is the acceptance of death a sign of maturity? And what does philosophy have to do with death and dying? Poets have perhaps most powerfully conveyed the emotions of survivors, as Wordsworth for example wrote:

> She lived unknown, and few could know
> When Lucy ceased to be;
> But she is in her grave, and oh!
> The difference to me!

Poets have upon occasion accepted their own mortality:

> Because I could not stop for Death
> He kindly stopped for me....

Among the more puzzling statements of Plato, none is more puzzling than: "Philosophy is preparation for death." How can this be? How does it fit in with the Platonic writings, which are all about living a virtuous life, and developing an ideal community? The most widely read of all the Platonic dialogues is *The Apology*, Plato's description of the death of Socrates. Socrates dies an ideal death, faithful to his principles, reviewing the achievements of his life, at peace with himself and the gods. His philosophic activity has prepared him to die well, which is perhaps the ultimate judge of the value of a philosophy.

Until the twentieth century, the vast majority of the world's population was "religious," predominantly Hindu, Buddhist, Moslem, Jewish, or Christian. But the century witnessed both the scientific criticism of religious belief, and the development of officially atheist states, like China and the Soviet Union. Religion offers the great assurance that this life is but preparation for a later, better life, free from suffering and pain. As one of the most ancient Christian liturgies for the deceased proclaims: "Unto thy faithful, O Lord, life is changed, not taken away." There is a world of difference between viewing death as a release from temporal bondage, and viewing it as the complete termination of consciousness.

Whether death is seen as the transformation to a new and better life, or as the final curtain, it takes a great deal of maturity to accept the reality of death, and the "loss" of everything and every experience that has been accumulated over a lifetime. Philosophy might offer the Socratic view that death is a liberation, the Stoic acceptance of death's inevitability, or the Epicurean assurance that death means release from the reality of pain and suffering. But a practical philosophy should go further. It should countenance the fact that death is a kind of framework that puts in perspective the whole of one's life. The inevitable reality of death means that each day is precious; each day is an opportunity for experience, for growth, for development, for doing things only the living can accomplish. Philosophy is an affirmation that thinking about life, and imparting meaning to life, is a task that must be renewed each day, with increasingly greater depth of insight and appreciation.

If you live to be 90, you will live 32,860 days. As modern culture is driven by the conviction of progress, each day in one's life should reveal some improvement over the previous day. Time should not be simply a repetition of what has gone on before. Kubler-Ross pointed out that dying is the last stage of life's growth. A whole lot of living should be packaged in, before you are ready for the final stage. The reality of death renders every moment of "mortal" existence all the more precious.

9
Aging and Retirement

There are those who age gracefully, some who age disgracefully, and some who simply age. In spite of all the favorable rhetoric about "things are getting better all the time," the fact is, there is some degree of degeneration involved with aging. Medically, degeneration is not that critical a problem. Beginning about age 30, different organs of the body lose capacity at a rate of approximately 1% a year. Fortunately, the body has built in a considerable overcapacity, and most organs can still function quite well at something less than 50% of peak capacity. The other good news is, that by eating a healthy diet and taking appropriate exercise, you can keep the deterioration to a very bare minimum.

There is abundant literature on the importance of keeping active mentally, physically, and socially, as the years accumulate. One of the best maxims regarding retirement is: "Don't just retire from something, retire to something." And that really means, retire to do something you really want to do. Just retiring "to" Florida, is not enough. The happiest retirees are people who have found a real purpose in their lives, whether that is making toys for tots, volunteering through some organization, becoming the best tennis player or golfer they can possibly be, or becoming involved in some civic, political, religious, or academic organization. Keeping the mind alert and interested is at least as important as keeping the body involved in physical activities.

Older people have concerns about money as well as health. Most people over 60 have at least one chronic health problem. It may be arthritis, heart disease, or cancer, more likely it is some lesser, but still bothersome, problem. Acute illnesses can occur at any age, but chronic health problems require some pre-meditated management. Financial planners insist that most people underestimate what their expenses in retirement will be. Social workers affirm that retirement communities soon differentiate the "haves" from the "have-nots," and financial planners argue convincingly that you do need to spend some time and effort insuring that your days will not run out before your dollars. Retiring "to" something insures that the retirement years can be filled with meaningful activities, and that dimensions of the personality that never had time to blossom, will receive the attention they so richly deserve.

10
Stress Management

Everyone has read the standard materials of stress management, and everyone knows that a little bit of stress is good, while prolonged excessive stress can be disastrous, even life-threatening. I would like to identify four "philosophical" sources of stress, along with prescriptions for handling them.

First of all comes the stress of the 51-49 decisions. Each day we are faced with hundreds of decisions, and many of them don't matter much: hot cereal or cold? Coffee or tea? But then there are major decisions, perhaps matters of life or death, career choices, advice for those who seek our counsel, and often the choices are not clear-cut. Sometimes the reasons pro and con simply balance out. Now these are the truly stressful situations....

There is also the stress of disappointing someone. In roundtable discussions, committee decisions, awarding of money, etc., there is pleasure in congratulating the successful, but there is stress in consoling the losers. Disappointing children is not without its stress on the parent.

Whatever our walk in life, we must at some time be the bearer of bad news, and we would be less than fully human if this was without its stress component.

There is the stress of time management. We all get 24 hours each day, but some of us seem to get a lot more done in that time, and others are victims of the saying: "The hurrieder I go, the behinder I get." Managing our time can be stressful, given the contradictory obligations we may have, the need to get more and more done in less and less time, and the abundance of information that cascades upon all of us, leaving us little time to sort out the important from the trivial.

For the 51-49 decisions, it might be wise to postpone these decisions as long as possible. New information may come to light, your subconscious may be able to come up with some blockade-lifting approach, or some outside force may intervene. Among the sayings of the sages, one of the best may be: "Deliberate slowly, act swiftly." Once a course of action presents itself, make the decision, and don't look back.

Disappointing people is painful. In the employment world, every new appointment is a dis-appointment for perhaps hundreds of applicants. Any good Board, or any good committee, looks over a range of proposals, and some proponents may feel strongly about their ideas, even if the ultimate decision maker knows the impracticality or even inanity of someone else's brainchild. Every choice you make may be a disappointment to someone. It is easy to say: "Let the losers down easily," but that is difficult to put into practice.

Time management is a huge challenge. It is the fortunate medical professional who has learned how to be hours behind, without being overwhelmed by stress. Most of the rest of us experience some "time anxiety" and suffer from not always being able to be "on time." If you realize beforehand that every event in your schedule wants all the time allotted to it, and just a bit more, it will be easier for you to glide from one event to another, and not feel guilty about being "late." It's easy to say: "Avoid over scheduling," but life is a matter of more things to do, than there are moments in which to do them. If you live to be 80, there will be over 42 million minutes in your life: presumably just time enough to fit everything in....

As for the stress of obstacles and things out of control, those I have known who handled stress best, had some "overarching purpose," some goal to which all else was oriented, which put this perspective on the obstacles of daily living: "Don't sweat the small stuff; and it's all small stuff." Each goal attained is a stressor put in its proper place.

And lastly, there are the universal basics of stress management: spend some quality time with friends who are "stress busters," take breaks when you need them, take vacations that are real getaways, and make sure there are some things that you look forward to each day that provide you with absolute delight. There is no stress reducer greater than love: love of persons, love of what you are doing, and love of the things that make life delightful. The mountain-climber enjoys the stress of the proportionate challenge: and keeping stress in proportion is what gets us to the top...of our own performance.

11
Faith, and Reason

Religious faith is regarded as a gift, as an enigma, and increasingly, as an anachronism. The great Religions of the world have some kind of Revelation, some kind of document that provides an account of a relationship between the Divine and the human. Judaism, Christianity, and Islam are all "religions of the book"(bible is simply the Greek for book). Each of these religions has "canonical" texts they have accepted as sacred and somehow divinely revealed. The first book of the Hebrew Torah provides a creation narrative, affirming not only that God is responsible for all that exists, but also that He has a "special relation" to His chosen people. The sacred texts of Judaism offer a historical narrative of how God has dealt with these people. There is prophetic analysis of various historical events, ranging from the exodus from Egypt to dealing with the Roman conquerors, and prayerful reflections represented by the Psalms and other poetic narrative.

The sacred books of Christianity are the Gospels, narratives of the life of Jesus Christ, and the various books and letters attempting to interpret the meaning of this "new," or "renewed" covenant. The sacred book of Islam, the Koran, is a narrative of Allah, the Compassionate, the Merciful, His dealings with the Prophet Muhammad, and what must be done to align oneself with the Will of Allah.

In the Western world, the vast majority of the population subscribed at least nominally to one of these three faiths right up to the age of science, in the seventeenth century. Reason delivered a series of blows to religious faith, beginning with the so-called "Copernican" revolution, overturning the comfortable Ptolemaic astronomy, that had been taken as supporting a biblical notion of the earth as the center of the universe. The second major blow was delivered by a man who had taken a theological degree and intended to become a country vicar, but instead took a voyage on the *Beagle* as a naturalist. Charles Darwin identified how species developed by natural selection, and so put human beings in much greater continuity with their animal kin, than religious minded people really wanted to believe. Evolutionary biology seemed to render unnecessary any kind of special creation, and meaning and purpose seemed to relate more to natural selection and a desire for species survival, than any eternal life in the company of the Divine. Freud saw no future for religious illusions: human beings are simply animals who engage in an inordinate amount of wishful thinking.

The decline of faith in the twentieth century had little to do with debates over the origin or age of the earth, missing links in the theory of evolution, or similarities between humans and other animals. As life expectancy increased, and as material goods became widely available, concern with this life displaced otherworldly issues. Coming to understand the "bible" as the religious self-understanding of a relatively primitive desert people, and not as so many whisperings into the ears of Moses, David, Matthew and Paul, has troubled many who would otherwise have found themselves religious believers. Religion is Hermeneutics: it is interpreting the world in a certain way. Biblical writers interpreted events as divine happenings; it may have been wind or drought drying up the Red Sea, (or "The Sea of Reeds,") but it was interpreted as divine intervention; it may have been people removing herbs and matzoth from concealment, but it was seen as miraculous feeding of the multitude.

Just as philosophy always buries its undertakers, so religious faith, whatever the arguments proposed against it, will be around as long as there are human beings. It may be misguided; it may be laden with magic, superstition, and wishful thinking. Still, faith is more than "the reasons of the heart" of which Pascal spoke; it is a way of perceiving reality, a mode of knowing, and a way of looking at the world. Faith is, as the sacred texts say, assurance of things hoped for, a certainty of realities not seen. Faith may be a grace, it may be a mode of mystical knowing, or it may be the result of wishful thinking. Whatever it is, some form of faith provides a rationale, a way of living, and a source of hope, for a great many of the world's people.

12
Is There a God?

The question of God's existence is inseparable from the question of what "nature" a God would have. Plato may be credited with offering an early "argument" that something must exist that is eternal and unchanging, and hence deserving of the adjective "divine." He was convinced that a sound society could not exist, unless there were some absolute and eternal values. In his writings, these values, or "Forms" turn out to be more "divine" than the gods who contemplate them. The gods of Greek mythology seem to have many of the weaknesses and foibles of human beings. Plato sought something beyond the human, something absolutely beautiful and true and good, and these are most truly "divine," for they are everlasting and ever the same.

Aristotle is serious about "theology," which he calls "first philosophy," or "wisdom." Aristotle's God is Pure Act, absolute Perfection, a pure and "infinite" act of knowing. God is the End or Goal of all, because all else is drawn toward the perfection of this substance, or, if there are many gods, perfect substances. (The very fact that there may be many such gods shows the distance between Aristotle and the monotheistic traditions that begin with Judaism.)

Medieval Philosophy, whether Jewish, Islamic, or Christian, simply applied the appropriate Revelations to the Aristotelian concept of God, and God became the Unmoved Mover of Maimonides, the Totally Remote of Avicenna, the Supreme and Infinite Being of Thomas Aquinas, the Perfect, and therefore necessarily existent Being, of Anselm.

For the most part, modern empirical philosophy found God-talk unrelated to the real world of practical knowledge, and abandoned discussion of a Supreme Being. As Wittgenstein said: "Whereof one cannot speak, thereon one must be silent." And curiously, for many people, religion became not a matter of going to Synagogue or Mosque or Church, but of choosing some kind of moral behavior that made sense, and worshipping whatever seemed most absolute, whether Beauty, or Goodness, or Truth, wherever it might be found. Writers as diverse as Martin Heidegger, Henri de Lubac, and Gabriel Vahanian counseled that worshipping any value short of the Absolute Value was bound to lead to some form of "idolatry," worshipping something less than God. And many are the critics who have pointed out that, devoid of an Absolute to worship, human beings may come to worship money, sexual pleasure, fame, or a panoply of lesser values.

19

One of the persistent problems of those who would speak favorably of God is the problem of evil. If there is a god who permits so much evil in the world (the Holocaust, the suffering of human beings, natural disasters, etc.) then he is either not all knowing, or not all-powerful, or not all good. For many of the "Death of God" theologians of a generation ago, the reality of evil obliterated the possibility of religious belief.

Two important philosophers of the twentieth century, Whitehead and Hartshorne, suggested that the real fault was with the Aristotelian conception of God. Just as evolution had become the most startling and yet most elementary discovery of the 19th century, so the conception of God as in process, as evolving, as including all consciousness as part of his existence, became the startling, if elementary, contribution of the process philosophers.

God is in process. God is not yet who he will become. God does not know nor effect the future, for the future depends on independent natural and human processes. All that conscious beings have ever done retains a kind of immortality, because it is forever held in the mind of God. There is evil in the world because of the limits of matter, and because of the real wickedness of human beings. God is not Absolute, but Relative: related to all that takes place, an interested observer, but not an intruder into the natural or human scene, which flows along according to its own laws.

Whitehead and Hartshorne regarded revealed religions as so many mythologies, attempts to explain the inexplicable, and both admired and encouraged religious practice. They find much that is "true" in traditional theology and religious practice, but propose that the idea of a God who is in process, who is tending toward what He will become, is a much more accurate concept of divine nature, than the Aristotelian notion of a Perfect Pure Act of Thinking, who thinks only of what is most perfect, his own divine being. Divinity is eternal, conscious being, in process of experiencing novelty and change, evolving, as has plant, animal, and human, seeking, but never attaining, absolute perfection.........

13
Proving God's Existence

"To those who believe, no proof is necessary; to those who do not ⏎
believe, no proof is possible." Philosophers have long sought demonstrations of God's existence, with not always convincing results. Others have found the arguments compelling. When Mortimer Adler was asked if he believed in God's existence, he replied: "I do not believe; I know."

The so-called "ontological" argument is as old as the eleventh century and Anselm, Bishop of Canterbury. Just think of God as the all-perfect being. If, in the line-up of attributes of this being, you exclude "existence," you are not thinking of the truly perfect being, for surely existence belongs to the true concept of the absolutely perfect being! Descartes suggested that the mere fact you can think of the all-perfect being must indicate the innate idea of that perfect being. Where could that idea have come from, he asked, unless God Himself deposited it there? Various philosophers have puzzled over the logic of this formula, but few are willing to go from any idea in the mind, to the existence of a real object.

Some contemporary philosophers suggest that Thomas Aquinas' formulation of the "Five Ways" was his essential contribution to philosophy. Aquinas says the clearest proof comes from motion: nothing is moved, he says, unless moved by another. Ultimately, you must come to a being that is the source of all motion, as you can't have an infinite chain of things moved by something else, and this Unmoved Mover, says Aquinas, is called "God." The second argument is a variation of the first: you can't have an endless chain of causes, you must come to a First Cause of all the "effects" you see around you. And, as you might guess, this Uncaused Cause is "God."

Some find his third argument most convincing. All around you see things that could be, or not be. But not everything could be contingent. You must ultimately arrive at some being that is Necessary, and the Necessary Being, the Being whose very essence is his existence, is "God."

The fourth argument is the most Platonic in character. There are degrees of perfection in things, as degrees of truth, goodness, or nobility. And also, says Aquinas, there are degrees of being, and some Being contains the highest degree of being, namely, "God."

The last argument is that even those things that lack intelligence seem to target themselves to some goal or purpose. If even inanimate things seem to have a purpose, that must originate in a Purposer who orders all things to their natural ends, and this "Purposer," as you might suspect, is called "God."

All attempts to prove God's existence foundered on the rocks of the "modern" theory of knowledge proposed by Immanuel Kant in the eighteenth century. Kant says the only sure knowledge we have derives from, and must return to, sensory evidence. There is no sense evidence of God, and therefore, God is but a "moral postulate," a basis for morality and piety, but not a legitimate object of knowledge, or of philosophical speculation.

Darwin's nineteenth century elaboration of the theory of evolution convinced some that matter can organize itself into ever-higher forms, and that seeking an explanation for the apparent order of nature outside the realm of nature, was conjecturing way beyond what the facts supported. Nevertheless, some contemporary biologists, like some current astronomers, have tended to look with new enthusiasm upon the arguments for purpose and design.

Typical of this restoration of the old ideas are the words of Frederick Turner: "Today the God of nature looks very much more like the God of the Old and New Testaments, and the God of other great world religions, than like the abstract God of the Enlightenment. Evolution is perhaps God's own vital signs." Or, as Einstein once wrote: "Science without religion is lame, and religion without science is blind." There is a great deal of popular support for Billy Graham's witty remark: "My God is not dead: I spoke with Him this morning." It is not just reasons of the heart, but reasons in scientific form, that have done so much to rehabilitate the notion that before the Big Bang, there was an Uncaused Cause, an Unmoved Mover, a Being who just had to be, and a Source for Purpose and Order in the universe. To anyone who would like to pursue the analysis of the arguments in modern form, I would recommend two books by Anthony Kenny, an Oxford philosopher of great fame: *The God of the Philosophers,* (Oxford University Press, 1979), and *The Unknown God,* (Continuum, 2004).

14
"Atheism"

In the middle of the twentieth century, the majority of the world's population became urban, and, thanks to Soviet and Chinese communism, officially atheist. Marx was only one of many nineteenth century philosophers who proposed atheism as the inevitable result of modern science and its more "objective" ways of knowing the world.

Two twentieth century French philosophers became the most literate spokespersons for atheism. Jean-Paul Sartre wrote a remarkable book, *Is Existentialism a Humanism,* which lays out with elegant simplicity the consequences of atheism. (As we have observed, a philosophy depends not only on the coherence of its logic, but also on the accuracy of its intuitions or assumptions. Sartre's starting point is atheism...) Putting the argument as simply as possible, Sartre says: "Since there is no God, there are no Divine Ideas, no human essence or nature that dictates what we must become or what we must do. In the human situation, existence precedes essence: we are, and we must choose what we will become." This is but one of the many varieties of "existentialism," philosophies that focus on the fact of existence, that we are, and what we will become is largely up to us. In Sartre's most famous book, *Being and Nothingness,* he says how lucky trees are, for they have an essence, they do not have a "hole in being," an emptiness that must be filled. Acorns become oaks, and have no distress over choosing what they might become. By contrast, human beings are a "project," an essence or nature to be achieved, always subject to revision and uncertainty.

Albert Camus is the other great French philosopher of atheism. In *The Myth of Sisyphus* he writes: "I don't know if this world has a meaning that transcends it. But I know that I do not know that meaning and that it is impossible for me just now to know it." Life is fundamentally "absurd" and without meaning, and true liberty means going on with life in the midst of its emptiness and absurdity. Philosophical maturity, says Camus, means accepting such a universe, and drawing strength from it amidst refusal to hope, and accepting the unyielding evidence of a life without consolation.

At one stage in his development, Sartre was a serious Marxist, convinced that communism offered the best hope for humankind. Eventually the depredations of Soviet Communism soured Sartre, and he was content to criticize the various French attempts at socialism. Camus kept careful watch on the French Algerian crisis, profiling it as a model of the absurdity of all political attempts.

Various other existential philosophers, from Martin Heidegger to Karl Jaspers to Martin Buber, present more optimistic philosophies of overcoming the human predicament. The atheistic existentialists proposed that we examine the consequences of affirming that there is no personal God, that existence only has the meaning we assign to it, that life has purpose only in terms of some quirk in evolutionary biology. For some, astrophysics and the expanding universe seem to cancel out the notion of Creation and Providence. Others respond like Hans Kung: "The more I reflect on the amazing results of astrophysics and again--like people from time immemorial--gaze out into the clear night sky, am I not to ask in all modesty: What is the point of the whole? Whither the whole? Whither humanity? Whither am I going myself?" For some, a thoroughgoing examination of Sartre and Camus lead back to a renewed exuberance for the Platonic vision, the intuition of purposefulness and meaning written deeply into existence, and for the human essence as something to be discovered and nourished, not something to be invented continually in the midst of a pointless existence. Sartre and Camus have brilliantly described both the assumptions, and the consequences, of atheism. Many will read and be enchanted. Others will have a renewed commitment to some form of theism, with its intimations of immortality and a personal divinity that shapes our ends, rough-hew them how we will...

15
"Christian" Apologetics

A common response to first hearing the term "Christian Apologetics" is, "Yes, Christians have a lot to apologize for!" While the modern word "apologize" means to beg forgiveness for a transgression, the classical roots of the word means "to offer a rational defense." Accordingly, "Christian Apologetics" has long meant that branch of theology most appropriately practiced by someone offering rational grounds for belief. (Curious you don't hear much of Jewish or Buddhist Apologetics. Judaism tried the apologetics route in the twelfth century with Moses Maimonides. While Maimonides has always had a devoted following within the Jewish community, the philosophical defense of Judaism has never been a matter of great importance. A character in Leon Uris' novel *Exodus* says: "We are the people of the Book, in the land of the Book." Judaism, in its purest form, is a Biblical religion, and the primary work of the Rabbi is to apply

Biblical Revelation to everyday life. Buddhism has many forms, but all of them depend on "Enlightenment," awareness of the way things really are, which comes as an act of intuition, not as a process of reasoning...)

Three basic problems of Christian Apologetics are: (1) the existence of God; (2) reconciling the evil of the world with an all-knowing and all-powerful God; (3) the relation between faith and reason.

It is obviously the province of philosophy to deal with these questions. Within University philosophy departments today, it is not difficult to find those who will say: (1) you cannot prove the existence of God: in fact, the scientific evidence seems to point the other way; (2) the prevalence of evil is incompatible with an all-good, all-powerful God; (3) the work of philosophy is to make no room for faith. Philosophy departments however are seldom monolithic; and, while denominational colleges are most likely to have departments whose members find harmony between faith and reason (Alvin Plantinga, author of *God, Freedom and Evil,* is perhaps the best example), secular university departments are not without their strong defenders of faith.

Philosophers have written remarkable books on the existence of God (A. Kenny, *The Five Ways*, and *The God of the Philosophers,)* on the problem of evil, (Howard-Snyder, *The Evidential Argument from Evil,* and on philosophers who have deep religious faith (T.V. Morris, *God and the Philosophers).* An excellent anthology of current apologetics (Jewish, Islamic, and Christian) is Stump and Murray, *Philosophy of Religion: The Big Questions.* Among the classic works by American philosophers, William James' *The Will to Believe,* and *The Varieties of Religious Experience,* have never been surpassed. Karen Armstrong's *A History of God* presents a remarkable summary of theological developments within the western monotheistic traditions. And, in opposition to those who say science has made religion obsolete, physicist Chet Raymo wrote: "The pieces are in place for a renaissance of religion: cosmic knowledge, the power for good, awareness of mystery, a sense of responsibility to all of creation, and a longing for union with the Absolute." (*Skeptics and True Believers,* 267).

Among the strongest proponents of the harmony of faith and reason was Etienne Gilson, who advised not to renounce religion for philosophy, nor abandon philosophy for religion, but rather keep the truth, and keep it whole. (See his *Reason and Revelation in the Middle Ages,* or *The Unity of Philosophical Experience.)* For Gilson, as for so many of the philosophers profiled here, the God of the philosophers is also the God of Abraham, Isaac and Jacob. Athens, the city of reason, becomes a sister-city of Jerusalem, the city of faith. And no apologies are necessary or permitted.

Lei Bammel and Megan Burrus, Beaver Creek, Colorado

16
Friendship

What is friendship? Why do people become friends? What nourishes friendship, what destroys it? We call some people "friends" with whom we have a working relationship, so we do some things for them, and they do some things for us. If the "usefulness" ceases, so does the friendship. Such friends may be people at work, neighbors, members of some group to which we belong. Then there are other "friends" who provide us pleasure or delight: these are the people it is fun to do things with, to travel with, to play or watch sports with, or to be good companions at the dinner table. Friends like these make life much more enjoyable.

Real friendship reaches to a deeper level. Some friends are "good" for us, even as we are "good" for them. These are the friends with whom we are more likely to discuss our dreams and aspirations, our emotions, our medical circumstances, our views of what life really means. For many, life's deepest friendships are provided by family members, people with whom we share some genetic basis, as well as some common culture.

While it is true that "like likes like," it's also true that "opposites attract." Sometimes our most important friendships develop with people who are very different from us, have challenging different opinions, and make us question our own values or ways of doing things. And then there are "soul-mates," people who, perhaps vastly different, seem to share our ways of looking at things, and share our values and aspirations. For a full and complete human life, it takes a large variety of friendships, but probably not a great many different friends. Real friendship takes time and cultivation, for it requires shared experiences and time for thoughtful conversation.

Real friendship also requires love: you come to love the character, the goodness, or the admirable qualities of your friends. And because of the presence of love, you scarcely notice shortcomings. Real friendship requires some lovable qualities in the friend, and the capacity to admire and appreciate those qualities. Lastly, real friends promote the growth of personalities: friends accept friends as they are, but quietly and subtly influence each other to move in new directions, to become more human, to think new thoughts, and to make progress in doing the things that really matter.

In his discourse on friendship (Books VIII & IX, *Nichomachean Ethics)*, Aristotle suggested that happiness, friendship, virtue, and leisure are four inseparable components of the good life. Without friends, life would indeed be poor, nasty, brutish, short, and hardly worth living.

17
Leisure

It is a commonplace to say: "We have too much stuff, but not enough free time." Among the examples frequently offered: "...we have a surfeit of stuff, but not enough time for ourselves and each other. Our morning coffee comes in 50 flavors, but we don't have time for a leisurely sip." Because people are so busy, they tend to spend more on luxury items, take expensive vacations, and display the wealth they are working too hard to enjoy. A very busy friend of mine said: "The people I know are taking more vacations, and spending more...they are looking for resorts and spas and massages and other comforts."

But the real issue is the "time poverty" most members of our society feel. What has changed in the last few years is simply the perception of time itself. We simply do not have "time" to do all the things we want to do. We have accelerated the pace of life, we have more activities clamoring to get into our schedules, we have more options of things to do, we have more information coming our way than we can possibly process, and we have more "demands" on our time than we can accommodate.

We try to pack more and more into less and less time, we try to do several things at once, and even retired people talk about having filled their schedule a month or two ahead. The question is, is this really the way we want to live? Is the goal of life to see how many activities we can get in, how many meetings we can attend, or how much money we can make, so that we can spend it on things we don't really need?

It is not uncommon to hear of people who wanted to maximize their income, so as to put their kids through college, take care of their financial obligations, and retire young enough to do some new things in their lives. Even among highly motivated people, making money is *instrumental* to the other things they really want to do with their lives. It takes some reflection to realize that the end of life is not to make a huge amount of money, or to get your name in the paper, or even to see how many things you can knock off your "to do" list.

Robert Louis Stevenson wrote: "To be what we are, and to become what we are capable of becoming, is the only end of life." In a book my wife and I wrote many years ago, *Leisure and Human Behavior,* we argued that **leisure is the realm of the intrinsically worthwhile,** of things you do for their own sake. The provinces of the kingdom of leisure are thinking, loving, communicating, doing good things for yourself and others, and becoming more of a human being in the process. You don't have to be at home in an easy chair to do these things: you can be anyplace, doing just about any thing. Leisure is an attitude, a way of being, and a way of doing things. It does require control over the pressure of time urgency, a sense of having to do many things at once, of not being in control of your own time and life.

We lose leisure when we let too many things or too many events dominate our lives. We regain leisure when we simplify, when we learn to say "No," when we learn to take time out for our selves and our priorities. Many retired people are not at leisure, because they have lost the sense of being free to choose how they will spend their time. To set out on the path of regaining leisure, you might begin by setting aside time for reflection, for reading, for organizing so that you can do everything you want or need to do. The best philosopher in this matter is Humpty-Dumpty, who said: "It's a question of who is to be master, that's all." Choose today to master your own life, control your schedule, and give leisure and leisurely behavior its rightful priority.

18
Meditation

A number of respected medical practitioners have recommended meditation as a fundamental exercise in good health. Meditation, in one form or another, has been practiced for thousands of years, for reasons religious, philosophical, healthful, and simply as an exercise in developing full humanity.

What is meditation, and how do you practice it? Meditation is essentially a calming and quieting experience, a turning off of the noise and distraction of everyday, and attentiveness to what is most basic and elementary, breathing, for example. The simplest form of meditation is to find a quiet place, sit comfortably, and spend ten minutes simply paying attention to your breath. (Dr. Andrew Weil said there is no medical prescription more important than re-learning how to breathe!) As we get busy, we tend to breathe very shallowly, and we can go days or even weeks, without paying attention to this most basic of vital experiences, our own breathing. Simply counting your breath can help focus your attention. Controlling your breath is the next step: breathe in for 5-10 seconds, hold your breath, and then breathe out slowly and calmly, and try to focus your entire attention on the act of breathing.

Rachel Bode, novice meditator

Is that all there is to meditation? You can dress it up in many ways, but that is the basis. You may make it a religious experience by incorporating the appropriate imagery, you may make an aesthetic experience by meditating on the sunset or on the moon, or any particularly striking natural phenomenon, or you may make it a calming and relaxing experience through the recitation of some "mantra," some phrase that has particular significance for you.

Dr. Herbert Benson has documented that the regular practice of meditation lowers blood pressure; Dr. Dean Ornish claimed that regular meditation reduces the risk of sudden heart attack, and Dr. Weil claimed that meditation boosts the effectiveness of the immune system. Perhaps it does these because it brings us back to our most basic self, puts us in touch with the roots of our pre-consciousness, and does something to establish a calm and tranquil center at the heart of our activity.

Among philosophers, Socrates had his meditative trances from which he could not be awakened, Plotinus had his transformative experiences of solitude, of being "alone with the Alone," and Thomas Aquinas was so transformed by his meditations that all he had written seemed like so much straw. Asian traditions are parallel: Thich Nhat Hanh, perhaps the greatest living teacher of ancient Buddhism, recommends the simple formula: *Breathing in, I calm my body, breathing out, I smile.* His books, *Peace is Every Step,* and *Interbeing,* can be great helps along the path to successful meditation.

By setting aside 10 minutes every day, you will open a new window on your own self-awareness, gain control over your own breathing and thereby your own life, and come to sense your participation in the mystery of existence. Your material being is part of the matter of the universe, your thinking is part of the web of thought that covers the universe, and your existing is a participation in that wonder of all wonders, your capacity to stand outside nothingness, and be a contributor to the on-going-ness of existence. The best cure for an overly-busy schedule is to set aside ten minutes a day of uninterruptible quiet time, when you center yourself, and find your proper place in the non-everyday world, the real reality behind the appearances of things.

19
Stem Cell Research

Stem cell research has become the grand meeting ground of Philosophy, Politics, and Religion. Stem cell research, with the promise and potential for the cure of some of our most dreaded diseases, evokes powerful emotional responses. One advocate for increased research begins his speeches with: "My son has juvenile diabetes and my mother is dying of Alzheimer's."

What are stem cells, and what are the moral issues involved, and why is stem cell research, which appears to hold out so many promises, so keenly debated? Stem cells are present in all adult tissues. Some are easier to locate than others, as those in umbilical cords. Those in the bone marrow, when stimulated, can produce all other blood components. It is not certain whether stem cells found in various tissues or organs are multipotential, i.e., can differentiate into any tissue or just that tissue in which it is found. There is a good chance that some adult stem cells are multipotential.

When adult stem cells are stimulated to differentiate, there is no compatibility problem, if the tissue is returned to the donor. The same is true with nuclear transfer. Stem cells are the blood cells that produce other blood cells. We are all walking collections of *adult* stem cells, for they are what give rise to all our normal blood components, like red cells, white cells, and platelets. Adult stem cells are normally located in the bone marrow, from which they can be harvested for transplant. "Adult" or "mature" stem cells are relatively easy to obtain, the easiest source being umbilical cords. The problem is, "adult" stem cells have already differentiated, that is, they are already on their way to becoming some particular bodily organ or tissue, whereas the earlier, totipotent stem cells, can become anything. It is expected that research on adult stem cells may produce benefits or even cures for at least a dozen different diseases. Researchers, however, are much more interested in *embryonic* stem cells, which clearly have the capacity to become any cell in the body. They may hold the clue to the solution to seventy or more diseases, and to complicated disorders such as spinal cord injuries.

Obtaining embryonic stem cells involves a very serious moral problem. Embryos are destroyed by the process of extracting stem cells from them. If the embryo is already a person, as some believe, you are killing this person to obtain the stem cells. As opponents of embryonic stem cell research point out, we would not permit killing children or adults to obtain various bodily parts for medical purposes. How can we tolerate using a human being at the very start of life as the source of cures for someone else's illness? This debate hinges on an issue that is as much scientific as it is religious or philosophical. If human life is present from the instant of conception, then the embryo is a human being, and deserves respect. Partisans on the other side of the debate contend that, just as an acorn is not an oak tree, human, personal life is not present in the embryo. It is unlikely that the two perspectives on this debate will ever reach agreement. The crux of the current debate is the source for embryonic stem cells used for research.

The principal sources of embryos for stem cell research are the surplus embryos from In Vitro Fertilization clinics, embryos that would otherwise be destroyed. The argument here is, since they are going to be destroyed anyway, why not use them for research? Embryos can also be made by uniting donated eggs and sperm, or by therapeutic cloning, which is done by nuclear transfer. Fetuses that have been aborted could also be the source of stem cells for research purposes, but for obvious reasons, this is very hotly contested.

Presuming that there are ways of obtaining embryonic stem cells that are morally acceptable, the larger question remains: is it wise or ethical to use human stem cells in medical research? The expectation of benefits from stem cell research is best expressed by this charter statement from the National Institutes of Health (which is the world's largest source of funds for medical research): "Scientists might be able to replace damaged genes or add new genes to stem cells in order to give them characteristics that can ultimately treat diseases."

There are three roadblocks to real progress from stem cell research. First of all, there are persistent immunological problems. Transplanted cells are targeted for destruction by the immune system. Scientists have yet to solve the rejection problem, without causing a host of new problems related to preventing the immunological response the body has to what it sees as an invader. This is a technological problem that presumably admits of some solution.

There are also embryological problems. We are not as good as nature is, in providing an environment for the growth of cells. An extraordinary number of teratomas, tumors that are odd mixtures of cells that have not received the right instructions, occur in animal experiments. This too is a technological problem, but it may or may not be solvable.

Thirdly, although animal studies done with mice have used cardiac stem cells to repair injured cardiac muscle, it is still not certain that we can produce consistent results without adverse side effects. This is what might be called the "Edison" problem. Edison experimented with thousands of filaments before he found one that would work as a light bulb. It may take years of experimentation to find a system that works, so that stem cells, whether embryonic or adult, can be "instructed" to become the kind of cells we want them to be, without debilitating side effects.

When researchers first discovered how to engineer recombinant DNA in the 1970s, the risks were seen as considerable, and the benefits purely theoretical. Within a few years, insulin was being produced, as was interferon. Is it possible that embryonic stem cell research can produce even greater benefits than did recombinant DNA? Is it possible that diseases that now appear to be incurable might be treatable, and that this could happen within a few years? With the three billion dollars California has committed to stem cell research, it is conceivable that major breakthroughs may be in the offing.

We may be at one of those watershed situations, where the thresholds of philosophy, science, and religious conviction will once again be challenged. We may be on the cusp of some major medical breakthroughs. As Dr. Homer Skinner observed, "Using embryonic or nuclear transfer stem cells will give researchers time to learn techniques to stimulate development of stem cells into various tissues. Once this is learned, then stem cells from the adult body can be harvested and made to do what is necessary—a new kidney, a new heart, etc.—and be used in the very donor's body. There would be no rejection problems, no ethical problems, no social problems, and no need for donors."

Understanding the science is a critical first step. Finding courses of action that are societally acceptable may prove to be a big hurdle, but not as big as finding the funding for research. And finally, as in all these bifurcating debates about issues of fundamental importance, not everyone will walk away happy. If the medical research does in fact produce cures for spinal cord injuries, for juvenile diabetes, Alzheimer's and Parkinson's diseases, will people with these ailments refuse treatment, on the basis of objecting to the morality of stem cell research? Is life, even that of an embryo, sacred, and not subject to use, so that good may result from the use of human tissue? These and other such problems will keep the stem cell debate on center stage for years to come. Meanwhile, the hope remains that stem cell research may produce breakthrough benefits, the likes of which we have never seen.

20
Environmentalism

When reporters pestered Gandhi for an interview during one of his times for silence, he wrote: "my life is my message." So too for all the great figures of environmentalism. Thoreau was the first great American environmentalist, and while his stay at Walden Pond was only two years, the fact that he wanted to live simply, to use no more natural resources than necessary, and that he wanted time to confront the really important issues of his life and his society, shows that his way of living was his message. The book he produced, *Walden,* is not just a treasure of American literature, but a milestone on the way to a truly "conservative" way of life. A few pertinent quotations: "To be a philosopher...is to so love wisdom as to live according to its dictates, a life of simplicity, independence, magnanimity, and trust. It is to solve some of the problems of life, not only theoretically, but practically." Not only did Thoreau think about his life, he had already begun to wonder about American materialism: "For a man is rich in proportion to the number of things he can afford to let alone."

Tree Hugger, Sedona Arizona

And perhaps the sentence that best summarizes the life and message of Thoreau: "I went to the woods because I wished to live deliberately, to front only the essential facts of life, and see if I could not learn what it had to teach, and not, when I came to die, discover that I had not lived."

Thoreau appreciated human society, but he thought if he were to have anything worthwhile to say to people, he needed times of being alone; and, like Thomas Jefferson before him, he was not enamored of spending all of one's life within the confines of the city. "In wildness is the preservation of the world." Thoreau is the first of the great American voices extolling getting back to nature, simplifying your life, confronting only what is essential, and living humbly, simply, and non-consumptively, upon the earth.

The lives and messages of John Muir, and of Aldo Leopold are much the same. They retreated to the woods, to see what nature had to teach them. All came back to the "city" to share their visions. And all preached a gospel of using natural resources wisely, of treating the natural world as "earth household," and not as a storehouse of resources to be consumed and then forgotten.

Lynn White's 1967 article, "The Historical Roots of our Ecologic Crisis," set off a fire storm of protest, because it was interpreted as blaming western religions for our excessively consumptive approach to natural resources. White simply pointed out that the "man's dominion over nature" passages had long been interpreted as affirming that God had placed all of nature at man's disposal. White's point was that the Benedictine notion of "stewardship" of natural resources seemed much more consonant with the sacred scriptures of both eastern and western religions.

True environmentalism is this: by our very nature we are consumers of natural resources: we require oxygen to breathe, we require nourishment to sustain life, we require mineral and energy resources to promote and develop human culture. As some Native American religions observed, the world is not a "profane", but a sacred space, because it is the avenue of expression of gods and human beings. Most of us could live much more simply and much more non-consumptively, and enjoy life more in the process. To use a phrase that Thoreau would have appreciated, "Live Simply, that others may simply live...."

21
(Liberal) Education

The cost of an education at some state universities is in the neighborhood of $25,000 a year. When you put dollar figures like this on education, it quickly awakens a discussion of the purposes and values of higher education. Is education all about jobs, so that parents and students can quickly recoup the investment? Is education about furthering maturity, so that people can become thoughtful contributors to the progress of society? Is education about learning what the past has to teach, so that the same mistakes will not be repeated? Is education about moral development? (If it is this, the headlines loudly proclaim our failures....). Or is education simply about problem solving, whether the problems are psychological maturity, parenting, earning a living, or achieving world peace?

During a University Presidential Search Committee meeting several years ago, I asked a consultant: "Does background discipline have anything to do with success as a University President?" His response: "It really doesn't seem to matter what someone's background is; the only thing that matters is that they have learned to solve a wide range of problems."

The same might be said for higher education. Whether the principal discipline is physics or political science, some approach to problem solving is an integral part of the discipline. Because of the range of problems discussed, one might be especially partial to such comprehensive disciplines as philosophy, political science, economics, and law, or one might be partial to engineering, a specifically problem-solving discipline.

The principle discipline or major may not be nearly as important as what else goes on during these privileged years of study. Entering a discipline too soon may stunt breadth of vision. The specialization featured by technical colleges comes at the expense of exposure to all the other things that are going on in the world. Higher education, whatever the job focus, should always be liberal, (from the Latin, *liber*, free, as in setting one free from narrow-mindedness.) The word liberal has taken on peculiar connotations recently, but in the context of education, it should mean: freeing one from pre-conceptions, from unexamined principles or convictions, and from reluctance to take in new information.

While having a specialization and a technical skill may be important in the initial job search, one must not overlook the importance of breadth of education. In a survey of graduates over a ten-year period, almost three-quarters had gone into careers that were only distantly, if at all, related to their undergraduate majors. A good education should enable one to process new information, and should develop an increased capacity for learning how to learn.

Some 2000 years ago, Cicero extolled the merits of liberal education by saying: "these studies delight in old age." As you grow older, you need to have the wider perspective that is only available if you can read and appreciate literature, music, and drama. You must be prepared to think your way through a new and challenging array of problems. Jobs and careers are very important, but preparing for the much wider range of what life has to offer, is more important still. To students heading off to college, and to their parents, one might say: "Do not abandon the wonderment of the range of human knowledge, in exchange for development of job skills." The liberally educated person will have the kinds of skills the workplace will require. Only the broadly educated person will have the kind of mental preparation necessary to face the unpredictable world of tomorrow, both in terms of the job market, and of the unpredictable challenges of adult life.

22
Music

One of the great classics of philosophical literature is Plato's *Republic*. Readers are often surprised to find, in this discussion of what makes for a great society, a lengthy discussion on the importance of hearing the proper kind of music! In a sentence with great contemporary significance, Plato wrote: "When the mode of the music changes, the walls of the city shake." And this, long before sub-woofers and mega-bass! Plato was concerned that children who listened to unseemly music would be unruly and irresponsible. And conversely, long before Shakespeare wrote about music having charms to soothe the savage beast, Plato thought that proper music had a soothing and settling effect upon the soul.

The music of the great classical period in western culture from Handel and Haydn, through Bach and Beethoven, represented a view of an orderly and meaning-laden world, a world of providential order, where harmony and tranquility were reflections of the divine spirit. With the twentieth century, symphony has often been replaced by cacophony, a succession of unpleasant sounds, reflecting the disorder and absence of harmony in the human world.

The President of a Recording Company said: "At no time in history have so many people listened to so much music." But what kind of music, and what kind of impact does it have on people? There is the bland elevator music that is easily tuned out, the explosive sound of hyper-amplified rock that obliterates all thought and all conversation, and the soothing sounds of new-age music, all competing across the radio and TV dials. (There is MTV and VH1, but where is the classical music channel? In fact, classical music stations across the country are losing out to "easy listening"...). What are we to make of music, and what is its significance? Is it just background, something to pass the empty time? Or does music have profound human implications?

Music, even in its most debased forms, has a philosophical significance, as it speaks to something deep within us: a desire for rhythm and harmony, and a need to express the ineffable. Music begins as pleasant sounds, and becomes an expression of the search for some kind of transcendence....

Gabriel Marcel, a modern French philosopher, said he often could not give answers to philosophical questions, but he could play them on a musical instrument! Music, at its best, speaks to a search for meaning, and is an attempt to express what is literally *beyond words*. Whether Gregorian chant, or a Bach Concerto, a country-western song or a traditional Andean

37

folk piece, music speaks of spiritual reality, of what is behind appearances, of matters too profound to be expressed by mere words.

As Yogi Berra might say, "You can hear a lot just by listening." Listen for the rhythm of the cosmos, and the harmony of the disparate and unconnected dimensions of reality. Music is profoundly and deeply philosophical, expressing dimensions of human existence too deep for words, too wonder-full for language. Change the mode of the music, and the walls of consciousness may be shaken or made sturdy, and perhaps we can begin to create harmony in the larger society. And to think this all could be, if we only were attentive to the philosophical power of music....

23
Of Virtues and Vices...

With a continuous stream of popular books about various virtues, it would seem there is nothing more to be said. But not a day goes by without some new challenge to understanding human virtue, and more painfully, human vice. Most of us think of ourselves as reasonably virtuous, and when we watch true life stories of reprehensible and heinous acts, we are driven to wonder how human beings could be so depraved.

How virtuous are we really, and how far away from vice do we really stand?

Does our virtue get tested only occasionally, or on a regular basis? What does it really mean to be virtuous? For Aristotle, once called "the master of those who know," a virtue was a habit of acting in a certain way that not only caused you to produce good actions consistently, but also made you into a good person in the process. Similarly, a vice was a disposition to act in a way that consistently produced undesirable results, and made a 'bad character" of the performer.

How does this relate to our everyday lives? Every day, our capacity for virtuous behavior is tested, sometimes trivially, sometimes gigantically. And most of us have surprised ourselves more than once, either by acting with unexpected nobility, or in a way we would rather forget. (Physiologists assert that the difference between the hero and the coward may simply be the time of the day, the flow of hormones, or some undetected physical source...) The acquisition of real virtue is a long-time task, (maybe a life-time pursuit...) and we may never know how virtuous or vicious we really were, until the very last tests of our lives have occurred. Those who work in Hospice situations get some inkling of how well or ill a lifetime of behavior has prepared an individual for the last challenge: dying well.

In the more everyday situation, the challenge is to behave progressively better, more nobly, more virtuously. Life is not an endless repetition of the past, but an opportunity to handle similar challenges more virtuously. As Herman Hesse has Siddartha say, in a novel of the same name, "We are not going around in circles, we are spiraling ever upwards." Part of the progress of life, is to take similar situations, and respond better each time.

The tests of virtue may occur with respect to integrity, to paying fair wages for labor, to discipline in one's own daily schedule, to fulfilling obligations properly, to following medical professionals instructions, or to identifying appropriate sexual behavior. It is curious how many people think "immoral behavior" means sexual misconduct, when immorality is probably much more widespread in other areas of human endeavor.

The Greek word *arete,* usually translated as "virtue," has the connotation of the pursuit of excellence. To be virtuous meant to excel in something. Aristotle, in his masterly analysis of virtue, says you won't get anywhere at all without the central virtue of prudence, which he also called "practical intelligence." But you need to be brave, to be temperate, to be just, to be in control of yourself, in short, you need to have all the virtues, if you are to be identified as virtuous. Aristotle says only the virtuous are really capable of friendship (for how can you be comfortable with those who are laden with vices?) He suggests the level of happiness you can experience in life is directly proportional to how virtuous you are. If you want to have friends and be happy, there's no two ways about it, you just are going to have to become even more virtuous.

24
Health

You know a quite a bit about what you need to do to be healthy: the real challenge is the motivation to do, and keep doing, the things that promote good health. Statistically, death rates during each decade after thirty are about double that of the previous decade. Some people appear to be genetically programmed to develop certain ailments at a certain point in their lives. But now the good news: your health is much more in your control than anything your genes have established. Many recent studies, particularly those on twins, have documented how much life style, diet, exercise, and attitude, have to do with maintaining good health.

The basic things you need to do to promote good health are reiterated in the popular press: eat more vegetables and grains, less sugar, less fat, less alcohol, and stay away from smoking and smokers. Modern life is stressful, and you need some effective way of dealing with stress. A pulmonary-function researcher claims that one of the best indicators of longevity is lung capacity: you can improve the working of your bellows, just by practicing deep breathing: inhaling as deeply as you can, expelling breath as forcefully as you can. And of course, there is no substitute for aerobic exercise, something that gets you really moving. "Pumping iron," lifting weights in some form, does good things for the body, as well as the spirit: people who lift weights experience fewer falls and muscular injuries, as well as less depression.

It is the motivation factor that keeps people doing the right things, and there are no motivators stronger than friends and family: people you want to be with, and whose company you really enjoy. I remember from my childhood that visits with my Uncle Henry and Aunt Loretta were always uplifting, and that my family always came home in high spirits, even after the briefest of visits. There are people who inject rays of sunshine into your life: try to do the same for them, and you will promote mutual longevity!

There is no better book on motivation than Viktor Frankl's *Man's Search for Meaning*. Frankl was a survivor of the Nazi concentration camps, and he observed that those who had a serious purpose in living were far more likely to withstand the hardships and tortures of such evil circumstances. "If you have a Why to live, you can put up with any How." Scott Peck's *The Road Less Traveled* bears the subtitle: "A new psychology of love, traditional values, and spiritual growth." The theme has been continued in the various books of Thomas More, such as *Care of the Soul:* life is more than getting and spending, eating and sleeping. Life is most meaningful when you have some reason for really wanting to get up in the morning and having at it, some large purpose that melts all the little goals into one large one. As the philosopher Hegel said: "Life has value only when it has something valuable as its object."

Your health and wellbeing is very much in your own hands. Cultivate a spirit of optimism. Look at the bright side of things. Spend time with people of cheerful disposition. And most of all, think of the great things you have to do, and the fact that you can only do them, if you nourish and cultivate the very best health your body and soul can sustain. Sure there are genetic and environmental factors, but the most important factors in your longevity are in your control.

Montezuma's Castle, Arizona

25
Cities

Americans have long had a love-hate attitude toward cities. Thomas Jefferson was convinced America would be a land of gentleman farmers, with no city larger than 40-50,000 people! Jefferson loved the land and loved agriculture, and while he appreciated great cities like London and Paris, he saw no reason why the American continent should become urbanized.

Archeologists keep finding evidence of the sophistication of the inhabitants of some very early cities, dating back thousands of years. Why did people citify in the first place, and what is this compelling attraction that cities exercise over people? Aristotle put it succinctly: people formed cities for bare subsistence, to afford protection and preserve food, but then found that cities alone promoted "the good life." And "the good life" is still what cities appear to provide: music, culture, conversation, commerce, trade, religion, and government. Every aspect of what makes us most human is facilitated by the kind of personal contact only large numbers of people living together can provide.

In a Platonic dialogue called *Phaedrus,* Socrates says: "Trees and countryside have no capacity to teach me anything, and my appetite is for learning. It is people in the city that teach me what I want to learn." Intellectual stimulation seems to be the hallmark of the successful city. All the great cities of the world have universities that are central to their fame and well-being: Paris, Boston, Toronto, Los Angeles, Rome, Berlin, Moscow, Beijing---every great city has one or more institutions of higher learning as a crowning glory. Major by-products of universities are cultivation of the arts, development of business opportunities, and the formation of a basis for commerce.

Cities offer an abundance of goods: modern cities are huge shopping malls, where all the goods necessary to facilitate "the good life" are available. That cities are also centers of political activity, and offer a wide range of religious worship, is almost taken for granted. But everywhere we are reminded of the dark side of cities. Cities can also be dens of iniquity, where every kind of vice can be found. Big cities suffer from congestion, pollution, and the very size of cities sometimes prevents the delivery of the basic goods and services for which people came to the city in the first place. Jane Jacobs wrote lovingly of the city of Toronto in the 1960s, but much of what she most loved about the city has been endangered by its own gigantism. Other huge cities, like Tokyo or Mexico City, have their great charms and work very well for those who know how to find their way around, but for many of their inhabitants they could hardly be said to promote "the good life."

Henry Ford, early in the twentieth century, said: "We shall solve the problem of the city by leaving the city." And indeed Americans in huge numbers get in their cars and flee the city whenever possible, not infrequently creating traffic and parking jams at National Parks and Wilderness areas. The path to solving the problems of the city is to take Aristotle more seriously. In his discussion of "The City," he says it must be a place where "leisure is abundant," and the citizens pursue the happiness that flows from the possession of wisdom and virtue, and not from the possession of external goods

Does your city promote the possession of wisdom and virtue? Do the citizens see external goods as means to the end of living nobly? Does your city produce a truly good life for its members? Aristotle said: "People come to the city in order to live, and wind up staying in order to live the good life." Some cities around the world manage to be very livable spaces, but many of our megalopolises fall far short of the ideal. Most Americans can solve their personal problems of urbanity by moving to a suburb, or by moving to a different city. The vast majority of the world's poor move to the slums of the big cities in the hopes of eking out a bare subsistence, but the dream of a good life in the big city has but a scant chance of realization. What Plato, Aristotle, Lewis Mumford and Jane Jacobs all proposed----a philosophy of successful urbanization---awaits some form of twenty-first century realization, and it may be long in coming.

26
Language

In academic philosophy, the twentieth century will be remembered as the time when philosophers discovered language, and its limitations. In the growing skepticism about philosophy's ability to know anything, philosophers turned first to explaining why science was so successful: it provided empirical evidence for the "truths" it reached, and could repeat experiments and verify the findings. Then philosophers turned to examine why philosophy had lost its credibility: there were no "proofs" for the big metaphysical, epistemological, or even moral claims it made. Philosophy turned inward, and studied how statements were made, how logic developed, and how empty was the language of previous philosophers.

The great debunker of philosophy as providing answers to big questions was Ludwig Wittgenstein. "Philosophy is a battle against the bewitchment of our intelligence by means of language." Just because language works for everyday situations, doesn't mean it is safe to make any big generalizations about the nature of reality. "What we do is to bring words back from their metaphysical to their everyday use." In other words, stop talking about God and soul, and talk about meat and potatoes: we can make "true" statements about things we use everyday. "The results of philosophy are the uncovering of one or another piece of plain nonsense and of bumps that the understanding has got by running its head up against the limits of language." So the real work of the philosopher is to lower people's ambitions: there are things you can know, and there are things you cannot know, and about the latter, you should just learn to be silent. And so the work of philosophy is to clarify everyday language, and stop abuses before they start. "Philosophy only states what everyone admits." Quite a comedown from the days of proclaiming dogmatic truths about God, Man, and the Universe! (Wittgenstein acknowledged the strong human penchant for wanting to talk nonsense. He concluded, go ahead and do it, but "just keep an eye on your nonsense.")

Philosophy was not alone in taking its lumps. Northrop Frye, in *Anatomy of Criticism,* claimed, "all texts are ironic, they have multiple meanings, none of them definitive." It is only a short step from there to de-constructionism, in its extreme forms stating that since our languages were developed by dead white males, it is hopelessly racist and sexist, and prejudices every attempt at honest communication. The ultimate limit is this: since no two people mean exactly the same thing by any word, all communication is impossible.

Noam Chomsky and other semanticists and semiologists have stirred the waters enough to come up with these saving conclusions: language is a convention that we establish so that we may communicate. Languages cause us to perceive the world in certain ways. Some Inuit languages have forty or more words for "snow," because it is perceived differently depending on its consistency or usefulness. This question is the focus of endless debate: do words cause us to perceive the world in a certain way, or does the world cause us to perceive it in certain ways, "because that's the way the world is?"

Carl Jung and Joseph Campbell and other "mythographers" provided a different solution to the language qualms of the twentieth century. Language is a way of structuring reality so that we can make sense of the world and of our lives. Language is an effective tool not just for conveying ideas, but also for communicating emotions. Note the content and power of these words of Joseph Campbell: "People say that what we are seeking is a meaning for life. I think that what we are seeking is an experience of being alive, so that our life experiences on the purely physical plane will have resonances within our innermost being and reality, so that we actually feel the rapture of being alive."

Leaving the great linguists aside, think about how well language works for you. How well do you use it to convey ideas? How well do you think you interpret what others say to you? How well do you use language to convey your emotions? I think you will find, for all the critical things said about language, that it seems rather effective at conveying ideas and emotions. We still have the problem of the limits of language, but practical people still know how to use language to convey what they need to express, despite the high anxiety philosophers continue to have about the possibilities of using language for lofty purposes, like solving metaphysical problems...

27
Continuing Medical Education

Continuing medical education is a requirement for health professionals in most states. Perhaps all institutions of higher learning should offer courses, free to the general public, on basic medical education. There are several potential benefits. There is something to the old formula: "Show me those who are their own doctors, and I will show you doctors who have fools for patients." We are forced to be our own physicians, partly because of the crisis in medical care, partly because of the continual revolutions in medical knowledge, and partly because much good new medical knowledge is so elementary, people could acquire it, with less effort than the average college course demands.

Such an approach could offer a necessary antidote to what has become a major medical problem: self-prescription and self-medication. Patients used to list two or three prescribed or self-selected medications, but it is not uncommon now for patients to list a dozen or more. There are very strong medications available over-the-counter, and many herbs and supplements that have powerful side effects. There is a lengthy list of medications that are not compatible with each other, and many others that influence the impact of other medications.

Some side effects, and some mutual interactions, can be quite serious. The twentieth century drug that has saved so many lives, penicillin, can have the very undesirable side effect of closing down bodily orifices, such as the eyes, the throat, etc. To cite some of the most commonly noted side effects, some erectile dysfunction drugs can cause the whole world to be perceived in hues of blue. (While that may be useful for a Picasso or Van Gogh, most of the rest of us would be somewhat distressed.) The Saw Palmetto, Pygeum-Africanum some men take to reduce prostate symptoms, can cause erectile dysfunction. L-Tryptophan was withdrawn from the market when this supposed sleep-inducer also seemed to cause the very undesirable side effect of sudden death. Valerian, which became the substitute sleep-inducer, has been known to cause depression, as well as persistent drowsiness.

Some vitamins and supplements are very effective. Antioxidants appear to reduce the risk of sudden heart attack, as does taking a quarter-grain of aspirin. Many who take chondroitin-glucosamine report reduced joint pain. Calcium supplements reduce the chance of osteoporosis. Men who take Selenium reduce the risk of prostate cancer.

How are we to know which medical paths to follow, and how are we to be up-to-date on the latest discoveries? It might be helpful if all institutions of higher learning were to offer public courses, team-taught by a physician and a professional health educator, on a no-fee or low-fee basis. Not only would this have the desired effect of keeping people up to date on necessary medical knowledge, it would take some of the burden off physicians, whose time is wasted by answering elementary questions, and whose time is somewhat squandered by repairing the damage due to unfortunate self-medication. It would also get more people to college campuses, where they might then come to learn other life-skills as well. Perhaps one of the most under-prescribed medications is continuing education. Such public courses on medical education might be the key to a renaissance of adult education in America, as well as answering the crying need of the general public for accurate, current, and useful medical knowledge.

28
The Truth About Retirement

There are as many different ways to retire, as there are people engaging in retirement. What works for one individual may not work for another. Life in Florida is long-awaited Paradise for some, hotter than Hell for others. Some delight in every aspect of retirement, some say it is the worst thing that ever happened to them.

What accounts for this wide range of responses? It is not just differences in character and temperament; it is something in human nature, and something in the nature of retirement itself. Aristotle and his successors made great use of the notion of *analogy,* and it may be pertinent to a clear understanding of the variability of retirement. Aristotle wrote that "perfections" are realized in each being according to differing capacities to exercise that perfection. This simply means that a word does not mean exactly the same thing each time you use it. The "goodness" of a meal is not the same as the "goodness" of your best friend, and the "beauty" of a sunset is not the same as the "beauty" of a smiling face.

We have a passion to be "univocal," to want a word to mean exactly the same thing every time we use it. Even as great a philosopher as Leibniz wanted to replace words with numbers, so they would have the same "quantity" every time they were used. But reality is not univocal, and words do not mean exactly the same thing every time we use them. A word has a different meaning, partly because each application is different, and partly because we grow and change, and interpret words differently, in light of our experience.

How does this analysis of how words are used apply to retirement? While people are alike in many ways, everyone is different, and what works for one person may not work for someone else, what works at one time, may not work at another. Aristotle observed that we learn by *imitation,* and learning by imitation can cause problems when it comes to retirement. We see what someone else has done, and try to imitate that pattern. That may work well when applied to learning some skill, such as playing a musical instrument or playing a sport, but it may be disastrous when it comes to a major life issue like retirement. You can "imitate" someone else's retirement only to a certain limited extent, before striking out on your own.

Successful retirement has to be a happy blend of "work" and "leisure," of things you really want to do, and of a certain amount of passivity, of letting the world go, and letting the world go by. The happiest retirees are those who find something they really like to do on a regular basis--the range of possibilities is infinite--and some capacity to sit back, and take delight in the world and its wonders.

Fortunate are those retirees who wake up in the morning with something they really want to do. And happy are those who are able to slow down the pace of things, find delight in what they were all too busy to notice, and have time to find joy in human nature, in nature, and the blending of the two in works of art.

For those who have retired, and for those who look forward to retirement, it is important to remember that retirement is a matter of imitating what you have seen elsewhere, and your unique, idiosyncratic approach. Retirement is *logical,* because it is the logical next step from the world of full-time work. Retirement is *dialogical,* because it should provide you the opportunity to engage in meaningful conversation. It is *analogical,* for it is realized in many different ways, according to the capacity of the person doing it. Aristotle would be pleased to see so many who have retired so well, delighting in the kind of perfection of life that a good retirement can bring.

29
Wittgenstein and the "Doing" of Philosophy

When *Time* magazine identified Ludwig Wittgenstein as the "most influential" philosopher of the twentieth century, I wondered how his thought could ever be translated into something useful and comprehensible. A distinguished professor of modern philosophy said that to understand Wittgenstein's early work, the *Tractatus,* all you need is a course in Formal Logic, and six totally dedicated months of your life. Wittgenstein's later work, *Philosophical Investigations,* is equally difficult.

Wittgenstein said of the *Tractatus:* "The whole sense of the book might be summed up in the following words: what can be said at all can be said clearly, and what we cannot talk about we must pass over in silence." Wittgenstein was an engineer by training, and was fascinated by language and its uses, perhaps as a result of his association with Bertrand Russell and other enthusiasts for "bringing our language back from its metaphysical, to its everyday use." In the *Tractatus,* he proposed a correspondence theory of truth: "A proposition is a picture of reality." He has an affinity for statements that have very clear-cut, definite physical references: "This red object is here, now."

Some years later, he prefaced a new book: "This book is written for those who are in sympathy with its spirit. This spirit is different from the one which informs the vast stream of European and American civilization in which all of us stand." Wittgenstein was fully aware of his iconoclastic activity, and because of that, he was in some sense the first post-modern philosopher, complete with an ironic sense of all use of language, and a rejection of any "big picture" philosophy.

To the question, "What is meaning? Wittgenstein responded: "The meaning of a word is its use in a language." Instead of the "analogical" use of language of the Aristotelian tradition, Wittgenstein introduces the notion of "family resemblances." Just as the members of any family resemble each other, so a word like "game" has certain family resemblances, whether applied to golf or peek-a-boo, chess or tennis. Words are pointers to things in our experience. Wittgenstein might appear to be a disciple of Plato, to the extent that he finds geometry as a source of excellent definitions, ("triangles are three-sided figures,"). But he is thoroughly un-Platonic on the use and definability of abstract terms like "knowledge," "being," "object," etc. Wittgenstein is loath to define staples of the Platonic dialogues like "courage" or "virtue," acknowledging only "ostensive" definitions, that is, pointing out individual examples of courage or virtue, without presuming to box in the virtue with some abstract definition.

Use words in their everyday sense, says Wittgenstein. "Philosophy is a battle against the bewitchment of our intelligence by means of language." Use words in their ordinary, everyday sense, or don't use them at all! Wittgenstein's point is that philosophy has had a long and painful history of "going beyond the facts," of verbalizing beyond the appropriate domain of language.

As seems fitting for such a critical thinker, Wittgenstein took long breaks from his academic positions, to work as a hospital porter, a monastery gardener, and a grade school instructor. His philosophy convinced him that what was important was *doing*, not seeing. In this sense, his whole philosophy can be seen as an ethics, a morality of "sound human understanding," of being immersed in the world, to which all discussion of language is but a preamble. He probably felt "enlightened," when he realized he could no longer "do" philosophy. As he wrote, "Philosophy only states what everyone admits." Bring words back to their ordinary meaning. Anchor yourself firmly in reality. "Do not seek the things that are above you."

So this most influential philosopher of the twentieth century has apparently epitomized philosophy by saying: Just carry on with your everyday life. Do not seek answers to questions that never should have been asked. Wittgenstein however left open a whole range of "experience" beyond language: "There are things which cannot be put into words. They *make themselves manifest*. They are what is mystical." The work of Wittgenstein was to proclaim very definite limits to philosophical discourse. Perhaps the words of the *Tractatus* are his only appropriate epitaph: "What we cannot speak of we must pass over in silence."

These are wonderful words, often quoted by philosophers, who simply cannot pass over weighty issues in silence. The words of Kant, the most influential philosopher of the eighteenth century, still echo down the corridors of philosophy: "What can I know? How should I act? What can I hope for?" Wittgenstein claimed that he had brought philosophy back to its most fundamental problems, and in doing so he has shown the fly how to get out of the bottle in which it was trapped. (It never should have been there in the first place.) Wittgenstein, far from putting an end to philosophy, forced philosophers to conceive of the doing of philosophy in a very different way. As one critic wrote: "The problems he aimed to resolve have obstinately refused to stay dead." Or, as Etienne Gilson, the great historian of philosophy said: "Philosophy always buries its undertakers." The fact is, professional philosophers simply think and write differently, in the aftermath of Wittgenstein. He has assumed his place in the pantheon of those who have made enduring contributions to the doing of philosophy. He has left Kant's three great questions unanswered, and pointed out how circumspect we must be, in our attempts to answer them. "What can I know? How should I act? What can I hope for?" Wittgenstein would say, the way you conduct your life is the only proper answer to such huge questions.

30
Heidegger: the "Other" Great Philosopher

What is the place of Heidegger in modern philosophy? What is his relevance to philosophy today? What possible importance might he have for the reader of this book? He has relevance for three reasons. First of all, he is an exemplar of the exuberance of philosophy. Philosophy comes to life in every generation, because of the power of some individuals, to express in a new and charismatic manner, the perennial power and importance of philosophical issues. Secondly, he serves as a reminder that even brilliant philosophers can make colossal mistakes, as he did in 1932 when, as University Rector, he gave a speech endorsing the then nascent National Socialist party. And thirdly, he is relevant because he speaks the philosophy that so many people have absorbed and lived, without putting it into so much philosophical language.

Heidegger says the philosophical tradition got it all wrong, when it tried to find the source and explanation of being in some transcendent other. The only path to understanding being is to strive to understand the human existent, in all its precariousness, all its fragility, and all its emotional intensity. The beginning of wisdom, says Heidegger, is to stop pretending that the overwhelming catastrophe of your life does not await you: your own death. You will be much wiser, he says, if you acknowledge that you are a being-towards-death, and that the threat of nothingness stands in the midst of your every action. The roots of morality are simple: you stand before the spectacle of the nothingness within your own being, and, with whatever consequences, you fashion yourself---as it were, out of nothingness.

Heidegger is the bluntest of this-worldly philosophers. The temper of the modern mind is to recognize the sheer materiality of it all. Face it, says Heidegger, when you die, as far as you are concerned, the world is dissolved. True morality is the voice of conscience, which is "the call of the nothing," the call of the only ultimate in a finite world, forcing you to shoulder the burden of your own impossibility, or worse, your own ridiculousness. Heidegger wants you to find the Ground of your Being not in a transcendent deity, but within yourself. He wants you to assume your divine function, that of imparting value to things. In various forms, Heidegger affirms that there is no God, and you must find the divine within the human. He might have said: "There is no God outside you or above you, but you have to accept that you are the being that is most sacred, the creative being who continuously overcomes the nothingness that surrounds you."

Heidegger endlessly repeats phrases like: "Within you alone transcendence takes place," and, "In understanding yourself you come into the presence of the holy." Heidegger cannot altogether avoid the language of the religious traditions, as if he had some longing to restore what has been lost. He says you need poetry as much as you need abstract thinking, and "poetically you dwell upon the earth." In poetry, says Heidegger, you can celebrate the sacred as much as you want to. Just don't mistake it for real thinking, for accepting the world as it is, for dwelling realistically upon the earth. Heidegger calls upon you to remember and celebrate being, and, in your Care and Concern, rejoice each day in your triumph over nothingness. In each of your actions, you do something to create being, to bring order out of chaos, to impart meaning in an otherwise meaningless world.

Heidegger has provoked strong responses, from Protestant theologians like Karl Barth, from Catholic theologians like Karl Rahner, from Hannah Arendt whose philosophical work is largely a response to his views, from William Barrett, in his book *Death of the Soul,* and from M. Scott Peck, in *Denial of the Soul.* It is the achievement of all great philosophers to state a case so clearly that either you subscribe to it and go where that takes you, or you look at the other side, the antithesis, and see that in a new and compelling light. Modern science has disposed us to think materialistically. Heidegger forces us to re-think the dimensions of radical materialism, either to see how we can rescue some traces of true humanism from it, or how we can transcend it, re-establish the roots of alternative points of view, and justify and explain our being upon the earth, our overcoming of everydayness. Like many philosophers, Heidegger leaves an ambiguous legacy. As if contradicting his early atheism, in his later years he became enamored of the phrase, *"Nur ein Gott kann uns retten,"* –"Only a God can save us."

31
Darwin's Dangerous Idea

Daniel Dennett published *Darwin's Dangerous Idea* in 1995. Dennett claimed that Darwin's dangerous idea was not simply evolution, nor his discussion of natural selection and the consequent survival of the fittest, nor the similarities between human beings and other animals, but the challenge to the age-old idea of teleology, that all things happen for a purpose. Dennett wrote: "If I were to give an award for the single best idea anyone has ever had. I'd give it to Darwin, ahead of Newton and Einstein and everyone else. In a single stroke, the idea of evolution by natural selection unifies the realm of life, meaning, and purpose with the realm of space and time, cause and effect, mechanism and physical law. But it is not just a wonderful idea. It is a dangerous idea." (21)

Dennett sees the Darwinian revolution as putting nails in the coffin of any attempt to build a rational theology, any attempt to be religious and avoid the charge of insanity or charlatanism. If religion is based on God as the final cause and ultimate explanation of all that exists, then, says Dennett, religion is no longer necessary. The fact of evolution, that species evolve, that higher life forms develop from lesser life forms, obviates the need for any explanation beyond the blunt data of evolution of species.

Dennett does not hesitate to list the consequences of his claims: "The kindly God who lovingly fashioned each and every one of us, and sprinkled the sky with shining stars for our delight--*that* God is, like Santa Claus, a myth of childhood, not anything a sane, undeluded adult could literally believe in. *That* God must either be turned into a symbol for something less concrete or abandoned altogether."(18)

So, what's left? Are we left with a meaningless universe, an impersonal cosmos, and a reality in which nothing is sacred? It takes several hundred pages, but Dennett finally concludes: "This world is sacred."(520) But how, in the absence of a God, can the world be *sacred*? Because it is the awesome outcome of design at work! "What is design at work? It is that wonderful wedding of chance and necessity, happening in a trillion places at once, at a trillion different levels. And what miracle caused it? None. It just happened to happen, in the fullness of time. You could even say, in a way, that the Tree of Life created itself. Not in a miraculous instantaneous whoosh, but slowly, over billions of years." (520)

In spite of the confidence and conviction with which Dennett expresses his ideas, the basic axiom or intuition at the root of it all needs to be questioned: Can natural selection by itself explain the order of the biological world? The Harvard paleontologist Stephen Jay Gould suggested that organisms evolve not by adaptation to the outside world, but by some kind of "pathways" mandated from within the organism. The fossil record does not show graduated change over time, but sudden sharp jolts, what Gould called "punctuated equilibrium." In a word, evolution of species is something that clearly occurred; that it occurred randomly is so unlikely, Gould says, as to be impossible.

If Darwin's most dangerous idea is the elimination of purpose built into things, of final causes, the evidence simply does not support the idea. Randomness has never yet produced order on any significant scale. While Dennett may assume that an infinite number of monkeys working on an infinite number of word processors might eventually produce Shakespeare, resurgent teleologists assert that that seems a less rational assumption than positing some Final Cause, some Source of Design, some Purpose beyond the random and unpredictable flow of events that of themselves, lead nowhere. Professors of philosophy, reflecting on both sides of the argument, are inclined to the so-called Scottish verdict: neither case is proved. Dennett has offered a brilliant argument for the prosecution, but the case is still wide open for further arguments from both sides.

32
Sigmund Freud's Dangerous Idea

Darwin, Freud, and eventually Bultmann, proposed ideas that were particularly dangerous for the future of religion. Darwin, with his notion of evolution by natural selection, seemed to offer an explanation for the apparent order of the universe, an explanation eliminating the need for some external Designer. Freud, the founder of psycho-analysis, and among the first to offer explanations for psychological phenomena, saw himself as a man of science, a cultural critic, and as one who could offer solutions for the great riddles of human existence.

His lasting claim to fame will doubtless be his enthusiasm for the "talking cure," a conviction that the neuroses or problems of adjustment that most people suffer, can be cured by a long course of talking the problems through. Few psychiatrists today subscribe to the simplistic principles of Freudian analysis. His convictions about the childhood origin of psychological problems, or the emphasis on sex and early sexual experiences, have been moderated by the test of time. Freud was serious about his atheism, and one of his best books is *The Future of an Illusion,* an attempt to ferret out the psychological roots of religion, and affirm its inutility in the modern, enlightened, scientific world.

Freud asserted that the root of religion is based on the child's sense of helplessness. We all need some defense against the crushingly superior forces of nature, and primitive peoples found gods everywhere, to protect them from nature, and heal them from their illnesses. Freud said religious ideas are illusions, and are infantile attempts to fulfill the oldest, strongest and most urgent wishes of mankind. The root of religion is a hope for some kind of Providence, a Father who watches over and protects us, prevents harm from befalling us. Freud affirmed that the evidence is everywhere, that bad things happen to good people, that rain falls on the just and the unjust, and that the only salvation for humankind is some form of rational ordering of society so that human needs are satisfied, without human impulses for sex and aggression doing us all in.

Freud asked: why do people believe? He answered that most people are believers because they adopt a religion their ancestors handed down to them, and it is forbidden to raise questions about the origins or truth of these beliefs. He concluded that once people realize the origin of belief is superstition and societal constraint, religion would soon vanish. As to the question about God the Lawgiver, Just Judge, and source of moral law, Freud says if you will just leave out God altogether, and admit the human origin of all regulations and precepts, we will all be better off.

Much like Marx, Freud said that by concentrating our liberated energies on our life on earth, we may ultimately achieve a state of things in which life will become tolerable for everyone, and civilization less oppressive. He believed the advance of science is inevitably accompanied by the decline of religion, as the contradictions of religion are altogether too palpable and too transparent.

Freud's dangerous idea encounters a fate similar to Darwin's. Freud committed the logical fallacy of "nothing but." Psychologically, religion may be a palliative, an escape, and a place of refuge in a time of distress. Historically, religions have been magical, superstitious attempts to control nature and the course of human events. But religion might also be what Carl Jung, Freud's one-time disciple and later antagonist said it was: the pathway of the unconscious to the roots of ultimate reality. Freud pointed out the obvious shortcomings of religious practice. As to the substance and ultimate source of the religious experience, Freud had little or nothing to say. The real "fallacy" in Freud's attack on religion lies in accepting psychological answers to what are really metaphysical questions. *The Future of An Illusion* is a brilliant book, exemplifying how well a case can be argued, given the initial assumptions. But in this, as in every philosophy, it is the initial assumptions that are most important. Freud's dangerous idea is rooted in taking ideas from one discipline and assuming they will solve or dissolve the problems of another discipline. Freud necessitated strong responses from philosophers of religion, and some of the vitality of that discipline is due to the strength of the arguments Freud elaborated. Where there is danger there is also excitement, and Freud has provided more than enough excitement for a whole generation of religious philosophers.

33
From Sartre to Buber

One of the most influential philosophers of the twentieth century was Jean-Paul Sartre. The fame and influence of a philosopher are dependent upon many things, the most important of which is the capacity to state clearly what many people are then thinking. Sartre was born in 1905 and died in 1980, and lived through the meaninglessness and despair so many Europeans suffered from the consequences of two devastating world wars, both of them fought largely on French soil. It is not surprising that Sartre saw *conflict* as the central truth of the human condition, and the assuaging of conflict as the central role of philosophy.

He saw resignation or acceptance as key to the task of getting through life relatively unscathed. If you understand and accept that life has no intrinsic meaning, that the only meaning life can have is whatever you impart to it, then the suffering and the inevitable conflict of human existence will be much less painful. Sartre's most famous phrase, *"L'enfer: c'est les autres,"* "Hell is other people," epitomizes the first step on life's journey. Recognize that values are irreconcilable, that in fact we live in the domain of irreconcilable differences, and the path to minimizing the conflict and de-emphasizing the differences becomes, if not clear, at least dimly visible.

Sartre says the human condition is rather pathetic, for we continually deceive ourselves, we play roles, and we are, deep down inside, "inauthentic." There is no royal road to authenticity, for there is no essence behind our existence, nor is there a permanent, enduring consciousness that is the loyal substrate of all our comings and goings. A stone really is what it is, and has no daily struggle to realize itself. But consciousness is a kind of "hole in being," an emptiness, for all my consciousness does, is make me aware of what I am not.

Of much less fame but of perhaps greater stature was the Austrian born philosopher Martin Buber. Born in 1878 to a Jewish family, what he lived through in the twentieth century was certainly equal to or worse than the existential experience of Sartre, but how differently he responded. Instead of conflict, Buber saw relation as the basic given of human experience. His most famous phrase, "I only become an I in relation to a Thou," is a perfect summary of his personalism. Human existence is essentially a being-in-relation-to-others, and what I am and what I become is a consequence of how I choose to relate to what happens to me, and to the persons who fill my consciousness.

Atheism is a kind of first principle for Sartre: how can you look around this world of conflict and think that an all-knowing and all-powerful God could be the source of it? And since there is no God, there are no divine ideas, hence no essences in things. There is only blunt, brutal existence, which, in some Darwinian manner, has organized itself so that we suffer the indignities of endless conflict.

By contrast, faith is a first principle for Buber: "Faith is not a feeling of the soul, but an entrance into reality." Buber inveighs against the materialism and the impersonalism of the times, and suggests that most people lead lives of desperate I-it relationships, treating others as mere things in the way, closing off the doors of perception that most clearly characterize personhood. Buber says the road back lies in the experience of others, in that perception which dawns upon us, as we relate to another as other, and not merely as a thing, an obstacle in the way. The light of the divine has indeed been eclipsed in our time, says Buber, but it has not been extinguished. Philosophers, he says, miss the point when they try to prove the existence of the Other, for it cannot be proved, but only experienced. Buber finds the root of a theology in human personal experience, for in the deepest of human relationships, something of the eternal Thou shines through. "Every particular Thou is a glimpse through to the eternal Thou." Human life is not conflict, but opportunity for encounter, for experience of what is Ultimate and Profound. In Sartre and Buber, we have two philosophers with similar experiences, but infinitely different conclusions.

34
Plato

"Western Philosophy," said Alfred North Whitehead, "consists of a series of footnotes to Plato." That may be an exaggeration, but Plato's influence, not just on philosophy but on the way people perceive and talk about things, persists to this very day.

First of all, in the doing of philosophy. Plato wrote *Dialogues,* to enforce the idea that philosophy is a never-ending discussion of the things that really matter. To the modern materialist, Plato would say: "OK, we have no physical experience of God, the soul, or moral values like justice. But these turn out to be the most important issues in our lives, so we have to talk about them." Plato would go on to say: "Search my writings as you will, you will not find definitive answers there: just provocations to make you think about these things. You will find viewpoints to think about some things in a certain way, but...."

There are indeed *viewpoints* that Plato espouses, and these have as much currency today as when he first elaborated them. He has an unshakable conviction that "human beings are basically good," they just need a lot of education to lead them along the right paths. The Greek word *paideia,* translated as "education of youth," really means "care of the soul," a concern with considerable contemporary overtones. Plato affirms that the only goal in life is to become as virtuous as possible, and he calls this *homoiosis Theo,* likeness to God. For political reasons he wants to make society as good and virtuous as possible. He needs to anchor society in some enduring truths, and these he calls The Forms, the ideal archetypes of things. If Truth is to be attained, conjectures Plato, Eternal Truth must reside somewhere, and Plato suggests these eternal truths have some form of independent existence. The "truths" of mathematics surely belong here, but so do the ideal models of justice and all the other virtues, as well as the perfect expressions of such ideals as Beauty and Truth.

Plato is the intellectual parent of all those who claim that there is an Invisible World which sustains this visible world, that there is an archetypal Goodness that is the model for all our little acts of goodness, and an Absolute Beauty, in which all beautiful things somehow participate. He is also the intellectual father of those who seek better political arrangements. His greatest dialogue, *The Republic,* is a discussion of what is necessary to bring about the most perfect society. He suggests that rulers need a very large dose of philosophy...so that they will not only know what the good is, they will know how to urge others to pursue it. One can argue that *The*

Republic is primarily a book about education: how do you educate people so that a more perfect society is possible?

Do you have a debt to Plato? To the extent that you are an idealist, to the extent that you try to bring about a better world, you owe something to Plato. To the extent that you passionately pursue goodness, that you strive for virtue, that you discuss the differences between right and wrong, that you strive to bring up children to be good people, you owe something to Plato. And to the extent that you are willing to think things through, to acknowledge that you do not have all the evidence and must suspend judgment on some very major issues, you owe something to Plato. Just as we enrich the lives of others by the things we do, so too Plato has enriched our lives, by the discussions he initiated so long ago. Aristotle would write: "Dear is Plato, but dearer still is truth." Plato would have appreciated that: he wanted his students not just to repeat what he had said, but also to think things through for themselves. Every time you engage in the exercise of thinking things through, you repay some of your debt, especially when you surprise yourself by arriving at an unexpected conclusion. After all, it was Plato who wrote: "The unexamined life is not worth living." And such examinations are bound to have surprising consequences. Whenever honest dialogues occur, the spirit of Plato is very much alive, and very interested in the outcome.

35
Are You a Platonist?

Among philosophers, about the nastiest thing you can do is to accuse someone of being a Platonist. Empiricism has ruled philosophy for a long time, and to be a Platonist means that you hold the mind apart from sense perception, as if the mind could think all by itself, without the help of what the senses have to offer. To be a Platonist means to be an idealist, to think that some ideal patterns exist, and all you have to do to reform human behavior or society, is to find these models, and impart them to society. But maybe being a little bit of a Platonist is not all that bad.

Recent events suggest some validity for at least some of Plato's insights. In the greatest of his works, *The Republic*, Plato suggested that the primary and ultimate human problem is politics: how do you enable people to get along, to work together to achieve true humanity? (The deeper message of this dialogue is that only through proper EDUCATION will the problems of society ever be solved. But that's another matter.) Plato avers that the only way you can have a "good" city, state, or country, is if the individual people who make up that society, are themselves "good." So the question becomes, how do you get people to become "good"? The answer lies in reforming the educational curriculum, so that "Truth," with a capital T, will prevail.

Plato is the first Greek philosopher to discuss at length the question of what is the good life for a human being. What is it that really makes people happy? His conviction is that the good life is only lived by virtuous people, and that only virtuous people are really happy. Plato provides endless examples to show that neither the miser nor the pleasure-seeker is happy, and the person who seeks honor and glory is seeking something external and transitory. Most of Plato's dialogues are discussions of how you become virtuous, and Plato's persistent theme is that thinking about it is the first step towards acquiring any virtue. Unless I think beforehand about what courage is, for example, I really won't know if my behavior is rash, or cowardly. Plato seems convinced that if you think about it long enough, you will have some insight into how you should behave, when your courage is challenged.

You have certain Platonist leanings if you believe in the primacy of Reason, and that by thinking, you can discern the "forms" of things, the way things ought to be. You have Platonist characteristics if your first principle is: "think before you act." If you think that reasoning things through will reach the truths you need for right action, you fit the Platonist profile. One of the great Plato scholars of the twentieth century, Huntington Cairns, wrote: "Plato's own philosophy rests on the doctrine that at the heart of things there is Intelligence at work endeavoring everywhere to fulfill itself." Platonists believe deep down that the real is rational, and that the rational ought to become real. In the modern world, most politicians claim to be "pragmatists," that is, finding solutions that will work. For the Platonist, it is important to find the Truth first, and workable solutions will inevitably follow.

Plato is a *transcendentalist*, that is, he believes there are ideal archetypes or patterns for all that is, and especially for human behavior. Jewish and Christian philosophers came to think of these patterns as ideas in the mind of God, but for Plato, the forms are themselves the highest reality, that which the gods contemplate, and perhaps imitate. If these eternal Forms or Models are the first principle of Platonism, belief in the primacy of the soul is the second central principle. The soul is the really important part of the human composite. And the soul should rule the body absolutely. Thoreau, perhaps America's greatest Platonist, wrote: "He is blessed who is assured that the animal is dying out in him day by day, and the divine being established."

It has been suggested that Plato is more "spiritual" than Judaism, Christianity or Islam, for his vision of the spiritual life includes a real negation of matter and the material world. The Platonic goal in life is a quest to become most like the absolute truth, beauty and goodness that characterize the divine. The prayer he offers at the end of the *Phaedrus* sums it up well: "Beloved Pan and all ye other gods here present, give me beauty in the inward soul; and may the outward and the inward man be at one. May I reckon the wise to be the wealthy, and may I have such a quantity of gold as a temperate man and he only can bear and carry."

There are worse things than being a Platonist. Perhaps it's time to acknowledge that the world needs Plato now more than ever, that society can only be improved if we have a vision of what the ideal society might be, that the real meaning of life is the pursuit of virtue, and that happiness resides much more in the nourishment of the soul, than of the body. Such convictions might be the key to a very beneficial Platonic Renaissance for the modern world.

36
Aristotle and the Modern World

Modern philosophy began with the skeptical doubt of Descartes, proceeded to the ethical "Perspectivism" of Nietzsche, and has ended badly with the incomprehensible babble of the post-moderns. However, every time philosophy does itself in, it has an opportunity to start anew. Perhaps re-discovering pathways long ago abandoned can help with that.

"All men by nature desire to know," said Aristotle, some 2400 years ago, thereby giving philosophy a good starting point. Aristotle assumed that the world was indeed knowable, that human existence was meaningful and purposeful, and that societies could be structured so as to achieve a "common good," insuring the best possible life for all its citizens.

"A small mistake in the beginning is a great one in the end," is an oft-repeated Aristotelian dictum. It might be said that Descartes' attempt to begin philosophy by being skeptical about knowing, was not just a small mistake, but a huge one, leading philosophy down a blind alley. Aristotle was, so to speak, a "realist," attempting first to know the world, and then talk about the nature of our knowledge. Every "realist" philosophy begins with some basic convictions about the knowability of the world, and the capacity to make statements that have some objective validity.

In building his ethics, Aristotle observed human behavior, and commented that those who live well and happily appear to be the people of outstanding virtue. Accordingly, his book on *Ethics* is simply a blueprint of the virtuous life. "Virtue is a state of character that makes the man good, and makes him do his activity well." (James Hillman, in his book *The Force of Character,* suggested that the real work of the older human being is building depth of character, which is but another way of saying, cultivating virtue.)

From the time of Galileo, the modern world has been obsessed with motion and change. In the coaching talk of Joe Paterno: "If you are not getting better, you are getting worse: there's no staying the same." We tend to assume that all change is progress, and that the force of evolution is ever upwards. But Aristotle, like the authors of the Hebrew Bible who endorsed "sabbaticals", envisioned some balance of rest and motion. Aristotle suggested the goal of motion, is rest! Paradoxically, rest is not doing nothing, but heightened activity. The particular "rest" that Aristotle most admires is leisure: activity done for its own sake, for the sheer delight of the performance. As Aristotle said: "Leisure seems to contain in itself pleasure, happiness, and the blessed life." Not for Aristotle is the modern life of frantic, restless activity. Life is not purposeless, random movement, nor is it idleness. For Aristotle, the meaning of life is fairly obvious: the goal of human existence is to become an actively virtuous person, thereby not only experiencing happiness, but also becoming a contributing member of society.

While Aristotle regarded "contemplation" as superior to action, taking an active role in the life of the community is important. He is no proponent of the ivory tower. "He who would live alone is either a beast or a god." His communitarian roots shine through his treatise on *Politics:* cities were founded first of all for mutual protection, then trade and commerce, but what they achieve at their best is the creation of the "good life" for their citizens.

Aristotle seems to live up to Plato's criterion for the true philosopher: "So the philosopher with his passion for wisdom will be the one who desires all wisdom, and not just some of it. Only the man who has a taste for every sort of knowledge and throws himself into acquiring it with an insatiable curiosity will deserve to be called a philosopher. And who are the genuine philosophers? Those whose passion it is to see the truth." Thus it is that Aristotle provides an opportunity for the rebirth of philosophy, and produces an ancient vision that has much to offer in these troubled and uncertain modern times.

37
"Who is Plotinus?"

Plotinus was born of Greek parents about 205 C.E. in Alexandria, eventually moved not to Athens, but to Rome, where he taught until his death in 270. He had many influential friends, and also ran an orphanage. He is called a "neo-Platonist," because he regarded Plato as the great fount of wisdom, and his writing clearly owes much to Plato. He had an extensive knowledge of Aristotle, the Stoics and the Epicureans, knew pious Jews and Christians, and was very interested in eastern philosophy, attempting a trip to India, but only getting as far as Persia.

Plotinus has been described as "the most metaphysical of all philosophers. " When Aristotle's works were catalogued, his book on the natural world was called "Physics," which is the Greek word for Nature. The large book that came next, and which dealt largely with the gods, was called "meta-physics," that which comes "after nature." Plotinus developed a rather intricate philosophy of how all things derive from "The One," how "The One" is unlike any being that you know, and how the purpose of life is to strive for some kind of union with "The One."

At the root of his philosophy is his mystical experience, some kind of contact with "The One," an experience more vivid than anything else in his life. "If anyone has seen It, he knows what I mean, how beautiful It is." This sentence summarizes his message: "I see a marvelous beauty and then most of all am assured that I am part of a higher order, attaining an excellent life and becoming identical with the divine."

Because of statements like this, Plotinus is called a pantheist or a monist. Nature mystics affirm that all things are divine, which makes them pantheists. The Indian tradition, which affirms "Atman is Brahman," is monist, that is, the individual soul is completely identical with the power behind the universe. But the One of Plotinus' metaphysics is really Other, and the goal of life is really becoming as like as possible to the One, not being subsumed or immersed in it. Mystics have some language trouble once they start speaking of "blending" or "mingling" with the divine order. (The medieval Christian mystic, Meister Eckhart, wrote: "The eye by which I see God, is the eye of God Himself." That sounds like the gap between Creator and creature so essential to Jewish, Moslem and Christian traditions, has disappeared...)

What are the practical consequences of such a metaphysical philosophy? Plotinus says people seek happiness in all the wrong places: it only comes from possession or union with the One, which can only be attained by the truly virtuous person. Self-mastery, and a certain amount of training in logic, are pre-requisites to the good life. Like all the great Greek philosophers, Plotinus is obsessed with the pursuit of knowledge; the passion for knowledge is one of the highest virtues, and just as performing a virtuous act makes the person performing the act good, so the act of knowing elevates the knower to a higher level of being. In the delight of knowing, Plotinus says, the knower "has a taste of eternity." Plotinus says "teaching is the real act of kindness," for it brings others along the path to wisdom...and contributes to the providential organization of the material world.

If, in your experience today, you should hear the voices of Goodness, Beauty, Truth, or the Oneness behind the multiplicity of things, attend to that voice, and respond to your higher calling. In this most un-metaphysical of ages, Plotinus has a message that is as contemporary as microchips. Plotinus affirms that there is an Ultimate Beauty hidden in the beauty of each beautiful thing--which is why art appeals to us--and there is an Ultimate Goodness concealed in good human actions--which is why we admire virtue, even when we don't practice it. There is a Unity behind the scattered multiplicity of our everyday activities, which is why our lives add up to something meaningful, no matter how hectic and uncoordinated things may appear. Even in this most un-metaphysical age, the voice of Plotinus rings loud and clear, conveying a message that is both metaphysical and mystical. "Those who have eyes to see, let them see."

38
Islamic Philosophy

While taking a class on Medieval Philosophy, I was so enchanted by the English translations of a variety of Islamic philosophers, I asked an Arabic Studies Professor how long it would take me to learn enough Arabic to read them in the original. "About eighteen years," was his immediate reply. That stilled my enthusiasm for reading them in the original, but I have maintained a fascination with this group whom I call "The Big Als," ranging from Al-Ashari to Al-Ghazzali, with a couple Ibns thrown in for free.

Virtually every "new" direction in Jewish or Christian philosophy or theology has its parallel among Islamic writers. In every age there are some Jewish and Christian writers who maintain that everything that happens is the direct result of God's agency, and that God Himself is beyond all human understanding, perhaps beyond all rationality. The first of the great

Moslem writers, Al-Ashari (d. 935) is in this camp. There are no "natural" laws, because the world is purely the result of God's volition. There is no human mind or human will, because God does the thinking and willing through us. Fire burns, not because it is its nature to do so, but because God wills it to be so. Among Christian writers, William of Ockham is the closest parallel: he says all theology begins with: "I believe in God, the Father Almighty." Being Almighty, means He can do anything He pleases, including squaring circles, or making fire cold.

Al-Farabi (d. 950) represents the kind of rationalism that goes beyond most Jewish or Christian writers. He sees philosophy as superior to revealed religion, which is just "philosophy for the masses." He sees Islam as free of illogical doctrines like the Christian Trinity, and as supporting a rational political organization of society, so that the Platonic Republic might come into being. All the same, Al-Farabi was a Sufi mystic, perhaps in reaction to the "legalism" of the Moslem clerics, whom he saw as creating a kind of rabbinic jurisprudence. For Al-Farabi, both reason and mysticism lead directly to the God most clearly revealed in the Koran.

Ibn-Sina (d. 1037) wished to reassert the primacy of revelation, suggesting that the Prophet Muhammad was the ideal philosopher, because he had insights beyond what human reason could attain. The truths God has revealed cannot be reached by human thought, so philosophy reaps the benefit of an advanced starting point. Since there is only One Truth, the mystic, the philosopher, and the ordinary believer have different ways of approaching the same Ultimate Reality. Ibn-Sina is likely the originator of the proof of the existence of God on the basis that there must be a Necessary Being who is the source of all contingent, finite being.

Ibn-Rushd (d. 1198) is the most "rationalist" of the Moslem faylasufs, (the Arabic word for philosopher), maintaining that while religion is for everybody, philosophy is reserved for an intellectual elite. He was a devout Muslim, and rejected any suggestion that there could be two truths, one of faith, one of reason. More than any other medieval Muslim writer, he had the largest collection of the writings of Aristotle, and became known to Jewish and Christian writers as "The Commentator," because of the depth of what he had to say about the Aristotelian texts.

The most influential of the medieval Moslem writers was Al-Ghazzali, (d. 1111), who said that although philosophy taught him a great deal about God, he had not come to know God Himself. After ten years of meditation, he affirmed that only ritual and prayer could give the believer direct knowledge of God. Like his Jewish contemporaries, he said the purpose of ritual observances was to develop unceasing consciousness of the Divine Presence. Devotion and reflection are all well and good, but the goal of all human activity should be awareness of the presence of God. In this, Al-Ghazzali is not that different from a modern Jewish writer like Rabbi Kushner, nor a Christian writer like Hans Urs von Balthasar, nor from a great many Protestant writers of the last three centuries.

Karen Armstrong has documented that fundamentalists, whether Jewish, Christian, or Moslem, manifest a deep disappointment and disenchantment with the modern world, and, in their enthusiasm for taking some scriptural texts literally, uniformly depart from the core values of compassion, justice, and benevolence that are at the roots of all the world's great religions.

We occasionally are exposed to the dark side and even malevolent practices of Jewish and Christian believers in the modern world, and we have had abundant evidence of Islam's negative confrontation with the western world and with western values. It is unfortunate that Moslems in Europe tend either to segregate themselves, or be segregated, not becoming participants in the mainstream of western European societies. Most Moslems in America, by contrast, have sought to Americanize as much as possible, struggling to balance the teachings of Islam with the manifold characteristics of American life. Some scholars claim the contrasts are irreconcilable, for the West preaches that self-direction and self-development are ultimate values, while Islam proclaims that all direction comes From Above, and that, as servants of Allah, self-effacement is the only goal appropriate to a devout Moslem. We still await the final outcome of these conflicting ideals.

Various critics have pointed out that in recent years the ancient values of Islam, such as social justice, equality, tolerance, and practical compassion, have taken a back seat to an Islam that sees itself in direct political, economic, and military confrontation with the western world. One can only hope that cooler heads will prevail, that the core values of Islam as elaborated by great thinkers from Al-Ashari to Al-Ghazzali, will surface, and that Moslems the whole world over will come to see that the heritage they represent has a role to play in the modern world. All of humanity could be better off by reaping the benefits from a great, noble and admirable tradition.

39
Moses Maimonides

In efforts to identify the ten greatest minds of all time, Plato and Aristotle constantly make the list. Not so well known but high on the list of candidates is Moses Maimonides, born in Moorish Spain in 1135, he spent most of his life in Egypt, dying there in 1204. He was Aristotelian to his roots, and Judaism never produced a more metaphysical philosopher. He lived at a time when Muslim civilization was at an apex, circulating Arabic translations of the works of Aristotle, Galen, and a host of other Greek and Roman philosophers and medical writers. He made his living as a physician, but his "hobby" was commenting on Jewish law, and Arabic philosophy.

He wrote a commentary on the Torah, in 14 volumes. He wrote 10 medical works. He wrote a text still widely used today, entitled "Thirteen Articles of Faith." But his most famous text was his attempt to consolidate religion and philosophy, *The Guide for the Perplexed*. With the popularity of Aristotelian philosophy in his day, many of his contemporaries had difficulty reconciling faith and reason, revelation and philosophy. Maimonides is inclined to award reason a certain primacy, for it is rational thinking that guides all understanding, including understanding the revealed word of God. Against the "fundamentalists" of his time, he pointed out that the Bible often speaks "figuratively and allegorically."

When Maimonides wishes to speak about God, he does so initially in the language of Aristotle: God is the unmoved Mover, the Cause of all motion. But in two ways he goes beyond the text of his philosophical master. He proceeds to a discussion of the attributes of God, all those things that might be said of God, such as: He is perfect, knowing, just, merciful, etc., and that He exists. Ah, says Maimonides, we use the terms as if we knew what they meant, but they only sound the same, so vastly superior is God to any of our concepts of Him! God has all these "attributes" in an utterly simple manner, so, complex creatures that we are, we do not have an inkling of what God really is.

The second contribution of Maimonides is even more startling. He says God is that Being, whose very essence is...existence! Maimonides may be the first metaphysician to get excited about the very fact of existence. Plato had said that to be is to be knowable; Aristotle had said that to be was to be a substance, a thing that stood on its own two feet. Maimonides says: to be...is to exist, to stand outside your causes, if you are a creature. What makes us different from God, is that his essence is Existence, whereas to us, it is accidental, it is something that just "happened" to us. Maimonides introduces this "mysticism of existence" into philosophy, and it will have a long and distinguished history.

Maimonides kept up a remarkable correspondence, and was in some respect the "Ann Landers" and "Dr. Phil" of his day, commenting on almost every aspect of health and personal psychology. To catalogue just a few of his comments: "Treat diseases with diet first." "Cheer up the patient, and make him and his family laugh." "May the love of the physician's art actuate me at all times. May I not be concerned with money or fame, but only with the good health of my patient." "The worst disease is to think you are more perfect than you really are." "Do all that you can so that you may maintain physical health and vigor, so that you can live well, and know God." And, one that shows his uniting of Aristotelian philosophy and his Jewish religion: "Be moderate in all things, and you will draw close to God."

Moses Maimonides was a very well rounded man, a participant in the learning and culture of his time, a kind of model for what a real human being might be in any age. No wonder that Jewish tradition has said, more than once, "From Moses, until Moses, there was none like Moses." So voluminous was his writing, so provocative are his commentaries, and so human and warm his advice, he deserves a place in the top ten.

40
Augustine, Kierkegaard, and Emotions

Among the great philosophers, the works of Augustine of Hippo and Soren Kierkegaard of Denmark are especially puzzling. Augustine, born in the fourth century, led a fairly wild life as a youth, but in his thirtieth year, he "got religion," and became the first great Christian theologian. His most famous work is *The Confessions*, an autobiographical, prayerful account of his conversion, and a statement of the reasons for his newfound faith. He was well versed in the philosophers of Greece and Rome, but the conclusions of the philosophers left him unsatisfied, until he became a believer. Only then, did things fall into place. Augustine's legacy is twofold: first of all, the world defies human comprehension, and only "by taking on faith," can you hope to begin to comprehend the nature of human existence. And secondly, "the reasons of the heart" Pascal spoke of so eloquently centuries later, is simply a basic Augustinian notion: God has left his imprint on us, and life is inexplicable, until one turns to and accepts

God. Augustine's most poetic statement is this: "Thou has made us for Thyself alone, and our hearts are restless until they rest in Thee."

Augustine claims that he is better off as a philosopher, because he is a believer. Notions of the unity of faith and reason have their anchor in his writings. God is the author of Nature and of Revelation, so the two must be in harmony. Augustine's religious faith, and his confessional style, give his "philosophy" an intensely emotional character, unrivaled in philosophy for 1500 hundred years....

Until Soren Kierkegaard came along, in the 19th century. He was deeply troubled by the cultural and religious turmoil of his time. He wanted to be religious, but everywhere he looked, he saw only the hypocrisy of the established churches. Was it not indeed impossible to be a Christian, within this Christian culture that had codified and removed the simple, direct "trust in Jesus" that characterized the Gospels? Was it not impossible to be "saved," when a churchly bureaucracy had replaced the spirit of Christ with a spirit of competing with others for the appearance of piety?

It is anxiety about his own salvation that leads him to write books with titles like "Fear and Trembling," and "Sickness Unto Death." Paradoxically, he is an intellectual writing difficult prose, to affirm that the intellect does not really solve life's major problems. Like Augustine, Kierkegaard affirms that faith is a higher mode of "knowing," because it goes beyond the powers of the human intellect. Kierkegaard becomes obsessed with the notion of faith: faith is venture, is risk, faith is infinite passion in the face of objective uncertainty. "Faith is riding on 60,000 fathoms, and being joyful."

The puzzle produced by Augustine and Kierkegaard is obvious: philosophers forsaking reason, and seeking for truth in the midst of human emotions. Curiously, so many scientists, passionate believers in the power of reason, turn to emotional response when life's largest questions loom. Months before his death, Carl Sagan, a most vocal modern agnostic, said: "It is as if I hear my mother's voice, saying: 'It's all right Carl: come join us'." And how puzzling the statement of Einstein, perhaps the greatest scientist of the century: "To the end, I remain a deeply religious unbeliever." Is there a level of truth reason cannot attain, and only emotion can lead where reason is dumb? Take for example the "truth" of the greatest of human emotions, the love you feel for others. Is there a "truth" in that experience of love that neither science nor philosophy can begin to touch? It is "truths" like this that writers like Augustine and Kierkegaard regard as of the greatest importance…

41
Philosophy and Science

Philosophy may have reached its apogee in the golden age of Greece, in the time of Socrates, Plato and Aristotle. It may have reached its nadir in the twentieth century, with Logical Positivism (only that which can be empirically verified is true--but that statement cannot be empirically verified) and Linguistic Analysis (scientists talk about things, philosophers talk about talk). Philosophy, which should be profound and meaningful reflection about what life really means, became a stultified and stuffy discipline, meaningful only to a few "professional" philosophers who seemed disconnected from the problems of the real world.

By our standards, "science" was rather primitive in the time of the Greeks, while it appears to have reached its point of maximum returns in our own day. Some scientists say that with the Theory of Relativity, Quantum Physics, and the Theory of Natural Selection, the great era of scientific discovery is over, and all that's left is mopping up operations. Even if the basic theories are in place, clearly a great many scientific discoveries remain on the horizon. Accordingly, science would appear to have a much brighter future than philosophy.

It has been wisely said that philosophy always buries its undertakers. Philosophy comes back to life for two basic reasons. First of all, all have to discover for themselves the philosophical insights they wish to live by. A philosophical question is always a new question, until you come up with your personal answer. Secondly, philosophical answers are more than verbal, more than linguistic, more than formulary. They require some kind of life re-orientation, so that as your perception of a philosophical position deepens, your personality and your behavior are called upon to change accordingly. Philosophy is not true to itself when it remains airy abstractions. Philosophy demands a "reformation of character," as the truth of a particular philosophy seeps into the bones of the individual. Philosophical statements may appear the same over time, but the assimilation changes, presumably deepens, as understanding of the "real meaning' becomes more profound.

Philosophy seeks to be wisdom about life, about the meaning of life, and how to live your life. Science, by contrast, is much more specific, much more targeted to precise answers. Modern science owes much to the development of mathematics, the most "precise" of all forms of human knowledge. Scientific studies provide us with statistics, for example, of what percentage of impotent men will benefit from Viagra, but it does not tell us much about why overcoming impotence is a good thing. Science provides us with precise mathematical measurements of how long it takes the light of the sun to reach the earth, or what percentage of scientists are religious believers. Science offers us fascinating insights into the composition of the material universe, as any visit to a planetarium or "Exploratorium" will readily tell you.

Science offers us precise answers to precise questions, and therein abides its special appeal. Scientists can get real answers to appropriately formed questions, and then move on to the next problem. Therein also reside its shortcomings, for science offers us little information about the really big questions: What is the meaning of my life? How ought I to act? What can I hope for? These are philosophical questions that do not admit of the kind of experimental study that makes for scientific answers.

Science can do much to improve the quality, as well as the duration of human life. (It might also terminate human life, if some day, some scientific experiment goes terribly awry...). Science can offer interesting theories about the origin of the universe, and about such questions as the likelihood of finding intelligent life on other planets. But science cannot answer the question posed by one of the greatest of modern mathematician-philosophers, Leibniz: "Why is there something rather than nothing?" Nor does science offer much in the way of an answer to the puzzling question: "Why do bad things happen to good people?" The goal of philosophy is not to answer these really big questions, but to encourage asking them, and not be satisfied with trivial responses. Philosophy is indeed the most life-long of all the intellectual pursuits....

Science deals with problems that admit of solutions. Philosophy deals with questions tinged with mystery, in which every answer is provisional, and every answer provokes further questions. Scientific questions presume the possibility of definitive answers. Philosophical questions simply indicate that you have focused on the larger mysteries of existence. Perhaps their very insolvability is what keeps human life so interesting.

42
How To Spend Your Money Wisely

Financial magazines frequently profile a new class of wealthy people: the recently retired. Many retirees who had well-managed pension plans have been pleasantly surprised by how much money they had. One lucky individual had accumulated a million dollars in his pension plan by the time of his retirement, and then had three consecutive years of more than 25% gains, and wound up with more than two million dollars. Greatly to his amazement, his financial planner told him he could safely spend $100,000 a year, and never run out of money. Planning for this kind of wealth is not something done by most people who were born in the depression-era, worked hard to put bread on the table and kids through college, and expected to retire on a limiting fixed income.

Is there a solution to this rather pleasant problem? There are many different things you can do with money, but there are three basic categories of expenditures pertinent to people who find themselves with more money than they know what to do with.

(1) You can spend so as to increase the total amount of pleasure in your life. We look upon hedonism as a vice, and look down upon those for whom the pursuit of pleasure has become the central aspect of life. But it is also a vice to be unable to find and accept pleasure. The body has many aches and pains, life hits us with many sorrows and hardships, and pleasure is something that softens the blows, and enables us to bear up through the hardships life sends our way. If eating were not pleasurable, we might forget to eat; if sex provided no pleasure, the human race might forget to reproduce; and dentists have been known to provide treats to children, partly to make the experience a bit more pleasant, perhaps partly to insure they will need to return . . . Pleasure has an important role in life, and spending money to increase one's regular pleasure, may be money well spent. You can easily spend money on food that is more nutritious as well as tastier, on furniture that is more comfortable, on better entertainment, on cars that get you places more enjoyably, and on doing a whole range of things that increase the total amount of pleasure in your life.

(2) Spending money just on pleasure only takes you so far. A second category of spending might be broadly labeled: "education." You should be willing to spend money on all those things that expand your mind, increase your understanding of the world, and help you come to grips with the larger mysteries of existence. Money spent on books, or taking courses, or any kind of learning experiences, is money well spent. Aristotle wrote: "Mind,

more than anything else, is what sets human beings apart." There are all kinds of educational experiences available, all kinds of travel experiences, wonderful Elderhostel programs, programs that involve nature, history, archeology, art---a million things to keep the mind active, alert, inspired, eager for ever more knowledge. Faust sold his soul for greater knowledge; no need to go that far, but money spent on good learning experiences is bound to be money well spent.

(3) Philanthropy is a third category of good ways to spend money. There are all kinds of worthy causes in need of support. Before you make generous contributions based on the latest TV appeal, you might want to call the National Charities Information Bureau (212-929-6300) and ask for their "Wise Giving Guide." The American Institute of Philanthropy (301-913-5200) provides a bulletin that grades each charity on the basis of what percent of donations are actually spent on the charitable purpose, and how well they fulfill their promises.

Seneca, perhaps the greatest of the Roman Stoic philosophers, wrote: "I shall always live as if I had been born for service to others . . .nothing shall seem to me so truly my possessions as the gifts I have wisely bestowed . . .the wise man lives happy in the present and unconcerned about the future." Surely Seneca would have loved to face the financial problem of some of today's retirees. He would have found a large number of great, good things to do with his money, including raising his own level of delight in life, increasing his learning activities, and doing some good things to improve the lives of others.

43
"Cui Bono?"

"Cui bono" is an odd Latin phrase that literally translates: "To whom is it for a good?" or more clearly, "What good is it?" or, as we would put it:" What should I do with my money?" This is a serious question for people of means and also of mature years. There is a bumper sticker that says: "I am spending my kids' inheritance." You may have heard of the will that reads: "Being of sound mind, I spent it all." But for some people the question remains: "What ought I to do with the money I do not need?" Stephen Pollan, the author of *Die Broke*, has a book entitled: *Live Rich*, in which he advises learning how to overcome the life-long habit of frugality, and spend money more freely. But that does not really answer the larger question.

One obvious answer to having more money than needed is: pass it on to the next generation, or, if they don't need it, the generation after that, or perhaps to elderly relatives who are in great need. The dilemma may be greater for those who do not have children. But if you choose to pass money on to relatives, the questions loom: How much money? When? Do I want to exercise control over how they spend it? We have all heard stories of children who either blew inheritances, or were "ruined" by them. People once grew up with strong "work ethics," which emphasized the value of hard work, frugality, and saving for a rainy day. Those are values that should never be spoiled by the sudden presence of a large inheritance.

Philosophers might suggest that we should want our children to live "nobly and well," and if our financial aid can promote that goal, well and good. But how many dollars does it take to enable them to live "nobly and well," and at what rate should it be dispersed? The federal government sets an annual limit to how much money can be given away free of gift tax, and in most circumstances that is enough to improve the opportunity to live "nobly and well." Warren Buffett suggested that while his children should experience some financial benefits from his will, "most" of his money should "return to the community from which it came."

There is no end to the "good causes" that could benefit from largesse. Around the world, millions of people starve to death each year, and even in the United States millions of people live lives of desperate poverty. Organizations like CARE and OXFAM render aid where most desperately needed. The *American Institute of Philanthropy* (301-913-5200) evaluates charities in terms of their cost effectiveness, and such guides, and your heart, can tell you something of where some portion of your moneys might go.

But what should you do with income that far exceeds your personal needs? You do not want to be too generous and "spoil" your children or grandchildren by depriving them of the rich rewards of work. There are limits to how much personal pleasure your money can buy. It does not take an Aristotle or a Gandhi to remind us that wealth should produce results, in terms of improving the lives of those in need--and not somewhere in the distant future, but right now. Aristotle would suggest that our first "duty" is to our family, then our community, and then the larger world. Gandhi would insist that those who most desperately need our aid should come first.

To whom is your extra money for a good? That is a choice, and the choice made is a reflection of moral maturity. The Stoic philosophers said we are all citizens of the world, responsible equally for those near and dear to us, and those far removed in space and time. If your money can alleviate pain and suffering some of it belongs there; if it can enhance the lives of those you love, some of it belongs there; and some of it should be spent to enhance the delight you take in life. Delighting in life should make you all the more anxious to share some of your wealth, with those who have not been so fortunate. You may have to give as much attention to the proper distribution of your wealth, as you did to its initial accumulation. The question becomes: to whom is it for the greatest good? And the answer may take some very serious thought.

44
Living With Affluence

Few Americans realize how affluent they are, or how accustomed they are to having their needs constantly expanding, and all their wants gratified. There are countries where the average annual income would translate into two hundred American dollars. Half the world's population does not enjoy what Americans presume to be basic sanitary conditions. But it is not just that our "standard of living" is higher than most of the rest of the world, it is our widespread conviction that an affluent manner of living is our birthright, and that spending money to the point of being deeply in debt is an integral part of the American experience.

A PBS special entitled "Affluenza" suggested that for many Americans, life is seen as one big shopping spree. Seventy percent of Americans visit shopping malls weekly, and Americans average six hours a week shopping, but less than an hour a week playing with children. There are more malls in America than there are high schools, and two-thirds of the space in newspapers is devoted to advertisements. The function of advertising is to keep consumers permanently discontent, always assuming that happiness will occur with the next purchase, and in a state of always needing new purchases to feed the addiction.

A veritable industry has grown up, offering advice on how to overcome affluenza by "simplifying your life." Among the books that may be helpful, Alan Lakein's *How to get Control over your Time and your Life* is perhaps the best for very busy people with myriad responsibilities. For those who simply feel overwhelmed by too many different things to do, Richard Carlson's *Don't Sweat the Small Stuff* is excellent. For those who really want to launch out and make big changes, Elaine St. James' *Living the Simple Life* is superb. For those who think they can never possibly earn enough money to pay all their bills and live as affluently as they deserve, Joe Dominguez and Vicki Robin's book, *Your Money or Your Life* is necessary reading.

But the best book of all is *Walden,* written by one of America's most distinctive philosophers, Henry David Thoreau. "A man is rich in proportion to the number of things he can afford to let alone." The theme of Dominguez' book was expressed by Thoreau 150 years ago: "The cost of a thing is the amount of what I will call life which requires to be exchanged for it." Thoreau worked hard enough to attain leisure--not to be idle, but to work at the things that really mattered: gaining some understanding of the universe and his place in it. "If I am not myself, who else will be?" And no one has written a better sentence describing the hordes of mall shoppers or evening pleasure-seekers than: "The mass of men lead lives of quiet desperation."

Diogenes is reported to have said: "With a little bread and a little water a man should be satisfied." By contrast, our civilization is built upon the notion of progress, that each year should be better than the past, each generation richer than its predecessor, with science and technology making life continually easier, healthier, more comfortable. Thoreau might suggest that our notion of progress has been distorted, that our ambition should be to become nobler, kinder, gentler, richer in the things that really matter, and not just having more stuff in storage. Thoreau stands as a gigantic statue, blocking the harbor of Affluenza, with his simple and disarming phrases...."my greatest skill has been to want but little...."

The more things you have, the more time you will spend repairing them. If you want to live the good life, stay away from the malls, tune out the advertisements, spend more time with people in meaningful activity and, instead of accumulating stuff, delight in being alive. Do things that are intrinsically worthwhile, and put in practice the Thoreauvian insights. The goal of life is not to see how much you can acquire, but how much you can do that is intrinsically worthwhile.

45
De-Cluttering

In getting control of your time and your life, nothing helps more than de-cluttering. It is easy to acquire things over time, difficult to dispense with them. As a result, we have more things than we know what to do with, and our precious time is consumed by attention to things that may not contribute much to our lives.

There are three main sources of clutter. The easiest one to do something about is your clothes. Here is a three-step program to eliminate clothes clutter: Move to southern Arizona; buy shorts and a T-shirt, and throw everything else away. That may be more drastic than most are willing to pursue, but the idea has its merits. Clothing is not only inexpensive, it is durable. Seventy percent of purchases at malls are for clothing! Most clothes last long after they have "gone out of style," and it is easy to add new garments to your collection, while neglecting to cast aside the old. The de-clutter formula: get rid of what you don't wear. The winter coat you no longer wear could be well used by someone else. Thoreau's advice: "Cultivate poverty like a garden herb, like sage. Do not trouble yourself much to get new things, whether clothes or friends. Turn the old; return to them. Things do not change, we change. Sell your clothes and keep your thoughts." If we pay too much attention to our clothes, we suffer by paying less attention to our thoughts.

The second avenue of clutter is information. Far more information is available to all of us than we can possibly process. Big libraries have millions of books. You can really only read one at a time. And while one might be curious about the whole range of human knowledge, you can only learn so much. Make up your mind about what is going to get through to you. Drop magazines and newspapers (and e-mails!) that no longer interest you. If a magazine arrives and your reaction is: "Do I have to read that thing?" you have probably subscribed long enough, and it is time to turn your attention somewhere else. The worldwide web puts an infinite amount of information at our fingertips, and we have to choose what is relevant to us, and what must be left for someone else.

The third avenue of clutter is activities. Just as there are many movies playing at your neighborhood Cineplex, there are endless activities and acquaintances waiting to claim your attention. One friend said he had played table tennis the last five years, and that was about enough. Another said he figured he had now devoted a sufficient portion of his life to the golf course, and it was time to pursue other sports. Activities may mean sociability, and there may be other, easier, more meaningful ways to be sociable. Aristotle suggested that it is difficult to be friends with more than a few people, because friendship requires time and attention, and while your circle of acquaintances may be ever enlarging, the number of people you can really spend quality time with, is limited. The number of activities in which you can engage meaningfully, also has its limits.

The removal of clutter is an endless battle. We live in a consumer society, and we are programmed to be good consumers. (A book by Donna Smallin may help: *Unclutter Your Home*, Storey books, $10.) Henry David Thoreau remains the patron saint of the de-clutter movement. His time at Walden Pond is the model of simplifying one's life. His detachment from material things, and from any one period of his life, is a model for all of us. "I left the woods for as good a reason as I went there. Perhaps it seemed to me that I had several more lives to live, and could not spare any more time for that one." (Perhaps a major source of clutter is our unwillingness to leave the past behind.) When our possessions begin to possess us, it is time to sort them out, and separate from what is no longer relevant.

As we free ourselves from clutter, we free the spirit within us, and have more time to be our selves, to cultivate the thoughts and activities that constitute the persons we are in the process of becoming. Things should be the instruments of human development; when they become obstacles in the way, it is time to put the de-clutter machinery into high gear.

46
American Tourism

When I checked into a motel in Washington D.C., the clerk said: "Are you here on business or are you *just* a tourist?" That being a tourist is of less value than negotiating some business or other is a conviction all too many people share. Tourism is not only one of the best things you can do with your time, it can also be an educational experience without parallel. With regard to the nation's capital, sure it might be important to go there to talk to your congressperson, or deal with one of the many federal agencies. But unless you go there sometime and just soak in the ambiance of the Washington Monument, the Jefferson and Lincoln Memorials, the War Memorials, the Smithsonian, the Congressional Buildings, including the library, you are missing some of the best physical expressions of what America is all about.

The same goes for the geological and historical wonders enshrined in our National Parks. Just touring, in whatever way is most appropriate, the wonders of Yosemite, Yellowstone, Zion, Bryce, the Grand Canyon, or any one of dozens of other stunning Parks, is a kind of cleansing experience, of emptying your mind of the mundane and everyday, awakening you to see the world as it really is: a place of spellbinding wonders. Every American should visit the great national historical shrines, from Independence Hall, to Gettysburg, to Williamsburg, and the many others that may have personal or local significance.

Being a successful tourist takes some time and some leisure, some turning away from everyday experience, some commitment of mind and energy to the questions that are really important. Is the world a beautiful place to live in? You won't know, unless you get out and have a real experience of natural beauty. What makes up our society? You won't really catch the flavor of it, unless you visit some of the great places of American History. Has the human experience really been worth it? You won't know, unless you take the time to visit a few repositories of artistic and scientific achievements....

Being a tourist is closely related to taking vacations. Curiously, the word "vacation" derives from the Latin verb *vacare,* which means to take a rest, take a break from your everyday tasks. As it occurs in Latin literature, it is consistently connected to coming to some important realization. A Latin version of the Psalms reads: "Vacate and videte quia Ego sum Dominus," which means: "Take a break, and become aware that I am the Lord." No small wonder that so many people interpret National Park experiences as having a religious dimension....

"Being a tourist" is not just killing time, and is not second fiddle to being somewhere on business. Being a tourist is one of the most important things you can do. Take a break, and see how your life stacks up. Are there things you should be doing to impart more meaning to your everyday experience? Maybe it's time for a real vacation, when you can put away the things of everyday, and have some sense of the things that are really important. While a visit to one or more of the great National Parks is highly desirable, there may be some tourist attractions more accessible to you. Don't wait for such grand tourist opportunities to come to you. Go out of your way, seek them out. The rewards of such adventures are beyond all reckoning. Being a tourist is, occasionally, one of the best things you can do with your time and your life.

47
The Ethical Turn

Contrary to the commercials, the most important decisions of your life do not revolve around your home mortgage. The biggest decisions of your life are, in one way or another, moral decisions. Some of the issues you have faced or will face: Must I always tell the truth? What do I owe to other people? What do I owe to my family? To the world? To God? What should I do with my life? With my sexual capacities? What do I owe to my community, my state, and to my country? What do I owe to future generations? How do I impart meaning and purpose to my life? Am I ever justified in taking someone else's life? Given certain circumstances, could I take my own life?

These questions are so large as to seem unanswerable, and most people take refuge in refusing to think about them, unless forced to. They are so universal they have been taken as themes by the world's major religions, and for most people, over the long course of human history, religion has provided guidelines and answers to the great moral questions.

We live however in an age that is significantly non-religious, progressively more secular, and decidedly pluralist. The answers provided by one religion cannot be imposed on non-believers, so reason, and hence philosophy, presents itself as the basis for a search for acceptable moral answers. Recent philosophers however have been loathe to provide moral advice, hinting that while philosophy might talk about the nature of moral language, its primary task is "conceptual analysis," getting clear about the words, as if the serious analysis of moral behavior was beyond the reach of philosophical reflection.

Moral issues have a stubborn way of staring us in the face, and the need for "moral education" becomes not just the stuff of editorials, but of headlines. There are heated debates about the posting of the Ten Commandments in public schools. The religious-minded see the Ten Commandments as the core of western ethics and civilization, while secularists balk at the clear favoring of at least one religious tradition in the first three Commandments. Accordingly, lively debates develop on the topic: "Do we need God to be good?" Those with deep religious convictions want those convictions posted in public places and taught in schools, while the more secular-minded want to keep religion out of the public squares.

Religion has two important ethical attributes: a set of guidelines for behavior, and a goal or purpose for that behavior. But religion needs a rational corrective, lest human sacrifices to Moloch or some bloodthirsty divinity can become the norm, or some other form of "irrational" behavior is identified as necessary, and identified as a public duty.

It is impossible to impose a religious-based ethic on those who do not share religious beliefs. What is needed is an ethic that outlines the characteristics of moral behavior and points out where meaning and purpose in life may be found. Such an ethic need not be in open conflict with religious-based ethics, but rather it might serve as the "rational basis" for an ethic that also has religious dimensions. What is clear is that ethics has come front and center in philosophical circles, as well as in the public eye. The most visible, headline issues of each day are ethical issues: rare is the newspaper that does not discuss medical ethics, business ethics or the lack thereof, the rights of children and other dependents, issues of how tax dollars "ought" to be spent, animal rights, or environmental issues.

What are the presuppositions of your ethics? Do you want to be an "ethical" person? What does that mean, and what does that demand of you? It may be more demanding than you think. It is easy to take ethics for granted, right up to the time when ethical convictions are put to some supreme test. Better to have thought about the foundations of ethical visions, before a time of testing presents itself.

48
Can Morals Be Taught?

Parents are sometimes surprised to learn they are in the business of teaching morals. Not all of us are parents, but almost all of us have been children at one time or another, and we have at least vague memories of gradually assimilating some convictions about how we ought to behave. How do we learn about morals? Are parents the most important moral teachers?

Having taught ethics classes to graduates and undergraduates for many years, I have more than a passing interest in this question. There would appear to be three basic approaches to teaching about morals. First of all, a "rule" approach: over time, society has established certain "rules," and, as a member of society, you are instructed to follow them. Religions tend to have "rule" moralities, and pleasing God or the gods is often the reason given for the rules. The extreme form of the rule morality is the story of God telling Abraham to sacrifice his son Isaac: it is not a question of doing what is reasonable, but of doing what God commands. For some parents, rule morality becomes an absolute: "Do this because I tell you to do it."

Such instruction may be effective moral initiation, but something more is needed, if an individual is to be able to make moral decisions of his or her own.

Many educators claim that setting good examples does the best moral teaching. It is not by "laying down the law" that someone acquires good morals, but by seeing the good example of a virtuous person, and seeing the happy results of that behavior. In the extreme instance, we have examples of someone losing their life in the attempt to rescue someone else. All around us, we do see little acts of kindness, and the example set by such people should be instructive to us all. While good example is helpful, a world full of people setting good examples will do little to convert the morally insensitive.

For the teaching of morals--and this is a business in which we are involved --there is no better approach than the examination and analysis of consequences. What happens to societies in which respect for persons is abandoned? What consequences ensue from accepting murder, or theft, or deceit? The best catalyst for moral reflection is a study of the consequences of what you might choose to do, in the light of the consequences of the actions of others on a larger scale.

On this issue, philosophers can be very helpful. The unanswered question of many of the Platonic dialogues is: Can virtue be taught? Aristotle's *Ethics* concluded that *prudence,* the highest of the practical virtues, could only be acquired by experience, and that only a person who has mastered prudence, can really be called virtuous. Kant is among the most important ethicists of modern times, and his three basic insights still evoke lively responses and intense debate: (1) always treat other persons as ends in themselves and never as means; (2) in every moral situation, act so that your choice could be a model for everyone, everywhere; (3) do what is "right" just because it is right, regardless of the consequences.

Can morality be taught in schools? Clearly some "laying down the rules" is a necessary starting point for any social group. And families, schools, and religions are all in the business of teaching morality by good example. But morality is best learned by examining the consequences of the choices people have made, and that is done in History, Social Studies, Political Science, and Anthropology--wherever the consequences of human behavior are studied. This kind of reflection should begin in nursery school and continue through graduate and continuing education. Even philosophers might have something important to say about morality and how to go about encouraging desirable moral behavior. Can morals be taught? We can certainly teach a lot about the need for morals, and the catastrophic results produced by those whose actions appear to be outside the moral sphere. If we are to teach morals, (and no one is exempt from imparting moral instruction,) the best place to start is by an examination of the consequences of actions that have moral consequences. As Humpty-Dumpty might say, it's a matter of consequences, that's all.

49
Ethical Theories

As has been said previously, all of us are philosophers; some just do it more consciously than others. We are also all ethicists, making major ethical decisions everyday, usually with little thought as to what "ethical theories" might underlie our judgments. In neither of these ventures do we start from scratch: great minds have gone before us, and sketched outlines that can be helpful to us in solving our philosophical and ethical dilemmas.

Many people are ethical "consequentialists," thinking that actions are right or wrong according to their consequences. Such thinking is ultimately "utilitarian," seeking the greatest balance of good and the least amount of harm. If you carefully examine the consequences of lying, for example, you can see that lying could lead to the complete breakdown of society, for unless you can rely on people telling the truth, human interaction becomes impossible. The consequentialist may derive a series of "rules" that under gird human behavior, in the light of producing the most desirable outcomes, and avoiding what is societally destructive.

Many people, wittingly or unwittingly, subscribe to the "duty" ethic of Immanuel Kant. Morally good actions are "categorical imperatives," because they are the right things to do, and they proceed from the "good will" of the actor. In a Kantian ethic, virtue is truly its own reward, and an act should be performed just because it is the right thing to do, regardless of praise or blame, or particular consequences. Kant is justly famous for his personalism: "Treat every person as an end, and never as a means only." The real Kantian imperative is that it is immoral to use other people for your own purposes. (John Rawls, a great Harvard Professor of Philosophy, in his classic text, *A Theory of Justice,* was the best modern defender of the Kantian ethic.) Having a society made up entirely of Kantians would provide an interesting experiment. According to some interpretations, the Kantian imperative is simply a form of this version of the golden rule: "What you would not have others do to you, don't do to them."

The ethical theory that derives from Plato and Aristotle is sometimes called "virtue ethics." Aristotle suggested the goal of life was to become a virtuous person. Aristotle's *Ethics* is a delineation of the virtuous traits of character a good human being should cultivate: justice, courage, temperance, prudence, friendliness, greatness of character, etc. There is elegance to the Aristotelian ethic, and once again, one could do worse than live amidst people whose highest aspiration was living the virtuous life.

Medical ethicists have elaborated an "ethics of care," in which sympathy, compassion, fidelity, love and friendship are established as the primary ethical values. This ethic stands in deliberate contrast to the self-centeredness, the "looking out for number one," the primacy of self-interest that has presented itself so universally in modern society. An emergency room physician once summarized his challenge as "Learning to love a perfect stranger, perfectly." May you be so lucky as to encounter a practitioner of this ethic if you ever need it!

The examination of cases, or "casuistry" is often found to be helpful when discussing ethical matters. If you analyze "typical" ethical situations, you might derive some conclusions about what is appropriate ethical practice in similar circumstances; if you elaborate enough cases, you might generate the "principles" you need to get you through all the ethical circumstances of your life. But every situation is in fact different, and guidelines for one set of circumstances may be changed radically by the presence of one small variable. Casuistry remains an important component of "doing" ethical reflection, but by its very nature it points to the need for something more substantial.

Most of us make use of all these approaches, sometimes citing principles, sometimes consequences, sometimes virtues or vices, sometimes circumstances. Given the challenge, one might be tempted to take refuge in Wittgenstein's words: "Ethics cannot be put into words. Ethics is transcendental." But ethics can be put into words. We do it all the time. The behavior of admirably ethical people stands as a beacon to the rest of us. And the actions of those who have inflicted irreparable harm indicate to us the importance of accurate, penetrating moral reflection.

The simplest moral questions are also the most important, and lead us most directly to building some larger theoretical structure. Ethical questions are ubiquitous; it is only satisfying answers that are relatively rare.

50
Basic Issues in Medical Ethics

Ethics is a form of rational reflection on human behavior dealing with questions like: How should I act? How should I treat others? How should I expect others to treat me? How should I relate to the world? How do I make my life meaningful? It would be convenient if we could draw up a list of rules, and say observation of those rules indicated good behavior, while their violation was always and everywhere undesirable. Unfortunately, human life is not that simple, and nowhere is this more evident than in the case of medical ethics.

We all make Doctor's appointments, and we are all treated, at one time or another, by medical professionals, but few of us give much thought to the ethics behind medical practice, or to what ethical principles stand behind the medical treatment we receive.

There are three basic principles widely voiced, and continually debated, within the medical community. The first principle is respect for the autonomy, or self-governance, of the patient. Most of us know about this through "informed consent," because before any major medical treatment, we sign a statement saying we understand and consent to what is going on. We have a right to assume we have been told all pertinent information, that our decisions will be accepted, and that we will not be "patronized." But there are limits: must autonomy be respected, if it might cause harm to someone else? Does a pregnant woman, for example, have a right to reject fetal surgery, if it would save the baby's life?

Beneficence, the second principle, is the most general: "Above all, do no harm." But, when we are suffering, we quite willingly accept the "harm" of injections or surgery, in the hope of greater good. We expect our medical practitioners to be guided by the principle of: Don't injure others, but help them. If you are terminally ill, and suffering terribly, does your medical practitioner harm you more by giving you, or by refusing to give you, a lethal injection? What is the real "doing good" here, which is what "beneficence" means?

To help resolve these issues, what some take to be the fundamental principle of all ethics becomes the central issue: the principle of justice. Justice means rendering to all what is their due. Does this mean that everyone is entitled to the same medical care? Does this mean the very wealthy should receive exactly the same medical care as the very poorest? Does this mean that very important people--business people and politicians for example--should not receive special care, even though their good health redounds to the benefit of many? The ideal of equal access is very appealing, but in practice those who have great funds, those who are famous, and those who are well connected, receive superior treatment.

From this glance at some of the principles of medical ethics, it should be obvious that the "right" course of action is not always clear. Since this is often the case in everyday life, no wonder that it applies in the realm of medicine. From our own experience we all know that the complexity of moral life makes any absolute hierarchy of rules and principles all but impossible. We also know of the great variety of moral principles and guidelines that seem to be part of the common wisdom of humankind. How to weight them in any given circumstance becomes the difficult moral challenge. The realm of ethics is a kingdom of a great many perplexing puzzlements. In spite of the apparent "relativity" of it all, there are some ethical principles most of us are eager to subscribe to, and hope others do too. The challenge lies in finding ethical principles with which we are comfortable, and then finding the society in which such ethical principles are practiced. We live in a time when all ethical principles are keenly debated, with strong advocates for opposing and sometimes irreconcilable points of view, and nowhere are these conflicts more evident than in the many difficult issues of medical ethics.

51
A Different Ethical Vision

Plato tells one of history's great ethical stories, under the heading of "The Ring of Gyges." Gyges is a shepherd who discovers a ring that can make him invisible. He is able to get away with all kinds of "unethical" activities, because the ring makes him invisible in the commission of his "crimes." Gyges can steal anything, murder anyone, have sex with whom he pleases, and get away with it. Plato asks: if you were completely free from any form of punishment, would there be any reason for you to act ethically? Plato says there is. Unethical, immoral, and illegal actions may produce their immediate rewards, but, says Plato, in the long run, only those who act rightly are really happy.

When you play a sport, and play it well, it makes you feel good. There may be some parallel with virtuous activity. It is not just idle chatter that those who act virtuously feel good for their action. But why does one feel good after performing a virtuous action? Is it just a matter of conditioning? Or is there some truth to a virtuous action being its own reward?

The first philosophers to espouse a theory of "natural law" were the Greek and Roman Stoics some 2000 years ago. They shared a conviction that there was a natural law inscribed into the very nature of things, and that activity in accordance with that natural law was not only good, but produced sense of satisfaction or well-being. The Stoics were perhaps a bit anthropomorphic, but they hinted that a bird finds delight in flying, a rock in cozying up to the earth, and the moon in shining. The theme was, when you do what nature intended, you feel good about it.

Aristotle assures us that only the virtuous person can possibly be happy. The liar cannot be happy if he always lives in fear of being found out; the coward lives a cringing life, and the intemperate person is the victim of passions. Only the virtuous person can handle the vicissitudes of life with equanimity, because only the virtuous person has the disposition to do the "right" things, whatever the circumstances. The life of virtue, Aristotle avers, turns out to be the most pleasant, because the virtuous person will not only do all things in moderation, the virtuous person will be lovable, and will therefore have friends. The virtuous person will have a capacity for contemplation, a capacity to rise above the trials of the moment, and have a certain timeless appreciation for both the delights and the tragedies of mundane existence.

One of the characteristics of American philosophy is its deeply "moral" character. Americans are often accused of being a-moral, of being business or production-minded, and of not giving much thought to the ethical or unethical character of their activities. America has certainly produced its fair share of remarkably immoral characters, but we have also a great many people with lofty moral visions. Even the much-maligned arena of politics has generated countless people who dedicated their lives to the betterment of society, and lived rather exemplary lives in the process.

John Dewey, whom some call America's most typical philosopher, was consumed with a passion to reform institutions, particularly educational and political institutions. He envisioned a society of free individuals in which all, through their own work, contribute to the liberation and enrichment of the lives of others, thereby producing the environment in which all can grow to their fullest stature. One finds in Dewey something of that natural law philosophy of the Stoics, and something of that aspiration to lofty virtue that so characterized the writings of Aristotle. If Dewey had the ring of Gyges, he would have made himself invisible, so as to effect some great genuine good, without having to take credit for it. Would you do the same, if, one of these days, you come across a ring with such magical qualities?

Tia and tiger friend

52
Peter Singer's Ethical Stance

Has life a meaning? Peter Singer, who occupies a prestigious Chair at Princeton University, avers that this is often regarded as the ultimate philosophical question. Unless you come up with some kind of answer, all the rest of philosophizing is just so much empty twaddle. As is clear from his long and controversial career as one of the most published, most quoted, and most vilified ethicists, Peter Singer thinks life does have a meaning, and he sees it in terms of choosing to live ethically.

Singer presumes a certain hierarchy of ethical convictions. The lowest level might be summarized as "eat, drink, and be merry, for tomorrow we die." Singer provides contemporary examples of the failures of such hedonism. The evidence is in, that those who most ardently pursue self-gratification turn out to be the unhappiest of people, endlessly seeking some new source of "meaning" in their lives.

People on the second level of moral behavior perform "good" actions and avoid "bad" ones on the basis of expecting rewards or fearing punishments. This is what Nietzsche described as "slave morality," acting not on the basis of some interior conviction, but out of hope, or fear. Singer is highly critical of the tradition of religious ethics, because it so often derives its motivation from hope of eternal reward or fear of everlasting damnation.

The next level of ethical behavior is practiced by people who have some vision of what is "right," and they try to do what they know they should, out of a sense of duty. This is the familiar Kantian ethic, and Singer acknowledges its appeal, but says that an ethic of duty falls short of a truly human ethic. In his war crimes trial, Adolph Eichmann said in sending people to the gas chambers, he was simply doing his duty, carrying out lawful commands. An ethic that can go that far astray, Singer suggests, has some fatal flaw. An ethic must not just be a form of social control, but must offer some rational motivation to the agent.

The highest level of ethical behavior, the ethic that imparts meaning and purpose to life, is an ethic of enlightened altruism, of committing yourself to a purpose that is higher than your own life and transcends your self-interests and petty concerns. The blood donor is the model: when you give blood, you do a good for some unknown other, while no particular benefit occurs to you. The highest ethic is a commitment to reducing the level of pain and suffering in the world. It is in this light that Singer committed himself to animal liberation and wilderness preservation, to population control, abortion and euthanasia (on the basis of reducing needless suffering) and to various programs to relieve starvation and homelessness around the world.

From Singer's point of view the highest ethic is to commit yourself, your life and your money, to doing good things for others. You do this not out of a sense of promoting your own self-interests, not out of a sense of duty, but out of a commitment to the ethical point of view. Singer's personal ethic is best summarized by the popular aphorism: Those who bring sunshine to the lives of others cannot keep it from themselves.

Far from being the "ethical monster" he has sometimes been depicted, Singer practices what he teaches. He is an ethical vegetarian, he is a sponsor of animal liberation programs, he gives 20% of his income to international aid programs, and he works as a public and visible advocate for the causes he espouses. Is life meaningful? It is, if you have purposes larger than yourself, and are committed to leaving the world a better place for your having been here. Singer has most vigorously criticized the "looking out for number one" ethic, and has attempted to take the best of traditional ethics, and raise it to a new level. Singer offers much to think about, in terms of making your own life even more full of meaning.

Singer's most popular books are *Practical Ethics*, and *Rethinking Life and Death*. The best critique of Singer is *Rethinking Peter Singer*, edited by Gordon Preece. Like him or despise him, he is one of the most important ethicists of our time.

53
Transplants

Organ transplantation is a very significant medical procedure. The first successful kidney transplant occurred in 1954, and now more than 10,000 occur each year. In 1967, Dr. Christiaan Barnard performed the first heart transplant, and now more than 2,000 occur annually. No area of medical ethics has provoked more moral and legal discussion than organ transplantation. The most publicized issue is the need for donors, and the need for a change in the public's attitude that would promote a willingness to permit organs to be "harvested" from those who clearly no longer need them. For every 200,000 brain deaths, only 2,000, or 1%, had consented to making their organs available. In some European countries, there is a presumption of consent; in America, unless consent is explicit, the presumption goes the other way.

Because no one dies in the process, kidney transplants are less controversial, but it does bring up the issue of the morality of consenting to surgery that does not benefit the donor, and this is frowned on by some religious traditions. U.S. Senator Orrin Hatch donated a kidney to his daughter, and basketball star Sean Elliot received a kidney from his brother. The major medical issue is donor compatibility. In India, where selling one's own organs is permissible, the moral issue of creating a "market" for human organs has been the source of intense debate. Moral discussion in America centers on the "good" to the person receiving the organ outweighing the "harm" done to the person donating the organ. Donation of an organ, or part of an organ, is not without its risks, and is regarded more as an altruistic act than as a duty.

Heart transplants are much different. The donor dies, and to remove a heart from a living person looks like homicide. To permit the removal of vital organs, the legal definition of death had to be changed. Death was once defined as "the cessation of circulatory and respiratory functions." Since organs can only be harvested if they are still in good shape,

Death was legally redefined as "the irreversible loss of all functions of the entire brain." (Some would specify: "functions above the brain stem," that is, the irreversible loss of all capacity for consciousness.) There is a moral issue here: are you really "dead" when your heart is still beating, and you are still breathing, even if those functions are being assisted by a machine? When your brain stops functioning, you are legally dead, but you will only "really" be dead when your heart is removed.

The most intensely debated moral question is: who gets the harvested organs? Do you do a liver transplant for someone whose alcohol or drug addictions destroyed the organ? Do you do a heart transplant for someone whose life expectancy is not very long? Do you do transplants to those who can afford to pay for them, or to those who are judged most needy or most valuable to the community by some medical board, or do you use some form of lottery?

A not insignificant aspect of the moral issues attached to transplant surgery is justification of the expenses. In an advanced technological society, we have an inclination to see just how much we can do, regardless of the costs. By a most conservative estimate, the 25,000 or so heart, liver and kidney transplants performed in a given year cost at least $3 billion. Annual expenses for complicated surgery can easily exceed $100,000. That money could provide basic medical care for a very large number of indigents, in this country or elsewhere. The very basic utilitarian principle of "the greatest good for the greatest number" flies in the face of billions of dollars spent to prolong the lives of a few, when millions could have their lives immensely improved, by the expenditure of the same funds.

We have clearly not solved our most basic ethical problems. The issue of organ transplantation is central to a host of bio-ethical problems that admit of no easy solutions, and should keep specialists in medical ethics occupied for years to come. These are issues individuals may show little interest in, until they happen to strike close to home, but every medical issue seems attached to every other one, particularly when some procedures cost a lot of money, and that money might produce greater benefits elsewhere.

54
Abortion

Few Supreme Court decisions have been so controversial, so divisive, and so full of philosophical implications as Roe v. Wade. The Supreme Court may have settled the legality of abortion, but it has not terminated the debate, for, as it acknowledged, medical, philosophical, and theological issues have been left open. For conservatives, human life is sacred, and human life begins at the moment of conception. (Biologists agree that all the organs necessary for human existence are present after about six weeks.) At one extreme, some aren't even sure they want to accord "human" status to the newborn. In the middle ages, 'quickening,' when the mother could feel the new life within her, was taken as manifesting the presence of human life. The Supreme Court prohibited abortion after 'viability,' the stage at which a fetus could make it on its own. With contemporary perinatal technology, this may be pushed back into the fifth month. The uncomfortable consequence is this: while an abortion is being carried out on one fetus, another of exactly the same age may have its life supported in a nearby high-tech neonatal unit.

Abortion has been practiced from ancient times; by the time of Hippocrates, the medical professional was not to facilitate an abortion. The Hippocratic Oath proclaims: "I will not give an abortifacient." The reasons for wanting an abortion then and now are manifold: pregnancy may be the result of rape or incest; pregnancy may affect the mother's physical or mental health; the woman may have more children than can be cared for; the fetus may be severely deformed; the female may not be old enough or mature enough, etc. Peter Singer presents a curious case: a woman is pregnant with a severely deformed child, which will require so much care no other child could be conceived. Singer asks, wouldn't the greater amount of happiness be produced if this fetus were aborted, so that an attempt may be made at having a healthy baby?

A most provocative article by Judith Thomson, "A Defense of Abortion," was published in 1971, and the argument it contained has since appeared in many forms. Suppose you awake to find you have been kidnapped, and your kidneys have been connected to the world's greatest violinist, whose kidneys will fail unless you help purify his blood. You are told not to worry; it is only for nine months! Does the person have a *right* to stay hooked up to you? Do you have a *right* to terminate the connection? Most of the arguments for a woman's right to choose have been based on similar illustrations.

There is no definitive answer to the abortion debate. Conservatives will continue to insist on the sanctity of human life from its first beginnings ("If the right to life is violated from the moment of conception, an indirect blow is struck also at the whole moral order."--Pope John Paul II.) Liberal thinkers will endorse abortion and "treating to die" in the case of the unwanted neonatal. (Catholics have 31% of abortions, exactly proportionate to the overall population, while the 6% of non-religious have 24% of abortions.)

With Roe v. Wade, the Supreme Court established the outlines of the abortion debate, but did not resolve the issues. As a practical matter, most medical professionals would far rather carry out abortions than have women who are determined not to be pregnant, effect their own abortions. Having a child is an immensely serious business, and were there licensing exams before attempts at pregnancy would be permitted, we might have a global underpopulation problem. The Utopian ideal would be that conception only occurred when parents were ready to love and support their offspring. Until that occurs, abortion is bound to be with us. As Peter Singer observes, societally we have abandoned the sanctity of life ethic, and replaced it with a quality of life ethic: quality of life of and for the baby, and for the mother. Such a step may have even greater implications than the Roe v. Wade decision of 1973. The abortion debate will continue as long as there are unwanted pregnancies, and as long as members of a society feel a sense of obligation to life, wherever it may be found.

55
Euthanasia: A Good Death?

Any discussion of euthanasia provokes lively debate. Euthanasia means "a good death," or, "dying well." One who succumbs, after an illness, after having put "all affairs in order", perhaps surrounded by loved ones, might be said to have died a good death. But the term has come to mean a death that frees one from pain. There are a number of organizations seeking to promote "death with dignity," the basic idea being that one should have the right to be freed from unbearable suffering, and that one should not be kept alive against one's wishes.

Western societies have never looked kindly on suicide. Curiously, the attempt to take one's own life in England until the twentieth century was a capital offense, punishable by hanging! We have been more lenient to those who attempt suicide, assuming that it is an irrational act, prompted by depression or some other curable malady. We tend to regard people who are terminally ill and asking to be released from suffering in a quite different category, although we acknowledge that depression and other psychological factors may weigh heavily upon them.

The issue of keeping someone alive on a respirator came before the Supreme Court of the United States because Nancy Cruzan had a car accident in 1983 and was left in a persistent vegetative state for eight years. The Supreme Court ruled that if there was evidence the patient did not want to be resuscitated, treatment could be discontinued. In the intervening years, and through dozens of court cases, the right of an individual to have respirators or feeding tubes withdrawn has become progressively clearer.

In 1989, Jack Kervorkian assisted Janet Adkins, a woman suffering from early stage Alzheimer's, to commit suicide. Kervorkian himself had been the defendant in cases without number, essentially testing the Michigan law that prohibited physician-assisted suicide. The legal and moral issues are still confusing, with partisans on both sides proclaiming the rationality of their respective points of view. The Supreme Court of Canada at first stated that someone with a severe disability could be helped to commit suicide, since an able-bodied person would be able to do so. But the Court quickly added, "no one has a right to commit suicide." In America that debate has centered around: what's the difference between turning off a respirator, and injecting a lethal drug? Isn't the doctor actually producing the same result? Perhaps in the second instance it is more merciful than in the first.

In the Netherlands, physician-assisted suicide is legal, and the law requires adherence to six regulations: only a medical practitioner may administer the drugs; there must be a clear, explicit request from the patient; the decision must be persistent, well-informed, and freely chosen; the person must be in unbearable pain with no hope of relief; there must be no other acceptable treatments, and there must be a second opinion from an independent medical practitioner.

Such regulations would appear to insure that only patients who are incurably ill and who have tried all alternatives are candidates for physician-assisted suicide. Those who have reviewed the history of the Dutch experience are not so sure. Richard Fenigsen for example claims that there are many patients who are euthanized against their will, and claims that if the law were applied in America, HMOs and others who have financial interests at stake, would see to it that patients who can be kept alive only at great expense, would soon become the victims of involuntary euthanasia.

Peter Singer writes: "Good medical practice...will come to be seen as including the provision of euthanasia." He further claims that the Dutch experience shows no evidence of sliding down the slippery slope towards involuntary euthanasia. Others write that legalizing euthanasia puts physicians in the contradictory circumstance of being committed both to the patient's health and to the patient's death. No one wants to experience unbearable suffering, but few of us want to be released before it's really time to go. Is there some reasonable, middle of the road answer to this thorniest of medical ethics issues? As in the case of the Roe v. Wade abortion decision, not even a Supreme Court ruling would bring this debate to an end. There are deep philosophical issues, which divide the two sides, and those issues admit of no easy resolutions.

56
Ethical Aging

Ethics is sometimes defined as the discussion of what one "ought" to do. The ethics of aging is fairly simple. There are a few easy guidelines everyone ought to follow. The tricky part comes in putting them into practice. Everyone ought to be physically active. Physiologists claim that bodily organs deteriorate at about the rate of 1% per year, beginning around age thirty. While some degree of deterioration is inevitable, appropriate exercise can condition everything from heart and lungs and brain to bones, muscles and joints. While too much exercise can be as harmful than too little, relatively few people are in danger from too much exercise.

The best exercises for most people of mature years turn out to be walking, bicycling, and swimming. Exercise as a "duty" is no fun at all, and if you are to persist, you must develop exercise routines that are enjoyable. Walking the same area repeatedly must become a meditation exercise, lest it become a bore and a chore. Some form of resistance (weight-lifting) is good for the body: it might save you from a hernia lifting groceries, or some other heavy object, like income tax forms. Recent articles suggest that weight-lifting exercises not only ward off osteoporosis, but also may help in preventing heart disease and cancer. You don't have to join a gym: keep a couple small dumbbells around the house and lift them while watching TV, or waiting for a brilliant insight into the world's political problems. Another important physical activity is stretching: just standing up and stretching from time to time is good for you, and many books illustrate positions anyone can learn. They do good things for your body, and perhaps, yoga practitioners maintain, for your mind.

Everyone "ought" to be mentally active. It's surprising how much education you can get just from reading the newspapers well. The art of journalism is to popularize big ideas, and the best newspapers and magazines do this very well. Scientific breakthroughs, great philosophic concerns, matters of political urgency, all are thought-provokingly profiled in the popular press. Conference centers, Elderhostels, and institutions of higher learning, all present golden opportunities for intellectual stimulation. Books and magazines can be sources of challenging ideas; studies show decreased brain wave activity after two hours of watching television. For most people, the greatest intellectual stimulation comes from conversation, and the people you talk to may do more than you realize to keep your mind sharp.

Social connections are also an important "ought" in terms of aging well. Human beings need other human beings: we need to be in contact with others. We all need to feel we are of some service to others. Families are built-in social devices, but most of us build "voluntary" families of those friends with whom we most closely associate. More than anything else, the social network we establish is what keeps us human. Among the friends whose contacts I value highly are family members, students stretching back many years, a wide range of university colleagues, people I exercise with, and others whose perceptions of reality are so different from mine, they might make me doubt my sanity, if I didn't already have some pretty clear convictions along these lines.

Aging ethically also demands the continuing acquisition of virtues. The older you are, the more likely you are to experience cancer, heart disease, and other life-threatening illnesses. It is only by developing the appropriate virtues that you can hope to take such large challenges in stride. Part of the wonder of being alive is the development of character, which comes by facing and overcoming challenges.

While the body may deteriorate with time, the capacity for achieving a whole range of "excellences" does not diminish. As the poet might well have said: "Grow old with me: the most interesting is yet to be...." Aging itself is an ethical challenge, and all of the virtues you acquire throughout your life, may have their most serious challenges in your later years. Aging is something we are all doing, all the time. Doing it well is the real ethical challenge.

57
Exasperation and Zen

"This is exasperating," said the saleslady, as she was unable to process my purchase. A man next to me was returning a newly purchased computer, clearly unhappy about the difficulties he had trying to make it work. Driving home, as I wound my way through heavy traffic, it gradually dawned on me: modern technological life is exasperating! When I got home I started working my way through the 88-page manual that came with my new cordless answering phone, I was beyond exasperation. Stronger measures were called for!

Small wonder that articles on depression appear with some frequency in the popular press. The endless stream of new devices we all have to learn to use--many of them not user friendly--can be downright depressing. It just could be that more people suffer from anxiety than from depression.

Our cave-dwelling ancestors surely had sources of anxiety: would that ferocious animal attack tonight, if the fire went out? If my sore foot doesn't heal, will I be able to hunt or gather, or resist attack? Will plants come back to life, after a winter as fierce as this? While modern life has produced conveniences no futurist among the cave dwellers ever could have imagined, it also has produced causes for anxiety that might make the cave-dwellers life look like an endless picnic.

Although the person returning the computer may be an extreme, we are all at the mercy of machines we really cannot master. At the time of the Ford Model-T, every driver was invited to be a mechanic. If you pop the hood on today's vehicles, there is very little you dare touch. In the electronic era, we are all surrounded by devices whose inner workings we do not understand, and on whose continued good behavior we are all dependent. Accordingly, there may be smoldering fires of anxiety within us all. Perhaps some of the bizarre behavior reported in the newspapers is the result of repressed anxiety. A heart disease study suggested that anger and anxiety correlated more highly with heart disease, than either high blood pressure or high cholesterol.

Zen practitioners have a defense against anxiety. Meditation is an attempt to bring anxiety to a halt, and say: *"All* that matters is the breath you draw right here, right now." Zen is an attempt to rise above the turmoil of the world and restore the perspective of "one thing at a time." The practice of Zen is an attempt to dismiss distraction, and focus totally on the present.

Several European philosophers have railed against technology, identifying it as the primary enemy. It forms the basis of Martin Buber's rejection of "I-it" relationships: technology disposes us to "thingify" all we meet, whereas "salvation" lies only in the depth of personal relationships, in "I-Thou" encounters. Karl Jaspers despaired of mass man in mass society at the mercy of mindless machinery.

It is not easy to overcome anxiety in a world in which there is so much to be anxious about. All of the wisdom traditions say: focus on one thing. Do one thing at a time. Take all things in stride. The same Gospels that counsel that one thing alone is necessary, also counsel: "Do not be anxious about what you shall eat or wear; for you count more than many sparrows." All this is more easily said than done, but it is still the only way of overcoming the inevitable abundance of exasperating events to which we are subject. Bertrand Russell said: "In a hundred years, will the outcome of all the things you worry about today, really matter?" It is, as Humpty-Dumpty pointed out, a matter of who is to be Master, that's all. Sources of anxiety are superabundant, but the mastery of anxiety lies within us.

58
The Spirit of Philosophy

We are all "philosophers" attempting to make sense of our existence. One might argue that more real philosophy is done in the popular press, than in the halls of academe. Philosophy is reflection on what really matters, and all of us are occasionally driven to ask: "What does it all mean? What does it all add up to?" These are the most urgent, and the most practical, of philosophical questions. And we need to learn to answer them for ourselves, for someone else's answers may not work for us.

Readers are often disappointed when they pick up the works of modern philosophers, because, far from providing answers to life's most puzzling questions, professional philosophers may obscure the central issues. The writings of philosophers may provide indications of how they developed their philosophies, but there is no substitute for philosophy brought to life, *viva voce,* listening to a philosopher work through the problems that perhaps have suddenly become ours.

Among the important, but now largely forgotten philosophers of the twentieth century, was Gabriel Marcel. I had the good fortune to hear him speak many years ago. He brought philosophy to life for me, and conveyed some of the lively spirit that animates real philosophical thinking. Reading the works of real philosophers should not be a matter of searching for answers, but of being stimulated to think through the major questions of human existence. The following quotation conveys something of Marcel's spirit:

"The imperishable glory of a Kierkegaard or a Nietzsche consists perhaps mainly in this, that they have proved, not only by their arguments, but by their trials and by their whole life, that a philosopher worthy of the name cannot be a man of conferences, and that he deviates from his path every time that he allows himself to be torn from the solitude which is his calling. It is only by clinging to this solitude that he remains at the disposal of those who await from him, if not a lead, at least a stimulation."
                              --Gabriel Marcel, *The Philosophy of Existence,* (93).

In developing our own philosophies, some happy balance of solitude and stimulation from those who urge us to think things through, remains a basic necessity. Solitude is hard to come by in the modern world, with pagers and cell phones and the mass media leaving us little peace and quiet. But some solitude is necessary for the doing of philosophy, and in the production of our own personal philosophies, some leisure--some freedom from the burdens of everydayness--and some solitude, some time to be alone, and let our thoughts mature--is an absolute necessity.

The spirit of philosophy is alive and well, in spite of the death knell so often proclaimed. As Etienne Gilson said, "Philosophy always buries its undertakers." Philosophy today is alive and well: it occurs in newspapers and magazines, it is the stuff of novels and plays and movies, and it is brought to life whenever anyone stops and asks: "Why am I doing this? What does it all mean?" The task of the professional philosopher is to stimulate people to do their own thinking, to wonder at the marvel of existence, and to strive to make sense of what existence has to offer, one awesome puzzlement after another.

59
Socrates and Celebration

Philosophers are often regarded as dour, heavy people, with serious problems on their minds. It is clear that taking advantage of solitude is essential for the doing of philosophy, and being willing to grapple with the puzzles of life is integral to building a philosophy that will mean something. However, if Socrates can be taken as the model of the philosopher, and if Plato portrays him accurately in the *Symposium*, then great philosophy is not absent from partying and celebration.

The dialogue called the *Symposium* is a narrative of an evening celebration where the wine flowed freely, and the participants were each called upon to talk about love. Socrates listens to them all, pokes fun at their shortcomings, makes a great speech, notices that he has drunk them all under the table, gathers up his stuff and heads for the market place, to begin another day of question and answer with anyone who comes along.

In the Platonic dialogues, Socrates will occasionally attain "ecstasy" in the process of discussing big ideas. "Ecstasy" is a Greek word that means literally, "standing outside your self. " While intellectual ecstasy is more widely available than many people realize, a happy life requires accepting opportunities for ecstasy whenever they come along. Ecstasy may be found in watching the glow of sunset or some other natural wonder. It may be found in doing some physical activity that suffuses the body with a distinctive sense of pleasure. But perhaps human beings are, deep down, "party animals," (Aristotle would prefer to say: "political animals," but he was clearly much less convivial than Socrates). One of the greatest sources of ecstasy is that kind of group quasi-mystical experience that occurs when you are in the midst of friends or family and your consciousness is blended with the group, and you become one with your fellow partiers.

Successful parties, like successful family reunions, provide these opportunities for ecstasy, when you let yourself go, become one with the activities, and find absolute delight just in "being there." Most of us are too busy remembering the past or anticipating the future, and few of us have really mastered the capacity of living totally in the present moment. "Conviviality" literally means "living well with others," and it often seems to be all too much a fleeting and quickly passing phenomenon.

Being fully human requires its moments of solitude; time to gather thoughts and make sense of the often-disparate data reality transmits. But true humanism also requires finding not just delight but ecstasy, a sense of being beside yourself, in the company of those whose companionship you truly enjoy, and with whom you feel a real sense of being "at home," no matter where you happen to be.

Philosophers too know not only how to have a good time, but how important having a good time is, in the overall picture of human life. There is a joyous philosophy available to us all. All we need is the time set aside, the blend of the right people, and the disposition to see things as they really are. *Atoms dance, and so should we.* Times of celebration should be opportunities for ecstasy, of feeling outside and beyond yourself, of touching the infinite within and the boundless without. Thomas Traherne, some four centuries ago, said: "You are never truly living until you awake each morning in Paradise." You can't do that unless, from time to time, some real sense of celebrating the wonder of existence pervades your consciousness. A failure to party is an unforgivably un-Socratic attitude. The dark moments of life can only be endured if the memory of the pure delight of celebration is always fresh, always easily reached, always within recent experience.

60
Sickness and Health

Some people seem to be healthy all the days of their lives, with good digestion, strong bones, the capacity to sleep well, and the disposition to take life's vicissitudes in stride. Most of us are not so fortunate, and know more than the occasional heartbreak of psoriasis, the anxiety of high blood pressure or cholesterol, or the aggravations of arthritis. It is not the minor aches and pains that are most distressing. At any age serious illness may strike. While the aged have a disproportionately large share of the obituary columns, terminal illness and death can occur to people at any age. Most people over 60 have at least one chronic illness, whether it is arthritis or diabetes, cancer, heart disease, or some other unfriendly malady. While the achievements of some seventy and eighty year olds is awesome, time takes its toll on our physical abilities, as well as on our overall health. Strength of character can be sorely tested, as we adjust to some of the inevitable changes brought about by the process of aging.

The focus should not be on what can no longer be done, but on what can perhaps be done better than at any previous age, or, what has never been attempted before. Capacity for love and compassion does not decrease with time, and "emotional maturity" in general is something that knows no age limit. While mathematicians and physicists seem to do their most creative work in their twenties and thirties, musicians, artists and philosophers not infrequently do their most valuable work in their later years. Bertrand Russell's best book, *My Philosophical Development*, was published when he was eighty-seven. Among the greatest politicians of the twentieth century, Winston Churchill, Konrad Adenauer, Charles de Gaulle and Golda Meir experienced their greatest successes after seventy. Spiritual leaders, whether Dalai Lamas or Popes, are examples of wisdom deepening with age. Overcoming illness at any age is not a matter of acceptance or resignation, but of resolution. It requires accepting the facts, acknowledging the limitations, and being 100% resolved to channel all available energies where they are needed.

Those who have overcome great hardships to lead meaningful and successful lives have done so because they had 'a destination that made it all worthwhile,' a goal that simply had to be reached, no matter what. Viktor Frankl, who survived the Nazi death camps when healthier and stronger people did not, said the phrase that kept him going was: "If you have a Why to life, you can put up with any How."

Illness is simply part of being human, unless genetic engineers take total control. Taking illness in stride, making the proper adjustments, carrying on with the business of becoming truly human, is the mark of ever-increasing maturity. If each day did not present new challenges, life would just be a dull repetition of problems we had already solved. Sickness visits us all; how we handle it may be the truest test of the character behind our surface appearances.

61
Priestly Celibacy

When contraception was a hot moral issue among Catholic theologians, an outspoken Archbishop said that when the Catholic Church accepted the morality of contraception, the encyclical letter would start out with the phrase: "As the Catholic Church has always believed and taught...."

In the intervening years, other issues have pushed hot buttons within the Roman Catholic community. Because Roman Catholicism is a very important pathway to spirituality, what goes on in the Catholic Church is of interest to us all. AIDS among priests and the clerical abuse of children has captured headlines, but they are but the surface manifestations of deeper problems. Most priests are poorly prepared for life in the modern world. The Church "that thinks in centuries," is slow to change, and the "updating" promised by Pope John XXIII seems to have stalled. Meanwhile, real life problems of real live people go without attention.

The traditional teaching on the celibacy of the priesthood has three pillars: (1) the priest is celibate so that he may attend to the needs of others, without the distractions of a wife and children; (2) the celibacy of the priesthood showcases spirituality and freedom from mere earthly concerns; (3) the priest is dedicated to God in a way that makes him radically different from everyone else.

In reality, there are "saints" who live lives that are remarkably different from the rest of us, and live on a plane of spirituality that is truly exemplary. But it may well be that a vast majority of priests would better serve their flocks, if they had the experiences of a loving family. (Marriage and children anchor a person in the real world in a way that no amount of solitude and prayer could possibly achieve.) Secondly, an understanding of the radical physicality of human nature has largely displaced the Platonic view of human nature as essentially 'a soul using a body'. The great Catholic theologian St. Thomas Aquinas concluded that human beings were "soul-body unities," and modern thought has done much to solidify this view of human nature. Thirdly, priests might be more "priestly" if they were more like the people to whom they minister, and for whom they strive to stand as a model or example of spiritual behavior.

The great philosophers of antiquity expressed little doubt that sexuality and sexual expression are basic components of human nature. The repression of sexual activity is not supernatural, but unnatural. At the same time that conservative theologians argue that God will give special graces to those who are celibate, sociologists produce statistics that the celibate life just does not work, save for a small minority. Widely accepted statistics suggest that some 5% of the human population is homosexual, so it should be no great surprise that some priests are. The Catholic Church has been loath to accept this reality, or to say anything to homosexuals except forbid them sexual activity. Society at large has moved some considerable distance toward accepting the presence and reality of homosexuality in the last few years. Can the Catholic Church be far behind?

There is an ancient Christian saying that "The voice of the people is the voice of God." Catholics, by their practice, have affirmed the morality of contraception. The Anglo-Catholic Church has struggled for at least four centuries with the issue of divorce. It seems eminently rational to most people that when a marriage fails completely, divorce is a morally desirable choice, and to condemn the divorced to a life without intimate personal loving relationships simply makes no sense.

Sometime in this millennium, perhaps there will be a papal encyclical that begins: "As the Catholic Church has always believed and taught: there should be a married clergy, composed of both male and female priests; same-sex relationships can be as nourishing and sacred as any other relationship; may the divorced be more fortunate in their new relationships. Children should be brought into the world in the context of a loving family…"

62
Dimensions of Leadership

When a new political season begins, all the old questions about leadership arise anew, almost as if they had never been debated. When we hear someone asking for our vote, we want to know what we are getting in return. Above all, we want leaders to be successful, to fulfill their promises, and, most simply, to make things better than they were before. It is distressingly easy to fail as a leader. It is not easy to meet others' expectations, and solve problems in a way that meets the needs of constituents.

Whether you think of leading the country, your company, or your local scout troop, several dimensions of leadership apply. When you are selected as a leader, it is expected that you will have a vision that provides direction. Leaders are not chosen in order to attend banquets and ceremonies; leaders are selected because of needs that can only be met by someone who has goals in mind, and ways to attain those goals.

Ultimately there are two extremes of leadership: the Chairman of the Board approach, where a board decides what needs to be done, and the Chairman's task is to figure out how to do it. There is also the Chief Executive approach, where it is your vision you must convey to others, convincing them that it is their own, and your task is to get everyone on the bandwagon. In the real world, the two extremes intermingle. In both, the leader must have some degree of open-mindedness, flexibility, and willingness to change. Being omniscient is an infrequent human quality, and being willing to learn from experience is an essential component of successful leadership. The leader must be a *perceptive* listener, able to discern good counsel from bad, and able to pick up on messages that are barely audible, perhaps disguised by body language, undue arrogance or humility, or uncertainty.

The leader must know what "public opinions" are out there, and which are majority, and which are minority, points of view. Few leaders attain universal assent. A huge challenge lies in hearing what critics have to say, and, instead of being defensive, being able to incorporate criticism into improved programs.

There comes a time in leadership when action is demanded, and the leader must not only be capable of exercising persuasion effectively, but of galvanizing people for action. The leader must be certain enough of the direction taken, that followers will not hold back in degree of commitment. The leader must have enough of a thick skin not to be overcome by carping critics. No matter how capable you are as a leader, there will be some who, either out of envy or some other emotion, wish to torpedo your leadership. You have to be able to brook opposition, deflect unkind or cutting remarks, and move on toward your goals.

To be an effective leader, you must have some degree of charisma. There must be something about you that sets you apart from others. It can be your voice, it can be your facial expressions, or it can be characteristics that are distinctively yours. Wherever it comes from, a leader without charisma will not be very effective.

Good leadership turns out to be a test of all the virtues: of willingness to make sacrifices, of courage, of temperance, of justice, of prudence. And most of all, true leadership will be a test of humility. When you experience success, you may wish to congratulate yourself, it may puff you up with pride, you may think you are now on the fast track, and can do no wrong. Several large corporations have suffered from the arrogance of their chief executives. No leader will remain in the forefront without some genuine humility, born of the awareness that great success is partly a matter of luck, partly a matter of having followers who really want to be led somewhere, and only a small part, the unique, invaluable contribution good leadership provides.

We all exercise leadership in one form or another. Exercising it well is no mean accomplishment. And many who have been successful leaders look back and wonder how they managed to accomplish what they did. When an opportunity to exercise leadership comes your way, do not be afraid to accept it, for it may do you some great good, and enable you to do some great good for others.

63
The Next Depression...

may be yours! One person in five will have at least one major episode of depression some time in life. It is not just the garden variety of feeling "blue" for a couple days, but an all-out, bottom-of-the-birdcage, and long-lasting depression. It can occur at any time, and be unrelated to "depressing" events. It may be related to the weather, and be part of a "Seasonal Affective Disorder" (SAD), or may be inversely proportional to external events. One of the classic cases of depression profiled a Caribbean islander who said: "I just can't stand all these blue skies!" Residents of the American desert southwest are more likely to suffer depression in summer than in winter: perhaps it is temperature extremes, perhaps it is cabin fever, or perhaps it is simply too much sunshine!

At an open forum for senior citizens in Tucson, almost half those attending acknowledged having had some experience with serious depression. A clinician present advised that depression sometimes occurred because of physiological changes, perhaps a decline in hormones like serotonin. Some depressions have a clear psychological origin, and correlate with sudden switches from optimism to pessimism, or with suddenly seeing the world filled with half-empty glasses, missed opportunities, and endless adversities. Some can trace their depression to the onset of a serious illness, or the loss of a job, or loved one.

The intensity of depression varies, as illustrated by two comments made at the open forum. "I am usually a very happy person. About once a month, I just feel so sad I don't want to get out of bed. Then, in a day or two, I am back to my usual cheerful self." The other quote provoked more concern: "I have had several lengthy episodes of depression in my life. I know I need help when I start wishing I were dead. I never actually think of committing suicide, I just start wishing something would happen to put me out of my misery." CBS News correspondent Mike Wallace said that in spite of everything working out so well in his life, without medication he would sink into a lethargic depression and cease to care about anything. Some people need permanent medication to overcome hormonal imbalances.

The advice to those who suffer from depression seems pretty simple: depression can occur to anyone at any time and is not something to hide or be ashamed of; depression can be overcome, sometimes with a short-term use of anti-depressant medication; most people who have had a bout of depression can lessen its severity, and the likelihood of its recurrence, by cultivating more optimistic attitudes, by exercising regularly, and by building friendships with people of positive outlook. It has been said that psychiatrists are simply "paid friends," and having someone to whom you can really tell your troubles may help keep you on an even keel, and even save you a lot of money.

Plato's philosophy has been summarized in the phrase, "life is basically good," but there are also philosophers like Schopenhauer, Nietzsche and Sartre, who take a very dark view of things. Religious writers like St. Augustine will affirm: "To those who love God, all things work together unto good." On the darker side, Camus wrote: "The absurd enlightens me on this point: there is no future." Along the same lines, American philosopher Thomas Nagel wrote: "Life may be not only meaningless but absurd." Clearly, the philosophers you choose to read can have a great influence on your outlook.

No matter how optimistic you are, life does have its depressing moments. The body has its own way of playing tricks on us. A series of depressing events may take their toll. But just as depression is not a desirable state for an economy, so it is not acceptable as a way of life. Emphasizing optimism over pessimism, taking positive action wherever possible, and spending time with people of cheerful disposition, all of these can help prevent, or at least mitigate, the next depression, even if it appears to be reserved exclusively for you. For the person of optimistic bent, there is always more to look forward to, more to be cheerful about, than there are reasons for negativity. *The simple fact that you are alive today proves that you have so far overcome every challenge that has come your way.* When you, or someone you know, show signs of the beginnings of depression, bring this fact to mind, and perhaps this simple observation will help ward off a potential bout of depression!

Gene Bammel

64
Gay and Lesbian Reality

Most of us are occasionally members of some minority group: a Jew amidst Christians, a male amidst females, an elder amongst kindergartners, etc. One of the toughest of all minority group challenges is to be homosexual in a society that places so much visible emphasis on heterosexuality.

A fact of life is that some people experience sexual attraction to their own gender. A friend once said: "Just as you are attracted to a pretty woman, I am attracted to particular men." Research supports the notion that sexual orientation has a genetic basis. Circumstances may have much to do with accepting and accommodating gayness, but something biological is at the root of it. The parents who recently accused a college of "turning our daughter into a lesbian," are working with very little evidence and even less wisdom.

Research suggests that most people go through a phase where they are much more comfortable emotionally with members of their own sex. At least 5% have at least one homosexual experience or love affair, and at least 2% of adults are predominantly homosexual. (Like much of the Kinsey report-style statistics, there is much room for skepticism with regard to the answers you get when asking people about their sexual activities....)

It is not uncommon to hear a gay individual say: "With all the potential for harassment and physical harm, do you think I would *choose* this lifestyle, if I could help it?" For some reason, heterosexual society suffers from homophobia, a fear of gay and lesbian individuals, either because it offers such a challenge to the dominant culture, or because of what Freud called "latent homosexuality," which might include some fear of having homosexual inclinations.

No wonder that gays and lesbians build serious support communities (among the most helpful and caring communities anywhere), when there are so many people out there who are not only not supportive, but downright hostile. Senator Barry Goldwater had a gay grandson, and because of his care and concern, was the most outspoken of all "conservatives" in support of gays and lesbians. The Senator's funeral was somewhat disrupted by a noisy protester waving a sign: "God hates fags." Extremists unfortunately sometimes get caught up in strange and inexplicable episodes of gay bashing.

Some Protestant churches offer deliberate and public support for the gay members of the community, while others have a "re-orientation" program, seeking to transform gays into heterosexuals. Some Roman Catholic documents accept a gay orientation, while affirming that homosexual activity among consenting adults is sinful. The Episcopal Church has struggled with the ordination of gays and lesbians, some Bishops accepting, others strongly opposed, even to the point of schism within the Church. The election of an openly gay Bishop rocked the Episcopal Church more than any doctrinal issue in years.

Gay people have the same needs for affection and sexual expression as anybody else. The song, "I can't live in a world without love," doesn't just play on heterosexual stations. The range of sexual practice in both groups is probably similar, ranging from the celibate, to the life-long relationship, to those whose sexual urges and the need for various partners seems almost out of control, and even to those who force themselves upon others.

Differences in sexual orientation are part and parcel of the diversity of the human species. Three centuries ago, John Locke surprised the philosophical community by advocating "tolerance," an acceptance of people of different political or religious persuasion. Perhaps that kind of tolerance and an accompanying level of enlightened understanding will be extended to gays and lesbians. To be intolerant of those who adopt different lifestyles is a form of absolutism that ill becomes the human spirit.

Chapter II.
Once More, With Feeling

II-65
What is Virtue?

If we are to "teach" virtue, we must have some idea of what virtue is. The problem is, the grasp of what is "virtuous" has clearly changed over time. Some of the greatest moralists have held views we would find abhorrent. Aristotle held there were some people who were naturally slaves, because "although able to understand reason, they are not themselves able to exercise it." Thomas Aquinas wrote that those who held heretical views were to be turned over to the secular power for prompt execution, lest they scandalize the faithful.

Is virtue purely "conventional," that is, something a particular group at a given time happens to agree upon? For example, is it "virtuous" for one group to exterminate another group they think racially inferior?) Or is virtue a matter of subscribing to a law "written into the heart of things," conformity to which makes for good actions, and makes the performer morally good? It would seem that virtue is deeper than what a particular group decides at a given time, but there is also a societal dimension to what we accept and praise as virtuous action.

There seems to be a kind of societal sub-conscious, through which a group gradually becomes aware of what is desirable human behavior. Americans abhor societies in which women are suppressed, or female genital mutilation is practiced. We tend to think these people just haven't yet "seen the light," and if we politely point out to them the error of their ways, they will change. (Is it ethnocentrism to think we have seen the right way, and those who practice genocide or gender-dominance just need our instruction? Or, is involvement in the practices of another society a response to a higher moral awareness?)

You cannot make anyone virtuous by imposing a certain course of action. That there is a "knowledge" component to virtue was pointed out by Socrates. Clear thinking about the consequences of actions is a big step along the road to virtue. But there is also what Aristotle described as moral weakness, and what St. Paul spoke of as knowing the right course of action but being unable to follow it. There are many paradoxes along the road to understanding the nature of virtue. We all know of bright people who are not virtuous by any stretch of the imagination, and we all know people who could not explain virtue if their life depended on it, but who have splendid moral instincts.

In the final analysis, the best instructor in virtue is a virtuous person. There are people who do "the right" things, and whose behavior does indeed become a model for the rest of us. Religious-minded people may attempt to follow the example of Abraham, Buddha, Jesus, Mohammed, or more recent saints. Philosophers may look to Plato, Aristotle, Kant, or perhaps to Kierkegaard or Sartre, or Bertrand Russell, for models of ideal behavior. (A question arises: was it easier being virtuous in the olden days, or, with the increase in knowledge and wealth, should it be easier to be virtuous in more modern times?) The pursuit of virtue, in whatever age, has not only an element of knowledge, but also a larger, more puzzling element of "inclination to do the right thing."

Kermit the Frog observed: "It's not easy being green." It is even harder to be virtuous, in a world in which vice is glorified, and moral depravity rewarded. One of the lessons of history is that only those civilizations prevail where virtue is pursued, and where the cultural goal is a progressively deeper understanding of the demands that morality makes upon us all. As psychologists have observed, moral consciousness is something that evolves gradually; so too our sense of moral obligation and moral excellence develops with time, experience, and opportunity. What virtue is, is thus an open-ended question, admitting of no simple, definitive answer, but requiring ever-new reflection, in the light of deepening and expanding moral consciousness.

Philosophy has been described as "the passionate pursuit of truth." The secret depth of personally meaningful philosophy is the passionate pursuit of truly virtuous living.

II-66
The "New" Psychology

The classical psychology of the nineteenth century emphasized how traumatic events of our past affected current behavior. Freudian psychoanalysis suggested that childhood experiences, and the emotional turmoil involved, left deep marks, and diminished our ability to cope with current problems. Jungian analysis found models or archetypes within the subconscious that served to explain some of the apparent irrationality of our behavior.

The new revolution in psychology proposes that it's not the past that matters so much, but current attitudes and convictions. Abraham Maslow may have been the instigator of this approach, but Mihaly Csikszentmihalyi, a psychologist with an ineffable name, has generated a large following. The recurrent theme of his books *Flow* and *The Evolving Self* is that the happiness we all seek depends simply on the control of consciousness. His studies over the years focused on when people thought they were most completely themselves. He developed his notion of *flow* from these studies: people felt they were most themselves when they were totally engrossed in something, when they had a challenge proportionate to their abilities, and some sense of success or achievement accompanied their activity.

Csikszentmihalyi observed that mental health did not mean healing your childhood memories, it meant being totally focused on something that deserved your full attention. (Some people say the best time in their lives was the time of greatest challenge: obviously you can do things to make any time in your life a time of greatest challenge...) His research included the creative moments of successful artists, the heroic exploits of athletes, and the everyday behavior of happy human beings.

George Pransky, author of *The Renaissance of Psychology,* suggests that the potential for healthy psychological functioning is close to the surface of us all, that psychological well being has a contagious effect on others, and that indeed it is control of consciousness that is the basis of happy and healthy mental functioning. How do you control consciousness? Pransky suggests it is a matter of tapping into *free-flowing thinking,* the sharp, keen, intuitive responses available to all, while reducing *process thinking,* or negative, self-critical, pessimistic thinking, to a practical minimum.

In his clinical practice, Pransky asserts he consistently promotes "vertical jumps" in self-understanding, as people move to a higher level of thinking, a renewed self-esteem, and a determination to get on with the business of living. Perhaps there is some connection between moving to the level of free-flowing thinking and the regular practice of meditation. Meditation is an opportunity to cleanse the mind of negative thinking, to engender a sense of acceptance and at-one-ment with reality, and a chance to initiate a mind-full approach to the tasks of daily living. This is more than the "power of positive thinking," it is a determination to elevate the plane of thoughts and emotions, to focus on the present, and to be "productive" of good thoughts and actions at a level higher than you have been requiring of yourself.

The Greek word "metanoia" is translated in the Bible as "repent," but it actually means, "have a change of mind," or, "change your attitudes about things." Apparently the "new" psychology has been around for a long time, we just haven't recognized it. The new psychology places a healthy emphasis on the present, and what activities most engross and delight one, and the kind of thinking one must do to live on the plane of acceptable challenges. Perhaps it is time to leave the old psychology behind, and try to live more on the plane of *flow*, of being engrossed in the present moment, and building on and working with, the fresh insights our minds eagerly seek to bring to the surface. As Heraclitus of Ephesus said long ago: "The world is new each day." By controlling your consciousness, you can do much more to make that world more to your liking, and in the process, you may produce a self much more to your liking.

II-67
Three Great Ideas

Great minds have puzzled over the question of the greatest ideas anyone has ever had. Among the oft-mentioned candidates: Newton's idea of Gravity, Einstein's idea of Relativity, Darwin's idea of Evolution by natural selection. Strikingly absent from such lists are those philosophical ideas that have a tremendous impact on the way we live our daily lives. From the myriads of great philosophical ideas, I would single out three for special current consideration: Pluralism, Tolerance, and Diversity.

(1.) Consider Pluralism first of all. William James, the great American philosopher-psychologist of the late nineteenth century, had a remarkable mastery of the history of philosophy. He asked if it were possible that from all this collection of diverse opinions, one could be right, and all the rest wrong? Some historians of philosophy surrender to skepticism, so difficult it is to choose between competing claims. James hit upon the novel idea that instead of right or wrong, competing systems were more or less "adequate" to representing what reality has to offer. Thus was born the idea of Pluralism: no one system is so perfect that it can lay claim to absolute truth, no one system is so "adequate" that it negates all the others.

(2) James might not have had the opportunity to view objectively so many different points of view, if not for his great seventeenth century predecessor, John Locke. In 1667, Locke wrote an *Essay on Toleration* that was a radical departure from the then current thinking. Like most British philosophers of the time, Locke was interested in practical politics, and his travels on the continent as well as his work for the British diplomatic services had convinced him that, far from imposing "the true religion" or "the true form of government" on others, enlightened people ought to learn to "tolerate" forms of religion and forms of government that differed from their own. As Locke surveyed European history, he was struck by the fact that opinions in one era that seemed so absolute and incontestable, in a century or two seemed outmoded and impractical. Locke's notion of toleration contributed to the American approach to religious tolerance, as well as to the basic American view of the right to self-determination in political matters.

(3) It is difficult to assign a single figure to the third great philosophical idea, in part because it is so new, and in part because it is the logical consequence of the previous two. Charles Darwin observed that diversity was one of the secrets of survival, but only gradually have human beings embraced diversity as a societal desideratum. All forms of ethnic cleansing are based on the rejection of the diversity principle. The world is in fact a richer place for the diversity of races, the diversity of religions, the diversity of political systems. Look at the damage that has been done by trying to make supreme one particular race, one particular religion, or one particular political system. While societies that accept diversity may not move as "fast" as societies comfortable in their absolutes, one might argue that the long-term results are always and everywhere preferable. In an open marketplace, one might assume that the best ideas, like the best products, will ultimately rise to the top. No heavy hand is necessary.

These three great ideas, Pluralism, Tolerance, and Diversity, have consequences for our everyday activities. They presume the acceptance of the other *as other*, the attentiveness to points of view that may be radically different from our own deepest convictions, and a sense that if we are patient enough, it will all come right in the end. We have the great good fortune to live in a pluralist society, where we are continually asked to be tolerant of views that differ from our own, and where we benefit from a wonderful diversity of people, ideas, and practices. Whatever the charms of absolutism, Pluralism, Tolerance, and Diversity make for a much more interesting society, and one that has a much better chance for long-term survival. Pluralism has become one of the "absolutes" of modern life.

II-68
Forms of Meditation

The best forms of meditation are the simplest: sit quietly for 15 or 20 minutes, and begin by observing your breathing: breathe in, breathe out. As you breathe, form in your mind the words: "In," "Out." Try to blot out all other words. Some meditators find it helpful to count "one" with each breath, or to count to ten and start over. Whatever your approach, distractions will come, as your mind wanders, or begins collecting thoughts, or reflects on your busy schedule, or your emotional challenges. It is helpful to come back simply to "In," and "Out," until you achieve the basic calmness or centeredness characteristic of good meditation. Meditation, incidentally, does not mean emptying your mind or having your mind go blank. On the contrary, it is preparation for a higher level of consciousness.

Meditation assumes many forms and over time, different approaches may be helpful. Stress-reduction meditation is facilitated by doing a body-scan. Focus on each segment of your body, and move gradually from toes to forehead. Some practitioners will say: "My toe is getting lighter, free from stress or pain; my ankle is getting lighter, free from stress or pain . . ." and so on. Some have used this formula before going to sleep, and find it helps produce deep and restful slumber.

Meditation can also be used as a tool for emotional mastery. If you are prone to anger, for example, you might make a mantra of: "I will not be angry today." Whatever emotion or virtue you are working on can be the focus or mantra of your meditation. You may find a solitary walk is the best and purest meditation exercise for you. Thoreau wrote: "a taste for the beautiful is most cultivated out of doors." The beauty of nature, far from being a distraction, may calm and relax you, and impel you to greater clarity of meditation. Meditation is not necessarily a solitary experience, but moments of aloneness and quiet are essential. Plotinus sought to be "alone with the Alone," and this may be best achieved in the open air. Some form of nature mysticism may easily present itself to the wilderness wanderer.

Meditation may lead to some form of prayer. Paul Tillich, one of the most important Protestant theologians of the 20th century, practiced a kind of resignation meditation captured in the phrase: "Accept, that you are accepted." A phrase appropriate to your needs and circumstances may present itself, and may become so powerful it will suffuse and irradiate your meditation practice.

For the prayerful, meditation may lead to something resembling mystical experience, as you bond with whatever Power drives the universe. The various yoga postures may have developed as techniques to calm and control the body, so that the Breath could be set free on its mystical journeys. For many, yoga becomes an essential component of the meditation practice. The gentle stretching represented by the yoga postures has been practiced for thousands of years, and may serve as a useful companion to the practice of meditation.

Our world super abounds with sensory experience, and we all suffer from the overload of receiving far more information than we can process. Meditation is a counter-balance to this sensory overload. It is a deliberate attempt to reduce experience to its most basic components. Your life is bound to improve if you commit some time each day to the deliberate practice of meditation. It may take you in directions as yet unmapped, but it will enable you to have greater control over your mind, your emotions, and the overall pattern of your life. What else is your mind except a capacity to concentrate, and what else is meditation but a method of focusing and intensifying concentration? Meditation is like the lottery: you can't win unless you buy a ticket. But unlike the lottery, with meditation, you win every time.

II-69
Knowing the Place

The basic work of philosophy is in part getting clear about words: not just knowing what the words mean, but the appropriateness of their use. The larger and more important work of philosophy is helping us understand the world in which we live. There is still truth in the old saw that science tells how the world works (and how to work the world), while philosophy tries to tell us something about why the world works, and, in the process, labors to establish a domain of values.

The work of astronomers and philosophers is well summarized by the conclusion of Eliot's poem "Little Gidding":

> We shall not cease from exploration
> And the end of all our exploring
> Will be to arrive where we started
> And know the place for the first time....

Such is clearly the work of astronomy: looking at the universe with awe and wonder, learning the mathematics necessary to understand something of the magnitude of the starry skies, and ending with greater awe and wonder at the immensity of what is at the end of the telescope.

Such is also the work of philosophy: we begin with the simplest questions: Why am I here? Where am I going? Does it all make sense? And after lengthy inquiry, observing how others, from Plato and Aristotle, to our post-modern contemporaries, have grappled with these questions, we at least have some idea about their true difficulty, and the importance of our answers.

Scientists from various disciplines are prone to extrapolate from their scientific information to larger philosophical conclusions. Thus the socio-biologist Edward Wilson generalizes from his studies of evolutionary biology, and concludes that materialist reductionism is the most tenable philosophical position. Evolution, says Wilson, provides incontrovertible evidence that matter is capable of organizing itself into ever-higher forms of order, and thus there is no need to posit anything beyond the realm of the material. He affirms that the purpose of life is preservation of the species, and that this is a high ethical calling: Wilson ends his book *Consilience* with an impassioned plea for a heightened environmental ethic, so that life on earth, in all its bio-diverse forms, may be preserved.

Many astronomers affirm that the order of the universe is remarkable, but that for science to assert any purpose in what the universe does, is going beyond its limits. Stephen Hawking said that given enough chances, in a realm of infinite possibility, this universe sooner or later would come to be, and the ultimate explanation of the order found can be expressed simply: we got lucky.

Other astronomers, going through the mathematics of probability of all the things that had to have occurred just the way they did so that life as we know could exist, (the so-called anthropic principle), try to put the facts before us, and let us reach our own conclusions. Wickramasinghe says: "The chances that life just occurred are about as unlikely as a typhoon blowing through a junkyard and constructing a Boeing 747." And various astronomers have said that, as an indirect consequence of their study of the universe, they have arrived at some kind of "faith" that there must be a Grand Designer behind it all. To make that Grand Designer a personal God requires a leap of faith, and clearly goes beyond science and philosophy and into the realm of religion.

Science begins with a kind of faith; a faith that the universe is intelligible, that our observations and mental activity accurately portray what is really going on out there. In this age of ambiguity, science may simply lead us to silence, to a kind of mystical appreciation for the wonder and mystery of existence. As Timothy Ferris says: "All who genuinely seek to learn, whether atheist or believer, scientist or mystic, are united in having not *a* faith but faith itself. Its token is reverence, its habit to respect the eloquence of silence." What we all do is eventually come back to our beginning, and re-cognize "the place" for the first time!

The Sphinx, Cairo, Egypt

II-70
Knowing Your Place

"A wandering Aramean was my father." So says Abraham, as he explains his lineage, and looks forward to finding his place in the "promised" land. Religious tradition is rich with the importance of finding the right place, whether the Bodhi tree of Buddha, the Salt Lake of Brigham Young, or the sacred space of many other traditions. For all of us, there is something about finding the right place, the place where we belong, a place that somehow vibrates with the harmony of our own personal destiny.

Geography, the lay of the land, has something to do with it. It has been suggested that ultimately everyone is either a mountain person or a water person, but that does not quite get it, for there are dedicated flatlanders too, and there are committed urbanities, and those who will not leave their privileged backcountry. When we find the terrain that is right for us, somehow it speaks to us, demands our presence, perhaps for a brief span, perhaps for a lifetime. Geography is not destiny, but destiny is intertwined with it.

Personality has something to do with it also. There is a *genius loci*, the particular spirit of a place, that has something to do with the kind of personalities that flourish there, and how the geography disposes people to a certain temperament and way of perceiving things. It is no great wonder that philosophy grew up in the tranquil Mediterranean climate that encourages one to wonder at the immensity of the universe, and enables one to converse outdoors year around. Philosophy is essentially discourse, and for that you need companionable people, a warm environment, and some degree of peace and tranquility. And no great wonder that the deserts of the middle east gave rise to Judaism, Christianity, and Islam, for deserts have a way of making people relate to what is ultimate, and of answering the most basic questions in formulas we would think of as religious. Diogenes Laertius said: "To do philosophy is to think like a Greek." To this observation one might add, to be religious, is to act like a Hebrew. The religion of Israel might be summed in the phrase from the book of Hosea: "I will lead her into the desert, and I will speak to her heart..."

There is more to sense of place than geography and personal fitness. You may not feel that you have found your unique place in the universe, without some strong sense of community, of like-mindedness with at least some of the people who surround you. Community can be fostered by the presence of people you strongly oppose, but unless you find people who share your attitudes and feelings, you will be isolated, and no sense of community will develop.

Modern America is built upon mobility. On average, Americans do not stay put in any one place for more than eight years. Most living octogenarians have made more than three major moves over their lifetimes. Perhaps this means that for most of us, no one place is an absolute, and that as we change, our geographic needs change, our personalities change, and what we can contribute to, and take from, a community, also changes. Maurice Brooks, author of *The Appalachians*, loved the Appalachian Mountains and the mountain people, but he admitted a quiet desire to spend some of his life in the Shenandoah Valley, and some of it in northern Arizona. Perhaps besides the sense of place, we also have a need to wander, to experience other places with their respective spirits, so that we can come back to the places that most deeply speak to us, and recognize them most fully for what they are. Home is not just where the heart is, it is where geography, personality, and community rise up to meet us, and say: "Welcome home. This is where you belong."

II-71
Gilson, Sartre, Levinas, Hadot

With persistent regularity, French genius manifests itself in the person of some intellectual who exerts a great influence on the rest of the world. While this phenomenon may reach as far back as Descartes, or perhaps back to Charlemagne, three twentieth century figures have had an extraordinary impact on philosophy.

In the 1920s, Etienne Gilson began publishing studies of the Christian thinkers of the Middle Ages, from Augustine in the fourth century to Duns Scotus and William of Ockham in the fourteenth. The academic world had come to assume that philosophy was either an ancient discipline as practiced by the Greeks, or a modern, more scientific discipline, in the tradition of Descartes or Kant or Russell. It was thought that religion so dominated the Middle Ages that nothing that could be called "philosophy" occurred there. Gilson documented, in book after book, that Jewish, Moslem and Christian writers had indeed done something that should be called "philosophy," and that writers as diverse as Averroes, Maimonides, and Aquinas, had produced philosophical insights that were of lasting value. Today, many philosophers acknowledge and make use of the philosophical arguments and positions taken by their great medieval predecessors, even when disagreeing strongly with their points of view.

In the mid twentieth century, Jean-Paul Sartre brought philosophy out of the University and into the coffee house. From Sartre and his colleagues, the modern world has taken seriously the lesson that philosophy is not an abstract academic discipline, but a continuing discussion about how to live your life, how to assume your fair share of political responsibility, and how to go about discussing life's most perplexing issues.

About the same time, Emmanuel Levinas began speaking out against the "secularization" of philosophy, affirming that the message of the Hebrew Bible presents a form of wisdom the modern world rejects at its own peril. For Levinas, the Biblical message is epitomized in Isaiah 6, when the prophet responds to the Lord: "Here I am: send me." As Levinas says, my right to exist shrinks to nothing, before my responsibility for the Other. I am fashioned and formed, he says, precisely by my responsibility to others. This, however, is Levinas' most famous utterance: "We are all responsible for each other; and I, I am the most responsible of all." What more telling indictment could there be, contradicting the rampant self-centeredness of the modern world?

Pierre Hadot's works have only recently become available in English, but he has exerted a monumental influence on contemporary French intellectual life. (The works of Derrida and Foucault are too well known to need comment here.) Like Gilson, Hadot began as an historian of philosophy, but with an emphasis on the Greek writers. Hadot has convinced his followers that such studies were not antiquarian classicism, but that the great writers of antiquity were indeed professors of wisdom, expressing by example "philosophy as a way of life," and not as some sterile, abstract doctrine of no relevance to anyone.

Hadot's book *Plotinus: or, the Simplicity of Vision,* examined the role that mystical experience played in the life and teaching of Plotinus, and how his life might be seen as a model for all those who wish to follow a more mystical path. Hadot himself has been much more influenced by the Stoics, and his analysis of their teachings forms the substance of his most important book *Philosophy as a Way of Life.*

The theme of Hadot's writings is that philosophy is an art of living--an art that is therapeutic--because it leads to a radically new way of existing. Hadot's point of view irradiates what you read on these pages. Philosophy is not some abstract academic discipline, but a practical, down-to-earth reflection on what we need to know to get us through each day, and make us better in the process. Philosophy, as Hadot says repeatedly, is a *way of life.* You are never fully living until and unless each day is a manifestation of your own personally developed philosophy. Fortunately, there are a number of French geniuses that can come to your assistance. Gilson, Sartre, Levinas and Hadot are but the tip of a very large iceberg...

II-72
Rediscovering Ancient Philosophy

Students tend to have three criticisms of Aristotle: (1) Aristotle at best expresses common sense points of view; (2) what he says is simply platitudinous; (3) whatever it is he says, it is irrelevant to the modern world.

Teachers have three responses to those who don't quite grasp Aristotle's wisdom: (1) there is some shortcoming on the part of the teacher; (2) there is some misunderstanding of the nature of philosophy, on the part of the student; (3) Wisdom is timeless, and just because Aristotle wrote 2500 years ago, in a language that is hard to comprehend, is no reason to downplay his thought. Teachers, of course, can always try harder, be better prepared, and cleverer at presenting Aristotle in modern terms. Aristotle's physics may be of little more than antiquarian interest, but his ethics and politics, and certain aspects of his metaphysics, are as interesting today as they would have been to ancient Athenians.

Taking Aristotle and the other philosophers of antiquity at their best, great historians, ranging from Toynbee to Gilson, have identified them as among the most brilliant people who have ever lived, and identify their legacy as one of the treasures of world civilization. Their works contain a great deal of wisdom about how to live our own lives, and how to foster the well being of society. Their philosophy is not empty words and airy abstractions, but an attempt to answer the questions most basic to living our daily lives well.

The best example I can find of the pertinence of ancient philosophy is Socrates' answer to a request for a definition of justice: "Instead of talking about it, I make it appear through my actions." Philosophy is not just empty words; it is a structure around which one lives one's life. Philosophy is the most *practical* form of knowledge, because it speaks to the issues we must have working solutions for, if we are to go about our everyday business. The philosopher is not a logic-chopper or a hair-splitter, but one who has some special insight into the way things really are, and seeks to arouse that perception in others.

A sentence from the Epicurean tradition, reads: "The discourse of philosophers is in vain, unless it heals some passion of the soul." The goal of the Stoics and Epicureans was to help us find our way in the universe, to offer practical advice about how to live wisely and nobly, and how to make sense of our own existence. These goals differ little from the ambitions of more modern philosophers. Perhaps the Stoics and Epicureans were more successful than most of our contemporaries, in offering practical advice.

Students often respond more favorably to Marcus Aurelius and Epictetus than to Plato or Aristotle. Plato is perhaps too "abstract" for the undergraduate mind, and Aristotle can appear trite or platitudinous. The Stoics and Epicureans speak of living life rationally, "in accordance with nature," and their philosophy has a psychological dimension to it that anticipates the work of Freud and Jung, and modern writers in the "self-help" tradition. Epictetus suggests the real task of growing up and being mature is learning to discipline not only desires and inclinations, but also assent: to know what to agree with, and what to oppose most vigorously.

There are those for whom the very word "philosophy" will forever be empty. There are others for whom the Greek and Roman philosophers are just so many dead white males. And there are some who, in the attempt to reject the doing of philosophy, will accidentally slip into doing it. As Aristotle said: "Even if you refuse to philosophize, the explanation of your refusal is an act of philosophizing." In the end, no matter how poor the teacher, or how strong the resistance to philosophy, philosophy always wins out. As Aristotle says: "Every art and every inquiry, and similarly every action and pursuit, is thought to aim at some good." What greater good could there be, than clear-headed thinking about how to live your life "nobly and well?"

II-73
Stoics and Epicureans

Two thousand years ago, the philosophy of the Stoics and Epicureans was much more popular, and much more practiced, than the philosophies of Plato or Aristotle. Quotes from Epictetus or Epicurus were much more likely to be on the lips of ordinary citizens. Classics scholars, and some philosophers, claim that the philosophy of the Stoics, in particular, is pertinent to modern concerns and contemporary life.

There are several features common to the Stoic writers. The Stoics were the first "cosmopolitans," (from the Greek, *cosmos*, world, and *polites*, citizen of.), affirming that none of us stand alone; we are each an important part of the Whole, and that each of us has some distinctive contribution to make. The Stoics are also moralists in a most grandiose sense: there is no evil but moral evil, and the perfection of human life consists in the purity of moral consciousness. This leads to the feeling of serenity and invulnerability popularly attached to Stoicism.

The Stoics are among the first to tout the absolute value of the human person. Epictetus was a slave, but no one "owned" his inner person; Marcus Aurelius was a Roman Emperor, but his sense of cosmic duty led him to see his life as a debt of service to humankind. The modern interest in 'human rights' owes much to his Stoic vision.

The one Stoic doctrine that has been widely quoted and even more widely ignored is: "Live in and for the present moment." There are dozens of different formulations of this in the writings of the Stoics, but this is perhaps the best: "Live as if you were seeing the world for the first and last time." Marcus Aurelius seemed especially fond of this version of the same thought: "If you see all that is there in the present moment, you have access to the totality of time and the world."

Stoic writers may have influenced the wisdom literature of the Hebrew Bible and the Epistles of the Christian Scriptures. When William Blake hoped to see a world in a grain of sand he was echoing the Stoic vision. Stoicism forms the nucleus of a great many self-help books, and Stoic philosophy figures prominently in the wisdom of daytime TV personalities.

Is Stoicism especially applicable to modern life? Clearly bearing up under misfortune is one important aspect of the Stoic legacy. Stoicism was simply an emphasis on one aspect of the Platonic heritage. Socrates might be identified as the first Stoic, with his phrase: "no harm can come to a good man..." Philosophy in these traditions is not a doctrine or a dogma, but a dialogue, an ongoing conversation between you and your world. Nobody can do philosophy for you, because it is the reflection on your personal experience, but Stoics and Platonists and others can show you the way to developing a philosophy you can live with. All the people you meet, all the books you read, are but sparks to illuminate your distinctive and original responses. Philosophy loses its way when it becomes a system like Hegel's, or a series of theses or propositions, or even a linking together of arguments, however logical or mathematical.

What you read in this book are not "definitive" statements, in part because they are meant to provoke or incite, not to end discussion. We all have a chance to learn from the wisdom of the past, but it only becomes "wisdom" for us when we appropriate it, personalize it, make it uniquely our own. Plato said that philosophy could never really be written down, because it must be spoken, heard, responded to. Good philosophy is alive with excitement and novelty, with enthusiasm for the unexpected and the original. The lasting glory of the Stoics is that they put us on the path to accepting the present moment with a mixture of delight and apprehension, because the world is not a locus of endless repetition. And, perhaps most important for us in the modern, troubled world, for the Stoics, the good in life clearly outweighs the bad, if only you focus on what is the reality deep-down of things.

II-74
The Place of Plotinus

I owe my textual understanding of Plotinus to John M. Rist's book, *Plotinus, The Road to Reality*. There are many anthologies of Plotinus, all of them useful summaries of his only book, a difficult text called *The Enneads*, Greek for "nine books." Plotinus wrote in very difficult Greek, sometimes in a puzzling oracular style, and he is not easy to understand. As to his personality, he was friendly, helpful, patient, ascetic, moral, and though seriously involved with people of importance, he was committed to taking care of orphans and other unfortunates. In his writings, he lays great stress on the importance of "retiring," separating from daily cares, to focus on "the eternal, and truly important."

Something like Spinoza, he was "a God-intoxicated man," and his mystical experiences are at the root of his life and philosophy. While his God is transcendent and "totally other," (Moslem mystics came to like this---it affords some understanding of the distant "Allah" of the Koran), God is also immanent, and His traces are found everywhere: "As a man walking on the beach leaves a footprint, so the One leaves a finite trace on the intelligible world..." In a phrase that influenced later theologians, Plotinus says: "The One exists in an infinite way, everything else finitely...."

The world into which Plotinus was born was suffering from 'a loss of nerve,' for a great cloud of pessimism and negativity hung over the Roman Empire at the time. Plotinus presented a contrasting optimistic view of human nature and of human purpose. The goal of life is not conquering more people, it is not accumulating wealth, it is *"homoiosis Theo,"* attaining likeness to God, becoming as God-like as possible. The soul has a vital spark, a drive to become more like the One. Two Christian saints, Augustine and Ambrose, were familiar with the writings of Plotinus, and a classic phrase of Augustine has clear Plotinian antecedents: "Thou hast made us for Thyself alone, O God, and our hearts are restless until they rest in Thee." Plotinus wrote: "The One is already present to those who seek Him."

In Plotinus' teaching, the soul, the intellectual and spiritual principle, is clearly immortal, but he says puzzling things like: "...it is our duty to attain immortality as far as possible." This may relate to his notion of purification, and might even have a trace of the notion of re-incarnation, of be-souling bodies until you get it right, and escape the wheel of re-birth. This idea occurred in Greek, as well as Indian thought, and Plotinus is never perfectly clear about the nature of soul, or why it inhabits a body, or what its independent existence would be like. "All things flow forth from the One, and all things return to the One." What later writers would call "the great chain of being," is clearly a Plotinian notion: being has levels or grades, different degrees or modes of expressing itself. (The poetry of Gerard Manley Hopkins reiterates clear Plotinian themes....)

How about faith? Plotinus uses the Greek word *pistis,* faith, to mean a low level of knowledge, based on sense evidence, of which you are not quite convinced. The prayerful and religious activities of his day he dismissed as so much "magic," as attempts to sway the gods, by people who simply had not had the transformative experience of the One such as he had. He had no need of a "leap of faith," because he had seen and touched the divine, and had no doubts about the validity of his experience. Plotinus could only say: "He who has seen It, knows what I mean."

Plotinus proposes the life of virtue and intellect as the road to "salvation," for one needs to be redeemed not so much from sin, as from emptiness and foolishness. The good life is the life of the sage, of the seeker after wisdom, and wisdom and goodness are ultimately inseparable. Temples are unnecessary, because the World is a Holy Place, irradiated with traces of the Divine. Historians of philosophy state that the influence of Plotinus was far greater than his relative obscurity would indicate. Perhaps this is exactly what you would expect from so retiring a seeker after ultimate truth and wisdom.

II-75
Both Sides Now?

For the ancient philosophers, philosophy is a conversion, a transformation of one's way of being and living. Philosophy is, above all, a quest for wisdom. For the Greeks, it was never a game of "I'm right, you're wrong." Too much of modern philosophy begins with "I shall defend the claim," and too much of what contemporary philosophers do begins with a quest for victory instead of a quest for wisdom.

Philosophers have been leaving the lecture halls and conference rooms, and making their way into the popular press. Daniel Dennett wrote an Op/Ed piece for the New York Times on "The Bright Stuff," in which he says it is time for "Brights" to come out of the closet. "What is a bright? A bright is a person with a naturalist as opposed to a supernaturalist worldview. We Brights don't believe in ghosts or elves or the Easter Bunny—or God." Dennett suggests history is on the side of the Brights, as more and more scientists, doctors, and nurses, even clergymen, align themselves on the side of the Brights. The Pew Forum noted that 27 million Americans are atheist or agnostic or have no religious preference. Robert Solomon's book *Spirituality for the Skeptic* is an attempt to retain some of what the religious traditions have had to offer, but now in an atheistic or agnostic context.

Particularly at Consciousness Conferences, understanding human mental processes as purely physiological actions is taken as the starting point for rejecting the notion that human nature has any kind of spiritual dimension. Simon Blackburn sums it up nicely: "Many philosophers argue, and I agree, that belief in the afterlife involves an indefensible metaphysics: a false picture of how we as persons relate to our physical bodies." Jonathan Miller, the Medical Doctor turned producer of "Beyond the Fringe" and now of a series of operas, says, "overcoming the travesties of religions" will be a major 21st century achievement.

If you follow the reasoning of "the brights," the conversion sought by philosophy would seem to be a conversion to atheism, or at least to agnosticism. But there is another side to the story. For some believers, "faith" is not a matter of reason or rationality at all, but simply submission of the will to Divine Revelation. In this, they follow the tradition Kant acknowledged in his *Critique of Pure Reason*, "I have therefore found it necessary to deny knowledge in order to make room for faith." *Fideism* becomes a position on the opposite extreme: "No matter what the weight of evidence, no matter what so many scientists prove, I will go on believing, because my faith in God is strong."

Most religious-minded philosophers, however, follow Alvin Plantinga in being as uncomfortable with this fideistic position as they are with the dogmatic atheism of the Brights. The position elaborated by John Rist in *Real Ethics* finds many supporters: even if reason can tell us little about the nature of God, it can produce a rational understanding that is supportive of what religious faith teaches.

Writers like Dennett and Rorty have become darlings of the popular press. This age has yet to find philosophical writers of a religious disposition of the caliber of C.S. Lewis or Abraham Heschel. C.S. Lewis founded the "Oxford Socratic Club," to bring together philosophers of diametrically opposing views, so that members could avoid spending their time listening to those who shared their own convictions. Members on each side would be forced to give full attention to the best available formulations of the views of their opponents. Given the absolutist convictions of those who espouse diametrically opposite points of view, perhaps it is high time for the revival of such clubs. Dan Dennet and Peter Singer opposite Richard Neuhaus and Norman Podhoretz. The fireworks that such clubs would provide would make Fourth of July celebrations seem tame, and the defenders of both points of view would come to a greater understanding not only of their own position, but of the reasonableness of those who think otherwise.

My Sister, Marion Young, in China

II-76
Confucius

"The wise man," said Aristotle, "knows things that are difficult, and knows everything, in so far as it knowable." In the years since Aristotle, the ambitions of philosophy in the west have been severely curtailed. What we call "science" has taken over the knowledge of nature that was once the province of philosophy. And academic philosophy has become so obsessed with logic that ethical and metaphysical questions are often used simply as illustrations of what is beyond logic.

In the East, there is a still a passion for the attempt to be "wise about life," and no eastern sage epitomizes this better than Confucius. Confucius was born about 552 B.C.E., thus making him a contemporary of the Greek pre-Socratics. Like the Sophists, Socrates' immediate predecessors, Confucius was interested in "right thinking about how society should be formed." And, like Socrates, the society into which Confucius was born, was in great disarray, with much concern for finding a better way of government. And very much like the presumed historical Socrates, Confucius was convinced you could not have a just society, unless you first have members who have a passion for justice.

Basic to Confucius' teaching is the observation that just as there is an order of the physical world, so too must individuals live their lives within a framework of a moral order. A ruler, said Confucius, must be "noble," in the sense of having a morally sound character, and a vision of how society must be ordered. This is quite similar to Plato's Republic, whose rulers are fit to rule, because they have a "vision" of what is "Good."

The Confucian notion that society is like a family, and should be ruled so that every member benefits, is still very much alive among some of the citizens of China today. To be human, said Confucius, is to have a special love for children, and to seek to treat everyone as you would your brother. Any visitor to China can witness examples of the fact that this is a philosophy that is still very much in practice.

The Sayings of Confucius that history has handed down to us make him sound like a member of the school of Practical Philosophy that grew out of Plato's Academy. Consequently, the sayings of Confucius sometimes have that "Chinese Fortune Cookie" character with which we have become so familiar. But there is a depth to the recorded sayings of Confucius beyond what fortune cookies can convey. Two shining examples will suffice: "A man of humanity, wishing to establish himself, also establishes others, and, wishing to enlarge himself, also enlarges others." "It is these things that cause me concern: failure to cultivate virtue, failure to go deeply into what I have learned, inability to move up to what I have heard to be right, and inability to reform myself when I have defects."

One could do worse than choosing Confucius as a personal philosophical master. Perhaps attentiveness to his wisdom can help build a new and better bridge of understanding between the Orient and the west. Until that happens, the application of his thinking in our own lives might be useful steps along the path to wisdom.

II-77
Buddhism, Plain and Simple

"The miracle is not to walk on water. The miracle is to walk on the green earth in the present moment. Peace is all around us—in the world and in nature—and within us." Thich Nhat Hanh has become one of the most widely read expositors of Buddhism to the modern world. With books like *Peace is Every Step: The Path of Mindfulness in Everyday Life*, he has made the teachings of Buddhism accessible to anyone who will take the time to read that book. For those who want the shortest possible summary formula, Baba Ram Dass' book will suffice: *Be Here. Now*. For an approach to Buddhism from a "western" perspective, Steve Hagen's *Buddhism Plain and Simple* has no rival.

Quite unintentionally, many philosophy professors drive their students to Buddhism. With a mind boggled by logic, concepts, clarification and argument, the student can easily be moved to Buddhism by attractiveness of the simple mantra: "Reality is what it is, and cannot be described. Reality is quite different from our concepts." Western Philosophy is analytic, taking concepts apart to the point of logical atomism. To someone exposed to symbolic logic and discussions of "Transcendental Idealism," the basic words of Buddhism are more refreshing than a summer breeze, more exhilarating than a release from prison. Listen to Thich Nhat Hanh: "The ultimate dimension of reality has nothing to do with concepts. It is not just absolute reality that cannot be talked about. Take for instance a glass of apple juice. You cannot talk about apple juice to someone who has never tasted it." In a word, concepts can be useful, but they are no substitute for real experience.

What is Buddhism? It is down to earth, empirical, based on direct experience, and does not depend on argument or discourse. It proposes that what each person must seek for his or her own enlightenment is direct experience of reality as it is. It is not abstruse, abstract, or metaphysical, but focused on immediate problems, such as how to overcome suffering. It is "therapeutic" in that it seeks to heal the ills encountered in everyday life. It is "psychological" in that it begins with human beings and their problems, and not with the universe and its origin and purpose. It is "democratic" in rejecting governments and hierarchies while attending to people and their everyday problems. It is "individualistic" in claiming that no one else can solve your problems, and that each individual must seek his or her own enlightenment.

129

Is Buddhism a religion or a philosophy? It can be both, or it can be neither. Some followers of Gautama Buddha "deified" him after his death, while other followers said: "If you meet the Buddha on the road, kill him!" And modern masters have said: "The only true Buddhist philosophy is to stop doing philosophy." Various "schools" of Buddhism, particularly the form known as Zen, teach a twofold doctrine of Mindfulness attained through the practice of Meditation, and Enlightenment attained by learning to live fully in the Present Moment.

Buddhist philosophy requires open-mindedness. Its basic principle is that no one concept, no one package of concepts, can begin to capture the whole of reality. Buddhism is just one of the many possible expressions of philosophy not as an academic exercise, but as a way of life. Civilization would be better served if, over the entrance to Houses of Worship and Community, the words of Thich Nhat Hanh were inscribed: "Do not think the knowledge you presently possess is changeless, absolute truth. Avoid being narrow-minded and bound to present views. Learn and practice non-attachment from views in order to be open to receive others' viewpoints." That is Buddhism, Plain and Simple. It also happens to be a very good philosophy, one we can all easily put into practice.

II-78
Confucius, Plain and Simple

"One may also observe in one's travels to distant countries the feelings of recognition and friendliness that link every human being to every other human being." This quote from Aristotle, who is widely regarded as the most influential philosopher in the western tradition, might serve as an apt introduction to Confucius, not only the most important sage in the eastern tradition, but whose teachings have had more direct and lasting influence than any collection of western philosophers.

Confucius, (or Kong Qiu, or Master Kong,) was born about 552 BCE, and died in 479 BCE. His teaching built upon an already long-standing tradition that the work of the wise man is to help create harmony in human society. This harmony is accomplished by balancing the two forces of yin and yang, the "soft and feminine" with the "hard and masculine." In terms of ethics, this means that harmony and responsibility are always more important than individual freedom and rights. A Chinese word that occurs with some frequency in Confucius' book *The Analects* is *Ren,* which is defined as a fusion of goodness, humaneness, love, benevolence, and human-heartedness.

The two greatest Confucian teachers have the same diametrically opposed convictions that occur in the western tradition. Mencius (371-289 BCE) proclaimed the basic goodness of human nature, while Xunxi (298-238 BCE) claimed that humans were originally evil and became good only through strict laws and harsh punishments.

The Analects contain pithy wise sayings that are no doubt the source of Chinese fortune cookies. The sayings may be simple: "If you do not consider the future, you will be in trouble when it comes near." "If you make a mistake, do not be afraid to correct it." They may be direct: "My ideals are to bring solace to the old, to be faithful to friends, and to cherish the young." They may be autobiographical: "At fifteen it was my desire to learn. At thirty I was established. At forty I had no more doubts. At fifty I knew Heaven's will. At sixty I could obey what I heard. At seventy I could follow my heart's desire and not transgress what is right." They may be quite personal: "Tell those who ask that I am a person who studies with such eagerness that he forgets his food, is so happy that he forgets his cares, and does not notice the coming of old age."

While Confucius applies the Asian rule of not speaking about that of which you have no experience, his writings affirm the sacredness of the universe, the importance of respect if not downright worship of ancestors, and while the writings seem to assume the existence of an afterlife, he keeps his focus on the here and now: "If we are not able to serve humanity, how can we serve spiritual beings? If we do not understand life, how can we understand death?"

Confucianism exerted great influence for over two thousand years not only in China, but also in Korea, Vietnam, and Japan. A western scholar wrote: "The East sees things in Confucian terms." A Chinese student of mine said: "Chinese studies for substance, western studies for function." Jennifer Oldstone-Moore, author of *Confucianism,* wrote: "To some, the end of explicitly Confucian states has meant the death of Confucianism. But others believe there is evidence that the tradition is too strong to be broken altogether, despite the sometimes severe strains placed upon it." Some years ago, I asked a Chinese grad student who was the most important Chinese philosopher. He replied: "Karl Marx." The odds are good that today the *Analects* of Confucius is much more important than *The Communist Manifesto,* perhaps even Mao's famous *Little Red Book.* Confucius' book *The Analects* is a philosophical classic that richly rewards the reader, whatever tradition they may come from.

II-79
Judaism, Plain and Simple

Most Americans have only a foggy idea of what Christianity is all about, and their understanding of Judaism is even foggier. Of the many recent expositors of Judaism, none wrote more clearly than Abraham Joshua Heschel (1907-1972). Spoken of as "the most significant Jewish theologian of the twentieth century," the titles of four of his books show the breadth of his concerns: *God In Search of Man, Man Is Not Alone, The Sabbath*, and, *The Prophets*. When two millennia ago Rabbi Hillel was asked if he could express the essence of Judaism while standing on one foot, he said: "Don't do to others what you wouldn't have them do to you." Heschel's answer was: "Judaism is not a matter of blood or race, but a spiritual dimension of existence, a dimension of holiness."

Judaism has two absolutes: first of all, Monotheism: "Hear, O Israel, the Lord our God is One," –Judaism arose as a contradiction to the polytheistic cults which flourished throughout the ancient Middle East; secondly, Sacredness: "Remove your shoes, for the ground you stand on is holy."—Ancient Judaism established a distinction between the Profane-the world God created, and the Sacred-the God who did the creating, and Who Is "Wholly Other." Reverence for the Sacred is the resounding keynote of Judaism. Out of reverence for the name of God, Jews leave out the vowel, writing "G-d." (The story is widely told: an undergraduate expresses her atheism by writing: "I don't believe in G-d.")

The current European Constitution omits any reference to a "Jewish or Christian heritage," which is unfortunate, for European culture would not be what it is without three influences from Judaism: (1) the universe is *personal*: life is not a battle of cosmic forces, but is more like a family relationship—as exemplified by God leading Moses into the Promised Land (eventually the nation of Israel); (2) the universe is *moral*: the Prophets not only rail against offending God, they proclaim that God demands a just and moral social order; (3) *nature*, as God's creation, has meaning and purpose, and man has a role to play in executing God's intent for creation.

Greek Culture walked the path of "Reason," and produced "rational reflection on the nature of reality." Judaism walked the path of Religion, for God revealed Himself by his actions in history, establishing a "Covenant" with Israel, a kind of legal agreement: "I am God Almighty: walk before me and be blameless, and I will establish a Covenant between you and me." In the light of this heritage, modern civilizations, whether western or eastern, have sought to establish some happy marriage of reason and faith, science and belief, investigation and acceptance.

Buddhism has an eightfold path, Islam its five pillars, and Judaism its four cornerstones: (1) Torah, (the first five books of the Bible), both a Constitution and a Presence, or, as one scholar said, "Out of *this* Jewish history, God is made manifest." (2) Talmud, a compendium of learning, a summary of debates, decisions, and wise sayings of the scholars, written about 2200 years ago. (3) The most troublesome cornerstone, *Aretz Yisrael*, "The Land of Israel." (Israel's leading newspaper is *Ha' Aretz*, "The Land.") The nation of Israel is about half the size of San Bernardino County, California. (Golda Meir, when she was Prime Minister of Israel, said: "How odd of God to choose for His people the only land in the Middle East that has no oil.") Beginning with Abraham, the conviction was enshrined that it is only in the Promised Land that Torah can be translated into the life of a nation. (4) *Mitzvah*: commands, duties. The *Mitzvoth* are the demands incumbent on every Jew—reverence for God, and the everyday acts of social life that express that reverence.

Judaism manifests itself in a variety of social traditions, ranging from the activities of the Pious Ones, the Hasidim, to the utopian vision of Karl Marx, and on to the Personalism of Emmanuel Levinas: "We are all responsible for each other, and I am the most responsible of all." Martin Buber created a modern Jewish synthesis in cryptic phrases like: "I only become an I in relation to a Thou." He is most famous for his book *I and Thou*, but *The Eclipse of God* is a brilliant critique of modern philosophy.

Judaism is a religion and not a philosophy, but it has produced an extensive panoply of philosophers and theologians. Philo of Alexandria (d. 50 C.E.) was the first to attempt a synthesis of Platonic philosophical ideas with Hebrew religion. Moses Maimonides (d. 1204 C.E.) wrote a *Guide for the Perplexed,* an attempt to dissolve philosophic conflicts, rich with aphorisms like: "Proper old age is a disposition to achieve moral virtue." Emil Fackenheim (d. 2003) wrote *To Mend the World: Foundations of Post-Holocaust Jewish Thought,* and, *What is Judaism?* Abraham Joshua Heschel has written very popular books, bringing Jewish tradition alive, and providing materials for anyone who would like to know more about Judaism. Heschel said: "I write for anyone willing to entertain the reality of the Sacred." The vision of man not being alone, and God being in search of man, stands in stark contrast to the modern secular spirit. Judaism stands forever as witness to the conviction of Absolute Transcendence. "Judaism is not a matter of blood or race, but a spiritual dimension of existence, a dimension of holiness."

II-80
Christianity, Plain and Simple

C.S. Lewis (1898-1963) was Professor of 16th century English Literature at first Oxford, then Cambridge. In 1931, he "became a Christian," and for the next thirty years, he gave speeches, radio and TV addresses, and wrote books, "in defense of Christianity." His most famous book, *Mere Christianity* (1944) was his attempt to express the common core of belief "in as simple a way as possible." The book provides his answers to questions like: Why believe in God? Is Christ the Redeemer? Is God a Trinity? And, What are appropriate Christian moral standards?

Years later, when asked why he wrote such books, he replied: "When I began, Christianity came before the great mass of my fellow-countrymen either in the highly emotional form offered by revivalists or in the unintelligible language of highly cultured clergymen. Most men were reached by neither." He was simply the best Christian "apologist," that is, defender of Christian beliefs, of the twentieth century. He founded "The Socratic Club" at Oxford, primarily to debate Christianity with unbelievers. He wrote an ingeniously simple defense of natural law morality in a book that is still timely today, *The Abolition of Man*. In *Miracles*, he defended various biblical events as "interference with nature by a Supernatural Power," and claimed that biblical miracles were just extensions of the everyday miracles nature provides.

He is best known for his series of science-fiction novels, *Out of the Silent Planet, Perelandra*, and *The Chronicles of Narnia*. *Perelandra* discusses a topic still debated today: What if there is a civilization on another planet that did not experience original sin? Is Christ still their "Redeemer?"

When I was working on an article on the various Greek words for love, I found Lewis had beaten me to it, with a book called *The Four Loves*. The Greeks carefully distinguished between what you are doing when you love a meal, a sunset, a person, a country, or a god. Lewis wrote with clarity I could only admire, but never imitate.

Lewis noted that a peculiar characteristic of modern times is that, instead of us being in the dock with God accusing us of our sins, we put "God in the Dock" (the title of a collection of his essays), and accuse Him of gross mismanagement of our affairs. The theme in these essays is: If God is omnipotent and omniscient, how come there is so much evil and suffering in the world? In his book *The Problem of Pain*, he discusses the redemptive value of human suffering—as punishment for sins, but seems nonplussed at animal suffering, even defending the "peaceable kingdom" idea that before original sin, all animals were vegetarian, the lion lay down with the lamb, and predators only preyed on fruits and vegetables.

In *The Screwtape Letters*, he explained the presence of some evils as the consequence of diabolical intervention. The book is purportedly a collection of letters written by one particular devil who is delighted that so few people believe in his existence, because that makes his work so much easier. Lewis' Christianity was unfailingly conservative, for example his 1948 article rejecting women as priests: "Only one wearing the masculine uniform can represent the Lord to the Church." And to the discussion about religious and secular ethics, he has a simple answer: "Morality is a mountain which we cannot climb by our own efforts." Lewis was Anglican through and through, but his favorite religious author was the Roman Catholic G.K. Chesterton, also a popular author and novelist, most famous for his "Fr. Brown" mystery stories, all of which have a religious theme. Lewis' favorite quote from Chesterton: "It is not that Christianity has been tried and found wanting: it is that Christianity has never been tried."

If you seek a plain but eloquent defense of Christianity, or if you simply want to give an honest hearing to a presentation of Christianity at its best, you can't do better than *Mere Christianity,* a mere book by no mere writer, C. S. Lewis.

II-81
Science and God

A great paradox: while philosophers have become progressively more atheistic, scientists have been busy suggesting that a God-initiated universe makes scientific sense. The Anglo-American tradition in philosophy, beginning with David Hume and proceeding through Bertrand Russell, John Dewey, Willard Quine, Richard Rorty, and most recently, Simon Blackburn, has rejected all the arguments for God's existence, not infrequently citing "science" as the basis. Arguments from design have most frequently been the target. While William Paley and others argued that, if you found a watch, you would presume a watchmaker, critics responded that while the gears and jewels of a device for telling time led to a watchmaker, the presence (or absence) of design in the universe is an improper analogy for the obvious purposiveness of some such device as a watch. Then along came Darwin.

As Simon Blackburn commented, "natural selection presented a scientific alternative to divine creation." For at least one hundred years,

Darwinian Evolution became the scientific dogma that made any God-hypothesis dubious. Darwin wrote in 1859: "All life is the product of undirected natural forces, chance, and natural selection." In the 1980s, Michael Denton published *Evolution: A Theory In Crisis*, citing an overlooked statement of Darwin: "If it could be demonstrated that any complex organ existed which could not possibly have been formed by numerous, successive, slight modifications, my theory would absolutely break down."

Scientific evidence was beginning to accumulate that while Natural Selection could explain how variations could occur in a living organism, it could not explain life itself, nor could it explain the presence of complex organs like eyes, every part of which must be in place before the organ functions at all. Cell biology became the root source of criticism of Darwinian Evolution. Until the 1950s, the incredible complexity of the cell had gone relatively unnoticed. A cell has forty different protein parts, none of which functions without the other.

Dean Kenyon published *Biochemical Predestination* in 1973, claiming that primitive cells emerged from simple chemicals in primitive waters, but no sooner had the book come out than Kenyon began doubting that simple attraction between proteins could possibly produce life. Kenyon asked: how could the first protein have been assembled without the help of genetic information? As he said: "Such instructions do not come from the chemicals." He went on to generalize: "Most researchers rejected by 1970 that the information necessary to build the first cell originated by chance alone." And he concluded: "Since you can pinpoint no chemical origin for life, the only alternative is Intelligent Design."

With the discovery of the DNA molecule and its incredible complexity, genetics seemed to provide the most compelling evidence for Intelligent Design. The next major step was an analysis of Information Processing. There are three billion characters in the DNA molecule, and that molecule somehow "knows" how to process that information correctly. As Bill Gates, who should know a great deal about computer code complexity, said, "DNA is like a computer code, only it is much more complex than any we have formulated."

Some scientists working in this area remind colleagues that science is "observation of the facts," and claim that their observation of the facts leads them inevitably to Intelligent Design. Philosophers as far back as Plato claimed that science was only possible because the universe had Forms or Patterns and was therefore intelligible. Plato would appreciate the comments of a contemporary philosopher of biology: "The universe is rational and comprehensible, underwritten by a supreme intelligence."

And his concluding comment is something Plato could have written: "You find rationality and comprehensibility and beauty right at the foundation of things."

In the 1970s, some scientists proposed "the anthropic principle," based on the notion that the universe seemed remarkably oriented to life. "The universe seems marvelously constructed to produce stars, planets, and life. Scientists have calculated that if the force binding atomic nuclei were just 0.5 percent different, the processes that forge atoms inside stars would have failed to produce either carbon or oxygen—key ingredients for life. If gravity were only slightly stronger or weaker, stars like our sun could not have formed. Yet physicists see no reason why the constants of nature are set just so. To some, this is all good news. Perhaps, as some religious people say, God exists and wanted it this way." (Charles Petit, USN&WR, Sept. 8, p. 40)

In a word, design is back on the table. Philosophical conferences are getting much more interesting, now that scientists are showing up, and giving philosophers something "new" to think about. To scientific discussions of matter and energy must be added discussions of the nature of information, its origins and its processing. It is an Unfolding Universe, and as scientists discover more about its nature, philosophers have more and more explaining to do, and the admonition about keeping an open mind becomes ever more imperative.

II-82
Facing Death

Funerals are difficult emotional experiences. The emotions and the distress of the bereaved may be well concealed, but the sense of grief is inescapable. Even when death has long been at the doorstep, the actual passing is not without its impact. Those who attend the funeral are properly called "mourners," for every one present experiences some sense of grief, some sense of loss, some sense that the world has changed.

The English poet and clergyman John Donne captured one aspect of it well when he said: "Do not ask for whom the bell tolls: the bell tolls for thee." When we attend a funeral, however focused our grief may be, some part of our emotion is the awareness that death is not just something that happens to other people, it happens to us, it will happen to us, and death drops a curtain on what we hold dear, what we have accomplished, what we have done with our lives.

The eminent philosopher Charles Hartshorne, who lived to be a hundred years old, was comforted by the thought that he would live forever in the mind of God. Hartshorne's philosophical reflections echoed a long-standing Jewish belief that human personality abides forever within the mind of God. As the Shema Israel Torah Network puts it, "The sum total of the human personality existing in God's memory is what lives on even after a man dies." For those who say living in God's memory is not enough, the Shema Network explains: "God's memory is not a static thing. The sum total of human personality may indeed exist in God's memory, but it can still maintain its self-identity, and remain in an active state."

The central words of one Christian funeral service are: "For unto thy faithful, O Lord, life is changed, not taken away." Christian theologians teach that belief in the Resurrection of Jesus was the central feature of early Christian preaching. His Resurrection prefigured rebirth of the Christian to eternal life. Theologians like Hans Kung have attempted to make this relevant to modern minds. Kung wrote: "Why hope for heaven? My answer is quite straightforward: out of an acceptance of life, out of a love of life. Precisely because we love life before death, we hope for a life after death."

As Socrates, ever the model of philosophers, faced his death, he said: "Either it will be a great liberation, and I shall be able to talk with the heroes of old, or it shall be like the deepest sleep I have ever enjoyed. Either way, I win." Socrates faced his death with equanimity, a capacity not always present among modern philosophers. Heidegger recommended daily awareness of death as a metaphysical exercise, but the fact that human existence is a "being-towards-death" seems to cut into the pleasure of everyday existence. There is a heaviness in the reflections on death in Heidegger's philosophy, dominated as it by the vision that life cannot last, that being is only temporal, that the greatest of human joys has the same staying power as a candle in the wind.

Death and awareness of death, for theologians and philosophers, as for all human beings, generates intense emotional responses. We want infinity, but we are limited; we want delight, ecstasy, bliss unmarred by pain and suffering. Nietzsche, by some identified as the greatest philosopher of the nineteenth century, in one of his Socratic moments, wrote: "All joy wants eternity, deep, deep, deep eternity." And perhaps that joyful longing for eternity is what makes funerals such deeply moving experiences. No life, even that of a centenarian is long enough. Having one's being-towards-death is a reminder of the challenge to live each day to the fullest, perhaps actualizing the capacity to place wonderful memories in the mind of God. Death reminds us of the temporal character of our being, that our opportunities are limited, and that we must make the most of every moment that comes our way. The death of a loved one reminds us that our being is inter-being, that our lives are intertwined with those we love, and that we have an obligation to honor their memory, by living our lives to the fullest. It is most important that, when we come to die, we must have a sense of having lived our lives to the fullest, and having done our best to live up to our potential...

Crematory ovens at Dachau, Germany

II-83
Do You Have Free Will?

Common sense convinces us that we have free will. We are aware of "making choices," we make decisions to go left or right, to choose a kind word, or to choose a food that is either good for us, or one that tastes "good." Common sense also tells us that if we were not "free," it would make no sense to praise someone for good behavior, or to punish someone for doing something bad. When the evidence is so universal, how could anyone believe that having free will is nothing but an illusion? Is it conceivable that if we were more accurate in assessing behavior, we could establish clear and inviolable causal connections between the genetic make-ups we inherited and the actions we choose?

The philosophic discussion of free will in the west comes in three distinct episodes: (1) Greek Philosophy: Plato and Aristotle formulated the common sense viewpoint that people are responsible for their actions, and their debate centered around educating people so they would know how to choose what is good. (2) Christianity shifted the debate into two new directions. St. Augustine said why, when I know the good I should choose, do I so often choose the evil I know I should avoid? Augustine says our will is not perfectly free, and this is caused by "original sin," the turning away from good and towards evil by our original parents, an act that darkened our intellects and weakened our wills. A long series of Christian writers, among them Aquinas, Scotus, Luther and Calvin, will struggle with the theological issue of God creating man "free" to choose good or evil, a "fall" from grace that disposes us towards evil, and the presence of freedom in the face of divine foreknowledge. Since God knows all, and God does not change, how can our choices possibly be free? Calvin and Augustine agreed that "predestination" is a fact, and theologians who follow them struggle to find ways to claim that what God knows is known because of our choices, and not that our choices are what they are because of what God knows. Spinoza thought he terminated the debate by saying: "If the falling stone were conscious, it too would think itself free."

(3) The third episode in the history of free will begins with Immanuel Kant, and his attempt to reconcile Newton's discovery of the laws of physics with free will. The more "scientific" one becomes, the more one tends to see the world as a great causal chain, each cause having an effect, which becomes a cause, and so on forever. The Laws of Physics determine all, and among some contemporary brain anatomists, busy probing the microtubules of consciousness, the only room for free will would have to come from the application of quantum mechanics, where some degree of indeterminacy seems to prevail, at least upon rare occasions.

Kant, ever the moralist, wished to defend human freedom and responsibility in the face of the overwhelming determinism of the physics of his day. He postulated that while nature operates in time and is part of the "appearances" of the world, the human will, which operates "beyond appearances," is outside time, and hence free from rigid determinism. Kant's more empiricist successors reject all talk of what is outside time, as hopelessly beyond human observation.

Contemporary philosophers like Dan Dennett go to great extremes, in the light of the current work in the "science of consciousness," to defend freedom of the will. At the same time the rest of us go about our business, secure in the knowledge that we really do make choices that could be otherwise. We are convinced that we merit praise for some of those choices, and that we are "blame-worthy" for others. We are convinced we are "moral agents," hoping to improve ourselves by the good choices we make, and hoping to build a better community by the influences we have on others. Paradox building upon paradox, we are bound and determined to be free, and as much as we would sometimes like not to be held responsible for our actions, down deep we seem to know that we are the authors of what we do. Do we have free will? We seem bound and determined to think so...

II-84
Lively Conflicts!

Having presided over a section of a Conference on "Conflicts of Religious and Secular Ethics," I am resolved that, should the opportunity present itself again, I will be better prepared. I am an ardent proponent of finding "common ground" between warring factions, and I have naively assumed religious-minded people would want to find out how much they had in common with secular ethicists. I expected that secular ethicists would delight in finding how many moral convictions they shared with the religious-minded.

Fireworks began with the first presenter, when the author of a book on St. Augustine accused the secularists of not just operating without faith, but of operating in "bad faith," indeed accusing them of being "professional liars," for, as he said, every secular ethic fails because of its inherent inconsistency. His presentation was based on three convictions: (1) Since God is the author of all that is, and has created human nature for specific purposes, failure to begin from that starting point is bound to lead to false conclusions; (2) given the doctrine of original sin, humans operate with a darkened intellect and a weakened will, and need divine assistance both to know the truth and to pursue the good; (3) all secular ethics ultimately reduce to the Kantian principle of "always treat other human beings as ends, never as means," and this simply falls short of the only "true" basis of ethics, which is the love of God, and the love of all humanity as God's children.

Fireworks continued with the first presentation by an uncompromisingly atheistic secular ethicist, who recounted the evils inflicted upon mankind in the name of religious truth, and proceeded to explain that (1) human freedom demands that people choose their goals and ends; (2) that religious ethics presumes first principles chosen by faith and not by reason; (3)

that, given the great variety of religious revelations, it is impossible to expect the human race to adopt some one religious ethic as universally acceptable, and (4) that it belonged to human reason, as expressed by the best application of positive science, to create a "common ground" ethic, that alone could form a basis for global peace and prosperity. Fortunately for all involved, other presentations were less confrontational, and areas of "mutual concern and agreement" were discovered, and some fair degree of civility prevailed.

The fireworks were not done for the day, however, for an explosive session occurred when a medical doctor presented her views on why she thought abortion was always and everywhere wrong, and other doctors were to be prohibited at all costs from performing abortions. She defended the claim that "Embryos are genetically unique human organisms, fully possessing the integrated biological function that defines human life at all stages of development." Her presentation was a strong and philosophically coherent rejection of abortion. It was quite 'secular,' making no reference to any religious tradition, and it spellbound most respondents.

The final presenter was supposed to resolve differences, note areas of mutual concern, and propose topics for the next conference. He chose to end on a somewhat partisan note: "What the word 'God' means, and whether God exists, will be debated between societies and also within them, until God determines that the time for debating is done." That the conference clearly did not bring people together, but rather polarized the participants, was evidenced by a summary statement by the first speaker: "If we find agreement, we do so at the price of self-deception." The second speaker of the day offered this rebuttal: "The tide of history is on our side." If I participate in a similar conference in the future, I will be hoping for greater charity on the part of the religious-minded, and less dogmatism on the part of the secularists!

II-85
Abortion and…

At a Conference on Medical Ethics a physician stated that she opposed abortion "not for philosophical, but for strictly scientific reasons." Her presentation was not favorably received by philosophers in the audience for two reasons: (1) she seemed to claim that because her statements were "scientific," they could not be called into question by mere philosophers; (2) her "scientific" statements about the nature of the embryo were taken by many to be a begging of the question, a clear presumption that the embryo was in fact a human person. As she put it: "Human embryos are living human beings precisely because they possess the single defining feature of human life that is lost in the moment of death—the ability to function *as a coordinated organism* rather than merely as a group of living human cells." The pertinent question is this: does the ability to function as a coordinated organism constitute human personhood?

Generally, philosophers are willing to leave to scientists discussion of the nature and characteristics of the embryo, but not the discussion of the nature of human personhood. The fact is, if embryos are human beings, a lot of human beings disappear long before much development in the womb takes place. There is a widespread conviction that the fetus is at least six weeks old before anything remotely resembling a "human person" takes shape.

Discussions of abortion polarize people like no other issue. There is no habitable middle ground between (1) Pro-life: from conception on, the conceptus is fully a human being, and (2) Pro-choice: an actual human being does not exist until birth, and until then, the pregnant woman has "rights" that supersede the rights of the conceptus.

Upholders of the "genetic" view claim that the conceptus is an actual human being from the time of conception. Upholders of the "developmental" view acknowledge that the conceptus is a "potential" human being, much in the manner that an acorn is a potential oak, but that its value increases as it develops, and consequently abortions in early pregnancy may be permitted.

Those who would permit abortion present a range of medical reasons, most notably the inability of some pregnant women to survive pregnancy, and the likelihood that a fetus will be severely deformed. Some present psychological reasons related to an unwanted pregnancy or an unwanted child. A scholar from India wrote, "No unwanted child should be brought into a world that already suffers from overpopulation." There are clearly a wide variety of social and economic reasons behind the fact that abortion is practiced worldwide.

A woman's absolute right over her own body is the argument most frequently mentioned by woman's rights groups. Such a supposed right may be vigorously countered by a statement like this: "One wonders if the woman's rights over her children once born are also absolute, so that she should be able to decide their lives or deaths as well."

When the Supreme Court ruled in 1973 that no state could prohibit a woman from getting an abortion "up to the point of viability of the conceptus," the Court avoided any statement about the conceptus as a human being, because "Neither science nor philosophy nor religion can seem to come to any conclusion on this point."

The issue is as murky now as it was then. If the conceptus is a human being, as some claim, then mass murder is occurring on a global scale. While the philosophical community is split on this issue, there is a widespread preference for the developmental view, which at least has the merit of relieving society of the charge of mass murder. Religious views seem unlikely to change, and statements made by scientists are often more philosophy than science. For those who see philosophy as a process of "clarifying one's thinking on a given issue," abortion becomes both the icon of an issue that begs for further clarification, and the dividing line between those who assume all philosophical problems can be solved, and those who despair of philosophy ever making any worthwhile contribution. Even the promise of "strictly scientific reasons" does not succeed in disposing of this thorny issue. The liveliness of the debate over Abortion indicates that there will be lively interchanges between scientists and philosophers for centuries to come. Analogies between acorns and fetuses soon break down, for as majestic as oak trees may become, no acorn has the potential to become a Socrates, a Beethoven, or an Einstein...

II-86
Rules or Consequences?

It seems to be just common sense to maintain that there are "certain moral rules we all abide by." That point of view is sorely tested by Professors of Ethics who propose this puzzle to their students: You have been in a cave with ten others, and you are about to emerge into a great tidal pool. The leader is a very fat man, who has become lodged in the only exit. As the tide comes in, it will drown all the members of your party, unless the fat man is removed. By chance, one caver has a stick of dynamite, and he proposes blowing up the fat man, thereby saving everyone else. You shrink back in horror, saying it is never right to take the life of an innocent person. The potential dynamiter says: "Rules be damned. Given the situation, we've got to look at the consequences." In this situation, do you want to abide by "certain moral rules," or do you want to temporarily suspend them, and live?

Immanuel Kant is taken as the spokesperson for a strict rule-based ethics. Lying, he says, is always wrong, for once you accept that some situation is an exception to the rule, (even the madman with a gun who asks where your friend is, or the Gestapo agent who asks if you are hiding someone), the floodgates are opened.

Anthony Kenny, an Oxford Don and a prolific writer of great books, is horrified at the unjust loss of life caused by the atomic bombs and Hiroshima and Nagasaki, and claims that America's breaking the rules against bombing civilian targets was one of the most immoral acts of all time. On the other side, Butch Mazzuca, a retired U.S. Marine, provided the following statistics: an invasion of Japan would have cost three million Japanese lives, and at least one million American lives. A blockade of the Japanese islands would have starved at least five million Asians. (Documents subsequently released showed the Japanese had planned to execute 500,000 allied prisoners the minute an invasion began.) Compare these numbers to the 200,000 casualties that resulted from the bombing of Hiroshima and Nagasaki. If you simply examined the consequences, you might be inclined to support President Truman's decision to drop the bombs. If you were a marine destined to be part of the invasion force, you would have had a vested interest in the atomic solution. It takes a very dedicated and perhaps disinterested observer of "the rules" to oppose breaking them in this situation.

There are ultimately three ethical starting points: *Rules, Consequences,* or *Virtue.* There are some rules whose absoluteness seems obvious: murder, rape, and child molestation among them. While it seems easy to build an ethics around "the rules" that make it possible for people to live together in peace and harmony, there are clear occasions where "the rules" don't seem to solve all the problems. Ethicians in the utilitarian tradition begin by examining the consequences of an action, asking, for instance, what are the consequences of not killing the fat man, or of not dropping the bomb? The governing principle becomes securing a greater good for a greater number. For those for whom neither examining the rules, nor discussing the consequences seems to work, *Virtue Ethics* begins with the premise that there is a human nature, and certain actions conform to, and perfect, that nature, while vicious acts detract from it.

All three approaches aim at happiness: Aristotle claims that only the virtuous person will truly be happy. Kant claims that a by-product of adherence to duty will be some sense of satisfaction of knowing you have done what is right. And John Stuart Mill wrote: "The creed which accepts as the foundation of morals 'utility' or 'the greatest happiness principle' holds that actions are right in proportion as they tend to promote happiness; wrong as they tend to produce the reverse of happiness."

Coming back to our initial moral problem: in terms of getting out of the cave, would it be virtuous to blow up an innocent man? Would any kind of rule-based morality justify the use of the dynamite? If you go in this instance with the greatest happiness of the greatest number, are you subscribing to consequentialism in other moral circumstances? Moving to the larger picture of moral decision-making, is it possible to move from camp to camp, as situations dictate, or must you be a dedicated subscriber to only one approach? Remember that while you think about these things, the water is continuing to rise....

II-87
Conservative or Liberal?

To a memorable melody, Gilbert & Sullivan suggested that every one is born either a little liberal or a little conservative. The two words are now bandied about so loosely that spending a few moments researching their origins may be helpful. The British Member of Parliament Edmund Burke (1724-1797) looked upon the French Revolution and shrunk back in horror. French writers like Rousseau and Voltaire had challenged the traditions of the monarchy, the aristocracy, and the Church. Burke thought the French Revolution provided positive proof that society could not flourish apart from well-established traditions, the corrective power of religion, and the constraints imposed upon the great unwashed by their betters. Most curious of all, Burke rhapsodized about the value of the incomprehensible mysteries of inherited institutions. Monarchy, said Burke, is there for a good reason. The value of an aristocracy resides in some kind of control by those who, by birth, breeding, or merit, keep the rabble in check. And what else is Religion, but adherence to laws established by an all-knowing and sovereign God? Joseph de Maistre (1753-1821) was an even more radical "conservative" of past traditions, claiming that only a return to Catholic Christianity could save the faltering political economies of Europe. "Conservativism," in its eighteenth century form, meant not just preservation of the status quo, but some kind of return to traditions that were being violated or overturned.

The slogan of the French Revolution, "Liberty, Equality, Fraternity," became the pattern for most of the social movements of the 18th and 19th centuries. Liberty, that is, Freedom, comes from the Latin word *liberalis*, which means first of all not being enslaved, not being servile, and so able to stand independently. Liberal Philosophy was elaborated in England by Jeremy Bentham (1748-1832) and in France by Benjamin Constant (1767-1830). This original liberalism argued for individual rights, for constitutional government, and for rational legal reforms. Liberalism in its origins meant, "maximizing the freedom of the individual." Liberals, looking at the mess the wars of religionists left behind, pleaded for religious tolerance, and the acceptance of diverse points of view. Looking at the limits governments placed on economic activity, liberals like Adam Smith pleaded for a free-market economy. Writers like John Stuart Mill (*On Liberty*) were not revolutionaries, but sought reforms of the existing institutions, so that the rights of individuals could be protected, and personal freedoms guaranteed.

Key American documents like the Declaration of Independence and the Constitution were drafted by Thomas Jefferson, Benjamin Franklin, and James Monroe, who had intimate knowledge of these European ideas. Jefferson's first draft of the Declaration read: "We hold these truths to be sacred." Franklin insisted he change it to read: "We hold these truths to be self-evident," preferring to emphasize reason and not religion, current philosophy, and not tradition.

Nowhere is the battle between "conservatives" and "liberals" more evident than in the interpretation of the First Amendment: "Congress shall pass no law respecting an establishment of religion." Conservatives see the Ten Commandments as upholding the traditions of our society, and therefore deserving of public display. As soon as Liberals read: "I am the Lord Thy God, Thou shalt not have strange gods before me," they see the establishment of one particular religious viewpoint, thereby infringing upon the civil rights of those not in the Jewish or Christian tradition. Edmund Burke would be furious about their removal from public places, while Jeremy Bentham would feel a great sense of relief. Perhaps it is the case that we are born Burkeans or Benthamites, unable to change from our initial conservative or liberal persuasions. Conservatives tend to be less tolerant of other points of view than do liberals. (Martin Marty, commenting on the First Amendment, said: "Those who are deeply committed, tend not to be very civil; those who are civil, tend not to be deeply committed...") We bandy these two terms about rather freely. It is helpful, from time to time, to look back and find the origins of the terms whose everyday usage may easily obscure their real meaning. It may be helpful to reflect that "conservative" once meant "defender of the status quo," while "liberal" meant one eager to try new things. Doubtless good government demands some happy balancing of the two approaches.

II-88
What do you mean when you say: "I Know"?

If you ask a philosophy professor to explain what knowledge is, you will be told that an answer will take at least one semester if not two, and that to prepare for the class, you will need to read at least Plato's *Theatetus*, Aquinas' *De Veritate*, Kant's *Critique of Pure Reason*, and Kuhn's *Structure of Scientific Revolutions*. Contrast that with Elizabeth Taylor's response to a police officer regarding a criminal investigation involving one of her friends: "I *know* Robert, and I *know* he couldn't do a thing like that."

There are three possible answers to the problem of knowledge. The simplest position is called *Realism,* and its lineage is traceable to Plato and Aristotle. Plato wanted to be sure that truth could be found; that it was objective, and that once having been seen, it could not be doubted. Plato suggested that there were "forms" or essences, and that once you grasped the eternal essence of whatever it was you wanted to know, you would have absolute certainty. Aristotle was a different kind of realist, affirming that there are "forms" in things making them to be what they are, and that knowledge was simply having the same "form" in your mind that "informed" the thing, making it to be what it is. Thomas Aquinas was also a realist, defining truth as "conformity between mind and thing." Contemporary philosophers prefer to call this "naïve realism," although many scientists concur that knowledge of the "real" world depends on the conformity between what you say about something, and the way it really is.

Immanuel Kant initiated a Copernican Revolution in the nature of knowledge during the "Enlightenment," the 18th century response to the revolutionary growth of science produced by Bacon, Galileo, Copernicus, and Newton. The basic theme is simple: knowledge is not a matter of things telling us what they are; knowledge is something the mind imposes on things! We produce our own objects of knowledge, by imposing certain forms on the information our senses bring to us. All our "ideas" are response dependent, artifacts of our own disposition to respond to things. Followers of Kant are sometimes called "conceptualists," because they see knowledge as the result of our own concepts. To the question: Why do some cultures perceive reality so differently from other cultures? The answer is simple: because we are educated to perceive reality in a certain way by the culture in which we are raised. The summary formula of Conceptualism is: "Beauty is in the eye of the beholder." For Realists, beauty is something objective, in the nature of the object. For conceptualists, the experience of beauty is what you contribute to the encounter with some object or event.

The third position regarding the nature of knowledge is Nominalism. There really aren't any forms or essences at all. We "name" things, and if we can get enough people to agree with our funny way of naming, then conversation is possible. But there really aren't any natures in things, there are just names that we find convenient to use. Reality, the nominalists would say, is simply a social construct. Nominalists tend to be utilitarian pragmatists: let's find a system that works, that perhaps produces the greatest amount of social getting-alongness, and encourage as many others as possible to think the same way, and at least we will have a system that helps us solve our everyday problems.

Try this thought experiment: Can you get through one day as a realist, presuming the objectivity of knowledge, and that when you know something, it is because that is the way it really is? If so, try a second day as a Conceptualist, imposing your categories on things, so as to make them knowable. Then try a third day as a Nominalist, literally seeing things from others' points of view, and trying hard not to think that your convictions are somehow anchored in the essences of things. And then ask yourself, do you know things because that's the way they are, or do you know things because you are imposing certain categories upon them? Do you know the forms or essences of things, or do you know only what your mind imposes upon things? At the end of this three-day experiment, you will know why it takes philosophy professors a semester or more to come up with answers to such simple questions!

II-89
Meaningfulness

In an unusually succinct statement, Freud commented: "The meaning of life derives from love and work." While the aphorism is brief, the truth is profound: if you expect your life to be meaningful, it has to be filled with some kind of love relationships, and some kind of activity you find worthwhile. Some people are lucky in love: they find a mate, have a relationship that grows and deepens over time, and offers new and surprising avenues of fulfillment. Some people are lucky in work: they find an activity that stimulates and delights them, find an environment that is supportive of their particular ability, and work happily and enthusiastically. Not everyone is so lucky, and some people have to work to find love relationships, and may never find work they really love.

Love has many forms, and many degrees of fulfillment. We regard the love of persons as the paramount expression of love, but we also speak of the love of books, of learning, of nature, of life itself. Love has also many levels of illusion. Erich Fromm, in *The Art of Loving*, suggested that one of the great illusions of the twentieth century was the conviction that love required finding the appropriate object of love: if you just find the right person, love will blossom, and forever-after happiness will ensue. Fromm pointed out that if you want to experience love, you must first become a loving person. As your capacity for love develops, the "right" objects of your love mysteriously appear. Happy families are the products of loving parents, and children, if they are lucky, are reflections of the love that "mature" parents have. The capacity for love needs a lifetime to develop and deepen; it is not accomplished in any 10-minute seminar or weekend workshop. "Love at first sight" only happens to people who are equipped to handle such a phenomenon.

What about work? Everywhere today we hear of unhappy workers, whether they are doctors, lawyers, professors, assembly line workers, or manual laborers. The world of work has become unpleasant, as worker efficiency has become an obsession. Professionals profiled in TV programs seem a far cry from what workers experience in the real world. Physicians and surgeons complain of the harassment of the insurance business and the factory approach of cost-conscious HMOs and the accountant mentality that applies poorly to the healing arts. Dedicated teachers complain of impossible working conditions, and there is hardly a line of work free of the stress to produce more, better, faster, often with less financial reward.

As the model for understanding love is the examination of a happy loving relationship, so too the model for understanding work has to be an analysis of someone doing something they find fulfilling and meaningful. It is helpful to separate "work" from the notion of paid employment, and from the definition as obligation, of doing what you have to do. Work is energy expended to effect change. We "work" at producing ideas, manipulating what is around us, making objects of art, cooking a meal, cleaning up our living space. (Isn't it curious that when we exercise, we "work out?") We all have models of work that we really enjoy, things we really like to do. At its worst, work is drudgery, laborious activity we would rather not be doing. At its best, work is activity we so much enjoy, time flies by without our knowing it. For some people, "retirement" from the world of paid employment means freedom to work at the things they most enjoy.

Is it possible that work and love are interrelated? Do people who have loving relationships find work that is meaningful and makes them feel good? Do people who work well at something they really enjoy, have a greater energy for really loving other people? Are there overlaps between love and work? Can you work at becoming a more loving person? Does the love you experience for others make the work you do more enjoyable? "The meaning of life derives from love and work." Had Freud never said anything else, this brief aphorism might have sealed his secure place in intellectual history...

II-90
The Timing of Retirement

Financial writers have produced a spate of books and articles on why retirement is a bad idea. The arguments boil down to three: (1) Financial. It will take considerable assets to replace the income from your salary, and given the reality of inflation, there is always the risk of outliving assets. The longer you are gainfully employed, the brighter the financial picture. (2) Personal. Given the increase in life expectancy, how many years do you really want to spend in retirement? Fishing and golf and bridge may be fun, but do you want to spend thirty years pursuing recreational activities? (3) Societal. The talents you have developed over a lifetime may still be needed. Society can ill afford the burden of supporting a large segment of the population living on social security, Medicare, and other government and workplace subsidies.

While the arguments have some merit, there are equal and opposite points that deserve a hearing. (1) How many years do you want to spend doing any one thing, or living in the same area? Your employment might be personally rewarding, but there might be some rejuvenation attached to doing something new, and living someplace different. (2) While biology is not necessarily destiny, your body does send various messages as you age. Somewhere around 40, most people realize they are not quite as strong as they once were. And somewhere around 60, most people acknowledge they do not have as much energy as before, and by this age, most bodies seem to have a chronic illness or two that demands attention. (3) People who have put in long hours at the office or factory or store, may realize a greater need for sociability, a desire to spend more time with family, or a capacity to do something good for society. Innumerable organizations are dependent upon the volunteer work of people of mature years.

For many, a major motivation for retirement is the increase in personal free time. Some people retire and begin the exercising they have omitted for too many years. Elderhostel, and the range of academic programs oriented to seniors, provide a level of intellectual stimulation surprising in content and awesome in variety. Older people make excellent students, having the time, the motivation, and the preparation, for thinking things through. Friendships may flourish among people who were once too busy to cultivate the fine art of leisurely conversation.

Retirement decisions are intensely personal, and the need to work, or the need to retire, may vary greatly from one person to another, or even from one year to another. "Bridge Jobs," and other forms of phased retirement, may be major elements of the "new" world of work and leisure. Retirement is essentially freedom: freedom to launch out in new directions, or, cultivate and revivify old patterns of behavior. There is no mathematical formula, no one right way for everyone. Some people who looked forward eagerly to retirement are back at work within a year. And some people who continue working might be much happier if retired. Retirement presents new options for self-expression. The world of work dictates how time and energies are expended; in retirement, abilities and proclivities that had no outlets, may now take center stage.

It may be helpful for someone approaching retirement age to read and reflect on the anti-retirement literature. But there is much to be said in favor of planning for the day when you can strike out on your own, do what you want to do for as long as you want to do it, and awake each morning with the questions: What would I most like to do today? How shall I exercise my freedom? How can I best express myself? What can I do for someone, just for the sake of doing it? There is much to be said in favor of the retired life. The Greek word for retirement is: *anachoresis,* which could mean: "to dance away from the crowd." That could be a convenient metaphor for what retirement is all about.

II-91
Bultmann's Dangerous Ideas

Rudolph Bultmann (1884-1976) is not nearly as well known as Darwin or Freud, but like them, he proposed some dangerous ideas, and his ideas may have had a greater impact on religious belief than either Darwin or Freud. Darwin looked at nature and saw the evolution of species by natural selection. Freud looked at religious belief and saw neuroses. Bultmann looked at the sacred scriptures, and saw mythology. Myth within the context of sacred scripture struck closer to home for most religious believers than evolution or neurosis.

Just as Darwin and Freud had important predecessors, the work of Ernst Renan and Sir James Frazier laid the groundwork for Bultmann's contributions. Renan, in the middle of the nineteenth century, applied the then current literary criticism to the Bible, and pointed out the very natural explanations of biblical miracles. Frazier, in the late nineteenth century, assembled the families of myths various cultures had developed, and pointed out how creation narratives, godly interventions in battle, virgin births, deaths and resurrections, had parallel stories in almost every religious tradition.

Bultmann was a devout and committed Christian, but he read the Bible with the open eyes of one familiar with Renan and Frazier. Miracles become interpretations of natural events; stories of virgin births become ways of pointing out the importance of the one thus born. Death and resurrection become stories of dying to the old, self-centered self, and rising to new life centered in concern for others. The liturgical year becomes an expression of dying and rising nature, of the harvest phenomenon on which all life depends.

Bultmann paved the way for radical de-mythologizing. The central story of Christianity is the Passion and Death of Jesus Christ, the God-become-man. Christian theology in the tradition of St. Anselm taught that since the offense of Adam and Eve was an infinite offense against God, only a being of equal rank could "atone" for it. Only the death of the sacrificial lamb, in the person of the God-Man, could atone for the offense against the majesty of God. Bultmann suggested that a great deal of primitive mythology went into the basic texts of the Christian religion. The teaching of the Pauline texts on atonement and justification combined the ritual sacrifices of Judaism with the juridical structure of Roman law.

Biblical fundamentalism can provide a position of great comfort and security. If the Bible is the literal truth, if each word is divinely revealed, and the whole Book is free from error, belief becomes a simple matter of subscribing to all that the sacred text contains. The biblical literalist does not need to harmonize the creation narrative with the fossil evidence, or with the scientific discussion of evolution, for if the Bible is true, what science says must be false.

Not to worry, said the followers of Bultmann. It is not the literal text that matters, but the truth behind the text. For these new interpreters, the Bible is the religious self-understanding of various desert nomads, who, by our standards, were rather primitive people. The real meaning of the Genesis narrative is not that God created it all in six days, but that God is responsible for all that is. The real meaning of the destruction of the Temple in Jerusalem is that God is not just a national God, but a God who is everywhere. The real meaning of the Crucifixion and Death of Jesus is that through suffering, we are born to new life, and life has meaning in terms of the kind of love that would lead us to lay down our lives for others.

Bultmann read the Bible as a very human document, as an expression of the religious experience of a given people, and as a model of the kind of contemporary religious self-understanding to which everyone is invited. No doubt it is more comfortable to think of the Bible as the transcription of divinely sent messages. However it is more challenging, and more realistic, to see it as an invitation to think about ways of being religious, and a reason to ask what religiousness really means. A reader might be driven to ask how the activities of a "chosen people" might become a model of religious practice always and everywhere.

Bultmann's ideas may be much more dangerous than those of Darwin or Freud. Taking religious writings seriously, but not literally, may be a greater challenge to belief than evolution or neurosis, and may demand more of the religious imagination than those of fundamentalist persuasion can possibly exercise.

II-92
The Appalachian Malady

The Appalachian Mountains stretch from the Deep South to southern New England. A famous sociologist once bewailed the woes of Appalachia. He profiled the long history of mountain people being taken advantage of by outsiders. Loggers came in and denuded the hillsides, leaving the natives with mudslides. Coalmines left slag dumps, and surface miners removed what was left of the natural beauty, and left a wake of devastation. The psychological impact upon the people was immense: their lands had been destroyed, their livelihoods removed, their dignity as a people deeply scarred. A sense of hopelessness and despair prevailed. A fear of the outsider was coupled with a fear of leaving, and the Appalachian Malady, a sense of futility, was widespread.

Appalachia has come a long way. Pockets of poverty remain, but a reinvigorated and diversified economy has developed, and the natural beauty of the area has returned, so much so that tourism has become a major source of local revenue. But the Appalachian Malady--a sense that you can't get anywhere, that escape from local problems is impossible, that circumstances cannot be improved, still lingers. Only the malady is no longer regionalized. It affects people in every area of the country, and in all walks of life.

If you want to see the Malady in its fullest blown form, visit almost any "inner city" in the country, and you will find a large number of people who seem to have given up hope, who have little sense of accomplishment, and no hope that they can make things better. In its milder form, many people are affected by the Malady. It is a sense that life has lost much of its meaning, that individuals are impotent in the face of larger powers, that the state of things is rapidly deteriorating.

Greek and Oriental visions of history were often cyclical, with a view that progress was balanced by inevitable deterioration, and that you could not escape the wheel of rebirth. Judaeo-Christian culture espoused the idea that history had a meaning and a direction, and that progress was not only desirable but probable. "Progress" has been called the dominant and all-pervasive American myth: that sheer hard work, and reasonable good luck, will improve the general state of affairs. Psychologically, its culmination is the "flow" doctrine, that happiness resides in the state of flow established when you (1) are neither bored nor anxious, (2) have challenges that are proportionate to your abilities, (3) have a sense that you are getting somewhere and making progress.

The Progress Myth is the anti-dote to the Appalachian Malady, and implies a series of convictions: (1) that what you do does make a difference; (2) that while all biological life does involve deterioration, it also enables continuous improvement in some areas; (3) that you really can get there from here, you really can make at least some things better, and (4) each day presents a challenge, the response to which can make you a more complete human being. What the astrophysicists have proclaimed about the ever-expanding universe has a psychological parallel: progress is not only our most important product, it is the most basic conviction you must have as you go about the business of making the world a better place to live. The Appalachian Malady, wherever and whenever it may occur, is a virus to be overcome by a powerful dose of the vision of continuous and unremitting progress.

II-93
Mastering Stress

Living in the modern world is stressful. There are dozens of little sources of stress, ranging from the answering machine that gives you a dozen options (none of them the one you want), to the traffic you encounter when you drive. Then there are the larger sources of stress, ranging from the problems in the lives of your family and friends, to your relationship to the world of work and to the larger world generally.

No matter your age or circumstance, there are particular sources of stress tailor-made for your situation. More important than the source of stress is your attitude toward it. You can take waiting in line at the market as a personal attack on your schedule, or as an opportunity to think kindly thoughts towards those similarly inconvenienced. You can take a traffic jam as a way to increase your blood pressure, or as an opportunity to compose a thoughtful letter to someone you love.

While the hunters and gatherers and farmers who were our cultural predecessors certainly had their sources of stress, the stressors were more predictable, and fewer in number or frequency. Cave dwellers had wild animals to fear, and farmers have always looked to the clouds with some anxiety, but the sources of stress were easy to identify, and the remedies had been passed down for generations.

Technology enables us to do more and travel further, but it also puts us at the mercy of innumerable machines. Who can master all the technology at our disposal? And who among us does not feel ambiguous about the communication technology that enables us to contact so many, but also puts us at the mercy of anyone who wants to contact us at any time or place? The workplace is awash with job insecurity, and financial markets move with lightning speed in directions that are seldom predictable.

What is to be done about all this? Researchers suggest that we must create "time out" zones for ourselves, and that we should practice some form of meditation. It is not easy, however, to create quiet times and places, nor can we easily find a center that cannot be disturbed. How nice it would be, to be able to simplify things, to combat the complexifying tendency of modern society. But how do you simplify your life? Can you ruthlessly toss out everything that is unnecessary? Can you accept that you cannot be master of all trades? Can you determine what is really important, and let the rest go? In terms of handling stress, there is no greater motto than: "Life is an unfinishedness."

If you are to survive in the modern world with its superabundant sources of stress, you must create a center of peacefulness, a source of inner tranquility, that cannot be torn apart, no matter what stressors come along. Try applying this version of Teresa of Avila's aphorism:

Let nothing disturb you, nothing terrify you
All things are passing and temporary,
Your deepest self is undisturbed.

The anti-dote to the tidal wave of the stresses of modern times is to insure access to this deepest self that rides out all storms, and awakes each morning refreshed and alert, ready to overcome the challenges of the new day. As Humpty-Dumpty said, "It is a question of who is to be master, that's all."

II-94
"...And The Grass Greens Itself..."

Life is a balancing act of involvement and withdrawal. Sleep is the best example of how we need to take time off from our activities. To be alive means to be involved and doing things, but it also requires stepping back and examining what we are doing. Underlying all our activities are some basic, often unexamined, convictions about what life means, and why we want to continue the adventure.

The vast majority of philosophers have extolled the goodness of existence. Some have exulted in "the rapture of being alive," while others have delighted in the life of the mind, the quest of making the world a better place, or simply sitting back and contemplating the joys of everyday existence. From the Zen tradition comes this poem:

Sitting quietly, doing nothing
Spring comes, and the grass greens itself....

There have been philosophers of the dark side of life, notably Schopenhauer and Camus. But even with them, hints of excitement about the human quest peep through. The real dark side is best represented by the Buddhist view that "life is basically suffering," and the goal of virtuous living is to escape the wheel of rebirth, the endless repetition of circumstances in which pain and penury prevail over delight and ecstasy.

Modern philosophers have been disposed to say that life is what you make it, and then they turn the task of being wise about everyday living over to the psychologists. The psychologists have obliged by speaking in terms of "peak experiences" and "flow," and have given advice about how to make the goodness of life outweigh the bad.

157

You don't have to cross the border far into Mexico or Central America to find grinding poverty and a daily struggle for the most basic necessities. Most Americans live in relative affluence, and so many of the good things of life are so readily available we take them for granted. The good cheer of so many of the impoverished proves that happiness is an attitude rather than a condition, and that it is not material things that produce happiness. To be happy, you have to believe that goodness prevails over suffering, and that, even in the midst of life's worst moments, something good will come of it. Herman Hesse wrote: "The loveliest joys are always those that cost no money." In the midst of poverty there can still be smiles, and amidst discomfort and disease, there is potential for some good, some heightened awareness, some hope, as Anne Frank said, that in the end, it would turn out all right.

Meaning can be imparted to life simply by walking out into the sunshine, by smiling at someone, or breathing deeply and enjoying what the present moment has to offer. Step back occasionally from activities, and appreciate the basic goodness of just being alive, of being who you are and what you are becoming, and of the friends and acquaintances you have. And for a moment, sit quietly, do nothing, and let the grass green itself.

II-95
From Entertainment to Leisure

One of the tasks of philosophy is "getting clear about words." Modern philosophers have sometimes regarded themselves as guardians of the language, attempting to assure that words are not used improperly. Philosophers have been major contributors to the Oxford English Dictionary, regarded as the Bible of proper word usage. Being clear about words is important, lest our conversation devolve into meaningless babble.

There are three words of general use and great importance whose meaning and significance is generally overlooked. Few people understand what entertainment is all about, fewer still understand recreation, and hardly anyone understands leisure. We live in a society obsessed with being entertained. People spend hundreds of dollars for tickets to rock concerts or sports events or spectacles at entertainment venues like Las Vegas. Evening programs are billed as "must see TV." But is entertainment anything more than an amusing way to pass the time? We all crave entertainment occasionally as a refuge from our cares, or as an interlude between serious concerns. To some degree, entertainment is a way of killing time. But Thoreau said: "You cannot kill time without wounding eternity."

Three Burruses (Harry, Ronald, Megan), Vail, Colorado

Recreation is that kind of activity that re-creates, restores, refreshes us. In some respect it is a break from the serious cares of life, so that we may return with a new enthusiasm for the concerns that constitute the center of our lives. Life as an endless round of entertainments and recreations would not have much meaning.

Leisure is not only superior to entertainment and recreation, it is superior to work! Leisure is the realm of the intrinsically worthwhile, the Kingdom of things done for their own sake. Leisure is about love, about honest and serious conversation, about teaching and learning, reading meaningful literature and discussing what really matters. Augustine, often heralded as the greatest of Christian theologians, wrote: "I was on fire as I read." For most people, work is a way of earning money, it is a means to the end of providing leisure, so that the best of human activities--thinking and loving and doing something for others--may be pursued. And for the fortunate ones who work at what they really enjoy, their work and their leisure become inseparable.

We all need the satisfaction that derives from some kind of work, some activity that is productive, something that makes us feel that our lives contribute something. From time to time, we all need to be entertained and recreated. But above all, we all need leisure, the openness to thinking and loving, coming to understand ourselves and those we live with, and the world around us. Leisure is in some sense the goal of life, for it is the

159

realm of our deepest needs and our highest aspirations. Philosophers as diverse as Aristotle and Sartre proclaim that the primary task of human beings is to know and understand the world in which they live! The moral of the story is, entertain yourself, be re-created when necessary, but save room for leisure, the realm of activities done for their own sake. Leisure is the Kingdom of the intrinsically and personally worthwhile, the inner sanctum where you both discover and reveal who you really are.

II-96
Transitioning...To Retirement

Life is a series of transitions. This should come as no great surprise to anyone, but the theme of dozens of popular books is simply that as you move from one stage of life to another, certain predictable problems accompany the movement. Innumerable are the psychologists eager to advise us that few of life's transitions will be easy.

Think for a moment of the big transitions in your life. Going off to school, going off to college, going off to work, getting married, having the first child--can there be any transition greater than parenthood? Many lesser transitions occur--moving, assuming new work responsibilities, civic or cultural involvement, and, eventually, for most of us, the transition we call "retirement."

For some, retirement is the toughest transition of all, precisely because it appears to be a withdrawal from virtually all the other transitions. The educational system is geared to preparing people for work, not leisure. Although parenthood is clearly a lifetime occupation, by the time retirement occurs, offspring generally have chartered their independent courses. The transition to retirement simply does not have the built-in structure that other important life transitions impart.

Three factors make the transition to retirement especially difficult for some people. Most important is the loss of the "identity" that has been cultivated for so many years. If you visit a retirement community, you will be surprised by how many people introduce themselves by saying: "I used to be..." --an accountant, an executive, a mayor, or whatever. Many retirees struggle to find a new self-image, a new way of describing who they are, throughout their retirement years. Some solve the problem only by going back to work. For many, volunteering their time and their skills becomes a critical element to successful retiring. Disengagement is a necessary aspect of retirement, but some form of re-engagement is the critical step in retiring successfully.

A second factor causing problems for some retirees is disappointment with recreational activities. Within a year or two, some have done all the hunting, fishing, painting, golfing or whatever activity they sought to center their lives around. A steady round of recreational activities can seem empty when there is nothing to be re-created from. For some would-be athletes, the aging body just cannot hold up to the rigors of "the amateur tour" a serious sports program may demand. At any stage of life, a healthy balance of activities is required, and over-emphasis in any one area has its drawbacks. Unrealistic expectations in any dimension can bring one back to earth with a resounding thud. Athletic activity is important to maintain good health, but aging bodies have a way of putting limits on just how much athletic participation is possible or healthy.

The third factor making retirement difficult for some is the realization that it is the penultimate stage. After retirement, the next stage appears to be death, and with retirement comes the obligation to reflect seriously not only about what your life has amounted to so far, but also about your will, your estate, and your choices about long-term medical care. While Socrates could say: "philosophy is preparation for death," and while he faced his own death with equanimity, facing death and accepting that death is the inevitable end that awaits us all, is not easy. When a lawyer asks: "What do you want done with your body?" the most natural response is: "I want to keep on using it." C. G. Jung said one of the hallmarks of maturity is accepting with serenity the fact of one's own inevitable death.

Why is the transition into retirement so difficult? Some enter into retirement too lightly, or with unrealistic expectations. Like any other of life's transitions, retirement has unexpected and unanticipated dimensions. But many of the crises of adult life are predictable, and becoming familiar with the literature on successful retirement can help prepare for what lies ahead. Life is an unending series of transitions, and no stage, however enjoyable, is permanent. Aristotle said: "During peace, prepare for war." During each stage of life, one must give some thought to what the next stage has to offer. Thoughtful conversation with those who have successfully moved on to the next stage often paves the way to smoother transitions.

Gene Bammel

II-97
Victory And Defeat

I happened to be in an outer office while an Athletic Director was firing an unsuccessful basketball coach. The A.D. shouted: "You told them they should go out and play their best basketball. What you should have told them was, they were a failure in life and failures as human beings unless they could pull off a victory." The episode left me wondering about the nature and character of college athletics. A letter to the editor in *The Chronicle of Higher Education* reflected a sentiment that is becoming more common: "Stop the sham! Accept that college athletics is a professional activity, pay college athletes appropriately, but don't pretend they are student-athletes playing games for fun!" It is time to ask: "What are sports? Why is winning so important?"

I watched a great tennis coach teach his players not only about how to play better and more competitive tennis, but also how to mature as human beings. This struck me as much closer to what college athletics should be all about. The tennis coach did some of the best "teaching" I have ever seen, as he led his players to understand more about how to play the game well, and in the process taught about handling competitive pressures and good sportsmanship.

Games should be good distractions from the "serious" business of life. Players get engrossed in them, develop skills, and learn something about how to collaborate with people, and how to compete. Players also learn something about self-control, while experiencing either "the thrill of victory, or the agony of defeat." There are some curious questions attached to playing games. Why is winning so much more fun than losing? If games are all about having fun, why can defeat be such a crushing emotional experience? There is some truth in the tennis adage that says: "Tennis is not a matter of life and death. It is more important than that." It is possible that, as people get older, the need for games and sports increases, even if the level of physical intensity diminishes. Senior Olympics programs may have as much to contribute to the health and wellbeing of senior citizens as youth programs do to the growth of character presumably produced from grade and high school athletic programs.

Games teach us valuable lessons about how to live our lives. Life itself is a competitive struggle, perhaps against nature to wrest food and livelihood from an environment that is not always cooperative, or perhaps against the very elements of our own bodies, that sometimes seem not to have our best interests in mind. Games serve as a kind of monitor of the level of competitiveness in various societies. Incredible sums of money are spent on professional sports, and some professional athletes who seem to have trouble stringing more than four or five words together, are paid enormous amounts of money.

Has sport simply gone ballistic in our society? Have college athletics become the tail that wags the academic dog? We need to come back to the basics of sport to keep some perspective on what athletic programs should be all about. Everyone needs some education in how to play sports well, and everyone needs some training in how to be a good sport.

Games and sports should be among life's most enjoyable activities. Peripheral concerns should not obscure the real purpose they have. No one wins all of life's battles, and losing a contest can make any player of any sport focus on what is needed in order to improve. Winning all the time would be rather boring, and is a sure sign that the appropriate level of competition is lacking. On the other hand, losing all the time is probably as harmful psychologically as it is physically. Engaging in sports should be a way of learning about life. One of the life-lessons from Joe Paterno, Penn States' justly famous football coach, is: "You are either getting better, or getting worse. You cannot stay the same."

Sport, in whatever form, is a lesson in personal growth. As an athlete, you either progress, or you deteriorate. The same is true in your personal life. And that is the essential message of sport, and why sport is an integral part of any educational program, whether grade school, college, or among senior citizens. Life is a balancing act of winning and losing, of learning to take victory and defeat in stride, of determination to get better at what you do. Perhaps the most important lesson of sports and games should be learning to have fun, delight, or even ecstasy, in the activity itself. With any luck at all, that lesson should carry over to other avenues of human endeavor.

II-98
True Management

Peter Drucker was the greatest management guru of the twentieth century. His very readable books tell you almost everything you need to know about management. Before you can manage others, you obviously have to know how to manage yourself, and there are three great tasks whose mastery takes a lifetime.

First of all, you have to learn how to manage your health. At some stages in life, you can pretty much leave your health to manage itself, but the older you get, the more attention your health demands. You have to find the eating arrangements that work best for you, and good nutrition does not happen all by itself, it takes some real effort on your part. There is abundant information available about how to eat a healthy diet, but unless you apply it to your daily intake, the information doesn't do you much good. We all need exercise, but our needs are idiosyncratic, and our abilities to exercise change with time. Exercise needs to be fun if you are to keep it up, and making exercise enjoyable can take some real thought. As you get older, you still need good sound sleep, but you may have to make some significant changes to insure that you get it. About half of mature adults nap on a regular basis, but working naps into busy schedules is not easy. Some companies have created napping arrangements, but not everyone who would benefit, is willing to catch a few winks in the midst of the busy day.

You have to learn to manage your work and your money. Some retirees make money management a full time job. Not everyone wants to do that, but the older you get, the more important money management can become. In practically every decade of your life, you will have some very important financial decisions to make, whether it is which job to take, which home to buy, which college to finance your offspring to, where to move, which investment plan to follow, when to quit work, when to start social security, or when to get someone else to manage your money. Good money management books are readily available, but Joe Dominquez' *Your Money or Your Life,* presents a wonderfully clear philosophy of money management in the simplest terms: Live with reasonable frugality; don't take needless financial risks, and take full advantage of whatever retirement programs come your way.

The last, and perhaps most important lifetime management skill, is learning to manage your emotions. Over the course of a lifetime, a variety of emotional events will come your way, and it is up to you to determine your response to them. It's your task to be sure that joy and delight and contentment outweigh the pain, aggravation, and grief that some events are bound to convey. There is no real happiness without emotional mastery, and only those who have learned to control their minds, will have mastery of their emotions. It is your interpretation of events that determines their meaning and place in your life. Management of emotions may be one of the greatest of lifetime achievements. The management of health and of money means little, apart from management and mastery of emotions. Adulthood inevitably involves the management of other people, whether through parenthood, or work, or community involvement. You cannot really manage other people, until and unless you have learned to manage yourself. That is a skill not even a careful reading of Peter Drucker can do for you. You can get some helpful hints from others, but just because of your uniqueness, your own self-management is a skill you must invent for yourself. This may be among the most challenging of all games, because it is a contest that lasts a lifetime. Management of others is impossible, unless we have first learned to manage ourselves.

Chapter III.
Searching for Wisdom

III-99
The Search for Wisdom:
Philosophy and Science

Philosophy may have reached its all time high in the golden age of Greece, in the time of Socrates, Plato and Aristotle. It may have hit bottom in the twentieth century, with the movement known as "Logical Positivism" (only that which can be empirically verified is true--but that statement cannot be empirically verified) and "Linguistic Analysis" (scientists talk about things, philosophers talk about talk).

By our standards, "science" was rather primitive in the golden age of Greece, and is producing its maximum returns at the present time. Some scientists say that with the Theory of Relativity, Quantum Physics, and the Theory of Natural Selection, the great era of scientific discovery is over, and all that's left is mopping up operations. Even if the basic theories are in place, clearly a great many scientific discoveries remain on the horizon, and science would appear to be much more fruitful than philosophy.

It has been wisely said that philosophy always buries its undertakers. Philosophy keeps rebounding for two basic reasons. First of all, all of us have to discover for ourselves the philosophical insights we wish to live by. A philosophical question is always a new question, until you have come up with your personal answer. Secondly, philosophical answers are more than verbal, more than linguistic, more than formulary. They require some kind of life re-orientation, so that as your perception of a philosophical position deepens, your personality and your behavior are called upon to change accordingly. Philosophy is not true to itself when it remains airy abstractions. Philosophy demands a "reformation of character," as the truth of a particular philosophy seeps into the bones of the individual. A philosophical formula may remain the same over time, but the assimilation of it changes, presumably deepens, as understanding of the "real meaning' becomes more profound.

Philosophy seeks to be wisdom about life, about how to impart meaning to life, and how to impart coherence to the random events that come your way. Science, by contrast, is much more specific, much more targeted to precise answers. Science is very much in the thrall of mathematics, the most "precise" of all forms of knowledge. Scientific studies provide us with statistics, for example, of what percentage of impotent men will benefit from Viagra--but it tells us nothing about why overcoming impotence is a good thing. Science can provide precise mathematical measurements of how long it takes the light of the sun to reach the earth, or what percentage of scientists are religious believers. Science may offer us stunning insights into the composition of the material universe, as visiting a planetarium or a science museum will quickly show. Nova Specials on PBS present some stunning images of the kind of achievements that are commonplace within the scientific community.

Science offers precise answers to precise questions, and that is its appeal. Scientists get real answers to appropriately formed questions, and then move on to the next problem. But science offers us little help about the really big questions: What is the meaning of my life? How ought I to act? What can I hope for? Such philosophical questions cannot be answered by the methods of experimental science.

Science can do much to improve the quality, as well as the duration of human life. (It might also terminate human life, with just one scientific experiment gone awry...). Science can offer theories about the origin of the universe, and about such questions as the likelihood of finding intelligent life on other planets. But science cannot answer the question posed by the mathematician-philosopher, Leibniz: "Why is there something rather than nothing?" Nor does science offer much in the way of an answer to the puzzling question: "Why do bad things happen to good people?" Philosophy may not answer these really big questions, but it encourages us to ask them, and not be satisfied with a trivial response. Philosophy accordingly is the most life-long of all intellectual pursuits....

Science deals with problems that admit of solutions. Philosophy deals with questions tinged with mystery, in which every answer is provisional, and every answer provokes further questions. Scientific questions presume the possibility of definitive answers. Philosophical questions simply indicate that you have focused on the larger mysteries of existence. It is their very insolvability that makes life so interesting...

III-100
The Paradox of Meditation

Meditation is such a simple activity it is a wonder so few people practice it. More people might practice, if they could just find a comfortable position, and sense they were benefiting from the activity. The getting comfortable part should be easy. Centuries of eastern practice have emphasized the use of the cross-legged position. If this works for you, that is well and good. If you have any degree of discomfort, you should find a more comfortable position. Simply sitting in a comfortable chair where you are free from distractions may be best. For some, stretching flat out on your back on the floor may be the most effective posture, achieving greater comfort and relaxation at the same time.

It is important to have the right approach to meditation. Meditate not for any specific purpose, but just to meditate. Do not include it in your list of productive activities, to be re-evaluated in terms of measurable results. This activity is an in-activity, because it is the leisure that imparts meaning to all your work.

As you relinquish any specific goals for your meditation, you will find that of its own accord it will produce some surprising consequences. You will come away from meditation in a more optimistic frame of mind, feeling that you can master the challenges of the day, and that you can impose meaningful order on the events of your life. Perhaps immediately after a meditation session, you may have clearer insight into how some problem may be solved, or how you should allocate your time or your energy. Meditation is essentially a clearing of the decks, an emptying of the mind, so that what is important may take center stage. As a consequence of meditation, you may gain some greater insight into how to go about the events of your life, and how to make the course of your life flow more smoothly. Meditate: do not try to focus on problem solution. Let things flow through your mind, as if you were a mountain, and clouds come and encircle you.

Meditation may produce some personal benefits, such as imparting a sense of greater peace in your life. It may produce some sense of the most appropriate mode of social involvement. We are all members of a larger community, and each of us has distinctive contributions to make to the wellbeing of that larger community. Meditation may provide us with both the insight into what our distinctive contribution can be, and the motivation to initiate and continue that involvement. One of the unavoidable consequences of meditation is insight into who we really are, and what we must do to play our special role in society. The purpose of meditation is not "finding your true self," but one of the consequences of meditation is a greater degree of self-awareness. Meditation is not a self-centered or egotistical activity, for one of the benefits of meditation is perception of inter-being, that we have our existence in the midst of others, and have some service to provide.

Set aside some secure time, find a comfortable position, and meditate just for the sake of meditation. Focus your mind on your breathing, and meditate with no specific purpose in mind. Do not be surprised if meditation becomes the root of major changes in your attitudes and dispositions. The result will be some beneficial modification in your behavior and activities. Meditation can easily become the most important moment of your day. Meditation is not killing time; it is the deepening and enriching of time.

III-101
Leadership

At one time or another, we are all called upon to be leaders. It may come as a surprise to us, as someone says: "Oh, you would be good at this." It may be an opportunity we have longed for, but thought beyond our grasp. Or it may be one of those events of everyday life that require the most astute exercise of leadership--like parenting, or settling a family or neighborhood dispute.

Whatever the circumstances, there are three characteristics of successful leadership that apply almost universally. The first and most important of which is: enunciating a clear vision of where you are going. Great leaders have this single-mindedness that almost appears to be an obsession. This is not to say the vision cannot be reversed: great leaders can bring the troops back safely, if that becomes necessary. In any exercise of leadership, even if it is leading a group around the block, a clear statement of where you want to take them is the all-important first step.

Being able to respond to larger challenges requires the second quality of leadership: charisma. The original meaning of the Greek word is "grace" or "favor." The charismatic leader has a certain grace or favor that causes others to say: "Wherever you lead, I will follow. I believe in you." Great leaders are trustworthy, they have a quality or feature that encourages people to say: "I am in your camp for good." It is this quality that enables people who run for political office to recruit hordes of volunteers, and to get voters to stand by them, even when their shortcomings are clearly evident.

The third quality of leadership is most elusive. Great leaders convince others that what they are doing has more than ephemeral consequences. Great leaders touch upon something absolute, something transcendent. America's founding fathers proclaimed a *novus ordo saeclorum,* a new order of the ages. A great leader conveys a sense of: "we are not just repeating what has gone on forever, we are launching out on a wonderful new path. Life will be forever better for what we do here today." It is not just large-scale events that require something of this elusive quality: every good leader does something to show the supreme importance of solving this particular problem in a magnificent way.

We are all thrust into positions of leadership from time to time. It may be an opportunity you have long sought, or it may be something you have to do, because no one else is willing. Whatever the circumstances, when the challenges of leadership come your way, keep in mind these basic principles: elucidate a clear vision of where you hope to go; do whatever you need to do to manifest your personal charisma, your unique charm; and convince your followers that something out of the ordinary, something that transcends the mundane and the everyday, can really be attained. You may not go down as one of history's greatest leaders, but you will accomplish *something,* and if you are a good leader, the world will be a little bit better, for what you have done.

III-102
Courage

A persistent theme of epic stories is the courage of soldiers in battle. Aristotle wrote: "War offers the truest test of the depth of virtues." No small wonder that we speak of the courageous efforts of everyday life as wars and battles. For some people, getting out of bed is an act of extraordinary heroism. Every stage in life has its appropriate demand for courageous action. With students it is the courage to take tough courses, to face exams, to face the uncertainties of the changing job market, to accept the challenges of living in the adult world. For young adults it is the courage to have children in an uncertain environment. And for others, it is the courage to overcome problems in relationships, or the courage to battle cancer, or other maladies. And for people of mature years, it may be the courage to grapple with serious illness, to overcome loneliness, to search anew for what makes each day meaningful and memorable.

Courage is an overlooked and misunderstood virtue, precisely because of its everydayness. Dramatic events demanding heroic response come to us but seldom. But the courage to go against the grain, to do the unexpected, to stand up to people whose views or actions deserve opposition--these are substantial challenges to the exercise of courage. It is convenient to be cowardly, to back away from difficult situations. It is easy to take the course of least resistance, easy to let someone else take a stand against wrongdoing. We all excuse ourselves from battles we feel we cannot win, but a pattern of self-excusing may contribute to a mindset of cowardice, something we do not want.

Life is full of events that require courageous response. It may be the onset of a serious illness, it may be responsibility for a friend or family member, it may be the need to take a public stand against prejudice or stupidity, or it may be the rescue of a stranger in need. The urgent question is, is there any way to prepare oneself for sudden and unexpected demands for the exercise of courage?

There are some "recreation" experiences that are deliberate and pre-meditated tests of courage: rock-climbing, whitewater rafting, spelunking are among the most popular. These may put courage to the test, and measure the potential of adrenaline supplies. But the real discipline of courage only comes by everyday practice, by overcoming the challenges of each day, and, when appropriate, taking the most courageous response. Only the practice of courage in the little challenges of everyday will prepare one for the inevitable moments in life when a great deal of courage will be called for.

Courage is not foolhardiness; it is not taking on inappropriate challenges. Rescue programs profile individuals who get in far beyond their depth, and complicate the rescue procedure. That is not the kind of public appearance anyone wants to make. Real courage means taking on the challenges that initially appear too big, and taking them in stride. You will be able to handle them more easily, if you have been regularly making courageous responses to smaller challenges. Aristotle noted that a virtue is a habit of behaving in a certain way. We become courageous by acting courageously in the little challenges, with the hope that when the big ones come our way, we will know what needs to be done, and we will do it. Courage is a virtue whose exercise we cannot afford to overlook until the time when we need to put it into practice. The school of virtues is one we must attend daily, and putting courage to the test is one of life's most important examinations.

III-103
"Growth"

"You are almost certainly much better than you think you are. More than you now permit yourself; you can be happier, stronger, and braver. You can be more loving and giving; warmer, more open and honest; more responsible and responsive. You can perceive worlds richer and fuller than any you now experience. You have it in you to be more creative, more zestful, and more joyous. All these prospects are within you. They are your potential."--From *Growth Games,* by Lewis and Streitfeld.

In 1954, Gardner Murphy published *Human Potentialities,* and it became the charter for the human potential movement. The claim is that we use less than ten percent of our brain capacity: what powers would be unleashed if we could learn to turn on our latent potential? Abraham Maslow was the most famous figure of the human potential movement, most notably with his discussion of attaining "peak experiences." Esalen Institute at Big Sur became the movement's capitol, offering programs in sensitivity training and mind expansion.

What has become of the movement today? Is it conceivable that we have lost our enthusiasm for personal growth? Have we given up on unlocking the hidden capacities of our brains? Have we become so immersed in our busy schedules that we have abandoned the hope that with tremendously expanded consciousness, we could accomplish far more, and still have energy left over for still greater achievements?

One might easily indict the educational system. Herbert Otto wrote: "In our educational system we kill intellectual curiosity. Statistics show that the average graduate from our colleges reads one book a year... The handwriting on the wall cannot be clearer." Yet everywhere, from kindergarten to graduate school, we hear of great new learning approaches, whether in magnet or charter schools or student-initiated research projects. Somehow none of them achieve the growth breakthroughs expected by the human potential movement.

There may be two reasons why the human potential movement has fallen on hard times. The first one is the length of time involved in any great step in human evolution. Doubtless we use only a fraction of our real potential. And clearly the demands and the technology of the new millennium are going to require greater exercise of our potential than has been customary. The second reason is harder to grasp. It is that we are not emotionally prepared for the kind of intellectual breakthrough the human potential movement envisioned. In every great era of human history, whether it is the axial period of some twenty five hundred years ago when so many religious and philosophical currents broke through, or the great era of the Enlightenment and the Scientific Revolution, some kind of cultural change in the emotional intensity of the populace had prepared the ground for such break-through events.

One might hope that the real revolution of the human potential movement is yet to be realized. Perhaps geopolitical events will create the emotional backdrop necessary for the next great breakthrough in the exercise of human consciousness. The words of Abraham Maslow ring clear: "If you set out to be less than you are really capable of being, you will be deeply unhappy for the rest of your life." Regardless of what happens to the movement, it is time for each of us to actualize more of our human potential. Today is a good day to get started, for none of us can risk being deeply unhappy for the rest of our lives!

III-104
The Reality of Death

An English translation of Johann Sebastian Bach's BWV 508 from *The Notebook for Anna Magdalena Bach* reads: "Art Thou with me? Then I go with joy...To my death, to my rest, for Thou art with me...." What has happened in the years since these words were written, that death is not approached with joy, but with anger, fear, dread, rejection? We live in a death-denying society, where we do not want to think about death, we do all we can to postpone it, we try to make sure it occurs behind closed doors, out of the view of the living. Death is the ultimate fact of life, the end that awaits us all, the framework that in some sense forces us to make meaningful each day and each event of our lives.

In the Jewish, Moslem, and Christian cultures of the Middle Ages, immortality or resurrection of the body was a basic article of faith. With the Scientific Revolution of the eighteenth century came a new materialism that is very much with us today. Some philosophers of consciousness confidently assert that when the last neuron is mapped, we will have identified all the components of human thought and emotion, and they will be found to have a purely material basis. Ecologists have registered concerns about the difficulty of feeding and retaining sanitary conditions for billions of resurrected bodies whose physical needs would have to be satisfied in perpetuity. Some theologians have suggested that it is the height of egotism to expect our humble capacities to deserve to exist forever. Some psychologists have opined that the hope for immortality is a denial of the importance of everyday existence, a failure to get on with the absolute seriousness of the possibilities each day presents.

There is much to be said for the awareness of death demanding that each moment of life be taken with appropriate seriousness. Rollo May wrote: "Death is the one fact of my life which is not relative but absolute, and my awareness of this gives my existence and what I do each hour an absolute quality." Other psychologists have discussed the value of heightened "Personal Death Awareness," claiming that once you have looked mortality squarely in the face, you will not want to return to your previous state of simple-minded unawareness.

No one has analyzed awareness of death more extensively than Elizabeth Kubler-Ross. She suggested that once a person becomes aware of impending serious illness and death, a stage of denial comes first, followed by anger, then some kind of bargaining, next a stage of depression, and finally, some degree of acceptance. Among the terminally ill, most have indeed accepted the fact that death is soon approaching, but some fight death to the very end, urgently seeking one more breath. Queen Elizabeth I is reported to have said: "My kingdom, for one more moment of time."

But what of those for whom death is some undetermined distance far into the future? Besides acknowledging that death imparts a framework that forces us to make each day of our lives as full of meaning as possible, what other meaning can death possibly have? For some, the possibility of life everlasting imparts a hope that life has an infinite value. Even as philosophers, ecologists and theologians have raised questions about immortality, scientists working on Near-Death Experiences insist there is evidence of souls separating themselves from bodies, having meaningful encounters with a "being of light," judging their own lives in terms of cultivating love for others, and then coming back to their bodies with a renewed sense of purpose and enthusiasm for life, as well as a conviction that there is life beyond the grave.

One might say: "What's important is to live each day to the fullest. If there is life after this life, I regard it as a great bonus." Awareness of death, acceptance of death, as well as hope that death is not the end of all, should encourage one to live as fully and as happily as possible. One might say: "There is no such thing as a good death, except for those who have achieved a good life." Awareness of death is not a dark and lugubrious matter, but a source of motivation to take each moment of life, exult in it, rejoice in it, and delight in the opportunities each moment of existence brings our way. Each moment of life gives us an opportunity to insure that something of us, in one way or another, abides forever. It is up to us to make the most of what life presents us with, moment by precious moment.

III-105
Achieving Identity

Few people have had as much influence on the psychotherapeutic professions as Carl Rogers. While the client-centered therapy he practiced has often been caricatured as repeating back what the client said, there was considerable substance to his approach, and a real philosophy of personality at the root of his therapeutic practice. Three basic principles form the nucleus of Rogers' therapeutic philosophy, and they are well worth revisiting.

(1) It is not easy to strip off the masks of false identity and become our real selves. It is very easy to pretend to be the person our parents or our friends or our society wants us to be, and very difficult to become the person we really need to be. There is a story about a Rabbi who says: "I wish I could be more like Rabbi Moses." Another Rabbi responds: "God will not ask you why you are not more like Rabbi Moses, but why you are not more like your self." It is convenient to be the person others expect us to be, initially difficult to become the person that emerges from the depths of our own character. Rogerian therapy teaches that you must discover yourself in your experience; you are not something you impose on your experience.

(2) When you become open to experience, and deal with events in the light of the authentic person within you, you begin to trust yourself, to trust your own organism, to trust your judgment of what you should do and how you should respond. The locus of evaluation becomes you, not the judgment of anyone else. The question Rogers proposes is: "Am I living in a way which is deeply satisfying to me, which truly expresses me?" This is not some form of arrogant self-centeredness, nor is it rejecting all that society suggests about appropriate behavior or the exercise of virtue. But it is a question of authenticity, of doing what flows from deep within, and not just accepting knee-jerk responses of expected or customary or superficial behavior.

(3) The third component of Rogers' therapeutic philosophy is the most important. It is the acceptance of identity as more process than product. To say "I am a doctor," or, "I am a lawyer," is to identify your self with some particular occupation. Whatever the occupation, it is part of who you are at the time, but it does not explain who you are becoming. Retirees for example may think of some identity as what they have attained, and many have an unfortunate habit of explaining who they used to be, and not focusing on who they are now, or who they are becoming. Identity is not

something any of us achieve once and for all, and we never reach some fixed state where all our problems are solved, or where we have magic formulas that dissolve every new challenge. We are in fact a stream of becoming, and never a completely finished product. Rogers approvingly quoted a patient as saying: "I haven't finished the job of integrating and reorganizing myself, but that's only confusing, not discouraging, now that I realize this is a continuing process."

Life is a process of gradually discovering who we are, and choosing what we wish to become. There is continuity in personality, but more importantly, there is growth, development, continual deepening. If our identities were completely established at eighteen, there would not be much point in living to a ripe old age. Maturity means being honest with one's self and with others about who we really are, what responses are unique to us, and how we need to change over time. Maturity means living in a way that is satisfying and truly manifests what flows from deep within. It is accepting that we are a process, not a product, and that each day enables us to become more ourselves. Physical growth may appear to stop at a certain stage, but the growth of personality knows no limits. It is what should make each day an exciting adventure. Each morning we embark on a voyage of discovery. What could possibly be more interesting, than continually finding out who we really are, what we can do, and how we can help others in their respective voyages of discovery? There is great wisdom in the saying of Plotinus: "You are ever on a voyage, but the voyage is within you."

III-106
Mexico

Mexico has a population of over 100 million people, at least one million of whom annually attempt illegal emigration into the United States of America. Why should the people of a country with such abundant natural resources be so eager to flee? Mexico is a land of many puzzles and paradoxes, not the least of which is great wealth in the hands of a few, desperate poverty for the vast majority. Mexico is the world's largest producer of silver, while the largest source of wealth for the country derives from the petroleum industry. Remarkable agricultural development characterizes southern Sonora and northern Sinaloa, and the dependable rains of the tropical south insure such abundant food harvests that agricultural exports are a major source of income.

So, what's the problem? The problem is political and historical. Spain conquered the land that is now Mexico, and for three hundred years the task of the Spanish viceroys was to export the local wealth to Spain. The Spanish colonizers treated the natives like slaves, and rigid societal classes became ingrained. After more than a decade of revolutionary struggle, Mexico became a republic in 1822. A century of political turmoil followed, including a declaration of independence by Texas in 1836, a war with the United States in 1848 which resulted in Arizona, California, New Mexico, Utah, and parts of Colorado being ceded to the United States. Mexico was briefly an "empire" under Archduke Maximillian whose regime was poorly supported by French soldiers, and the country then suffered a long dictatorship under Porfirio Diaz.

Pancho Villa and Emiliano Zapata were heroes of the revolutionary activity between 1910 and 1917, when a new constitution, somewhat modeled after that of the United States, was adopted. Since then, Mexico has enjoyed comparative stability, interrupted by occasional earthquakes, assassinations, devaluations of the peso, and uprisings by dissatisfied indigenous people. Apart from such episodes, things have been relatively calm and tranquil.

Three-quarters of the population are mestizos, people of mixed European and Native American descent. Indigenous people compose fifteen percent of Mexico's population. Some, like the Tarahumara, strongly resist assimilation, and do not consider themselves Mexicans. Ten percent of the population is of purely European ancestry, and exercise a disproportionately large share of political and economic control.

The geographic diversity of Mexico is remarkable. From the northwestern deserts of Baja California and Sonora, where annual rainfall may be less than three inches, to the snow-covered volcanic peaks of central and southern Mexico, to the clearly tropical forests of the Yucatan peninsula, you can find almost every life-zone somewhere in Mexico. Vera Cruz receives over sixty inches of rainfall a year, fourteen inches in September alone. The Monsoon rainy season is July through September, and much of tropical Mexico receives about six inches of rainfall in the month of August.

It has been said of Brazil that it is, and always will be, the greatest country of the future. Mexico's possibilities are somewhat more limited. Agriculture will be limited by the amount of water that can be captured and stored for irrigation, as well as by the limits of the soils. There are limits to natural resource extraction, and limits to the other economic enterprises, except of course for tourism. Mexico is an interesting country to visit, with well-known resort communities like Cancun and Acapulco, archeological sites like the pyramids, Mayan centers like Chichen-Itza, and Palenque, colonial cities like San Miguel de Allende, Alamos, San Luis Potosi, and many others, along with puzzling archeological ruins like Paquime.

Canada, the United States, and Mexico were all founded by European colonial powers. Canada has retained the British parliamentary system, and a constitutional commitment to "Peace, Order, and Good Government." The United States established the primacy of freedom, and of government by the people. And Mexico? It still struggles with finding the form of government appropriate for a land with such a powerful colonial heritage, such a mixture of population, so many natural resources, and such a history of intractable problems.

Danzante, Monte Alban, Mexico

179

III-107
Healthy Lifestyles

Lei at Aria Spa in Vail, Colorado

The diet of many Americans derives from four basic food groups: pizza, alcohol, ice cream, and chocolate. And for some Americans, exercise is a matter of searching for the remote control. The evidence is overwhelming that there are healthier lifestyles available, and that lifestyle changes may do more to improve health and longevity prospects, than any combination of medication and surgery.

No one has done more popular research on the benefits of exercise than Dr. Ken Cooper, and the books he has published with *Aerobics* in the title all present the same basic message: if you cannot find time to exercise, you must find time to be ill. As a man of mature years, Cooper said twenty minutes a day of moderately vigorous walking is all he needed to sustain his cardiovascular-pulmonary systems (and perhaps all his orthopedic system will permit...) Younger people may need more, and getting into good shape may require a disciplined program. For optimal health, think of setting aside an hour a day for some combination of stretching, aerobic activity, and working out with weights.

There is no lack of those who would be your diet-masters, and in spite of the popularity of Atkins' low carbohydrate diets, the evidence compiled by researchers like Pritikin, MacDougall and Ornish is incontrovertible. Dr. MacDougall was an intern in Hawaii, and was puzzled by the good health of his aged Asian patients, compared to the heart disease and cancer of their middle-aged offspring. The elderly were eating an Asian version of a vegetarian diet, their Americanized descendants were feasting on fast foods at popular American restaurants. Thirty years of research have documented the benefits of vegetarianism. With the abundance of fresh produce available, the drift toward appreciating the taste of fruits and vegetables should help overcome the long-standing conviction that meals saturated with fats and sweets provide the greatest satisfaction.

Two San Francisco cardiologists, Friedman and Rosenman, were convinced that heart disease was caused primarily by the sense of time urgency, the excessive competitiveness, and the perpetual anger or anxiety or experience of stress Americans seemed to feature. Research has not always supported the thesis of their book, *Type A Behavior and Your Heart,* but the underlying theme, that the mind-set you bring to your daily activities is of critical importance, has caught the attention of health professionals. The claim is that the more positive and optimistic your outlook, the better your chances of avoiding health crises, or overcoming them if they assail you.

To borrow terms from the economists, there is macro-attitude and micro-attitude. Macro-attitude means developing an overall positive outlook on life, a conviction that you can be the master of events, and that you can bring about good results. Micro-attitudes are what you bring to individual events. In terms of exercise routines, runners or joggers who are not having a good time probably will not persist in their activities. Exercise routines that are enjoyable and have some social component are more likely to be kept up over time. While ascetics may be happy with a diet of bread and water, most of us want to make mealtimes enjoyable and somewhat festive. Vegetarians who do not learn to make their meals tasty and appealing will soon return to their meat-eating habits.

The message is clear: if you want to live a long and healthy life, find forms of exercise you really enjoy, and devote a reasonable amount of time to them. Find ways of eating that provide the nourishment your body needs, and provide you with the appropriate pleasures of eating tasty meals. Develop attitudes that say: I am glad to be alive; there are fun and important things for me to do; there are interesting people to meet, interesting places to go, interesting ideas to think about. Developing a healthy lifestyle requires cultivating the right macro-attitudes. With good basic attitudes in place, you will find approaches to diet, exercise, and time management that will enable you to make the most of each day. You will so delight in being alive, that you will not want to do anything to diminish that great, good feeling of effervescent good health. A healthy lifestyle is a happy combination of diet, exercise, and positive attitude, and the combined approach is your best bet to not only exceeding your statistical life-expectancy, but to enjoying each day along the way.

III-108
After Post-Modernism, What?

At the beginning of the twentieth century, philosophers, artists and architects who were doing something that departed radically from the past, were called "modernists." Picasso's works seemed remarkably different, Frank Lloyd Wright constructed buildings unlike anything conceived by his predecessors, and philosophers combined logic and language in an unprecedented manner. By the end of the twentieth century, philosophers, artists and architects had moved far beyond the modernists, so what else could they be called but "post-modernists"? The relevant questions are: What do post-modernists teach, who are their standard-bearers, and why should we be interested in them?

The Western Tradition began with the flowering of Greek Philosophy some twenty-five hundred years ago. What characterized the work of Plato and Aristotle was a conviction that reality was knowable, and that there was some correspondence between the mind and reality. At the basis of post-modernism is a rejection of this view of knowledge, and a conviction that what we take to be "reality" is a state constructed by the mind, not perceived by it. I make up what I know. My consciousness is radically subjective, and what I know, is not what you know. I constitute my world by my ideas, and when I use words, there is no reason for me to think that they will mean to you exactly what they mean to me. The world, in a word, is radically subjective. Your statements about reality, however strange they may seem, are just as valid as anyone else's. There is no truth; there are only "points of view."

The most important word for post-modernists is "deconstruction." The meaning of what anyone has said is unique to that speaker, and your interpretation of another's words is also subject to being taken apart, for your words express only your view, and hence deserve to be de-constructed in the same manner. Most post-modernist writers follow the pattern of the master of de-construction, Jacques Derrida, and write in a manner that is difficult to comprehend. Critics claim that scholarly conferences of post-modernists are attempts to put other people on, to appear profound without actually saying anything of substance, to obfuscate the simple by making it utterly incomprehensible. The writings of post-modernists have been called "pomobabble," post-modern babble, suggesting that simple ideas are being translated into something obscure, thereby creating the impression of profundity.

Another key figure of post-modernism was Michel Foucault. His writings can be interpreted as a reaction to Jean-Paul Sartre, the leading figure in French existentialism. There is something comprehensible in Sartre, something that stands in continuity with the Greek tradition: the conviction that you can make meaningful statements about reality, and that human beings can communicate meaningfully with one another. Foucault was obsessed with the abuse of political power, with the evil of one group dominating another, with the impossibility of communication between the empowered and the powerless. Foucault returns to the basic questions of how are we to live, and to what values can we hold fast, but he is pessimistic about arriving at meaningful answers.

Just as the pre-Socratics, with their relativism and attempts to appear wise without actually being so, set the stage for the golden age of Greek Philosophy, it is just possible that this round of skepticism profiled by the post-modernists will usher in a new era of philosophic and scientific optimism, based on convictions that the world is knowable, that human beings can engage in meaningful communication with one another, and that purpose in life can either be discovered or invented. Perhaps post-modernism has fertilized the soil for a great new renaissance of ethical and political reflection. The thinkers of the Enlightenment may have been too optimistic: we cannot know everything, and science cannot master the whole world. The post-modernists have been too pessimistic: there is a great deal we can know, a great deal we can agree on, a great challenge for human intelligence to make of this, if not the best of all possible worlds, at least a very functional world, in which progress, achievement, and a sense of going somewhere, are the keys to a great new, post-post modernist world. We just have to find a better name for it…

III-109
Intuition

The word "intuition" comes from a Latin word meaning "to look at, to contemplate, to have insight into." It has come to signify some capacity to obtain direct knowledge without having to go through a lengthy chain of reasoning. It has been suggested that the work of each of the great philosophers is based on some key intuition, some original way of seeing into the heart of things, thereby intuiting the way things really are. The intuition behind Plato's philosophy, for example, is that there are forms or essences concealed in things, and that mind has a capacity to grasp these forms or essences. For Plato reality is fundamentally intelligible, and the act of knowing these forms or essences is the most important of human activities.

The twentieth century can boast of at least three philosophers whose intuitions set them apart and guarantee them a lasting place in philosophical history. Martin Heidegger's major work was entitled *Being and Time*, and his basic intuition centered on the temporality of being, the fragility of existence, and the consequent narrowness of the window of human knowing. Like a prophet wandering in the wilderness, his work questions how we seem to have gone astray, how we have misread the vision of the great Greek philosophers, and how we ought to re-examine the tradition. Our very being is shrouded in darkness, and we must hope for the illumination which might come from a re-opening of the question of being, of what our being means, of what must anchor and support the fragility of temporality. Two words focus the basic intuition of Heidegger: *Sorge,* which means, "care," and *Angst,* usually translated as "anxiety." We are "the shepherds of being," but we are poorly equipped to handle our responsibility, and we have much to be anxious about.

Jean-Paul Sartre also harkens back to the Greek beginnings of western philosophy, but Sartre thinks he is closing the door to the Platonic tradition, while opening the window to those Greek and Roman stoics who took a much darker view of life. The title of his major book, *Being and Nothingness,* expresses his intuition very well. His intuition is that there are no essences, no forms in things, being is radically formless and void, and the only meaning life has, is whatever you assign to it. You are the creator of your own being, the designer of your destiny. There is a nothingness at the very heart of being, and it is up to you to create essence and form, and impose it upon reality. If a Biblical phrase could be used to sum up Sartre's philosophy, it might be this: "The earth was without form and void, with darkness over the face of the abyss." Sartre thought the wars of the twentieth century provided ample proof of the irrationality and fundamental absurdity of human existence.

A much different kind of intuition forms the basis of a third great twentieth century philosopher, Alfred North Whitehead. His major work is *Process and Reality,* and while his language can be incredibly difficult, the basic theme of reality as process, of becoming and change as the fundamental law of being, is everywhere apparent. He proposes a new theism, a way of talking about God as a being in process, instead of the static, immutable God of the western tradition. This quote summarizes Whitehead's primary intuition: "Neither God, nor the world, reaches static completion. Both are in the grip of the ultimate metaphysical ground, the creative advance into novelty. Either of them, God and the world, is the instrument of novelty for the other."

Not only does a novel theology but also an ethical and political philosophy develop from Whitehead's intuition that reality is process, change, development, growth, for even God is a being in process, a being who is not yet what he will be. Whitehead's most readable book, *The Aims of Education*, begins: "Culture is activity of thought, and receptiveness to beauty and humane feeling." What a world of difference from the somber temporality of Heidegger, or the dark forebodings of Sartre!

We have here three great philosophers of the twentieth century: an agnostic, an atheist, and a new kind of theist. Philosophies are built on intuitions, and people adhere to philosophies whose intuitions most closely resemble their own. The real work of philosophy is to unravel the consequences of those intuitions, to see what ethical and political points of view are most in harmony with the fundamental insights. Undoubtedly it is by their consequences that the fundamental intuitions are best evaluated. The biblical injunction retains its full force: "By their fruits you shall know them . . ."

III-110
Time and Retirement

So many people think: when I retire, I will have all kinds of time. The fact of the matter is, many retirees have only two complaints: There aren't enough hours in the day, and there aren't enough days in the week. How can it be that people freed from the necessity to labor, freed from the dictates of the forty plus hour work week, still do not have enough time? Where does the time go, and what can be done, for everyone, and not just retirees, to create, if not time abundance, at least time sufficiency?

A Ford Foundation Grant enabled me to travel to remote towns in Greece and Mexico where electricity and other modern conveniences had not yet found their way. What most characterized the inhabitants was the absence of time urgency. They all had a daily round of activities, and the evenings were characterized by food, music, and conversation, and an early bedtime. I have not since met any group of people who were so well rested, and so free of the stress of always having more things to do than time allowed. Is it possible to live in the electronic world without being victimized by too many things to do, and not enough time?

One would think that retired status should put one well on the road to imitating the life-style of these remote villagers. Most retirees fill their schedules with the things they really want to do, --which may include unexpected ventures in art, learning, or politics-- coupled with the things we all have to do, ranging from house maintenance to medical appointments and community obligations. The curiosity is that the things you want to do begin to consume larger and larger amounts of time, and the things you have to do generate progressively greater urgency. The odds are that as you get older, you will spend more time in "health maintenance," and if you are lucky, you will be able to spend more time exercising and taking good care of your body. With any luck at all, you will have more time to spend with friends and relatives, and this might indeed be some of the highest "quality time" of your whole life. But the sense of time insufficiency may still prevail.

The basics of time management apply to every stage in the life cycle. You have to list the things you need or want to do, you have to establish priorities, and you have to "budget" the time you will allot to the various categories of your activities. At any life stage, you have to prevent unwanted time-consumers from devouring your time. You have to decide what information you want to flow into your daily life: do you want to read the daily newspapers and the weekly magazines? How much TV do you want to watch? How much time do you want to spend browsing the Internet? How much time sunset gazing?

Specialists on time management from Alan Lakein to Stephen Covey emphasize micro-management, the handling of mail and phone calls, determining how much travel is necessary, and how to budget time so that the most important priorities receive attention when you are at your best. Perhaps macro-management is more important: how do you really want to spend your time? What are the issues that really matter? What is it you really want to accomplish this month, this year, or over the next ten years? Only when these issues are settled, can you determine the micro-details of what to do at various times of the day.

After I retired from the University, I enrolled in a course in Plato's *Dialogues*. I read them more intently than I did in graduate school, and I spent more time with the scholarly literature than I did when I prepared for comprehensive exams. I allotted a very considerable time for my Plato studies, because that was in keeping with my overall larger goal of coming to a better understanding of philosophy and the contribution of the great Greek philosophers. For me, that activity was in the realm of "the intrinsically worthwhile." That course, and some similar scholarly endeavors, has been among the most rewarding activities of my retirement years.

If you are to manage your time well at any stage of life, you must determine what is in your realm of the intrinsically worthwhile, commit time to that, and eliminate activities that do not contribute to your life goals. As a social human being, you may want to maximize the opportunities you have for personal interaction. You are then ready to go with the flow of where your inclinations lead you. With a little bit of luck, you will have time for everything important, you will feel good about how you are spending your time and your life, you will improve your capacities to think, to love, to relax, and perhaps you will even have time left over, to read the occasional good book in philosophy!

Harry Burrus and Augusta Stengle, Mason, Texas

III-111
Theories of Aging

Professor Stephen Hawking has written: "The eventual goal of science is to provide a single theory that describes the whole universe." Within the realm of physics, the challenge is to find a "Theory of Everything" that can harmonize the general theory of relativity, with quantum mechanics. Quantum mechanics includes an element of uncertainty that appears to contradict the demands of relativity, so physicists have their work cut out for them.

At a far less abstract level, gerontologists have proposed two apparently contradictory theories to explain what occurs to people as they age. The first describes historical experience: as people age, they do withdraw from a number of their accustomed roles. Retirement from work is the most obvious change, but a number of other changes occur gradually. For most people, the work of parenthood becomes less central by the time they reach their sixties. Grandparenthood usually goes through several stages, sometimes including considerable involvement, usually decreasing, as grandkids get older. Civic, political, and volunteer involvement may reach a peak sometime after retirement from paid employment, but within a few years, most people feel they have made their major contributions. The extreme form of this disengagement theory produces the eventual picture of the elderly individual, largely withdrawn from social activity, sitting in a rocking chair gazing at the sunset.

While this picture may be an accurate description of what occurs in some cases, it is not the model of aging most people want for themselves, nor does it describe very well the aspirations of "The Pepsi Generation." The so-called Activity Theory of Aging suggests that successful aging means the withdrawal from certain roles, only to emphasize new ones. Parents who no longer spend all their time raising children, and workers who no longer spend their days in the workplace, find new and challenging roles as they develop identities that may have long slumbered beneath the surface. The occasional person of mature years publishes a novel, becomes famous as a painter or sculptor, but many people find artistic outlets in various ways, producing beautiful woodwork, attractive pottery, or literary works that promote self-understanding. Philanthropy, in one form or another, becomes a new role and new source of meaning for many active people of mature years. For others, the amateur athletic career that was put aside provides some challenge, some companionship, and ample exercise.

Healthy aging means some balance of retreat from old roles that are no longer necessary and incorporation of new activities that provide meaning and excitement. Retirement provides an opportunity to re-think old patterns, perhaps initiating a new dietary program, a renewed commitment to exercise, a greater opportunity to be involved in arts and culture, and a new group of people with whom to socialize. It also has its hazards, as one may rest too much or too little, not get enough exercise or far too much, and have too much time for the pleasures of the table or the bar. Like any other stage in life, the exercise of intelligence can make the difference between success and failure in the displacement of old roles and the acquisition of new ones.

Physicists may one day find a theory that balances general relativity with quantum mechanics, an achievement that may not appear to have any great impact on most people. But a choice of a pattern of aging has immense personal consequences. It is up to individuals to find a balance between retreating from accustomed roles and actively engaging in new forms of behavior that provide that vital spark that makes you say: "I really want to get up and get at it, because there are things I really want to do." If you lose that spark, at whatever age, it's time to abandon the outworn and outmoded, and become active in new and meaningful ways. We can leave relativity and quantum mechanics to the experts, but everyone needs to make some choices about the most desirable and acceptable patterns of aging. To no small degree, you are what you choose to become.

III-112
Plato and Political Realities

More than a century ago, Thoreau wrote: "Most men lead lives of quiet desperation." The desperation has not been so quiet lately, as more and more Americans have concerns about the current political environment. The conviction is widespread that Congress does a poor job of representing the best interests of the American people. Qualified candidates sometimes do not run for office, not just because they know every aspect of their lives will be subject to minute scrutiny, and not just because they know they must raise a lot of money, but because they are convinced that American political life is dominated by Political Action Committees, and that a kind of plutocracy, a government by the rich, has taken over. No one runs for Congress anymore without accepting millions of dollars from special interest groups. Big companies fund candidates of both parties, not because they like their policies, but because they want those who are elected to remember who paid to help elect them.

The current political situation bears a strong resemblance to Athens in the time of Plato. Plato was overwhelmed by the fact that his city had rejected Socrates, in his mind the wisest man who had ever lived. The people of Athens had become accustomed to the practice of sophistry, preferring the appearance of wisdom to wisdom itself. The professional sophists were accused of attempting to make the weaker argument appear the better—

an argumentative form that preferred victory to truth. Plato rejected all this, claiming that there are ideals, particularly political ideals, that can be established and pursued. Much of his most famous dialogue, *The Republic*, is a discussion of the kind of education it would take to produce the wise statesmen and women required to make a society function as perfectly as possible. He wants a society that promotes the best interests of all the citizens, not just benefits to some particular class. He worries especially about plutocracy, a concern that the rich, just because of their wealth and prominence, will exercise undue political influence. He is no "democrat," for he thinks "rule by the people" is rule by the uneducated mob, and much of *The Republic* is devoted to developing a system of education that will produce citizens who are capable of exercising enlightened leadership.

Plato maintains that true politicians must passionately pursue wisdom, "philosophy," but for him philosophy is not some abstract empty discussion, but reflection and concern about how best to fashion human life. Putting his words into contemporary English, he writes: "Until philosophers are statesmen, or the politicians of this world become imbued with the spirit and power of philosophy, or until political greatness and the passionate pursuit of truth and goodness meet in the same people, nations will never have rest from the tribulations that assail them." In America today, lofty political ideals remain in place, and no doubt there are candidates of whom Plato would have been proud who can make a difference in how the nation is run, and who can bring us closer to the Platonic ideal of a nation that works for the benefit of all its citizens, and not the special interests of a privileged few.

None of us are free to shy away from political involvement. For some, it is the demand to run for office. For many, it is the requirement to think about the nature of the political situation, to step out from the shadows, and do something to promote the candidacy of the most qualified, the ones who most represent not just the Platonic Ideal, but the ideals of Washington, Jefferson, and Lincoln, and all those who have sought to bring out the best in human nature, and the best that any political system has to offer. Human beings are political animals, and we have to live up to our responsibilities. That demands thought and action, reflection and involvement. In our day, as in the time of Plato, such political involvement will not be without a considerable amount of controversy. Could it be the case that political controversy is an unavoidable component of the human predicament? And could it be that Plato stands as a permanent reminder of the importance of ideals, and of the passionate commitment to putting in place the best possible government?

III-113
On Finding a Master

"He who is his own master has a fool for a teacher." Or as lawyers phrase it, "He who is his own lawyer has a fool for a client." The admonition to seek advice from appropriate sources is universal. Few tasks are more difficult, however, than finding the right master, at the right time, offering the right advice. A financial magazine suggested this procedure to find a good financial planner: Get recommendations for at least five planners; interview them, examine their credentials; get references to clients similar to you whom they have advised, and call and talk to these people. Then, have a trial session with the best candidate, and see if you are compatible.

It would appear that if you are to go to all this trouble to find a good financial planner, the search for someone to give you advice about how to live your life should be even more thorough and painstaking. The fact is, from time to time we all need advice about life's most important issues and apparent impasses. This advice cannot just be generic; it has to be tailor-made for our situation and circumstances, by someone who knows something about our history and us. And it must be accessible at the proper time, because life has a way of posing problems to us for which we are ill prepared and poorly forewarned.

In previous societies, seers, oracles and priests were sources of advice for life's major problems. Our era has seen the triumph of the therapeutic, where therapists of one stream or another have attempted to find the hidden sources of our problems, and proposed to help us out of life's confusing mazes.

Peter Kramer's book *Listening to Prozac* is critical of the therapeutic profession, stating that drugs effect more "cures" than any form of psychotherapy. (There are parallel but opposite texts suggesting drugs mask the problems, but do not solve them, the way psychotherapy does.) Medication and psychotherapy may still leave the larger problems of life untouched. The burgeoning "self-help" sections of bookstores show the seriousness of the search for soul-satisfying solutions. Books have become the spiritual masters for a vast array of the reading public. *The Road Less Traveled* was a best seller for over a decade, being displaced by ever-new versions of various kinds of soup for the soul. Many TV talk shows are essentially public therapy sessions, some of them very good, some of them pandering to the lowest common denominators of human behavior.

While books are helpful, most people need the kind of personal assurance only conversation can provide. Clubs, whose apparent purpose is Contract Bridge or Sewing or Tennis, provide opportunities for serious and meaningful conversation, in which the most important and sensitive issues can be discussed. While close friends are our most available sources of counsel, there will be times in life when a mentor, a master, a sage, or someone who has gone before us into uncharted land, may become necessary. This may be a brief encounter that occurs purely accidentally, or it may be the result of a deliberate journey, or it may come from someone we have known for a long time and whose perception we acknowledge. It is sometimes a case of: "When the pupil is ready, the master will appear."

In the journey of life, we all learn much by mentoring others. Sometimes we best understand our own experience when we try to help someone else through similar circumstances. It is unlikely that you would know so much, nor would you be the person you are, unless the right masters had been there, when most you needed them. One of the basic laws of life is inter-being: we have our being in conjunction with others, and just as we can be of help to others, others may have a vital role to play in our growth. It takes some humility and some common sense, to seek out and accept advice and counsel, even when the right master, the appropriate teacher, the knowledgeable guru, appears. But finding the right counsel at the right time can make the difference between traveling the right path, and stumbling around in the dark. "When the pupil is ready, the master will appear." Even then, it must be a happy marriage of perception on the part of the pupil, and wisdom on the part of the master. It takes both perception and luck, to find the right counsel, from the right person, at the right time and place.

III-114
Universities and "Senior" Students

In the 1950s and1960s, American Colleges and Universities were expanding at rates never seen before. The model seemed to be: for anything anyone wants to study, a program will be created. Even small colleges developed wide ranges of inter-disciplinary programs: American Studies, Afro-American Studies, Russian Studies, Cognitive Studies, Multicultural Studies, Women's Studies, etc. By the 1980s, Colleges and Universities realized the expansion could not go on forever. Mission statements became the key, and "areas of excellence" became the motto for funding and development. Universities began to look at "niche marketing," looking for clientele groups whose demands could be met, with the expectation that funding would follow.

Public Universities have marketed themselves as "engines of economic growth," and as "paving the way to the careers of the future." By the end of the twentieth century however, universities were seen less as the crowning glory of a city or state, and more as an economic and even social drain. Into this mix loomed the world of Elderhostels and other "Life-Long Learning" programs. While producing some income from otherwise underutilized facilities, it also produced a new level of consciousness for all involved. Instead of "economic growth" or "preparing people for careers," these programs approximated an even older university ideal, that of learning for its own sake. They offered courses covering the whole domain of human knowledge, from Astronomy to Zoology, from the simplest of artistic activities to the abstruseness of the highest mathematics.

Such programs meet not only the need for learning, but also the needs for community and companionship that may be especially intense among a senior population. People of mature years have a wealth of life experiences to share with one another, but they may also have experiences of losses that are catastrophic, ranging from deaths in the family to a variety of declines in physical or mental abilities. Just as undergraduates learn so much from peer experiences, so too the people of mature years who enroll in these programs learn from each other in terms of coping with misfortune and adapting to vastly changing circumstances.

Universities have many different missions. They should be "engines of economic growth" as they research new areas of enterprise. They should enable people to pursue careers that benefit society and that make them productive citizens. But Universities must not lose sight of the fact that these are by-products of the formative mission of the University, the pursuit of knowledge for its own sake. A University ought to be a place where the whole range of human knowledge can be explored, and where all who want to learn, will have their needs satisfied. Nowhere is this obligation more clearly met than in the provision of programs for people of mature years, who want to learn more about how the world operates, about how human beings interact, and about how to become more fully human.

Universities may have abandoned the aspiration to be all things to all people, but they can still be the providers of intellectual and personal stimulation to all those who are eager to learn, and have the time and disposition to reflect on Gauguin's three questions: "Where do we come from? What are we? Where are we going?" The astrophysicist Stephen Hawking asked parallel questions: "What is the nature of the universe? What is our place in it and where did it and we come from? Why is it the way it is?" No matter how practical or professional the program, a university education that does not do something to help students of whatever age grapple with these larger questions is failing in its basic responsibility.

President David Hardesty of West Virginia University emphasized "transmission" as the unique character of higher education. Universities differ from corporate research laboratories--where knowledge may be pursued, but with practical application as the primary purpose. They differ from libraries, where knowledge may indeed be pursued, but discussion, or changing minds and behavior, is not the primary goal. Universities are places where attaining knowledge, and transmitting that knowledge to others, is the primary reason for being. Without students, there are no universities; without discussion and the open exchange of ideas, something essential is missing. Stephen Leacock, a Canadian economist with a humorous bent, said if he were founding a university, he would start with a common room where people could gather and talk, then add a library, and if he had any money left over, hire professors.

Universities are remarkable achievements, as are the senior citizens who have weathered many storms, and who might now benefit from the opportunity to share their experiences, and deepen their understanding of their lives and times. Universities and senior citizens have much to offer each other. It is not just that retiring baby boomers create a new market for colleges and universities: their very presence on campus enlivens the critical mass, providing different perspectives, and perhaps, purely by accident, acting as "role models" for much younger students.

University campuses might reap considerable benefits from expanding the range of contacts between students of diverse ages: the exuberance of youth might be tempered by the wisdom of age in a manner beneficial to both groups. The presence of youth does something to rejuvenate people of more mature years; and people of mature years can have an energizing and stimulating effect on younger students. Colleges and Universities are missing the boat if they fail to give serious consideration to the inter-generational dimensions of life on campus, for they will be foregoing the opportunity to transmit knowledge to those most in need, and failing to live up to the basic charter of higher education, that of providing a place where all ideas may be entertained, where all forms of knowledge may be pursued, and where human interaction may produce benefits of unexpected magnitude.

III-115
Your Board of Directors

You probably have a Board of Directors and don't even know it. A Board of Directors is a very helpful form of self-government. No one person can possibly handle all the information necessary to survive in this complicated world. Most corporations are run by a Chairperson who has a Board of Directors, people of wide-ranging intelligence and with some particular expertise.

A bad Board of Directors is made up of people who think exactly like the Chairperson. An even worse Board is made up of people who are totally opposed to the Chairperson. A good Board is made up of people with diverse backgrounds and perspectives, who respect each other's expertise, and who earnestly desire the best possible outcomes. Your personal Informal Board should be composed of at least four persons. Your vice-chair should be someone you trust completely, who could in fact step in and make decisions should you become incapacitated, or briefly "out to lunch."

A second member should be a medical professional, who could supply essential information about the state of your health, your readiness to undertake demanding roles, and how your health needs correspond with your activity. This may be your family physician, or someone who has enough medical knowledge and enough awareness of your physical condition to tell you what you need to know.

A third member should be someone whose judgment you trust, and who has offered good advice on previous challenging occasions. As you go through life, you bump into people who seem especially *simpatico*. They may be older or younger, a long-time friend or a relatively new acquaintance. Perhaps they have already experienced some of the ventures you plan to launch out into, perhaps they have done things you have only dreamed of doing, or perhaps they are simply an outstanding processor of pertinent information. They may be more familiar than you are with new technologies, new approaches, and new ways of seeing things. Whatever their distinctive qualifications, you need on your Board someone whose horizons are appreciably different from yours.

One great advantage of a personal and informal Board is that it never has to meet as a group! You can consult Board members one by one, only letting other Board members know of controversies if you deem it appropriate. There are many advantages to governing yourself with this kind of Board, not the least of them, having someone quietly to blame, if things go wrong! You have probably had an Informal Personal Board of Directors all along, and just never thought of it this way. You may want to keep it as your little secret, or you may want to let these people in on it. Whichever way you choose, your self-governance may well improve, just because you have parceled out some responsibilities to those who know you so well, and you have clearly identified those whose advice and counsel you know you can count on when challenging events occur in your life.

III-116
Three Personal Laws of Physics

At a "Physics For Everyone" symposium, the physicist-in-charge of the demonstrations said: "If it moves, it's biology. If it smells, it's chemistry. If it doesn't work, it's probably physics." Physics in fact provides the basic frame within which we all work, and, like it or not, we are subject to Physics' most basic laws. There are three laws of physics that apply to everyday life. The first is at least as old as Newton: A body once in motion tends to stay in motion. The personal application of this is: get off your duff, and start doing something! Once you are doing something, you tend to find other things to do. Keep doing things until the obverse law asserts itself: a body at rest tends to stay at rest.

The second law comes from quantum mechanics. There is, at the micro level, a degree of discontinuity in the world. The Newtonian universe was one in which the future was expected to be a replica of the past. We are comfortable with the tested, the tried and true, and the repetition of what worked before. As futurists, we all tend to extrapolate, to expect that trends currently in vogue, will continue indefinitely. Modern life, however, is filled with discontinuity. The future tends less and less to resemble the past. There are now millions of cell phone users in the United States; there were none a few a decades ago. Changes in telecommunications, health care, and computerization will affect your life in sudden and dramatic ways, rather than in the gradual way we all expect change to take place.

Entropy is the physical law that says: left to themselves, things tend to disorganize. Imparting and retaining order is one of the most challenging of all our physical tasks. You must impart order to the information flow that comes your way: you must choose what to process, what to omit, what to discard. You must also impart order to your daily activities, some "schedule" that insures all the important tasks will be tended to. You must also leave adequate room for serendipity, the invasion of your world by the unanticipated and unexpected. Disorder is only tolerable if some kind of organizing structure is there, so that the serendipitous may be incorporated into some kind of continuity.

The practice of meditation can help with the application all three physical laws. Meditation is a "rest" exercise that should lead to ordered activity. Meditation should leave the practitioner open to the possibility of quantum leaps, of movement into new and unexpected directions. And meditation should help to overcome entropy, as order is imposed on an otherwise chaotic universe.

There's no escaping the "laws" of physics. The challenge lies in applying them creatively. On the human level, it means resting fully when it is time to rest, being 100% active and involved when that is appropriate. It means openness to change, when some radical departure presents itself. And it means learning how best to keep things from falling apart completely, when entropy most threatens. Humpty-Dumpty clearly had some problems with the law of gravity, but his words of wisdom are universally applicable: "It is a question of who is to be Master, that's all."

III-117
Philosophers on Drugs

There are at least two different "wars on drugs" going on in America. One is the war to eradicate supply, as exemplified by the billion dollar allocations to military forces in Central America to prevent the growth and export of drugs. The other, much less publicized, is the war against American citizens who have been "users" of marijuana, cocaine, heroin, or other "recreational" drugs. Some 35% of the current prison population is there for drug-related offenses.

We may be fighting the wrong wars. We have spent far more money attempting to interdict the supply, and far too little curtailing the demand. Even if we shut down the supply of drugs from abroad, local suppliers would be quick to adapt to the demand. More marijuana is grown today than ever before. Methamphetamine labs can produce far more dangerous chemicals than most of the imported drugs.

Some public officials, realizing law enforcement is fighting a war it cannot win, have pleaded for the legalization of drugs. Joseph McNamara, a former police chief, said: " Why does the thought of responsible citizens controlling their own lives without government coercion seem so threatening?" McNamara noted that drugs were not illegal until Congress passed the Harrison Act in 1914. Others have suggested that, despite spending more than $1 Billion annually on the "war," drugs are "cheaper, more potent, and more powerful than ever."

Is legalization the answer? It might diminish the crimes committed in order to obtain drugs; it might sharply diminish the numbers of people in prison for victimless crimes; it might enable police forces to focus on other, more pressing problems. Against legalization stands the evidence of those countries like the Netherlands where it has led to more addicts, and addicts who are harder to treat. James Q. Wilson has argued that compulsory treatment for drug offenders, a program of "testing and control," and a large-scale commitment to counseling would do more to diminish the drug problem, than any amount of dollars spent on cutting down the supply. As Wilson says, "demand will produce supply."

Among philosophers, some argue that we should be free to use our own bodies as we see fit. Both Aldous Huxley and Alan Watts argued that the choice to experiment with drugs should be up to the individual. John Stuart Mill, the greatest of libertarian philosophers, argued that the only justifiable reason for restricting human liberty is to prevent harm to others. It is however the clear conviction of the vast majority of drug specialists that not only does the unbridled use of drugs cause harm to the individual, it also inevitably inflicts harm on others. Even Mill acknowledged that full liberty could not be granted to those who were unable to be rational about their activities.

We should commit our resources to diminishing the demand for drugs. Aristotle said that the goal of human life is to move towards the perfection of human nature. Drug use, despite the testimonials of some happy users, does little or nothing to enhance, enrich, or ennoble the human character. The challenge is to create programs, including after-school activities, recreation experiences, counseling and guidance opportunities, and work environments that so focus attention on what is stimulating and satisfying, that the demand for drugs sharply diminishes.

It has been suggested that for alcoholics and drug users, there is some unsolved philosophical problem at the root of their addiction. Some addictions are simply chemical dependencies, but there is often some unsettled anxiety, some discomfort about one's place in the universe, that functions as the root cause of addiction. Is it too Utopian to think that the proper use of various public educational programs might do more to stem the tide of drug addiction, than any amount of money spent on curtailing the supply? If there is something at the root of addiction that might be called a "philosophical" problem, shouldn't philosophers, and philosophically minded counselors, be somehow engaged as major contributors to the solution? Working along these lines may produce greater benefits than anything we have tried so far...

III-118
Philosophy Is Everywhere

Everyone practices Philosophy; some just do it more publicly, more explicitly, more visibly than others. Everyone needs philosophy: it helps us grapple with what makes our lives meaningful, and it makes us come to terms with the challenges of the day, and of the world. Some might claim that philosophy is the hardest and most recondite of all the forms of knowledge. Philosophy might appear to be the domain of experts, locked into some arcane discipline no one else can understand. George Schlesinger wrote: "There exists virtually no popular literature to offer a nontechnical yet authentic account for the perusal of the intelligent layman." (*God and the Philosophers*, p. 249.) By contrast, Henri Bergson, a philosopher who managed to write in clear and elegant prose, wrote: "The essence of philosophy is the spirit of simplicity...always and everywhere, complication is superficial, construction is an accessory, and synthesis an appearance. Philosophizing is a simple act." ("*La Pensee*," quoted in Hadot, *Philosophy as a Way of Life*, p. 125).

How could it be otherwise? Philosophy is insight into the way things really are. It may be espoused in a simple axiom, expressed emotionally in poetry or drama, or conveyed artistically by simple, evocative images. Above all, philosophy is not some arid, empty, abstract discipline. It tells us something about how to live our lives, how to be rational, how to impart meaning to our everyday existence. As Hadot wrote in *Plotinus, Or, The Simplicity of Vision*: "Might it not be the case that the greatest lesson which the philosophers of Antiquity--and above all Plotinus--have to teach us is that philosophy is not the complicated, pretentious, and artificial construction of a learned system of discourse, but the transformation of perception and of life?"

Philosophy should not be mistaken for Logic, or the work of those scholars who produce difficult essays designed to puzzle even the most erudite. As Marcus Aurelius said: "The work of philosophy is simple and discreet. Let us not get carried away by the swollen puffiness of solemn affectation." (*Meditations*, 9, 29.)

Philosophy is about life in all its dimensions. It is everyday thinking about everyday matters. It may be trivial or profound, pertinent or irrelevant, widely accepted or blatantly controversial. Good philosophy manages to meet us where we are, and speaks to us about what matters most. When philosophy appears difficult or incomprehensible, we need only wait for the next wave, the next impulse, the next turn of events, which will bring the issues back down to earth, and force philosophy to help us interpret what we encounter. When professional philosophers abdicate their responsibility to the general public, popular philosophy will be found in magazines and newspapers, often disguised as editorials or comics, but endowed with that kernel of insight someone may need, to produce the appropriate response. Philosophy must in fact be one of the simplest of all human activities, for we are all doing it, all the time. The challenge is to do it well.

III-119
Doing Moral Philosophy

The "method" in the madness of these essays is Socratic midwifery. Socrates said that he knew nothing, and that he simply served as a "midwife," bringing out of people what they already dimly knew. The goal of those who practice philosophy in the Socratic manner is to make people think clearly about things they have overlooked. The midwife simply brings to birth what is really already there.

The Socratic philosopher believes that truth is really attainable, and that the process of thinking things through is not just producing hot air. Truth does not need to be expressed in a verbal formula, nor does it require a neat package of syllogisms. As Socrates put it: "I cannot define justice, but I can demonstrate it by the way I live my life." Philosophic truth is not a matter of words or arguments, but of living one's life in a certain way.

Greek Philosophy began with questions like: "What is really real? What is the world made of?" Such questions have largely been handed over to physicists and astronomers, and philosophers sometimes try desperately to make philosophic sense of answers given by the scientists. Modern philosophy's obsession has been with the question: "What can I know?" The nature of knowledge, the limits of reason, and the nature and proper use of the mind, have been the preoccupations of philosophers from Descartes to Wittgenstein. Discussions of the nature of knowledge have become exceedingly technical, and it is difficult to simplify the arcane statements of those whose obsession is the nature of knowledge itself.

Philosophy comes down to earth with the perennial question of human behavior: "What should I do?" Few of us get through a day without some puzzling moral situation confronting us. These moral questions are not only the substance of Congressional and Supreme Court debates, but of everyday conversations. Is abortion permissible? Is physician-assisted suicide moral or immoral? Is capital punishment justified? Do I give money back if a cashier has made a small mistake? How much should I give to the less fortunate? How careful must I be when figuring my taxes? Should I tell the truth even when it hurts me, or someone else?

James Q. Wilson in *The Moral Sense* argued that it is the loss of a moral sense that is the reason why crime has increased around the world. He claimed that if civilization is to survive, the "relativism" that has been so widely embraced must be overcome, and something of traditional moral values must be reestablished. The possibility of civilization perishing because of the loss of any moral sense should be enough to make the discussion of morality a front-burner issue in every household.

As a founding member of a Hospital Ethics Committee, I argued that the ethical "charter" we established must have a philosophical, and not a religious base. My hope was that a secular ethic based on reason could be accepted by everyone, and that religious convictions might motivate some to go well beyond the secular ethic. That debate is still alive today, and I still have the hope that reason, manifested by some form of rational decision procedures, can point the way to a desirable standard of moral behavior. My hope is that Socratic midwifery can be successful in bringing forth satisfactory answers for most of our moral dilemmas. Moral issues are the clearest examples of philosophical problems that require progressively deeper and deeper insights. While philosophy may not be able to solve all our problems, doing philosophy well is an important component of every good solution.

III-120
John Wesley and Immanuel Kant

If Immanuel Kant is the pivotal figure in modern philosophy, John Wesley plays a similar role in the modern religious response to Kant. When Kant wrote *The Critique of Pure Reason*, he removed the philosophical support for Christian belief that had been in place for centuries. He attempted to show the severe limits of human reason, exemplified by his demolition of the proofs for the existence of God. Kant said our minds are shaped by the categories of space and time, and since God is neither spatial nor temporal, we can have no knowledge of him or his existence. As Kant later said, he "destroyed reason, in order to make room for faith." Faith for Kant, as for Luther, did not mean a low level of knowledge, but trust or commitment, unsupported by rational arguments. Faith was to become "the reasons of the heart," and the "will to believe" was to become God's test of the depth of one's faith.

"The religion of the heart" was precisely what John Wesley had experienced during a Moravian prayer meeting in Aldersgate Street, London, in 1738. Kant's preference for "religion within the limits of reason alone" would have been no obstacle for Wesley, who was convinced that doctrines about God were useless and could in fact be damaging. What Wesley experienced was "God continuously breathing, as it were, upon the human soul." The Greek word "en-thus-iasm" means "God [breathing] from within," and Wesley is at the heart of the great "enthusiast" movement in modern religion. (Ronald Knox's book *Enthusiasm* is an excellent history of the movement and its meaning.)

Blaise Pascal had spoken of "the reasons of the heart that the mind knows not of," and he inscribed on a scrap of paper: "You would not seek Me unless you had already found Me", and kept it close to his heart. The Roman Catholic response to this wave of enthusiasm was to invent a brand new devotion to "The Sacred Heart of Jesus," with an intensity of emotion hitherto uncommon in Catholic circles. Within Judaism, the cool rationalism of Moses Mendelssohn and Spinoza had come as a response to the Kabalistic mysticism of Isaac Luria, but the tradition of the Zaddikim, the God-intoxicated ones, has always had a small but "enthusiastic" following in Judaism.

Wesley had provided an acceptable answer to Kant's claim that knowledge of the world offered no rational proof for the existence of God. Wesley could simply say: "Look within you: the voice of the Lord cries out to all who will hear Him." Wesley pries open the door that Kant seeks to keep shut. The more you put limits to reason, the more passionately the will to believe may seek to express itself. Wesley is much more in tune with the quasi-mystical Neo-Platonic tradition in Greek philosophy than was Kant, who was after all a child of the age of Newton. In the third century Plotinus had written: "If God were absent from the world, he would not be within you either." And in the fifth century, Augustine, the first of the great Christian philosophers, wrote: "I sought Thee without, but Thou wert within."

Kant is the curator of the primacy of science in human knowing. Wesley is the keeper of the ancient tradition, the conviction that science is only one small part of knowing, and the heart has reasons that are quite legitimate, even if the mind doesn't quite know what to make of them.

III-121
Orthodoxy

It seems that every community has some vision of orthodoxy, "right teaching." We hear of Orthodox Jews, Orthodox Presbyterians, and "The Eastern Orthodox Church." The Vatican has recently spoken of "Orthodox Catholic Teaching," as opposed to those described as "cafeteria Catholics," who pick and choose from among the doctrines and practices of the Church. The passion for orthodoxy is deep seated. At conferences of "secular humanists", there is a very clear "orthodoxy" among the atheists present, and deviation from official teaching is a form of heresy requiring some kind of excommunication. Among politicians and some journalists there is a very clear orthodoxy: either you subscribe to the correct way of thinking, or you deserve banishment to the nether regions. Recent debates over legalizing drugs or the controversies about the death penalty are good examples of the unyieldingness of the 'true believers,' of those who, once having had the vision of what is 'right,' become intolerant of all those who do not subscribe to their views.

Philosophers can be as absolutist as anyone else. It is not uncommon for articles submitted to scholarly journals to be rejected with a slip that reads: "This article is not in step with current opinion on this matter." A few years later, and "current opinion" may well swing around to what then becomes the new orthodoxy.

Philosophy should be the very breath of tolerance of novel opinions. Philosophy only progresses because someone challenges received convictions. While Cicero said: "There is no position so foolish but what some philosopher has maintained it," the history of philosophy provides rich evidence for new arguments resuscitating old convictions, and newer logic calling into account established positions.

The important question remains: Can you be so sure of your current position on any matter, that no argument to the contrary could dislodge you from your conviction? Is there any orthodoxy so absolute that it is beyond all questioning? "Dogmatism" has been defined as "proclamations no amount of contrary reasoning can contravene. Some serious Christians, troubled by the chinks in the armor of their previous religious dogmatism, can find comfort in a statement by an eminent Anglican cleric who wrote: "Cling fast to the person of Christ, and as for all else, be uncommitted." G.K. Chesterton's *Orthodoxy* has a parallel in C.S. Lewis' *Mere Christianity*, both texts seeking to defend "orthodox" Christian teaching from the ravages of modern thought.

Gene Bammel

Whatever positions prevail, there are few who can live without some support for their own personal orthodoxy. Its root may be the Torah, it may be Jesus Christ, it may be the Koran, it may be the Constitution, or the U.N. Charter. It may be derived from Art, or Literature, Philosophy or Science. It may be rooted in the bond of love within a family. Whatever it is, it should be tolerant of other orthodoxies, other true teachings, and other visions of what is the one true way. After all, it is not ortho-doxy, true teaching, that matters as much as ortho-praxy, the right way of doing things. A world in which everyone sought the right way of doing things would be a much better world than one in which the only thing that matters is having the right teachings...

III-122
Tolerance and Morality

The Spanish Inquisition was built upon the premise: "Error has no rights." This justified torturing Jews and heretics, and putting to death those who dared to speak out against the atrocities. "Error has no rights," assumes that the speaker has the truth, and can afford to be intolerant of those who are in error. On the other extreme, tolerating everything would lead one to say: one person's actions are as justifiable as anyone else's, and there is no criterion by which to judge one morality as acceptable, and another as objectionable.

Anthony Kenny suggested in *A Brief History of Western Philosophy* that moral philosophers could be divided into absolutists and consequentialists. Absolutists think some kinds of actions are intrinsically wrong and should never be permitted, no matter what the consequences. (Telling a lie to save the world, for example.) Consequentialists think the morality of actions should be judged by their results. Absolutists tend to think in terms of natural law or natural rights. The Tribunal at Nuremberg, for example, found the Nazi war criminals guilty of "crimes against humanity," for actions that everyone, everywhere, and at all times, should find repulsive.

By contrast, consequentialism has dominated contemporary moral reflection. Medical ethics, for example, raises questions in terms of the desirable consequences of permitting stem cell research, abortion, or euthanasia. The acceptance of Euthanasia may be taken as resulting from a deepening understanding of what morality demands. Advocates for the practice maintain that there was a time when the prohibition of assisting someone in dying made sense; today, when we know that even with the best pain medications, some patients are suffering intolerably, it is morally

204

incumbent upon the physician to ease the transition from painful existence to the "good death" that means the removal of all pain.

Even in the midst of the triumph of consequentialism, something of the absolutist morality remains. Three elements are necessary for morality: a moral community, a set of moral values, and a moral code. We are brought up into a moral community, and we acquire a basic moral vision as parents, siblings, and playmates gradually socialize us. We develop our own moral values in the process, and values such as sharing, fairness, truth telling, and comradeship, gradually develop in the socialization-education-humanization process.

Every society does something to establish a moral code, an awareness of what is praiseworthy, and what is to be condemned. We laud our heroes who go into burning buildings to rescue someone, and we imprison teen-age mothers who smother their babies. The moral code of our society has identified racism and sexism as morally unacceptable. But moral puzzlements remain: why do some members of every society flaunt the established moral code? Why do some societies develop moral codes that deviate wildly from the rest of the world? Can consequentialism by itself guide us to a universally acceptable moral code?

If consequentialism is taken to mean providing the greatest good for the greatest number, the following example exposes its weakness. Suppose a hundred sadists derived immense delight from the torture of one man. In terms of the greatest good for the greatest number, the torturing wins out hands down. The example shows the inescapable need for something larger in our morality than a near-sighted view of consequences. There are actions so heinous, so obnoxious, and so inhumane that they ought everywhere and at all times to be prohibited. We are continually made aware of immoral communities, immoral values, and immoral codes that go beyond the limits of conceivable tolerance, and that we condemn as simply "wrong." It is not uncommon for criminals, caught in the act of some terrible crime, to say to the arresting officer: "I'll get even with you for this." Such people are simply "outside the moral sphere."

A successful morality examines consequences carefully, but retains as "absolutes" some notion of what human beings ought to do. Moral sensitivity is not some knee-jerk reaction, nor is it something that can be learned by rote while listening to someone else. It would instead appear to be a life-long learning process. It is no easy matter to develop an ethic that tolerates the tolerable, while being intolerant of forms of conduct that do not measure up to what is *humanly* acceptable. Those who would proclaim that "error has no rights" may wind up being intolerant of themselves, as they find that their own previous moral convictions may have been contaminated by a variety of errors that maturity and deepening insight have made manifest. Tolerance is the virtue of humility applied to our own and to others' gradual moral awakening.

III-123
Why do Philosophy?

There are at least four good reasons why you should do philosophy. First of all, you should do philosophy because it provides some important truths about human existence--and we all stand in desperate need of pursuing these truths. (This implies that truth is attainable, and that a mind properly focused can attain these truths--a matter of no trivial importance.) This may put you at some distance from most academic philosophy. It is not uncommon for professional philosophers to begin presentations with some variation of: "I shall defend the claim that...although x is causative of p, the presence of p does not imply x." Such presentations remove academic philosophy from the real concerns of people who most desperately need to benefit from real philosophy. As Schopenhauer phrased it: "Generally speaking, university philosophy is mere fencing in front of a mirror." Far from leading to any valuable truth, many see philosophy as a waste of time, or as words awaiting some useful application. As Voltaire said of metaphysicians: "They are like minuet dancers, who, being dressed to the greatest advantage, make a couple of bows, move through the room in the finest attitudes, display all their graces, are in perpetual motion without advancing a step, and finish at the identical point from which they set out."

We should do philosophy because it gets us somewhere. Real philosophy is progressively deepening insight into life's most basic questions. It is not just abstract speculation, but a guide to living life well. The models of philosophic existence are seen most clearly among the ancients: Socrates, Aristotle, Epictetus, and Plotinus. These people lived their philosophies, and tried to help others to live "in accordance with right reason." Socrates condemned the sophists for taking money for their teaching: his point was that philosophy is intrinsically worthwhile, and should be done for its own sake, and not for any financial return. Aristotle exhorted his followers to lead the life of the mind, and to exercise the virtues necessary to follow reason unclouded by passion. Epictetus wrote: "A carpenter does not come up to you and say: 'listen to me discourse about the art of carpentry,' but he makes a contract for a house, and builds it...Do the same thing yourself. Eat like a man, drink like a man...get married, have children, take part in civic life, learn how to put up with insults, and learn to tolerate other people." Plotinus wrote on the importance of seeing life as a process of self-development: "Never stop sculpting your own statue." We should all do philosophy because it is the most practical, the most down-to-earth of all disciplines.

We should do philosophy because it is a most enjoyable pursuit. What could be more delightful, than discussing, to the best of one's abilities, the most important human concerns?

Ultimately, there is a very selfish reason for doing philosophy. It provides you with your identity. The poet Gerard Manly Hopkins wrote: "What I do, is me." The doing of philosophy is simply an integral part of your being. We all have a need and a capacity to do philosophy, and to live our lives in peaceful accord with the philosophical voice within us.

There is an optimistic spirit at the root of philosophy. Perhaps it derives from the Greek philosophers of antiquity, who, despite all the adversities of life, never wavered from a conviction that goodness was at the heart of reality. As Plotinus wrote: "What is ultimately good is gentle, mild, and very delicate, and always at the disposition of whomever desires it." Doing philosophy is a conditioned response to the mystery and grandeur of what goes on everyday, but is so easy to overlook. The challenge of philosophy is in bringing us back to what is right there in front of us, ever awaiting our enlightened response, hoping that we will see it as it really is…

Chapter IV.
Making Progress

IV-124
Truth and Progress

One of Francis Bacon's most famous essays begins: "'What is truth?' said jesting Pilate, and would not wait for an answer." Bacon hints that had Pilate been patient, he was talking with someone who might have given him the best imaginable answer. The nature of truth may be the thorniest question of philosophy. Lengthy graduate seminars fail to provide satisfactory answers, so do not expect too much from what may be presented here.

For the "realist," truth is a property of utterances that correctly represent the world the way it is. In the realist formula, truth is a correspondence between thought and thing. For the Platonic realist, you have the truth when you see the "form" or essence of the thing. Platonic dialogues often appear to be a search for a "definition," a verbal statement of the essence of something, whether a table or a chair, justice or beauty. Aristotelian realism said you have "the truth" when the form that is in the thing, is also in your mind.

Realism suffered a mortal blow when the artists of the Renaissance noticed the importance of Perspective: where you stand determines how you see things. Immanuel Kant put this in philosophical terms when he said that "truth" was a construct of the mind: the mind applies certain categories so as to make "things" knowable. We know the appearances of things, but not things in themselves. When Nietzsche concluded that perspective is everything, the search for "truth" dissolved into relativism: all statements are relative to your perspective, and every utterance is simply "a point of view."

The nature and attainability of truth became the hottest philosophical topic of the twentieth century. Thomas Kuhn, in *The Structure of Scientific Revolutions*, (one of the most influential philosophical books of the twentieth century), proclaimed a social construct theory of truth. "Truth" was whatever the dominant body of scientists agreed upon at a given time. When too many conflicts arose, a new "paradigm" was established, and scientists worked within that paradigm until it too became obsolete. Kuhn suggested the transition from the Ptolemaic to the Copernican astronomy was indicative of how "truths" change over time, one paradigm replacing another, depending on how reality was being constructed by the interested parties.

Richard Rorty, in *Truth and Progress*, summarized his own changing attitudes about truth. Sounding at one stage much like an ancient Stoic, Rorty said truth was "warranted assertibility." He softened that to say: "Truth is what our peers let us get away with saying." Rorty's conclusion: the only criterion we have for truth, lies in the justification we offer for our statements.

This point of view revived the Vienna Circle's commitment to "verifiability:" the need to point to some empirical evidence to justify any truth claim. Since no empirical evidence supports the proposition: "Truth is what is empirically verifiable," it seems there is no truth to truth! Sir Karl Popper, whom some regard as the most overlooked philosopher of the twentieth century, concluded that "Falsifiability" was the best criterion of truth. What would falsify the claim "All crows are black?" Well, finding one white crow would be pretty effective! The bottom line for Popper: there are "truth claims," but every claim is subject to revision, should new evidence occur, such as the presence of one white crow.

Wittgenstein, like Popper, claimed there were limits to the kinds of questions for which you can expect truth-full answers. Both agree with the common sense view that truth is indeed attainable, but only for those questions for which empirical evidence may be gathered. "Does God exist?", "Is the soul immortal?", such are not proper questions, because they are outside our real experience. As Wittgenstein said: "What we do is bring words back from their metaphysical to their everyday use."

Like Kant, Wittgenstein has made the world safe for science, but left the bigger questions untouched. As he said, "We feel that even when all possible scientific questions have been answered, the problems of life remain completely untouched." But then, are the really important truths unattainable? Does philosophy have nothing to say about the meaning of life? The most quoted of all of Wittgenstein's aphorisms is: "Whereof one cannot speak, thereof one must be silent." When you use language beyond the proper domain of its application, you are talking non-sense! Wittgenstein seemed to acknowledge the inevitability of asking the questions that seemed to produce non-sensical answers, so he said: "Keep an eye on your nonsense."

Is truth attainable? Philosophers seem more fascinated than others with the simple truths like 2+2=4. But what are our chances of knowing the "truth" about God, abortion, euthanasia, or the best forms of government? The Socratic dialogues seem to leave every statement subject to future revision. Aristotle, by contrast, often seems downright dogmatic in his proclamations, ending one text with the statement: "Since now, all truths are known." Later Greek philosophers would maintain that truths are best expressed by living life in a certain way. Truths are not so much properties of propositions as they are attitudes, expressions, and affirmations of certain ways of existing.

Wittgenstein leaves us puzzling over the problem of existence: "It is not how things are in the world that is mystical, but that it exists." Mathematics offers us truths that seem incontrovertible; the "truths" of physics continue to contradict many of our common sense attitudes. People with opposite points of view may hotly contest statements about government or about morality. What is truth? We know that many of our "truths" are provisional, subject to revision should new information occur; we know that people see things from different and often irreconcilable perspectives. Nevertheless, we are convinced that there are some truths that we can reach, some we can live our lives by, and some that we would die for. That we seem to attain so many of these truths is indeed a most puzzling phenomenon, enough to humble the greatest of philosophers.

IV-125
"To Teach Is To Touch Others Forever"

I have "loved wisdom" for as far back as I can remember. When I was in high school, my brother took me to one of his philosophy classes, and I was completely captivated. That year I began reading William James, and went on to tackle Kant's *Critique of Pure Reason,* which I did not understand at all, but it wetted my appetite for the many questions it raised. While I taught History of Philosophy and Ethics, I spent most of my academic career working in what might be called "applied philosophy," ranging from philosophy of work and leisure, to environmental and medical ethics. I have had three great teachers, and their influence has continued to affect my every philosophical thought.

My first and most important teacher was Etienne Gilson. As an undergraduate and graduate student at the University of Toronto, I attended his lectures for several years. He was an historian of philosophy, and the great philosophical questions came alive for his audience, as he deftly pursued problems from their Greek origins, through Jewish, Moslem, and Christian writers, and into the modern era. Gilson wrote more than 40 books, including *Being and Some Philosophers, God and Philosophy, The Unity of Philosophical Experience,* and *The Spirit of Medieval Philosophy.* His most important contribution was showing how difficult it is to do philosophy without being familiar with its history

A second important teacher for me was Pierre Hadot. His book *Philosophy As A Way Of Life* taught me what to look for in reading the Greek philosophers. Hadot was professor of classics at the College de France, and was disturbed by the modern disregard for Greek thought. Modern philosophers have been obsessed with technical details; Hadot pointed out that for the Greeks, philosophy was not a technical discipline, but a way of dialoguing with reality, in fact a way of living, with a mind wide open to what reality has to offer. For the Greeks, said Hadot, philosophy was a "spiritual exercise," a way of coming to grips with the challenges of everyday existence. Philosophy is a matter of learning how to cope! Hadot was convinced that philosophy reached its apex with the Stoics and Epicureans, who were masters of learning how to take life in stride, and how to respond positively to whatever "perfect storms" time had to offer.

The third teacher who was critical to my philosophical development was Anthony Kenny. He was long the Master of Balliol College, Oxford, and "retired" to become the Master of Rhodes House, the academic home for Oxford's Rhodes' scholars, and then retired a second time to become a Fellow of St. John's College, at Oxford. He was educated at the Gregorianum in Rome, wrote his doctoral thesis on "Religion and Linguistic Philosophy," and has written more than twenty books, among them: *Wittgenstein; Frege; Descartes; The Five Ways; Aquinas on Mind, A Brief History of Western Philosophy,* and *The Unknown God: Agnostic Essays.*

From these three great teachers, and from many others, I have learned respect for all those who have searched dispassionately for philosophical truth. I have learned something of the awesome power of pure philosophical insight, whether expressed by Plato, Aquinas, Spinoza, or Nietzsche.

Philosophy comes alive in the hands of such great masters. For all of us who "do" philosophy, (and every one of us does philosophy!) we have the opportunity to see as far as we do, because we are able to stand on the shoulders of giants like these. Gilson observed that philosophy always buries its undertakers. Hadot noted that philosophy is nothing unless it is a way of life. Kenny added that philosophy should haunt the lives of every person who grapples with the daily problems of human existence. With teachers like these, the future flowering of philosophy is indeed secure.

IV-126
Revelation

Is Revelation the sacred word of God, or just the earthly word of man? Stained glass windows in churches depict an angel whispering into the ears of the biblical writers. Accordingly, for many believers, the Bible is simply the revealed word of God, every word dictated by God and transcribed by the biblical co-author. Such "literalism" is not the prerogative of Southern Baptists, but can be found among Jews, Catholics, and a wide variety of Protestants. Such literalism has always been well represented in Islam.

Modern biblical scholarship might be seen as a process of "de-mythologizing," of interpreting the literary styles of the various biblical authors, and separating the archaic format from the "truth" of the narrative. The most obvious example is the Genesis account of creation as the work of seven days, complete with God walking in the garden to enjoy the cool evening breezes. The biblical literalist either rejects evolution on the basis of this account, or strains to accommodate scientific discovery with the biblical narrative. The biblical scholar stops the discussion short: the "revelation" is that God is the originator of all that is. The account of the seven days, like God walking in the garden, is just a story to enable readers to grasp the "fundamental" truth, and is not to be taken "literally."

The ancient biblical writers subscribed to a three-level universe, with heaven above, the earth in the middle, and hell below. Copernicus and Galileo had to overcome centuries of unquestioned commitment to the three-level universe, which put earth clearly in the center of all creation. The infancy narratives in the Christian Gospels pose similar problems. Matthew uses an elaborate genealogy to show that Jesus has David for an ancestor, while Luke takes the ancestry of Jesus back to Adam, and keeps angels busy informing a variety of people about the divine pregnancy. The whole point of the narrative: "Jesus is really important." It was a literary convention of the time to accord kings and prophets with glorious ancestry, and Jesus deserved no less.

Modern biblical criticism attempts to say: "Don't get bogged down in the archaic world views, or the literary forms of a given era. Look for the truth behind the narrative." Religion, in whatever form, is an attempt to say there is more to reality than what philosophers have to offer. Philosophers, after all, have only human reason for a guide, and everyone knows that reason has its limits. Biblical literature is an explanation of the interplay between God, humans, and the universe. For believers, its human basis should not make it any less "divine," or any less a "revelation." Reduced to its simplest elements, biblical faith means: (1) God is the creator of the universe; (2) He has not abandoned his creation; (3) a distinctive 'moral' response is required of the believer.

The Hebrew Bible contains some of the best religious poetry ever written. What more comforting thought could you come up with, than what Jeremiah has God say: "I have loved you with an everlasting love, therefore have I led you, taking pity on you." The book of Job is a brilliant literary narrative of what most writers call "the problem of evil." (Some say religion is a response to the presence of evil in the world; others say such evil makes religion impossible.) There is a persistent ethical dimension throughout the biblical literature, as exemplified by lines like these: "How can one claim to love God, whom he does not see, if he does not love his brother whom he sees?" The Koran has a recurring mystical theme: "Is He not closer than the veins of thy neck?"

In every biblical text, a "revelation" is supposed to occur. The reader is challenged to see with the eyes of faith. "Faith" has been variously described as a "gift," a "leap," "an act of trust," a "non-rational act of will," as "picking up where reason leaves off," or as "wishful thinking." Whatever faith is, it involves some removal of a veil, some form of disclosure, some invitation to a deeper insight into the way things really are.

Philosophical literature frequently uses the metaphor of "seeing." Refugees from Plato's cave are invited to "see" the sun, and see "the Good" as having the same role in the intelligible universe as the sun has in the material universe. How curious that the Bible frequently uses the metaphor of hearing: "Now hear the word of the Lord." "A voice said to me..." "He who has ears to hear, let him hear." "Faith comes by hearing...." "If today you should hear his voice, harden not your hearts." Could it be that faith is to the audible universe, what philosophy is to the visible universe? Or could it be that what philosophy is for the human word, faith is to the divine word? "Let those who have eyes for seeing, see, and those who have ears for hearing, let them hear." There are some scientists and some philosophers who claim that modern discoveries have made it impossible to believe in any of the purported documents of Revelation. But it is clear that Religion, like Philosophy, always manages to bury its undertakers.

IV-127
William James, Marcus Aurelius, Friedrich Nietzsche

So you are ready to read some real philosophy, but don't know where to begin? And you don't want to spend a whole lot of money? Dover Books has a deal for you! Dover exemplifies the philosophy of doing something for the good of doing it, and not just for making money. Dover has an incredible selection of great books, and none of them cost very much money.

If you like what your have heard about the Stoics, Marcus Aurelius' *Meditations* is available for a pittance. There is something about directly reading the words of a great philosopher, something of the spirit of really thinking philosophically, that no secondary source can quite convey. See how rich are the words of Marcus Aurelius: "As physicians have always ready their knives and instruments for cases that require their skill, so do you have principles ready for the understanding of things divine and human, and for doing everything, even the smallest, with a recollection of the bond that unites the divine and the human to each other. For neither can you do anything well that pertains to man without at the same time having a reference to things divine; nor the contrary."

Perhaps the Pragmatism of William James has appealed to you. The Dover edition of *Pragmatism* is inexpensive, offering 116 pages of perhaps the best single work ever by an American philosophical master. James is as down to earth and "pragmatic" as you could possibly hope for: "For the philosophy which is so important in each of us is not a technical matter; it is our more or less dumb sense of what life honestly and deeply means. It is only partly got from books; it is our individual way of just seeing and feeling the total push and pressure of the cosmos." And James offers what is often taken as a one sentence summary of pragmatism: "'The true,' to put it very briefly, is only the expedient in the way of our thinking, just as 'the right' is only the expedient in our way of behaving."

Friedrich Nietzsche sought to unmask the deceits of philosophy. He wrote in a plane, aphoristic style that lends itself to easy reading, until you suddenly awake to what you have almost assented to. Nietzsche saw himself as not only proclaiming the end of the religious era, but as the transformer of all values, the guide to new moral vistas. In *Beyond Good and Evil*, Nietzsche wrote: "To recognize untruth as a condition of life: that is certainly to impugn the traditional ideas of value in a dangerous manner, and a philosophy which ventures to do so, has thereby alone placed itself beyond good and evil." To be ignorant of Nietzsche, and not to read his own words, is to miss one of the great shapers of the modern mind. His "Perspectivism" has been adopted by philosophers of science like Thomas Kuhn, by philosophers of religion like Art Holmes, and by great intellectual historians like Jacques Barzun. (Dover sells *Beyond Good and Evil* and *The Birth of Tragedy*, his great commentary on Greek civilization, in very inexpensive editions.)

Walt Whitman could say: "I loaf and invite my soul." But I say: loaf, and read some great philosophy. The real work of professors of the History of Philosophy is to get their students to read the books of the great philosophers. When Dover makes it so inexpensive, you can't go wrong. Their website is: www.DoverPublications.com.

IV-128
Three Useful Maxims

When a friend was in the process of assuming a new job with considerable responsibilities, she showed her good sense by coming to a philosopher for advice. Now generally it is not a good idea to ask a philosopher for advice: they tend to love the sound of their own words, and they are seldom very practical people. But since I happened to be the philosopher, the advice was brief, and seemed down to earth. These three simple maxims may be helpful to you as you take on new tasks or increased responsibilities.

(1) "To put something new into your life, something old must be discarded." It is easy to say yes to doing something new, but most of us fill up our time rather well, and while doing something new may be stimulating and exciting, it means you must devote less time and energy to something you are currently doing. While keeping track of where the moments go is not very exciting, it can be very informative. Those who perform this exercise are surprised at how much time "watching TV" consumes of their weekly 168 hours. Some very productive people watch TV hardly at all, or "multi-task" while listening in. In practical terms, putting something new into your life means something old has to go. If you remember that there is no such thing as "must see TV," cutting out some TV time may

be a fruitful first step. It may be difficult to eliminate some other things that you are accustomed to doing, but there are times when it is necessary to put new things into your life, and to discard activities that, while long practiced, are less important.

(2) While our expectations of ourselves should be high, there is a realistic limit to what any one of us can do. Accordingly, the second maxim is: "All you can do, is all you can do." Put forward your best effort, and learn to let go. It pays to expect much of our selves, but there is a limit to what any one person can do at any given time. Do your best, move on, and do not waste time second-guessing yourself.

(3) "Learn to rise above it all." This third maxim has its roots in Stoicism, western religions, and Zen Buddhism. Greek writers used the word *ataraxia*, which is customarily translated as "tranquility," but that doesn't quite get it. It means "imperturbability," or, caring and being concerned, while being master of the situation. Teresa of Avila put the western religious response into poetry:

Let nothing disturb you, nothing dismay you;
All things are passing, God never changes.
Patience attains all that it strives for;
Whoever has God lacks nothing;
God alone suffices.

The Zen Buddhist tradition offers an excellent summary of all three maxims: Do not lose yourself in dispersion and in your surroundings. Practice deep breathing, to come back to what is happening in the present moment. Be in touch with what is wondrous, refreshing, and healing both inside and around you. Plant seeds of joy, peace, and understanding within yourself. This will facilitate the work of transformation in the depths of your consciousness. We all stand in need of transformation, and the assumption of new responsibilities, the start of a new year, the move to a new location, starting a new and healthier way of living-- any of these can serve as the summons to a new level of consciousness, and a new way of discovering who we are in the process of becoming. "To put something new into your life, something old must be discarded." "All you can do is all you can do." "Learn to rise above it all."

IV-129
"Otium"

"*Otium*" is the Latin word for "leisure." "*Neg-otium*" means the denial of leisure, and is the word for "business." Curiously, our word "otiose" has come to mean, "producing no useful result." What a falling off there has been, in understanding the primacy of leisure in a meaningful human existence! Why do so many people extol and long for retirement, if not the hope for a real experience of leisure! Leisure is a most important component of living well, and to underestimate its importance is both unwise and unhealthy.

In the Jewish tradition, the Sabbath is "a day of rest," but not of empty idleness. The purpose of the Sabbath is an *imitatio Dei*, an imitating of God, by looking back on the work of the previous six days, and seeing that they are very good! In the book of Genesis, God looks upon his creation and sees that it is tov *miod*, "exceedingly good." Judaism has sought to restore a sense of Sabbath as a "sacred time," when the usual affairs of everyday life are put aside, and there is time and energy to focus on what really matters most, that which is of absolute, and not passing, importance.

The Christian tradition has seldom been without some admiration for monasticism: retreat from the world, in order to make sense of the world. One of the Psalms says: "Be still, and acknowledge that I am God." There is presumably a religious motive in the New Testament injunction: "Come apart, and rest awhile." Religious traditions maintain that life is not just frantic movement, but should be activity with some purpose or goal in mind. And in the midst of incessant change, it is important to retreat from time to time and ask: "What am I doing, and Why am I doing it?"

The popularity of Zen Buddhism in America owes much to the practice of meditation, of taking "time out" from busy-ness, to come back to basics, and count not just breaths, but blessings. Zen suggests that the remedy for anxiety is to live life fully and completely in the present moment. The Abbot of the Tessajara Buddhist monastery was asked how a man of his small size could lift so much weight, as boulders were being moved from the building site. He replied: "When I lift, I am doing nothing else but lifting." Life comes to us one breath at a time, one problem at a time, one boulder at a time. We are in error if we model our lives on the computer's capacity for multi-tasking. And we make a major mistake if we think the goal of life is to see how much more we can accomplish in ever less time.

If we are to live, we have to be busy, we have to accomplish things, and we have to get the jobs done. But if we are to live well, we must cultivate a sense of leisure, a sense of delight, not only in what we have done, but also in the sheer joy of being alive, of breathing, of seeing, of sensitivity to the world around us. Someday "otiose" will lose its negative connotation, and simply mean being at full-blown leisure. To be fully alive, you need to become a person of leisure, that is, you need to learn to be otiose, in the best possible sense.

IV-130
Getting the Point...

I was "educated'" and "trained" to do history of philosophy. "Educated," because I was taught to think for myself in matters philosophical, and "trained," because, like an athlete, I was schooled in certain preferred ways of doing things. One of the essential skills of the historian of philosophy is being able to pick out the wheat from the chaff, the central message from the foreground and background. For example, the most popular edition of the *Dialogues* of Plato is 1600 pages, *The Basic Works of Aristotle*, 1500 pages. Most great philosophers were voluminous writers, and, if you are to make sense of them, you have to separate the important from the much less important.

The skills employed in reading the great philosophical texts can be applied equally well to the study of religion. Listening to televangelists, I come away with the sense that, with respect to the Hebrew Bible, or what Christians call "The Old Testament," the televangelists had focused without exception on the secondary, and neglected the central message. There seems to be an obsession with the historical character of the Bible, with the date of the Great Flood, or with the location of Noah's ark. You even hear of the skeleton of a whale large enough to have contained Jonah. Jonah, like the book of Job, is clearly a story meant to convey a deeper truth. To focus on finding whalebones, or the courtyard of Job's discussions, is as foolish as searching the Arctic Circle for Santa's home.

To a historian of philosophy, the message of the Hebrew Bible seems perfectly clear. The God of the Hebrews is not like the gods of the other ancient Middle Eastern religions. He is not interested in ritual sacrifices or temple services, but in social justice, and the exercise of human compassion. The Hebrew Bible might be summed up in what Hosea has God say: "What I want is merciful love, not sacrifices; obedience, not burnt offerings." To anyone trained in any form of literary criticism, in the Hebrew Bible there is a clear development of teaching, from some very primitive and intolerant formulas, to the developed doctrine of the prophets and the wisdom literature.

It has often been said that the difference between religion and philosophy is this: religion is essentially obedience to a divine command, whereas philosophy is relentless critical inquiry. Is religious obedience to be taken as slavish observance of a Divine Will? Can such a God command anything He wishes, or is there some "reasonableness" to the Divine Will? Jeremiah has God say: "Deep within them I will plant my Law, writing it in their hearts." But what is the Law the prophets worry about violating? It is lack of compassion for those who suffer, and absence of concern for the poor and the downtrodden.

Philosophers, loving wisdom, are compelled to pursue it wherever it may be found, which may include biblical literature. To anyone who reads "the book unlike any other book," it seems clear the essential message occurs in a great many texts similar to Hosea 6:3: "Let us humble ourselves, let us strive to know the Lord, whose justice dawns like the morning light." "Justice" is clearly a matter of dealing rightly with other people, of feeding the poor, and comforting the distressed. To a philosopher reading the sacred text, the God of the Hebrew Bible seems much less concerned with supra mundane floods and arks, and much more concerned with down-to-earth issues of dealing decently with others. Martin Buber once suggested that biblical religion could be summed up in the phrase: "I only become an I in relation to a Thou." Maybe someone should remind the televangelists of this.

IV-131
Whatever Happened to Real Philosophy?

"In my youth," said Dr. Johnson, "I wished to become a philosopher; but cheerfulness kept breaking in." Philosophers are thought of as either morbidly serious people, engaging in disputes no one can understand, or as people wasting time by discussing what everyone already knows, or what is beyond the realm of real knowledge.

But what is it that philosophers do, and is the occupation of philosopher as outdated as that of a shepherd, or town crier? Plato thought the philosopher was the most important man or woman in a society, because only the philosopher had a real vision of the good toward which society should be moving. Aristotle saw the work of the philosopher as an end in itself, and as productive of the only truly happy life, because the philosopher "knows all things, in so far as they are knowable."

The philosophers of the ancient and medieval world were accorded a place of importance in society, because they were the presumed experts in separating appearance from reality, and because they provided some practical wisdom about how to live morally and well. Cardinal Newman expressed this vision in the late nineteenth century when he said: "To have mapped the universe is the boast, or at least the ambition, of philosophy."

Karl Marx had no patience for such a lofty vision: "Up till now philosophers have sought to know the world. The important thing is to change it." Marx and his modern successors are philosophers of change and process: according to them it is foolish to chase after the immutable ultimate of the Platonist, essentialist vision. Real philosophy is done in the trenches, in determining what current needs are, and how best to get humanity out of the wretched state to which it seems prone. John Dewey, who got philosophy out of the colleges of liberal arts and into the colleges of education, business, and law, said that realizing *process* is the one universal absolute, is "the most revolutionary discovery yet made."

The drift of modern philosophy is this-worldly, anti-essentialist (there are no essences or natures in things, all is in process...) anti-absolute, and anti-dogma. One model of the truly modern philosopher is Richard Rorty, who proclaimed this as the charter for philosophy: "My candidate for the most distinctive and praiseworthy human capacity is our ability to trust and to cooperate with other people, and in particular to work together so as to improve the future."

There are centers of academic philosophy where refinements of modal logic, the mystery of consciousness and other arcane topics are hotly debated, but in the minds of many, these are not the main streams. Philosophy, real philosophy, has long ago abandoned the academy, and taken up residence in movies or novels or the cartoons in the daily newspapers, or the works of journalists and TV commentators. Philosophy always buries its undertakers.

University philosophy departments exist as laboratories for the conduct of philosophical experiments, and for the training of apprentices, and occasionally genuine philosophical reflection. Real philosophical work today is done in politics, in movies, in novels, and also in hospitals, in law courts, in popular journals, and everywhere where serious thinking about important issues needs to take place.

More than two thousand years ago Aristotle wrote: "For it is owing to their wonder that men both now begin and at first began to philosophize." Sources of wonderment are all around us, and real philosophy has moved out of the university and into the marketplace, or wherever people gather and respond to the wonder of existence, or ponder the reality of love, of war, or the meaning of life. Philosophy is too important to be left to the academics. After all, doing philosophy well is the calling of every human being.

IV-132
Religion and Politics

Religion and politics are inseparable, in part because both tend to claim absolute allegiance. You cannot understand global politics, unless you have some grasp of the various ways religion and politics intermingle. At one extreme, you have one of the greatest politicians of all time, Gandhi, who saw no need for conflict between the two. "I am a Moslem, a Hindu, A Christian, a Jew: and so are you. We are all the children of God." Gandhi was the ultimate practitioner of the conviction that there are many paths to the mountaintop, and the path you are on should make no difference in your politics.

In the modern world, Islam appears to be the most intolerant of the global religions. And yet the Koran, the sacred book of Islam, bids every Moslem recite: "For our God and your God are one and the same." While every religion seems to have its modernists and its traditionalists, Islam throughout its divisions is deeply committed to the inseparability of politics and religion. Islam minimizes the difference between the sacred and the profane, the religious and the secular. For Islam, the *ummah*, the community of believers, is sacramental, a sign of God's presence. Islam lends itself to political theocracy, a rule by religious figures, whose authority is complete and unquestionable. Iran's ouster of a very western Shah and his replacement by an Ayatollah, is a prime example of this Islamic ideal. Islamic leaders who have clearly secular agendas, nevertheless claim to draw their power from the desire to see the Koran and the accompanying Sharia, Islamic Law, made absolute.

Religion is an attempt to do and to proclaim "the will of God." The danger to which every religion is subject is irrational absolutism attached to the claim of knowing the will of God. The motto of the Christian crusades, one of the most irrational of all politico-religious campaigns, was "God wills it." Religion can easily be taken captive by some form of irrationalism, as evidenced by the onslaught of televangelists. Islam and Christianity have occasionally strayed into an unhappy voluntarism: an act is good or bad because God wills it so, and not because of anything intrinsic to the act itself. When such voluntarism, such extreme commitment to "doing the will of God" prevails, philosophy must arise and exercise its proper role of rational reflection, trenchant criticism, and clarity of vision. It must say: "Wait a minute. Let's think about this."

Religion is an attempt to discern and do the will of God. Philosophy is rational reflection on the way reality operates. Politics, as Aristotle observed, should have as its goal the provision of a good and happy life for the citizens of any community. Today, citizenship is as much global as it is local. For religion and politics to get along, philosophy should be welcomed as an essential arbiter, a critical contributor to the kinds of issues whose peaceful settlement is important to not just the well-being, but to the survival, of the human race. Politics and religion appear to be universal aspects of the human condition. Philosophical reflection has a critical role to play to insure that the two get along, and add to the progress of human wellbeing.

IV-133
Understanding Anti-Religionists

We live in a "secular" society, with a large component of people for whom religion makes no sense. Those who are, or who wish to be, religious, need to be aware of the mind-sets of the anti-religionists, and should have some reasonable responses to them. Moslem, Jewish, and Christian philosophers debated similar issues a thousand years ago, culminating in widely held convictions first of all that truth is one, because the truths of religion and the truths of science cannot be in disagreement; and secondly that faith is not irrational, but has continuity with the truths reason can attain. As one medieval writer put it: "Grace builds on nature, and does not displace it." Throughout the Middle Ages, the issue was what validity reason had in a religious worldview. For people in the modern world, the issue is the validity of religion. To get a handle on this issue, one must understand three different points of view expressed by the anti-religionists.

(1) *Religion has done more harm than good.* Various historians have looked at the long heritage of religious conflicts, of Moslem or Christian vs. Jew, Moslem vs. Hindu, Protestant vs. Catholic, and concluded that so many wars have been conducted in the name of religion, and so much harm has been generated as a result of religious absolutism, that the world would be better off without religion. Islam, for example, has been faulted for various violations of human rights, and for its apparent preference for a manner of life that flouts the demands of modernity. Examples from various traditions might be cited as instances of the human and

cultural destructiveness for which religions must assume at least some responsibility.

(2) *Religion is a hoax.* Freud suggested religion is a psychological crutch for those who are too weak to face the harshness and cruelty of the real world. Nietzsche portrayed religion as a morality by which the weak of the world overcome the strong. And anthropologists claim religion has been used as a means of social control, keeping a ruling class dominant, and a servile class seeking rewards in a heavenly kingdom.

(3) *Religion is not intellectually respectable.* There are those who read Frazier's *Golden Bough* and Joseph Campbell's *The Power of Myth* as if they taught that all religions are fabrications, stories made up to explain the puzzles of everyday existence to an ignorant populace. Some of the most influential modern intellectuals have been vigorously anti-religious. Some regard Immanuel Kant as the father of modern atheism. His *Critique of Pure Reason* poked holes in the traditional proofs for the existence of God. Carl Sagan found nothing in his cosmological research to justify positing the existence of a divine being. Stephen Hawking, in *A Brief History of Time*, found no astronomical reason for positing a first cause of the universe. The theory of evolution is interpreted by some as eliminating the need for identifying any Supreme Orderer of the universe. E.O. Wilson in *Consilience* said that as the scientific method is more widely applied, traditional religious beliefs would gradually disappear. Daniel Dennett in *Consciousness Explained* offered 'scientific' reasons for abandoning all beliefs in the 'old fashioned concept of 'soul.' Reducing "mind" to what the brain does is a major aspect of much current consciousness research.

Gallup Polls find that 8% of the American population is atheist, and that the percentage is higher among physicists and astronomers. What is the response of the defenders of religion? Are there valid arguments against those who say that religion historically has done more harm than good? Are there good arguments against those who say that religion is for the weak and downtrodden, just so many fairy tales to get them through the day? Are there equally powerful arguments against the attacks by prominent scientists like Sagan, Wilson, and Hawking? Or is it the case that religion has lost its intellectual respectability, and is essentially fighting a rearguard action? Those who wish to pursue what religious apologists have had to say in defense of belief might find Stephen Barr's *Modern Physics and Ancient Faith* helpful. Those bothered by the conclusions of neuroscience might find: *What About the Soul? Neuroscience and Christian Anthropology*, an anthology edited by Joel Green useful. It is incumbent upon religious believers to read and understand the viewpoints of the anti-religionists; those who are disposed to be anti-religious have an equal obligation to understand what the best defenders of faith have to say. At any rate, the debate continues, and is not likely to come to an end anytime soon. If it did, human conversation would be immensely impoverished!

"Old" City Hall, Munich, Germany

IV-134
A Medieval Interlude

When scientists have problems, they turn to some kind of "laboratory," some place where experiments can be conducted, hypotheses tested, evidence gathered, and conclusions drawn. The "laboratory" for philosophy is its history, for it is unlikely that any philosophical problem will not have been discussed in some form, by someone, somewhere, and probably at great length.

The current debates between those who reject religion and those who would uphold it have their closest parallel in centuries of debate between Moslem, Jewish, and Christian, scientists, philosophers, and theologians in the high Middle Ages. Greek philosophy, in particular the work of Aristotle, gradually spread from Islam, to Judaism, and finally to Christianity. All three traditions shared a conviction that philosophy could clarify the "concept" of God, and help remove the anthropomorphisms, as well as the superstitions, of popular religion. The Arabs who were the first to latch onto Greek learning quickly came to revere the power of science: it provided useful knowledge of the physical world. Medieval Moslems invented al-gebra (an Arabic word meaning reduction), and made significant contributions to both astronomy and medicine. For these medieval Moslems, science was simply "rational thinking" and should be applied to Scripture, for example, to help make sense of it, and to overcome apparent contradictions. Within the larger Moslem culture, there was a lively debate between believers who wanted nothing to do with philosophical or scientific speculation, and the ardent advocates of such reflections.

For some Moslems, philosophy was superior to faith, because it was rational analysis of the way things really are. For others, faith, being inspired by God, was unquestionably superior. It is possible that at least one Moslem theologian thought that there were two irreconcilable truths, one of faith, one of philosophy or science. One of the quirks of medieval Moslem philosophy was the suspicion that God could do anything He pleased, including squaring circles or making a rock so heavy He could not move it. According to this belief, if He wanted the world of "super-nature" to be different from the world of nature, that was His privilege.

Moses Maimonides, the greatest figure of medieval Jewish philosophy, said that since God is the author of both nature and revelation, there could be no contradiction, for "Truth is One." (Logic clearly prevails, even in the divine realm!) Maimonides saw the task of science and philosophy as helping to understand what God has created. Since we do not know God as He is in Himself, our goal is to understand Him by studying His activities, His effects, and His creation. For Maimonides, science is a kind of holy mission, and doing science is a mitzvah, a divine command. As to which approach is superior, Maimonides says: "The Rabbis speak with authority on Law, all else is the domain of science." And by "Law," he means the Torah, the divinely revealed sacred text.

Thomas Aquinas was a master synthesizer of the thoughts of his predecessors, as well as having a remarkable capacity to add something distinctively new. Aquinas asked: If we have nature, why is there any need for Revelation at all? He answers: These Truths are as difficult to reach as they are important, and even brilliant minds could spend their whole lives struggling to attain them. Aquinas said God in His mercy provides Revelation, so that all may know early on the truths that are necessary for salvation, and begin practicing them. For Aquinas, faith provided "knowledge" of what God has revealed about Himself, so is clearly superior to what reason can attain.

Several lessons can be drawn from this narrative. First of all, the writers of the medieval period had great respect for the thinking, as well as the religious practices, of the other traditions. Today's "multi-culturalism" is a revival of this spirit of the best of the medieval writers, and should be more widely imitated. Secondly, in Moslem, Jewish, and Christian traditions, not only did faith triumph over philosophy, in each case mystical religion became the answer to the puzzles posed by philosophical questioning. The breakdown of medieval philosophy occurred because of this loss of nerve, this flight to mysticism. While mysticism is an important component of the religious quest, it does not provide answers to philosophical problems. The most important message to be drawn from the works of the great medieval writers, whether Jewish, Moslem, or Christian, is that it never pays to give up on what reason may attain.

IV-135
"Answers"

Medieval philosophers, whether Moslem, Jewish, or Christian, worked within a community of believers. This was an age of faith, and the statement of Anselm would have been well received in any one of the three communities: "Unless I believed, I would not understand." Modern philosophy gradually severed itself from this faith context, and current philosophy has modeled itself on science, which takes nothing on faith. While system-builders like Hegel and Whitehead have always had supporters, the dominant voice among modern philosophers was well expressed by the comment of the Greek skeptic Arcesilaus, who said: "The proper attitude of the philosopher is to suspend judgment on all important topics." Bertrand Russell, the best-known philosopher of the twentieth century, said that philosophy was simply the application of cold, hard logic to the problems at hand.

In this environment, it is somewhat of a paradox that the philosophy of religion is enjoying a rebirth of interest. While "philosophy" strives to be as neutral as possible, individual philosophers seem eager to take sides. Some, in deference to their faith, practice philosophy only to dismiss it. According to St. Paul, philosophy would appear to be superfluous: "Let no one cheat you by philosophy and vain deceit, according to human traditions, rather than according to Christ." This is the only use of the word "philosophy" in the New Testament, and it is not very complimentary. The "wisdom of this world," is something Paul puts aside, so that he may simply "preach Christ." Christian philosophers quickly responded that Paul must have been talking about philosophy poorly done, for elsewhere faith is described as "a reasonable service." On the other end of the spectrum, there are adamant atheistic-minded philosophers like Paul Kurtz who say that philosophy has made religion superfluous, and we have reached an era in human history where people are rewarded for living for today, and no longer need fairy tales of a divine being who is the rescuer of last resort.

Should philosophy be seen as firmly on one side or the other? Philosophy is in part a method, a way of thinking logically and clearly about things, but it is also a "principled" discipline, and it draws its principles from fundamental, basic intuitions that come from everyday experience. To interpret the world theistically, or a-theistically, is more a matter of fundamental first principles than a matter of philosophical conclusions. Speaking from the religious perspective, Laura Garcia wrote: "Ultimately it is always a matter of hearing the voice of God as addressed to oneself, as calling one's own name, and of choosing to listen and obey." On the other side stands the well-known and controversial Princeton philosopher Peter Singer who says none of the theistic positions "are rationally defensible." Singer's basic intuitions are of a universe devoid of the divine, and he claims that as people become "more scientific," this view will prevail.

The interplay of the two positions is epitomized in the title of Alasdair MacIntyre's book, *The Religious Significance of Atheism.* Mircea Eliade provided testimony to the fact that this dialogue can never end. In *Patterns In Comparative Religion,* he wrote: "The history of religion can, in the last analysis, be expressed in terms of the drama of the losing and refinding of those values, a loss and rediscovery, which are never, nor can ever be, final." The debate continues, because the human mind stands ever in need of new, and revolutionary, intuitions---insight into the way things really are. For all of us, intuitions are unpredictable, as evidenced by the fact just as today's atheist may become tomorrow's believer, today's believer may become a most ardent atheist.

What does a believer have to lose by the practice of philosophy? Is it not possible that the believer stands to have belief deepened and strengthened by the activity of philosophy? While it may be difficult for the true believer to accept, the truth of the matter is that atheism is not a "foolish" or irrational position. Faith and Un-faith both begin from very basic intuitions that are deeper than reason. Life is a process for gathering evidence that corroborates or disproves our intuitively held premises. It takes a lifetime to find out what our own intuitions are, leave alone the process of reasoning that corroborates or takes them apart. The reason we need to live a long time, is that it takes so long to sort out these most basic and fundamental issues, and find out where we really stand. With a great breakthrough in self-awareness, Martin Luther was able to say: "Here I stand. I can do no other." Discovering where we really stand is no simple task.

IV-136
Working and Living

Aristotle observed that all human activity was goal-oriented. We do not behave randomly; we act purposefully, with specific ends in mind. Nowhere is this clearer than with respect to work. Work is rarely a goal in itself. We usually work to achieve some specific target. The interesting philosophical question is: What is the ultimate goal of all our strivings?

The student works to get a diploma or a degree. Then one works to become established, to marry, to raise children, put them through college, and then to be able to afford retirement. What happens when one stops working for a living? Margaret Mead once said that men died when they retired, while women kept right on cooking. The current crop of retirees is the healthiest, wealthiest, and best educated ever, and consequently has the highest expectations, but what those expectations are is far from clear.

Work, the environment of work, and the need to work, all impart meaning and structure to the worker's life. When the worker retires, new structures of meaning must be identified. For most retirees, what was only a hobby or of passing interest becomes of much greater importance. For some, a sport long neglected assumes center stage. Clearly retirement is an opportunity for the physical exercise that has been neglected, but just as clearly, sports are recreations, and not ends in themselves. Successful retirement means freedom to move from the level of the "instrumental," to the realm of the "intrinsically worthwhile."

The Intrinsically Worthwhile has four dimensions. The first is self-discovery. At different times in life, you have to come up with a deeper understanding of who you really are. If you have been busy working, the odds are you have not had time to ask the basic self-discovery questions. You are more than your functions, more than a money-tree, more than a payer of bills and a consumer of goods and services. In the midst of exercising these functions, it is all too easy to overlook the person behind the functions.

The second dimension of the Intrinsically Worthwhile is discovering what your world is really like. The knowledge revolution changes our picture of the world with alarming regularity. But there are basic convictions about the world that must either be re-enforced or cast aside.

Is the world an endless array of purely random events, or does it have some comprehensible order? Is there purpose built into the world, or is purpose a purely human enterprise? At different times in our lives, we have the chance to move to a new level of intellectual or spiritual life, and retirement is the last, best hope of getting it right.

The third dimension of the Intrinsically Worthwhile is your role in society. What is your relation to other people? Are other people simply obstacles in your way-simply occupants of the parking places you would like to have--or are they all your neighbors and part of your community? Are world affairs someone else's business, or are you a participant in social, economic, and political life? Does your presidential vote really count? Do you have civil responsibilities as well as civil rights? And if so, are you obligated to exercise them?

The last dimension of the Intrinsically Worthwhile is the most important. It is learning to be at peace with your place in the universe. One may work in order to live, but one lives in order to be as fully alive and vital as circumstances permit. As one of the great medieval philosophers wrote, first you exist, then you engage in purposeful activities, and finally you take peaceful delight in what you have done. Finding and engaging in the activities that provide "peaceful delight" is the fulfillment of the earlier dimensions. While aging inevitably includes some forms of deterioration, there are other aspects of life that can continue to improve. The real "work" of life is not subsumed in earning a living, but in becoming all that you can be. Your most important achievement in life is what you have made, and are making, of your self. After all, you too belong to the realm of the Intrinsically Worthwhile.

IV-137
Nature Mysticism

"Mysticism" lost its allure in the seventeenth century. Descartes expected "clear and distinct" ideas would replace the fuzzy religious and philosophical thinking of previous centuries. The older view had accepted that much of the world remained incomprehensible, and that the root of reality remained mysterious, perhaps only appropriated by a kind of incommunicable mystical experience. Sir Isaac Newton was even more determined than Descartes to dispense with the mystical and mysterious, hoping to find mathematical formulae that would explain precisely how every aspect of the universe really worked.

Sedona, Arizona

Pascal and Wesley both responded in defense of mysticism, and its importance for religion. For Pascal, mathematician that he was, the heart had its reasons the mind knew not of. For Wesley, the encounter with God was a transformative experience, a kind of mystical union beyond words or rational explanation. Wesley's Methodism and Jonathan Edward's Great Awakening were invitations to listen to the God who speaks from within.

Coleridge and Wordsworth produced poetic responses in the form of nature mysticism. The tradition of so-called 'romantic' poetry (romance meaning back-to-nature, or back to the wondrous middle ages, not at all the modern sense of 'romantic,') culminates in the lines of Masefield, as he explained that the reason for his repeated visits to the seashore was:

To mingle with the universe and feel
What I can ne'er express, yet cannot all conceal.

The nature mystic is transformed by the experience of nature, and seems prone to return to everyday life revitalized by the depth of the encounter.

Emerson and Thoreau are the prime American exponents of nature mysticism. Thoreau's travels, as well as his experience at Walden Pond, taught him of the transformative power of nature, and of the wholesomeness and purity of the natural, uncorrupted world. Emerson has a unique blend of religious and nature mysticism: "In the woods we return to reason and

231

faith. Standing on the bare ground, my head bathed by the blythe air and uplifted into infinite space, all mean egotism vanishes. I become a transparent eyeball; I am nothing; I see all; the currents of the Universal Being circulate through me; I am part or parcel of God. I am the lover of uncontained and immortal beauty."

Emerson unites traditional theistic mysticism--the soul is 'oned' with the transcendent God--with nature mysticism, where the soul is merged with the natural world. The practitioners of more conventional religion fear that nature mysticism is a form of idolatry, mistaking the creature for the Creator. But clearly, at least in Emerson's case, the natural world is the sacrament of God's presence, the transparent vehicle of His self-revelation.

In its essence, mysticism is a transformative union with the object of one's devotion. Plotinus, "the father of western mysticism," describes his experience as "being oned with the One." The nature mystic knows the ecstasy of being 'oned' with nature, of being elevated and transformed by the experience of mingling with the universe and feeling what no words can express. Far from being idolatrous, this may be but a step in the direction of showing how short sighted was the mechanistic vision of Descartes and Newton. We are surrounded by a reality we cannot express in words or formulae; we can only open ourselves to the experience, and hope to be "oned" with the mystery that surrounds us. Being fully awake and alert to one's surroundings may be inseparable from some degree of nature mysticism.

IV-138
Constructing a Personal Theology

"What makes my life worthwhile?" is a question with a wide range of possible answers. The first responses are usually on the psychological level. Why do particular events or people provide meaning in my life? What is it that I do that makes me feel good about my everyday experience? Answers to these questions are deeply personal, and while they change from time to time, there is considerable continuity in what satisfies our psychological needs.

On the next level in the quest to make life worthwhile, the appropriate answers are in the philosophical arena. In making life worthwhile, some expression of our personal ethics and values is necessary. Some may have lengthy statements of this, complete with quotations from philosophers ancient and modern. For others, the most basic personal philosophy may only reach the verbal stage in crisis situations, or in moments of blinding insight when there is a sudden realization of what really matters.

Most westerners have clear theological or a-theological convictions. We speak rather glibly of our "Judeo-Christian" heritage, and our culture continually reminds us of the importance of religious beliefs in human history. Nevertheless, Pew and Gallup Polls show that fewer and fewer people go to church or synagogue, and fewer people identify with the religious tradition in which they were raised.

Theology as "reasoned discourse about God" reached its peak in the middle ages with writers like Ibn-Sina, Maimonides, and Aquinas. The conviction that reason could tell you anything important about God was gradually abandoned; God became the object of a "sixth sense," an awareness of the Infinite that was beyond words. Theology as "the feeling of absolute dependence" found its clearest expression among romantic writers of the nineteenth century like Keats and Schleiermacher. For Keats it is a feeling of "creative imagination" that brings you to the God of your personal devotion. Nineteenth century "theology" ended with a series of thinkers who proclaimed the obsoleteness of the religious enterprise. Atheism became fashionable with the writings of Marx, Nietzsche, and Freud. But theology, like philosophy, always manages to bury its undertakers.

Theology in the twentieth century sought desperately to revitalize the numinous elements of the religious traditions. This was exemplified by answers to the century's two greatest concerns. Teilhard de Chardin responded to the triumph of science by inventing an imagery drawn from the scientific concept of evolution. Teilhard wrote that the whole of creation is evolving towards its Omega Point, when all things will indeed return from Whence they came. Alfred North Whitehead responded to the greatest theological problem of the twentieth century, the pervasive problem of evil, by saying that "God is the Great Companion, the fellow-sufferer who understands." Dietrich Bonhoeffer expressed it more captivatingly: "Only a suffering God can help."

Where does that leave us in the twenty-first century? Does the tradition have anything to offer, or have we outgrown all the ancient religious concepts? Has Psychology convinced us that all religious longing is simply an attempt to fulfill childish wishes? Has Modern Philosophy demonstrated that all language about God is misappropriated? Has Theology, as a "science of God," been completely discredited, and is it impossible to build a personal theology that provides answers for our deepest questions of meaning?

There are no off-the-shelf answers to life's leading questions, and each of us must generate answers that are uniquely ours. Ludwig Wittgenstein, the most influential philosopher of the twentieth century, indicated (a) we cannot take someone else's answers as our own, and (b), we need to spend a lifetime exploring our own answers to life's largest questions. Wittgenstein left himself open to the transcendental questions, in formulas that are brief and to the point: "It is not how things are in the world that is mystical, but that it exists." "Feeling the world as limited whole--it is this that is mystical." "We feel that even when all possible scientific questions have been answered, the problems of life remain completely untouched."

We all have a need to construct our own personal "theologies," because we all must come up with distinctively personal answers to what it is that makes our lives worthwhile.

IV-139
Judeo-Christianity and Mysticism

Political campaigns persistently trumpet the importance of our "traditional Judeo-Christian values." While there is much that is similar between Judaism and Christianity, it is a great mistake to lump them together as if they were just two different ways of practicing one religion, or as if one were just a cultural variation of the other. Karen Armstrong's *History of God* shows the similarities among the three great monotheist religions (Judaism, Christianity, Islam), but also delineates the chasm of differences.

Differences between Judaism and Christianity are most apparent when it comes to mysticism. It has been suggested that all religions are simply "institutionalized mysticism," because the root of religion is the propagation of some presumed direct experience of God. There are eminent scholars who claim there is no such thing as 'Jewish mysticism,' precisely because Judaism makes such a clear distinction between the Creator, the Holy One of Israel, and His creation. And there are those who maintain that Christianity is intrinsically mystical, whether rooted in scriptural statements like "I and the Father are One," or in the Pauline mysticism exemplified by repeated expressions of finding "all things in Christ."

One might argue that Judaism is intensely mystical, and that the piety of the Hasidim, a sect that celebrates the joyous ecstasy of the Divine Presence, is a model of what is essential to the practice of Judaism. Such Jewish mysticism is intensely 'this-worldly.' It is based on the Genesis creation narrative where God finds His creation to be "exceedingly good."

The world is God's handiwork, and experience of the world leads the pious Jew directly to God, the Author of all that is "good." The celebrated *mitzvoth*, devotional practices, are meant to be constant reminders of the Presence of God in everyday activities. The Sabbath is resting from trivial activities, to celebrate and delight in the Shekinah, the Divine Presence. What else could mysticism be, but a celebration of the Presence of the Divine?

By contrast, Christian mysticism is generally otherworldly. The basic Christian text is the saying of John: "Do not love the world, or the things of the world." Christianity, in its early years, was heavily infected with a Platonic philosophy that saw this world as but a shadow of the Divine World, and this life as but a testing ground for the Real Life that comes hereafter.

Modern scholarship has a vested interest in emphasizing the continuity between Judaism and Christianity. While the similarities are extensive and important, the differences are deep-seated and pervasive. As Ruth Gelman has written: "Jews work to bring holy spirituality to elevate our everyday, mundane practices." While Christians seek to do the same, Christianity retains an otherworldliness, an emphasis on the transcendent realm to which all things are destined to return. For Christians, the Messiah has come, and matter has been irradiated by the Divine Presence. ("He became flesh, and dwelt among us.") In Christian practice, material things are only symbols and images of the Divine Reality. Judaism, and in particular Jewish mysticism, has always emphasized God's presence in human history, His involvement in everyday affairs, His availability in the reading of the Torah or the discussion of Jewish Teaching. (God's absence in the Holocaust is the scandalous and puzzling noninvolvement of God in human existence.) Christian mysticism is practiced most ardently by monks and nuns in remote monasteries, whereas Jewish mysticism is the everyday responsibility of the devout Jew.

There is a great deal of truth to the notion of a "Judeo-Christian heritage," for the community of beliefs and practices is considerable. But there are deep-seated differences, nowhere more apparent than in the contrasting views of mysticism as practiced by the two faiths. What should not pass unnoticed is the complementariness of the two practices, the need for two different ways of going about the process of being deeply and profoundly religious. In an era of secular dominance, the two approaches have much to offer each other, the world, and all those for whom mysticism is an important component of any understanding of the human predicament.

Gene Bammel

IV-140
Progress!

Nothing characterizes the modern world more than the commitment to progress. Nomadic civilizations are content to repeat for generations the same way of doing things, but we moderns have come to expect signs of progress everywhere. When Francis Bacon wrote *The Advancement of Learning* in 1605, he suggested that the new "scientific method" would produce more new knowledge in the ensuing forty years than had occurred in the previous four thousand. Modern science has produced the appearance of continuous improvement with new technological advances from which everyone can benefit, even without "knowing" any science.

The progress of philosophy is much different. Philosophy does not progress, unless philosophical insights are personally appropriated and applied. I do not need to understand Newton or Einstein to make use of gravity or relativity, but I do need to understand something of Aristotle or Kant if I am to make use of them in the development of my personal philosophy. We all live by the philosophy we have developed; the pity is, so much great philosophy has been done by the philosophical masters, and so little of it has been assimilated by those who most desperately need it. Everyone needs philosophy, and everyone needs to make progress in developing a personal philosophy.

Philosophy has three basic problems. What is real? What can I know? How should I act? An individual's philosophy only progresses by attaining increasingly deeper insights into these problems. Is the external world just an illusion? Do I make up my picture of external reality, and is my picture just as valid as anyone else's? Or is there something "objective" about reality, and do I need to conform my picture to accommodate what others think is really real? All of us have the limits of our knowledge tested daily, as we listen to various reports that make demands on our credibility. What counts as "knowledge" is no small question, and we have to filter the claims of politicians, journalists, scientists, and the innumerable commercial messages we receive each day, to see which pass our "truth" test, and which deserve further debate.

We need deepening insight into the question of how we should act. Should I give to everyone who is in need? Who deserves my attention right now? Should investing be done with a social conscience? Can I come right out and tell boldfaced lies, or must I always tell the truth? Does religion have any claim on me, or anything to say about how I should behave?

236

Do my beliefs affect my political activity? Do I have political or social obligations, or can I safely turn them over to the experts?

So you see, it is not a question of doing or not doing philosophy; philosophical problems enter into our daily existence whether we want them to or not. The real question is simply: how well will we do the job of philosophizing? No one else can philosophize for us, although the tutors out there are endless, and range from Plato to Wittgenstein, and from the famous, to the friend or neighbor who challenges your most basic assumptions. The rewards of philosophy include deepening insight into the human condition, and greater appreciation for what each new day has to offer. Philosophy richly rewards all those who accept the responsibility for doing it; the challenge is to do it as well as possible, and have some sense of making real progress in answering the questions that really matter.

IV-141
Religious Thinking

The twentieth century was a particularly difficult time for practitioners of the world's three great monotheistic religions, Judaism, Islam, and Christianity. All three religions went through three distinctive phases in the last one hundred years.

Phase (1): *Religion is essentially "social gospel."* Early in the twentieth century, some prominent figures from each of the traditions agreed that religion was most properly manifested as social concern. The two most applicable biblical quotations were: "I desire mercy, not sacrifices," and: "How can one claim to love God whom he does not see, if he does not love the neighbor whom he does see?" Religion was interpreted as social concern, commitment to social justice, having compassion on the poor and unfortunate, more than as cultic observance or ritual performance. This led to raising the question: why do you need "religion" at all? Why not just do these social service activities, and leave the religious doctrines and practice behind? And if the goal of religion is to transform society, why not just do the transforming, and leave religion out of it?

Phase (2): With the development of modern science, the conviction spread that *atheism is the irreversible fate of humanity.* Theologians like Paul Tillich said the notion of the transcendental God "out there" was dead, and religion was essentially the expression of an "ultimate concern," whether that was wilderness preservation, world peace, or raising your children to be model citizens. A series of "death of God" theologians built upon the comment of Friedrich Nietzsche that God was dead, and claimed that now humankind was "free" to choose its own destiny, and the superstitious worship of a tyrannical deity was something we were better off without. Rudolph Bultmann and Joseph Campbell convinced two generations that looking for the "truth" behind the myths of biblical literature was the real challenge to those who would be religious. The "divinity" of Jesus came to mean that he was the exemplar or model of what humanity can become, willing to lay down his life for the wellbeing of others. Philosophers like Paul Kurtz and Richard Rorty celebrated the progress of mankind, based on imagining all the citizens of the world living for today, and not for some future heavenly reward.

Phase (3): *Religion is not dead; it only sleeps.* For those who would still be religious, profound expressions of the vitality of religion could be found in various quarters, perhaps most powerfully in the works of Martin Buber, Emmanuel Levinas, and Hans Kung. Martin Buber is best known for his book *I and Thou,* a discussion of what happens when the encounter with another person is found to be an ineffable experience. Buber wrote: "Faith is not a feeling in the soul, but an entrance into reality. It is not to be proved, but to be experienced." Buber claimed that in the greatest depth of human encounters, something of the presence of the divine Thou is experienced. Levinas built on Buber's work, suggesting that the Other is "always beyond me," a Presence that exceeds my grasp, and is best revealed by the sense of responsibility that overcomes every person who experiences a profound ethical demand. Levinas: "We are all responsible for each other, and I--I am most responsible of all." And Levinas said we are all in the position of the various biblical characters that hear the voice of God and respond: "Here I am; send me."

A third resuscitating theologian was Hans Kung. The authentic teachings of the tradition are still believable, and faith is the act of overcoming the negativity and emptiness otherwise presented by daily life. Kung wrote: "If I believe in an eternal life, I know that this world is not the ultimate reality, conditions do not remain as they are forever, all that exists--has a provisional character." The essence of monotheistic religious belief, whether Jewish, Moslem, or Christian, is that God is the central figure in the great drama of reality. He may be variously understood as the Ground of Being, the Fellow Sufferer who understands, or the Simplicity behind complexity. As Kung wrote: "My life will acquire fullness of meaning and the history of humanity reach a confirmation only with the evident reality of God; the ambiguity of life and all that is negative are overcome definitively only by God Himself." The three great monotheist religions continue to practice some form of social gospel, have sought to overcome the reports of the death of God, and have developed theologies that apply the insights of tradition to contemporary reality. In spite of all the challenges of the twentieth century, religion, like philosophy, always manages to bury its undertakers.

Chapter V.
Some Contemporary Concerns

V-142
Which Mad Ludwig?

Ludwig II was King of Bavaria until his death in 1886. He spent most of his rule building castles, castles that had nothing to do with defense of his kingdom, or with the real politics of dealing with Prussia or Austria. Twentieth century philosophy was dominated by another Ludwig, this time an Austrian who spent most of his life in England, was so chronically depressed his life was a constant meditation on suicide, and was so obsessed with logic he periodically translated his sentences into their logical symbols.

Ludwig Wittgenstein was born in 1889 and died in 1951. His life was part of the span of the greatest golden age of logic the world has ever known, beginning with Gottlob Frege about 1870, and culminating with Kurt Gödel, who died in 1937. Frege was convinced that not only should mathematics be reducible to pure logic, so should philosophy! The enduring masterpiece of this search for mathematical absolutes is *Principia Mathematica*, co-authored by Bertrand Russell and Alfred North Whitehead, published in 1910. The best expression of the limits of logic came from Kurt Gödel in the 1930s. This is a succinct expression of his famous theorem: "For any consistent formal system M, a sentence in the language of M can be constructed which is neither provable nor refutable within M." What that means is: no matter how thorough your axioms, you cannot construct a system so perfect that it doesn't need help from the outside.

Wittgenstein was an engineer and mathematician by training, but became interested in the problems of logic, and sought help from Bertrand Russell, at the time a fellow at Cambridge. Within ten years, Wittgenstein had written a brief philosophical masterpiece, called *Tractatus Logico-Philosophicus*, which begins with the sentence: "The world is everything that is the case," which sounds like something a logician might say. Wittgenstein acknowledged obsession with the problem of how he ought to live his life, how he could be in some sense "ethical." Late in the text he says: "It is clear that ethics cannot be expressed. Ethics is transcendental." And further on he writes: "There is indeed the inexpressible. This shows itself. It is the mystical." He concludes the text with an astounding sentence: "Whereof one cannot speak, one must pass over in silence."

Some thirty years later, and a year after his death, his second major book was published, *Philosophical Investigations*. This text contains an extensive philosophy of language, lengthy discourses on other philosophical problems, and retains that same disparagement of philosophy. "So in the end when one is doing philosophy, one gets to the point where one would just like to emit an inarticulate sound."

Wittgenstein thought he had shown the limits of philosophy, that he had demonstrated the emptiness of metaphysical or ethical statements, and that he had proved that philosophy is essentially applied logic. Did Wittgenstein succeed in putting and end to the doing of philosophy? Anthony Kenny, one of the greatest commentators on Wittgenstein, says there will always remain an irreducible core of problems amenable only to philosophy: theory of meaning, epistemology, philosophy of mind, ethics, and metaphysics.

Wittgenstein did much to alter the language and context of modern philosophy. After Wittgenstein, no one can doubt the primacy of logic and the importance of the analysis of language. Part of the achievement of Wittgenstein was an appreciation for just how much his predecessors had achieved. Wittgenstein spent very little time reading his great philosophical antecedents, but he came to appreciate their greatness. As he wrote: "How remarkable that Plato could get so far! Or that we have not been able to get any further! Was it because Plato was so clever?"

Reading any great philosopher leads one back to the key questions: How do I know what I know? How can I be sure of what I know? Are my actions all that they should be? Where does that "should" come from? Philosophy is reborn every time someone asks the most important philosophical question: "What is it that makes my life meaningful?" One would be madder than mad Ludwig not to pay attention to Wittgenstein's aphorism: "We feel that even if all possible scientific questions be answered, the problems of life still have not been touched at all..."

King Ludwig's Neuschwanstein Castle, Germany

V-143
Flight to Mexico

Two of my friends decided to move to Mexico. Major motivation for one was the lower cost of medical care, which she described as "almost as good at a fraction of the cost." The second just wanted to go somewhere where global events with tragic implications would be less frequent.

Most North Americans know little about Canada and less about Mexico. Spanish colonization of Mexico began in earnest in the 1520s--a hundred years before the English became serious about settling the eastern seaboard. The natives encountered by the English were mostly nomads and hunter-gatherers. The natives of Mesoamerica had already established agricultural surpluses, which made large cities possible, and afforded the leisure to develop writing, mathematical systems, astronomical observatories, and sophisticated political and religious practices.

Spain's expropriation of the natural resources--not just gold and silver but the indigenous fruits and vegetables like corn and tomatoes-- sparked rebellion, and by 1821, Mexico gained a troubled independence. In 1846, what Mexicans call "The North American Invasion" removed from Mexican control what are now California, Nevada, Utah, Arizona, New Mexico, and Texas. When those North Americans were engaged in their own civil war, the French saw an opportunity to seize Mexico, and installed the underemployed and idealistic Habsburg Prince, Maximilian, as Emperor.

Benito Juarez, a poor Zapotec Indian who had played a major role in writing a constitution for Mexico, regained the Presidency in 1867, seeking a "Reform" of Mexican politics, based on mutual respect, an independent judiciary, and fair treatment of indigenous peoples.

Upon his death, Porfirio Diaz assumed the presidency, and he "dictated" policy until his death in 1910. On the positive side, he secured foreign aid, developed infrastructure and manufacturing, and sought "modernization" wherever possible. On the negative side, by the time of his death, 90% of Mexican land was owned by 1,000 families. A few of them owned "haciendas" bigger than some American states. Something of this vast difference between the well off and the very poor has characterized Mexico to the present day.

The "Revolution" of 1910 put a "democratic" government in place that controlled Mexican politics until the election of Vicente Fox, a former Coca-Cola executive. Mexico remains a nation with many troubles, much political division but comparatively little social unrest, rich natural resources, and great prospects.

It is said that Mexican "Philosophy" is mostly derivative, debating the problems bequeathed to the modern world by our common European heritage. But there is also something else about Mexican philosophy, for something of the character of the people and of the indigenous concerns keeps coming through. There are two distinctive fascinations that characterize the work of major Mexican philosophers. Issues of social justice dominate the pages of philosophical journals, not without persistent reference to Benito Juarez' search for a way to provide freedom and justice for all, yet peppered with an interest in both Marxism and liberation theology. The second issue raises the delicate matter of religion and politics, church and state, the sacred and the secular. In 1861, the Catholic Church owned about half the land of Mexico. Church holdings were peremptorily secularized, and to this day, the government owns the land on which churches stand.

Mexico is a Catholic country, where churches are within easy walking distance of each other. It is also a country where a very rigid wall separates church and state. It is instructive that while American presidents end their speeches with "God Bless America," Mexican presidents end theirs with: "Viva Mexico," "Long Live Mexico."

The Government has made contraception a national policy, and religious leaders seldom criticize what the President and Congress support. In most respects, Mexico seeks accommodation with the modern world, while preserving its ancient roots. Mexico has huge problems to solve; for example, the smog generated by Mexico City's 20 million inhabitants obliterates the sun on most days. Many of those problems affect the United States: illegal immigration creates a cheap labor pool for American employers, medical and social nightmares for the cities that take care of the indigent. Mexico has wonderful prospects, if it makes headway in solving its political, economic, and social difficulties. For U.S. citizens, the lower cost of health care and the more limited immersion in global politics is hardly reason to move there. But it is a wonderful country to visit, full of friendly people, warm sunshine, lovely beaches, and, oh yes, philosophers whose voices are actually heeded in political assemblies.

Gene Bammel

GPR V-144
Famous Physicists

I have spent my life among people of great intellectual power. (In spite of some appearances to the contrary, universities really do attract and retain people of real brilliance.) When I reviewed promotion and tenure files from every college within the University, I was amazed at the diversity of ways people exercised intelligence. There were physicists and mathematicians whose formulas and theories made my head swim, musicians whose explanations of compound rhythms were spellbinding, specialists in various literatures who found influences and symbolism well beyond what my untutored mind might have discerned.

It is clear that intellectual power manifests itself in many different ways and through many different disciplines. A historian of ideas pointed out that the greatest minds of the thirteenth century turned inevitably to philosophy and theology, while the greatest minds of the twentieth century were attracted to physics. But I wondered, even if this is the case, might not the greatest minds in whatever disciplines, have something profound to say about philosophical and theological issues? Remarks from eight of the greatest physicists of the twentieth century might suggest that, in their heart of hearts, they really were philosophers. From my perhaps somewhat prejudiced point of view, this might indicate that philosophy is really the most important of all disciplines, and that granting PhD's, "doctorates in philosophy," is but public acknowledgment of this simple fact. Read these quotations, and see what you think.

--- Erwin Schrödinger (whose specialty was wave mechanics): "Whence came I, and whither go I? That is the great, unfathomable question, the same for every one of us. Science has no answer to it."

---Albert Einstein, (relativity theory): "Science can only be created by those who are imbued with the aspiration toward truth and understanding. This source of feeling, however, springs from the sphere of religion. Science without religion is lame, religion without science is blind."

---Werner Heisenberg (originator of the uncertainty principle, hence the subject of the bumper sticker: "Heisenberg may have slept here."): "Only by leaving open the question of the ultimate essence of a body, of matter, of energy, etc., can physics reach an understanding of the individual properties of the phenomena that we designate by these concepts, an understanding which alone may lead us to real philosophical insight. The philosophic content of a science is only preserved if science is conscious of its limits."

---Louis de Broglie (moving electrons somehow produce waves): "These scientific theories establish between the phenomena a natural classification, allowing us to sense the existence of an ontological order which is beyond us."

---James Jeans (the evolution of gaseous stars and the nature of nebulae): "God is a mathematician, and the universe begins to look more like a great thought than a great machine."

---Max Planck (nature is not continuous, but comes in discrete points, or quanta): "Those forms of religion which have a nihilistic attitude toward life are out of harmony with the scientific outlook and contradictory to its principles. Science as such can never really take the place of religion."

---Wolfgang Pauli (neutrino as overlooked component of atoms): "From an inner center, the mind seems to move outward, so that the spirit serenely encompasses this physical world, as it were, with its Ideas. This mysticism is so lucid that it sees out beyond many obscurities which we moderns dare not and cannot do."

---Arthur Eddington (proof of the relativity theory): "Whilst I contemplate a spiritual domain underlying the physical world as a whole... there is an immediate knowledge in the minds of conscious beings which lifts the veil in places." Eddington, more than most, wanted to be sure that philosophers and theologians did not base their view of God on some scientific theory: "The religious reader may well be content that I have not offered him a God revealed by the quantum theory, and therefore liable to be swept away in the next scientific revolution." On his office door, Eddington posted this note: "Something unknown is doing we don't know what."

Some simple observations: (1) All of these great physicists were in a sense Platonists, convinced that all reality is imprinted with intelligible form, and that human spirit has the potential for contact with ultimate spirit; (2) all of these physicists deserved tenure in some philosophy department, as did in fact happen to the great mathematician, Alfred North Whitehead; (3) Great brain power, and great intellectual stimulation, continue to manifest themselves in physics labs and other places, inside and outside of university environments. A passion for wisdom seems to characterize all great minds.

(To find these and other quotations from great scientists, see Ken Wilber's book, *Quantum Questions*.)

Mosque at the Citadel, Cairo, Egypt

V-145
What Happened to Islam?

There have been a number of excellent TV documentaries on Islam, such as: "Islam, Empire of Faith." Such programs show the beginnings of Islam, its golden medieval period, and the power of the Ottoman Empire. If you watch a program like this, you may come away asking, "What happened? How is Islam today related to that previous glory?"

The answer is complex, and has political, social, and religious aspects. Tribal warfare was as characteristic of the ancient Middle East as were battles between the various native tribes of North America. Part of the wonder of Muhammad is his success at diminishing such conflicts, and Islam at its best has been very successful at generating a community of interests between peoples of different languages and heritage. Western Political Philosophy has its roots in the quest for the common good that Plato and Aristotle proposed as the glue holding society together. Eastern Political Philosophy found a similar expression in thinkers as various as Confucius and Nagarjuna and the conviction that the wellbeing of the individual family rested in harmony with the rulers of the city, the state, and the region. No such societal visions ever pervaded the Arabic cultures of the Middle East.

Most religions have enjoyed a period when philosophical reflection generated some rational support for religious beliefs. Judaism has benefited from the philosophical genius of Philo of Alexandria in the ancient world, Moses Maimonides in the medieval world, Martin Buber and Emmanuel Levinas in the modern world. Christianity found a Platonic synthesis of sorts with Augustine, an Aristotelian synthesis with Aquinas, and has had its philosophical mettle tested by Kant, Heidegger, and a variety of contemporary philosophers. Both Judaism and Christianity have also had "orthodox" reformers who sought to reject the meddling of the philosophers. In general, philosophers perform a valuable service, by keeping theologians honest. Part of the tragedy of Islam is that, in its attempt to adhere to the Koran, it turned its back on philosophy.

Modern Islam, and particularly the Islam of Saudi Arabia, is dominated by the thought of Muhammad ibn al-Wahhab, who died in 1792, but whose Koranic literalism is taken seriously by those who teach in Saudi-sponsored madrasas. Jews and Christians long ago determined that some passages of their sacred scripture were pertinent to a given time and place, but were not to be taken as literally true. For example, Leviticus 24:13 says: "Take the man who has blasphemed out of the camp, and have all the community stone him to death." Deuteronomy 22:11 says: "You shall not wear clothes woven with two kinds of yarn, wool and flax together. No woman shall wear an article of man's clothing." (Fortunately for Wal-Mart, our culture no longer feels bound by those commands!) Joshua 6:21 says, upon the capture of Jericho: "Destroy everything in the city; put everyone to the sword, men and women, old and young, sheep and cattle." Not even the most destructive modern warfare does that!

The Wahhabi school interprets everything in the Koran literally. And so in Saudi Arabia today, thieves have a hand chopped off, adulterers are stoned to death; women are prevented from playing a major role in public affairs, or even driving. In Iran there are posters displaying the size of stones most effective for stoning someone: not so small as to be painless, not so big as to kill immediately.

The decrees of the Taliban were simply the extreme of Wahhabic Islam. Just a few of their decrees: (1) Anyone who has shaved his beard shall be arrested and imprisoned until the beard grows back. (2) Female doctors and nurses are not allowed to enter rooms where male patients are hospitalized. (3) To prevent kite flying, kite-shops in the city shall be abolished. (4) To prevent music, if a cassette is found in a shop, the shop shall be closed and the shopkeeper imprisoned.

The Hebrew Bible and the Christian Testament lend themselves much more readily to philosophical reflection than does the Koran. Biblical scholars today discuss the "development of doctrine" that occurred over the thousand years or so of biblical writings. One individual wrote the Koran over a period of less than twenty years. It bears the marks both of its brevity and of its desert origins. Surah Rome 41: "Surely Allah does not love the ungrateful who disbelieve." In a lengthier context, or with opportunity for interpretation, that statement might be appropriately modified, but with a literal approach, it could be life threatening.

In the cultures of the Moslem world, there is a tendency to think that God is not only beyond what reason can grasp, He is beyond reason, and beyond what we think of as rational. Jews and Christians are happy to say God is beyond human comprehension, but are loath to say that God is not reasonable. (Einstein: "God does not play dice with the universe."— Which Einstein meant as a rejection of quantum mechanics.) Surah Rome 51 says: "Allah creates whatever Allah will; and Allah is all-knowing, all-powerful." One might argue that Islam has gone too far in stressing the transcendence of God. Even for moderate Sufi writers, God is so transcendent as to be completely incomprehensible.

The literalism of Wahhab is not the only approach to the Koran, nor is it the path most favored by Sunni or Shiite mullahs. No doubt the reform of Islam must come from within Islam, but as several western writers have suggested, there are many helpful hints non-Muslims can convey. Among them, the suggestion that you can be profoundly religious, and a serious reader of sacred scriptures, without feeling obligated to take everything there as literally true.

Religions tend to have some component of universalism. Isaiah 65: "I was there to be sought by a people who did not ask." John 1: "The light was in being, light absolute, enlightening every man born into the world." There are signs of more universal concern in the Koran: "So who fails to be religious? The one who rebuffs the orphan and does not feed the poor. Woe to those who pray, without paying attention to their prayers; they appear to pray, all the while depriving the needy."

Islam is not a religion of murder, violence, or hatred. Perhaps the awakening of Islam to a new golden age is not far off. The powers of darkness that have been so influential, will be overcome by the voice of reason, and all the world will be the better for it.

V-146
Reading The Book of Job Today

Handel's text for the Book of Job, Chapter 19, vs. 25ff. read: "I know that my Redeemer liveth, and that he shall stand at the latter day upon the earth; and though worms destroy this body, yet in my flesh I shall see God."

Translations, and textual analysis have come a long way since Handel's time, and both the Jerusalem Bible and the New English Bible translate the text in this manner: "But in my heart I know that my vindicator lives, and that he will rise last to speak in court; and I shall discern my witness standing at my side, and see my defining counsel, even God himself, whom I shall see with my own eyes, I myself and no other."

Now I am no biblical exegete, nor literary critic. But no one can read the Book of Job without realizing it is a kind of literary masterpiece, replete with all the figures of speech known to the ancient world. Joseph Campbell would point out the "mythical" structure of the book, without demeaning in any way its sacred character. A myth is a story told to point to a deeper truth. The Book of Job begins: "There lived in the land of Uz a man of blameless and upright life named Job who feared God and set his face against wrongdoing." And then the story unfolds of Job's tribulations, and of his foolish comforters who try to explain to him why bad things happen to good people. The book ends with this sentence: "Thereafter Job lived another hundred and forty years, he saw his sons and his grandsons to four generations, and died at a very great age." The beginning and end indicate the "story" character of the narrative, and excuse the reader from taking the events as literally true. But for all who have experienced how unfair life can be, and have seen good people suffer while others of dubious merit have prospered, the Book of Job offers sources of timely earnest reflection.

How does one read the Bible? I have listened to, and learned much from, biblical scholars, but I note there is great disparity among them. I favor the interpreters, whose work is well exemplified at this website: www.Quodlibet.net/. With respect to the Hebrew Bible, I find great help from: www.Tikkun.org/. A very different approach occurs in www.messiahrevealed.org/. I lament that so many modern people dismiss the Bible as a book no longer relevant, I rejoice that so many literature departments offer courses in the Bible as Literature, and I wonder at the religious establishments who struggle to see to it that the Bible is kept relevant for modern people.

Even thoroughly modern people can wonder that so many evildoers seem to prosper, and so much wickedness appears to go unpunished. Philosophers from Plato to John Rawls have struggled with the concept of justice: justice means doling out to everyone what is due them. Does justice permit revenge? Is vengeance part of justice? And how is justice to be tempered by mercy? Elie Wiesel, on the fiftieth anniversary of the liberation of Auschwitz, said: "Merciful God, do not have mercy on those who had no mercy." And the philosopher Robert Solomon (no relation to the King) wrote: "The emotions are the stuff of which our conceptions of justice are constructed and in which they remain anchored. Without emotion, without caring, a theory of justice is just another numbers game."

Injustice arouses our emotions, and the events of 9/11, 2001, aroused American emotions like few other events in modern history. Those better versed in the Bible, of a greater religious bent than I, may find appropriate texts to channel or direct their anger. I take some consolation from Isaiah 57:21: "There is no peace for the wicked." And I find my work vindicated to some degree by Isaiah 50:4: "The Lord God has given me the tongue of a teacher, and skill to console the weary with a word in the morning; he sharpened my hearing, that I might listen like one who is taught." Finally, the theologian Hans Kung has written that his conviction about personal immortality is bolstered by the fact that justice is not always accomplished in this life. The Book of Job is as relevant today as when it was written. Why do good people suffer, while at least some of those who delight in inflicting pain on others, seem to prosper? A modern version of the book of Job might well begin with the refrain: "There ain't no justice." Then, the book would go on, trying to convince the reader that justice and fairness always win out, but finally admitting that the problem is simply beyond human comprehension.

V-147
High Costs of Higher Education

If you are, or will be, paying the costs of higher education, you may well ask: How come higher education suddenly costs so much? For several years, tuition hikes at most state universities have increased by 5%, to 10%, or more. As state legislatures decrease the amount of state funding, the demands on parents and students are only likely to increase. While the financial and personal returns of higher education are unquestionable, the escalating costs have generated many questions both about how much students should pay, and what constitutes the character of the education received.

Parents and students are surprised to learn that tuition covers less than 20% of the expenses of running a university. Fairly typical of the revenue sources of most major state universities is the following account from one major university: State Appropriations 35%; Gifts, Grants, and Contracts, 31%, Tuition, 20%, Investment Income, Services, and Federal Support, 14%.

Where does the money go? 45% is spent on Instruction and Student Services, Research 12%, Public Service 8%, and the rest is divided up between Scholarships and Plant Upkeep. Personnel salaries make up about 85% of total expenditures in each category.

The budgets of major universities exceed a billion dollars annually. If you visit any major campus, from Harvard to UCLA or any institution in-between, you will be surprised at the size of the campus and the numbers of students and faculty milling about. What you will not see is the tremendous cost of the infrastructure, ranging from advanced technological devices in research laboratories, to the vastness of library holdings, or the intricacies of student services, including Internet connections, recreation facilities, and arrangements for student security in dormitories and classrooms.

This leaves the much larger questions unanswered. What are all these physical facilities for, and what is the goal of this large investment in human potential?

I was a member of a response team to a legislative initiative entitled: "Higher Education: Preparation for Life's Work." Taken for granted in the initiative was the conviction that the primary purpose of higher education was to prepare people for financially rewarding employment in the new, postindustrial economy. While it is clear that legislators can best sell the funding of higher education to their constituents by convincing them that it will improve the employment prospects of their offspring, interpreting higher education simply in terms of its vocational or technical training fails to grasp what is at the heart of the educational endeavor.

Whether the purpose of higher education is understood in terms of unleashing the human potential, or of preparing for citizenship, something more grandiose than vocational or technical training is at the nucleus of higher education. Being successful in a career is something of a byproduct of having a larger vision of one's role in society, of one's growth as a human being and as a member of many different communities.

Where funding comes from for higher education, how much a society should spend on educating its youth, and the content of educational programs are very large questions. For the benefit of society, higher education must remain a priority budget item both in family finances, and in state legislatures. Aristotle was not just whistling in the dark when he said that the fate of empires depends upon the education of youth. Education is too important to be left in the hands of legislators, unless, that is, they are educated enough to know that a state can have no higher priority than the education of its citizens, whether children, adolescents, adults, or even senior citizens.

V-148
Pain Management

Few of us are exempt from feeling pain from to time. . Pain is a good thing, because it tells us something is wrong. But too much of a good thing is a bad thing. And too much pain can be a very bad thing.

In case such a bad thing comes your way, you might want to remember that there are four dimensions to successful pain management. The first and most obvious is appropriate medication. For minor pains, aspirin, acetaminophen, ibuprofen, and other such analgesics, usually work very well. For more serious, prolonged pain, your medical professional's pharmacopoeia will find the best answer. Even with expert assistance, different dosages and even different drugs may have to be checked out, before the best answer is found.

The second dimension of pain management is meditation. Innumerable biofeedback experiments have demonstrated that there is a mind over matter phenomenon, and that meditation carefully practiced can help overcome even the most intense pains. Deep breathing, focusing on a single number or a soothing image, and telling your body to quiet itself, can all contribute to the management of discomfort.

Exercise is a third dimension. Some people who are in intense pain find any form of movement out of the question, but for most pain sufferers most of the time, some simple, regular form of exercise will contribute to the reduction of pain's intensity. One woman who suffered intense pain claimed that working in her garden, and then walking calmly around in it, was the best therapy she ever discovered.

As part of the mind over matter issue, concentrating or focusing attention on some one activity may be a very effective palliative. A professor I knew many years ago had a body devastated by various illnesses. Preparing and teaching classes, as well as the concentration necessary to produce articles for publication, was his most effective therapy. If you canvass the volunteers at almost any volunteer organization, you will find several who will testify that the best way to mitigate their own pain is to focus on some service to others.

Every religion includes some forms of worship, some approaches to prayer. For some religious believers, petitionary prayer, asking God or the gods to do something, is the most important aspect of religion. But most religions affirm that the highest form of prayer is at-one-ment with the all, or being at peace with the universe, or with the Creator and Designer of the universe. However, as one minister was fond of saying: "Do you think God needs to be reminded of your pain?" Among the theologians of almost any religion, you will find discussions of Acceptance, or Resignation, or Obedience to the Tao, as the highest fulfillment of religious belief. Although there is lively controversy over various aspects of religious healing, statistics are clearly in favor of those who find religious belief and practice as important approaches to dealing with pain.

A famous scholar of religion was attending a world congress of religions in India. His roommate happened to be an editor of a magazine of skeptical inquiry. Both had attended an afternoon session which featured a Sanyasin who proclaimed that since the god of healing was blind, you needed to ring a little bell to remind the god of your needs, and what part of your body was hurting. On the way to their lodging, the skeptical roommate fell through a grating, cutting his body badly enough to need medical attention. The scholar of course assisted his suffering roommate in every way he could, and as he was leaving the next morning asked if he could get anything for him. "Well, you could get me one of those little bells," came the reply....

V-149
A Brief History of Philosophy

If you always knew you should take a history of philosophy course, but never had the time, here is the briefest history imaginable. If you have had a very good course in the history of philosophy, this might help reorganize your knowledge. For all practical purposes, Western Philosophy begins with Socrates. For whatever reason, a peculiar passion for rational inquiry developed in the northern Mediterranean, about six hundred years B.C.E. The Athenian Greeks developed an unusual interest in asking difficult questions, not only about how a city should be organized, but also about how people should go about living their lives.

Socrates was the most passionate inquirer among them all, so much so that he antagonized his fellow Athenians, and they accused him not only of not believing in the traditional gods, but of actually corrupting the young, by his ceaseless questioning. On trial for his life, and asked why he carried on this relentless questioning, he replied: "The unexamined life is not worth living." That may seem like a rather bland statement, but it is the foundation stone of Western Philosophy. Philosophy is simply passionate, relentless questioning, particularly about those matters that everyone takes for granted, or that seem so simple, no one need inquire about them. When asked the reason for such endless inquiry, Socrates replied: "Remember, it is no ordinary matter we are discussing, but how we are to live our lives."

The Dialogues of Plato are dramatic applications of the various questions the historical Socrates presumably asked. After the death of his master, Plato took upon himself not only to illustrate the kinds of questions Socrates debated, but also to create a Theory of Ideas, --a discussion of the nature of knowledge and how we come to know-- that probably went far beyond the actual questions of the historical Socrates.

Aristotle was a student of Plato's, and might be called the first great encylopedist, for he attempted to synthesize all the knowledge available in his time. Accordingly, he wrote texts on biology, physics, astronomy, ethics, and politics. His most enduring work however, is a treatise that might be called: What is the nature of reality? Since it seemed to cover so much more than Physics, a Greek librarian called it "Meta-physics," that which comes after studying Physics, or physical reality.

Over the next several centuries, philosophy developed many new modes of expression, as found in the works of Stoics and Skeptics, as well as new followers of Plato, appropriately called, Neo-Platonists. Philo, a Jew living in Alexandria, attempted to reconcile the Hebrew Scriptures with the writings of Plato. Four centuries later, the Christian writer Augustine attempted something similar. For the next thousand years, religious and philosophical questions are inseparable, and some brilliant philosophizing is done in a religious context, by thinkers as different as the Moslem Avicenna, the great Jewish teacher Maimonides, and the Christian Thomas Aquinas.

Descartes, who died in 1650, established the modern approach of rationalism: all problems are solvable if you just think rationally enough. British empiricism, an approach pioneered by John Locke, is the antidote to all this rationalism, maintaining that, no matter how clear your thinking, if you don't have good down-to-earth evidence for what you are saying, you are just whistling in the wind.

Kant is the central figure of modern philosophy. To paraphrase Senate inquiries, the key philosophical question becomes: What can I know, and how can I claim to know it? Modern philosophy is obsessed with the question of the nature of knowledge, in part brought on by Kant's awareness that "science" seemed to be so successful at answering questions decisively, while philosophy belabored the same old dilemmas.

Kant's offspring range from the "Idealism" of Hegel, the inverted idealism of Karl Marx, the Positivism that culminates in the work of Wittgenstein, the very American Pragmatism of John Dewey, and the varieties of existentialist response from Kierkegaard to Martin Buber.

Contemporary Philosophy has not yet cured itself of the malady of what is called "Post-Modernism." Comic writers of the late nineteenth century had already parodied the theme of post-modernism: "When I use a word, it means just want I want it to mean, that's all." Academic philosophy departments have sometimes seen themselves as simply logic departments, analyzing the logic of language, and helping to determine what makes for good scientific inquiry. That process drove many traditional philosophers to history, or history of ideas departments, to comparative literature programs, or to "applied philosophy" in medical, law, or business schools.

But Socratic Inquiry is making a comeback. When the work of the logicians is done, when scientists have had their say, the really important questions remain unanswered. Philosophical questions constitute the beginning and the terminus of all rational questioning. What Socrates said is as true today as it was 2500 years ago: the unexamined life is not worth living, and what we are doing in philosophy is no trivial matter, for when we do philosophy, we are trying to come to grips with the meaning behind the conduct of our very lives. Philosophy cannot do without its history, nor can the human race prosper, without the doing of philosophy. This history is much too brief, but the History of Philosophy will be around for as long as there are human beings to raise big questions.

Gene Bammel

V-150
Philosophy as Enlightenment

Socrates is the cornerstone figure of western philosophy, with his passion for inquiry, his commitment to rational argument, and his conviction that reasoning things through is one of the most admirable capacities of human beings. *The Dialogues of Plato* are dramatic illustrations of Socrates using his capacity for clear thinking about moral issues, demonstrating to generals that they really do not know what courage is, to city officials that they do not have a clear notion of what justice is, and to just about everyone, that they think they know what they do not really know. Socrates somewhat reluctantly accepts the oracle's saying that he is the wisest man in Athens, just because he alone knows that he does not know.

Modern Anglo-American philosophy has emphasized the passion for logic and clear thinking, but has minimized that other characteristic of Socratic philosophy, the passion for enlightenment. In the Socratic tradition, enlightenment means knowledge of who you really are. It means being free from illusions, and above all it means going about living your life as if it really mattered.

Having found a firm basis for knowledge, Immanuel Kant explicitly proclaimed the goal of his philosophy as the attainment of enlightenment. He begins his famous essay on Enlightenment with two Latin words: *Sapere aude*, "Dare to think for yourself." The point of the essay is a simple one: do not be guided by illusions; do not believe something just because someone has told you so. Be responsible for your own ideas, as well as your own decisions.

Having determined that city life and drawing room conversations were not helping him to progress as a human being, Henry David Thoreau retreated to Walden Pond, where he wrote: "Most men lead lives of quiet desperation." A century and a half ago, Thoreau was concerned about the budding American consumer culture, and he warned that happiness did not lie in what you had, but in what you were. His writings are unlikely to be quoted in advertisements for consumer goods, for he says things like: "The more you have of such things, the poorer you are."

Modern psychologists are often the most outspoken advocates for the enlightenment tradition of philosophy. Erich Fromm wrote: "The main task in life is to give birth to yourself." And an influential modern psychologist, Abraham Maslow, wrote: "If you set out to be less than you are really capable of being, you will be deeply unhappy for the rest of your life." That is wonderful testimony to the tradition of philosophy as self-knowledge, and of the passion for Enlightenment as inseparable from awareness not only of who you are, but who you are capable of becoming.

Not even this brief glance at Philosophy as Enlightenment can exclude the Buddha, who explicitly sought Enlightenment, and did so by forgetting himself, by becoming so immersed in the stream of reality that a separate consciousness, or self-consciousness, became a burden. Nor can it exclude Stoic writers like Marcus Aurelius, whose prime concern was Mastery of the Emotions, and whose watchword became: "Discipline thyself." It must also include the personalism of a Martin Buber, and his famous phrase, "I only become an I, in relation to a Thou." We are indeed social beings, and we can only be enlightened by our involvement with others, both by what we do for them, and what they do for us.

"Enlightenment" has two senses: it means being awake to your world and your surroundings, but also an enlightened being is one whose burdens are lighter, and who will spread good cheer to others. It has been said that angels can fly, because they take themselves lightly...

V-151
Something Was Lost...

A century ago, "higher education" meant some exposure to the Classics of Greek and Roman literature. In most colleges and universities, at least one professor in ten was busy teaching students how to read Latin or Greek. As vocationalism and professional preparation came to dominate American higher education, the role of the Classics, and the prevalence of Classics professors, rapidly diminished.

While much has been gained by this process of modernization, something irreplaceable was lost. You cannot know who you are, unless you have some knowledge of where you came from. The popularity of books like *Founding Brothers* and *John Adams* and others about early American patriots shows Americans have a great interest in understanding the source of their values and the origins of the American form of government. Novels with political themes are always popular, while movies on the Revolutionary and Civil Wars attract large audiences.

The roots of American democracy are not in eighteenth century figures, but in the writings of Plato and Aristotle. The liveliest discussions of how to live the good life are not in self-help books, but in the writings of Cicero, Seneca, and Marcus Aurelius. To have no knowledge of the classical roots of the problems we face is to have a very large educational deficiency. As we face the "clash of civilizations" that dealing with terrorists imposes, we desperately need some clarity in understanding how civilizations can be quite diverse, yet have a community of interests. We need to understand how political convictions can appear to be irreconcilable, yet be resolved by reasonable reflection.

In terms of self-knowledge, and in particular about accepting the aging process, no writer has expressed it better than Cicero: "A person who lacks the means to lead a good and happy life will find any period of his existence wearisome. But rely for life's blessings on your own resources, and you will not take a gloomy view of any of the inevitable consequences of nature's laws. Everyone hopes to attain an advanced age, yet when it comes, they all complain!"

One could argue that the greatest single writer of Roman antiquity was the emperor Marcus Aurelius. No wielder of great political power was ever more aware of the universality of humanity, nor of the lack of real distance between those who lived in palaces and those who were homeless. If, in your daily rounds you have to deal with people who are sometimes difficult, listen to what Marcus Aurelius has to say: "In the morning say to yourself: today I shall meet with the busybody, the arrogant person, the ungrateful, and people who are deceitful, envious, or antisocial. All these things happen to them by reason of their ignorance of what is good and evil. But since you know the nature of the good that it is beautiful, and of the evil that it is ugly, and that the nature of the person who does wrong is the same as your human nature, do not let yourself be injured by any of them, do not be angry with those who wrong you, nor let yourself hate them. For we are made for cooperation, just like the rows of the upper and lower teeth. To act against one another is simply contrary to nature, and makes no sense."

Harvard and Yale (and Henrico College in Virginia) were founded as Divinity schools, for the training of Christian ministers. Curiously their training involved a mastery of Greek and Latin literature, and familiarity with the writings of Cicero, Marcus Aurelius, and a whole host of "pagan" authors. For us today, not to be familiar with them is to be cut off from some of the wellsprings of who we are. How are we to help other cultures get back on their feet, unless we understand more of the common humanity we all share, and unless we cultivate a finer sense for the authors of classical antiquity? Clearly we have gained much by our commitment to education as preparation for professions, but we lose something irreplaceable, if we permit ourselves to grow callous to cultivating our humanity, which is best done by some reading of the texts of the great masters of classical antiquity.

V-152
The Morrill Act

Justin Morrill of Vermont had been a member of the House of Representatives for seven years, and had fashioned several bills to foster education in those skills Americans most desperately needed. On July 2, 1862, with a devastating civil war in its early stages, Abraham Lincoln signed into law the Morrill Act, "donating public lands to the several states and territories which may provide colleges for the benefit of agriculture and the mechanic arts." More than eleven million acres were sold, and successive congressional actions saw to it that each state, whether tiny Rhode Island, or huge Texas, would reap "perpetual" benefits. Every state has at least one land-grant institution, and the original intentions of Justin Morrill have been attended to faithfully, while the size and success of the land grant ideal would leave him speechless.

Part of the land grant legislation was to make education accessible to all. As Townsend Harris phrased it: "Open the doors to all...Let the children of the rich and the poor take their seats together and know of no distinction save that of industry, good conduct, and intellect." Education was to be primarily practical but not devoid of classical learning, and was to be as inexpensive as possible.

The most frequently quoted statement about the Morrill Act is the following: "We must keep our root system in the people. Land-grant institutions should take a much more active outreach in the state's public education system, and at the same time serve as an engine of economic growth." When William Friday said that, he probably did not realize that virtually every university administrator speaking to the general public or to members of a state legislature would begin requests for funding by quoting at least part of that statement.

What is the situation of universities today? Thanks to the Morrill Act, American education is very much the envy of the world. Land-grant universities have taught the agricultural and mechanical arts, and have gone on to teach the whole range of human knowledge. They have become major research centers, and have developed new ways to enter into public service.

In recent years, England has sought to make higher education much more widely available; Germany has expressed concern that its higher educational system fails to turn out people who are prepared to work in an increasingly technological society, while Spain has produced more college graduates than its economy can employ. While some form of the American model has been adopted throughout Europe, state legislatures in America, faced with budget shortfalls, have been cutting back on state funding for higher education, and land-grant universities have been hit especially hard in the process.

American colleges and universities have been engines of economic growth, and more importantly, they have enriched the lives of almost everyone who has had the opportunity to reap benefits from participation in higher education. Many citizens who have never set foot on a university campus have benefited from university research, from extension programs, and from the community involvement universities have engendered.

A most perceptive comment on the importance of the land-grant approach to higher education came from the founder of Common Cause, John Gardner: "An excellent plumber is infinitely more admirable than an incompetent philosopher. The society which scorns excellence in plumbing because plumbing is a humble activity and tolerates shoddiness in philosophy because philosophy is an exalted activity will have neither good plumbing nor good philosophy. Neither its pipes nor its theories will hold water."

The Morrill Act promoted a philosophy of education that is both practical and theoretical. Sometimes the most practical of all knowledge is theoretical; but there is no doubt that society only prospers when it knows how to solve its most practical problems. If Justin Morrill could convince Abraham Lincoln to establish the Land-Grant system in the midst of the trying times of the Civil War, higher education deserves appropriate financial support, even in these trying budgetary times.

V-153
Moral Acts

You cannot get through a day without running into serious questions of morality. Like it or not, you cannot resolve your daily round of moral problems, without resorting to philosophy. Today, as in the time of Socrates, moral relativism is very much the fashion. Moral relativists claim that reason does not really help us solve our moral dilemmas, because morality is simply a matter of what satisfies us emotionally. Such relativists say: "Murder, ugh!" Child pornography is wrong, because it is emotionally repulsive. But is it just the emotional response to acts of terrorism that shows how "wrong" they are?

The emotions with which we respond to certain actions may be a good starting point for moral reflection, but there are good reasons why we find some actions morally admirable and others despicable. The moral reasoning we do with children begins with the language of right and wrong, just as the insanity defense in the courtroom is based on being able to distinguish right from wrong. If an action is "right," not only do we prescribe that it should be done, we are somehow disposed to stretch our prescription from this individual action here and now, to any similar action in all times and places. From such human experience, society develops a rule-based ethic, a morality to which we are invited to subscribe, because long human experience has shown that certain forms of behavior work, while forbidden behavior does not.

Moralists seem especially fascinated with honesty. Every moral code has some rule about not telling lies. An extreme form of rule-based morality says, you can never tell a lie in any circumstance, because society breaks down if you cannot depend on people telling the truth. Such an absolute morality fails in test cases where telling the truth would obviously cause some great catastrophe. Professor Alan Dershowitz of Harvard Law School says a purely rule-based morality can be seen to be inadequate in the case of terrorism. The normal rule is that you do not torture people, including prisoners. But if you have a prisoner who knows where and when a nuclear device is set to explode, would it not be the moral thing to do, to torture that individual, so that we might save innumerable people?

A larger moral theory acknowledges how helpful rules are in promoting morality, but insists that the goal of moral behavior is doing what is good, and that in the long run, what is "right" is what leads to "the good." The challenge lies in making judgments about the hierarchy of goods. In the case of the terrorist, it is not good for him to be tortured, but there is the higher good of saving the lives of many people. (One might also argue that engaging in Terrorism places the perpetrator "outside the moral sphere," where normal rules of morality do not apply.) In the case of deliberate deception, the good of the life of the person you may be saving by telling a crazed killer his intended victim is not there, when the person is right beside you, is a greater good than the practice of honesty in all times and all places.

Each day brings with it a variety of moral dilemmas. In the midst of the South African AIDS epidemic, local priestesses told men that the cure for AIDS is having sex with a virgin, with the consequence that very young girls were being raped. The moral question is not just how can such stupidity be rampant, but what moral demand is made upon the person becoming aware of such inhuman practice, to intervene and prevent further horror? The finger of guilt will forever be pointed at those who knew of the Nazi death camp horrors, and did nothing to stop them. Morality is not just "private behavior," for it measures our involvement as citizens of a much wider world.

Moral judgment may begin as emotional reaction to particular situations, but it is rooted in a perception of right and wrong, a reasoned description of what is good behavior, and what detracts from "the good" that should be attained. Reason may not be able to resolve all moral dilemmas, but our actions, and the moral judgments we are called upon to make everyday, stand to benefit immensely from rational reflection on what it means to be a moral agent, what it means to be responsible, what it means to identify what is good, and how to accomplish it. To be human is to be a moral agent, and becoming fully human, requires being prepared for the demands of moral excellence that come our way. Our moral decisions do much to express who we really are, and what we are becoming. This is no trivial matter; as Abraham Lincoln said early in his career: "I will prepare myself, and when the time comes, I will be ready."

V-154
Political Morality and the Middle East

We all like to pretend that politics is somebody else's problem, and that our personal involvement doesn't really matter. By the very fact that we are all moral agents, that our moral activity reaches into everything we do, and that many of our actions have consequences that reach far into the political arena, we are involved in politics, whether we want to be or not. Given the global village (or better, "global city") our world has become, we each have a very direct interest and involvement in global politics. Political problems in other parts of the world are also our problems. Middle-Eastern expert Stephen Cohen wrote: "This Israeli-Palestinian war is not just a local ethnic conflict that we can ignore. It resonates with too many millions of people, connected by too many satellite TV's with too many dangerous weapons." Journalist Tom Friedman cited an Arab student who said that eight small suitcase sized nuclear bombs could eliminate the whole problem of Israel. It is frightening that the world has come to this, frightening that a student could say such a thing, frightening that such a catastrophe is indeed possible, and terrifying that the situation in any part of the world could lead to a global nuclear holocaust.

The world of just a few years ago was divided into a small number of absolutist camps. Several religions claimed to have the one true orthodoxy, and hurled anathemas on other religious approaches. In the political sphere, a Soviet premier promised an American president that his grandchildren would live under socialism. All the while, American politicians hoped that we could make the world "safe for democracy."

As the shortcomings of every form of absolutism were revealed, the western world retreated to a moral relativism, an acceptance that tastes and social customs differed, and that the morals of certain groups of people were in fact incompatible with the moral visions of some other group. "Live and Let Live" became the accepted truism. Nevertheless, in the midst of espousing this moral relativism, it was not difficult to identify some behavior that was simply unacceptable. It was clear that while some matters could be left up to personal choice, down deep there was a "human dimension" that simply could not be violated. Wherever genocide occurred, moral outrage followed.

Rejections of relativism and pleas for pluralism often came from unlikely quarters. Early in the twentieth century, Ataturk, the father of modern Turkey, proclaimed that while countries might vary, civilization was one, and that for any part of the world to isolate itself, was to fail in the civilizing process. Turkey is still unique in that part of the world, for the pluralist vision represented by Ataturk has not been the pattern for the nations of the Middle East. Is it the case that the path away from absolutism and to pluralism, must first pass through some form of relativism?

Ishai Menuchin, a Major in the Israeli Defense Forces, wrote that it is "morally impossible to be both a devoted democratic citizen and a regular offender against democratic values." He is committed to fighting for the independence of Israel, but he declines to "undertake acts of repression aimed at the entire Palestinian population." His moral and political dilemma is not uncommon. Reinhold Niebuhr, one of the most influential Christian theologians of the twentieth century, in his book *Moral Man and Immoral Society*, explained how difficult it is to be a moral person, when you are surrounded by those who would treat you immorally. Niebuhr posed the question: How can your political action be moral, when those who oppose you, do not share your sense of what is or is not moral? This question divides moralists to this day. Alan Dershowitz has said terrorists act "outside the moral sphere," and hence it is moral to torture a terrorist so that some malicious plot may be thwarted; on the other hand, the Israeli Supreme Court has determined that it is never permissible to torture a captive, even to save the lives of others.

Conflicts in the Middle East have the capacity to escalate into a devastation that could engulf us all. Many of the test cases for the resolution of global political issues have Middle Eastern signatures. Books like *Understanding The Contemporary Middle East* by Deborah Gerner and Jillian Schwedler, can help separate fact from fiction in an area in which so many people know so many things that just aren't true. The larger moral and political question remains unanswered: how do you respond morally, to those who would act globally, with terrorist actions that could be disruptive of civilization itself? The only escape is the phrase with which Ph.D. dissertations usually end: "much more research needs to be done."

V-155
Morals

A Professor of Ethics at the University of Toronto used to begin his oversubscribed classes with this admonition: "The very taking of this course will place a higher standard on your moral behavior." That warning alone would bring the class size down to more acceptable numbers.

Morality is something like time: as long as nobody asks us to explain it, we know exactly what it is. Just as Socrates tripped up so many Athenians who thought they knew what the various virtues were, so do most of us get caught up short when we try to explain the basis of our moral convictions.

We do not live in a homogeneous moral culture. A time there was when most members of a community shared some basic religious upbringing, and the elements of moral reflection were taken in with mother's milk. Not only have religious convictions fragmented, the numbers of people who identify themselves as "secular humanists," or who have deliberately stepped away from any religious affiliation, grow every year. The comfortable world of certain and unquestioned moral convictions has simply vanished.

We do not need the testimony of Toynbee, Gibbon, or Spengler to point out how civilizations collapse when agreement on basic moral issues cannot be reached. Some component of the decline and fall of every great civilization has been accompanied by the collapse of public morality, the absence of agreement on what is right and wrong, even the cessation of dialogue on moral matters. In America, we appear to have consensus on some moral issues: we shudder at the thought of pedophilia; we incarcerate mothers who have taken the lives of their children, and we condemn terrorism in all its forms as a contemptible crime against humanity. But we are clearly divided on such issues as gay marriage, abortion, and euthanasia.

How do we decide what is moral and what is immoral, what is right and what is wrong, and what "situations" allow for the bending of particular rules? The prescription against taking the life of another is easily suspended when your own life is in danger. One of the longest debates in western philosophical history centers around the justice of war. In the last hundred years, the debate has moved from defending yourself when your life or your country is threatened, to the deliberate taking of life in capital punishment, then to whether abortion is the taking of innocent human life, and finally to euthanasia, the taking of life when living has become unbearable.

Are some crimes so hateful, that the appropriate punishment for the perpetrator is the taking of his or her life? Does capital punishment work as an effective deterrent to others who might commit such a crime? Does a fetus gradually become a human being, or is it human from the instant of conception? Is there a certain level of pain no one should have to tolerate, even if death is the only release?

Moral reflection begins with questions of what increases or decreases the amount of good in the world. There are no completely private acts, for each of my actions involves others, and presumably each of my thoughts in some way affects my relations with others. If I am in the habit of thinking kindly towards others, my actions are likely to be much different than if I think of every person as an obstacle in my way. Whether I choose to wear orange or green today may have no apparent moral consequence, but if I happen to choose clothing that is in some way offensive to those I encounter, it becomes a matter of some moral consequence. The presumption is that pornography is not private, for the viewing of it will influence the attitude and the behavior of the viewer.

As a free society, we are committed to fostering as much freedom of choice and expression as possible. But amidst all this freedom, what do we do to educate the public about making "free" decisions that are also moral? Can the news media be responsible for continuing moral education of the general public? Should not *Continuing Education* be an integral part of every college degree, because new questions arise, new contexts develop, and minds must be opened to new approaches to old problems? Most professions have conferences whose avowed purpose is updating the skills of the respective professionals. But we have nothing comparable for updating the skills of the general public in terms of increasingly complex moral realities.

Rabbis, priests, ministers and imams often claim people need synagogues, churches and mosques, because we all need to be preached to, we all need to be admonished, we all need to be awakened to the ever new moral demands that are placed upon us. The vision of the Professor who said taking his class would impose a higher moral standard on all those who took it, should be much more widespread. Those who have taken such courses no longer have the excuse of not having thought long and deeply about the moral matters we all take for granted. While we might wish the rest of the world would tune in to a higher level of moral reflection, such deeper thinking must begin at home. There's no escaping it. Just by reading this page, the demands upon your moral life have been raised. What are you going to do about it?

V-156
A Celibate Priesthood?

To those who would cultivate some form of spiritual life, and to those who regard moral action as the manifestation of personality, the recent saga of pedophile priests is most disheartening. The Catholic Church is not inclined to discuss the issue of celibacy, but it is clearly a critical concern.

The first question is: Why require priests and nuns to be celibate? Catholic writers provide three answers. The theological response: the celibate individual gives witness of the life that is to come, "where there is no marrying or giving in marriage." The celibate individual shows, by his or her example, that "life in Christ" is more important than any possible earthly concern, no matter how biologically based.

The second response has its roots in the New Testament. In the letters of Paul, he says the unmarried man may be busy about the Lord's business. This has been interpreted to mean that the priest, brother, or nun, having no family of their own, can devote themselves completely to their religious duties, ranging from prayer, to social service, to spreading the word of God.

The third answer is that the chaste, celibate life is in some way holy, set apart, in the sense of the Hebrew word kadosh, meaning something that is "completely other," transcendent, not part of everyday expectations. Just as we notice someone who is exceptionally tall or short, so the celibate person appears as one set aside from the normal course of events, different, in some way, sacred. The celibate life is presumably an act of witnessing to the total commitment to holiness made by the individual, and to the primacy of the sacred.

There is an economic dimension to celibacy: as Jewish and Protestant congregations are well aware, it costs more to support "a clerical family," than to support just one individual. The very large sums the Catholic Church is paying out in lawsuits may do much to neutralize the validity of this as a reason for celibacy.

Can celibacy in the modern world be justified? Whatever any individual wants to do for noble purposes certainly deserves admiration, but for any organization to demand of its members something that so goes against the grain of human nature is certain to be a source of problems. Catholic seminarians are prone to say: "Yes it is an unnatural existence, and we can only do it because of God's grace." As recent events show, that supernatural assistance is not always forthcoming, or something is drastically wrong with the capacity to comply.

Some will say that just as it took the Catholic Church centuries to accept the discoveries of Galileo, it will take centuries to assimilate the teachings of Freud and the insights of modern psychology. There is more to it than that. First of all, quite apart from biological imperatives, there is a matter of maturation as a human being, developing a capacity to love and receive love, and all the other aspects of maturity that are brought about by the effort to develop a loving relationship. Quite apart from the odd situation of a celibate Catholic priest giving marital advice, there is the element of only being expert about something when you know it from extensive personal experience.

There is another easily overlooked but extremely important issue. In our own personal growth, we do reveal ourselves to ourselves, action by action. No seventeen-year old, and no forty year old, really knows all the dimensions of his or her personality. Seminarians who today reject pedophilia and homosexuality as abominations, may, with the passage of years, find those dispositions as long latent parts of their personalities. As someone once wisely said, it is much easier to find a young saint, than an old one.

Widely accepted statistics show that about 5% of priests are in fact homosexual, about the same as the general population. When all the dust has settled, probably fewer 1% of priests are pedophiles. Terminating priestly celibacy will not alter the fact that some priests will be homosexual, and some will be pedophiles. Current diocesan administrators and rectors of seminaries are eager to point out that much more extensive psychological counseling, and more thorough personality analysis, may insure that the candidates who do make it through, will be less likely to cause problems.

This current episode, as traumatic as it is, may move the Catholic Church to make celibacy optional, but it seems unlikely. It will certainly do more to make priests responsible to their congregations, and Bishops legally responsible for the wayward actions of clergy. As religious scholar Jack Miles has asked: "What do we go out to see when we go to Church? I submit to you that we go out to see someone demonstrating in public that he or she has a deep and real relationship with God." (*The Changing Face of*

God, p. 72.) Those in our midst who would in some way be spokespersons for God, already set themselves apart as kadosh, as holy, as having some responsibility that is absolute and transcending normal concerns. Let them get on with the business of cultivating what is of transcendent importance, while not denying very basic earthly concerns. God, said St. Augustine, is so powerful that he can bring good out of evil. Perhaps this crisis in the Catholic Church is one of those opportunities.

V-157
Irreconcilable Differences and the Middle East

To begin to understand the current situation in the Middle East, you need both a vast knowledge of history and a philosophy of history. Some approach history as if it is all a matter of particular heroic individuals, be they Alexander the Great, George Washington, or Winston Churchill. Others approach history as having some kind of built-in determination, whether that is economic, technological, or a quest for freedom, or some other compelling value.

In terms of the current quagmire of the Middle East, it seems clear that irreconcilable cultural differences between Arab-Moslem traditions and Israeli-Jewish traditions play a powerful role, while the absence on either side of the kind of charismatic leadership that a Gandhi, for example, exercised so well in India, prevents progress toward a peaceful solution.

Tom Friedman, in the *New York Times*, has proposed a three-point solution for the intractable problem. The first point: Israel must withdraw from the areas captured in the 1967 war. Point two: Do not trust the PLO to stop the suicide bombing: if they think this strategy would work, they would not stop deploying it to the death of the last Palestinian, or the last Israeli, whichever came first. The critical question: How do you enforce a withdrawal from the conquered territories, without putting the rest of Israel at risk? Friedman goes directly to point three: a quote from Middle East expert Stephen Cohen: "The only solution is a new U.N. mandate for the U.S. and NATO troops to supervise the gradual emergence of a Palestinian State--after a phased Israeli withdrawal--and then to control its borders."

Americans wish we could avoid being peacekeepers for the rest of the world--so much American blood has already been shed in this thankless task. Besides, a peacekeeping force is not the model for solving internecine conflicts. In the Middle Eastern situation, not only are there irreconcilable differences between the principle players, but the security and prosperity of the rest of the world depend on some acceptable solution being accepted by the parties involved.

Western Civilization has been heavily influenced by belief in the power of reason, and of the capacity for people to get together and reason things through. Oriental civilizations have had a long-standing and powerful commitment to the view that there are forces operating that are beyond comprehension or control. These two contradictory visions are nowhere better in conflict than in the location where east meets west: the Middle East!

The Middle East is the nexus of conflict between competing basic convictions about the human predicament. Western rationalists would like to impose their vision on Middle Eastern cultures that are imbued with a sense of Kismet, of Destiny beyond human designs, of being but the agents of higher powers whose ways and goals are inscrutable. The reason that solutions like the one proposed by Tom Friedman have such difficulty even getting to the discussion table, is that the parties most directly involved in the fray, have a sense of being directed by forces beyond the bounds of human understanding. Both Palestinians and Israeli Jews lay claim to the dictum: "History (and Divine Power) is on our side."

While articles in the popular press provide basic building blocks for understanding the current situation in the middle east, Bernard Lewis' book: *What Went Wrong? Western Impact and Middle Eastern Response* presents a point of view widely respected by U.S. and U.N. diplomats. A very different perspective is offered by William Bennett in: *Why We Fight: Moral Clarity and the War on Terrorism.* Lewis' book is a summary statement by one who has devoted his life to understanding the history and culture of the Middle East. Bennett's book proposes philosophical answers to the historical and cultural questions Lewis raises.

Successful historical outcomes are the flowing together of powerful forces manipulated by people of greatness. Today, the powerful forces are in place; all we need are people of greatness to harness them.

V-158
"Conceived in Liberty..."

There are many reasons for patriotism, a high level of commitment to one's country. Americans have good reasons for a very high degree of patriotism. Pericles said of Athens that it was to be a "model for the nations," a phrase Abraham Lincoln applied to America, and proceeded to call it "humanity's last, best hope."

The Gettysburg Address has been called "the greatest speech in American political history." The speech was rich in religious imagery--words like "dedicate," "consecrate," "hallow" are sprinkled throughout. Lincoln said the rebirth of the United States, made possible by the sacrifice of these honored dead, "will ensure that democracy and liberty will not perish from the earth." The fuse for the Civil War may have been the right of states to control their own destinies, but the central issue was the granting of freedom to those who had been created equal, but had been enslaved. The War was seen as God's punishment on America for not living up to a key tenet of the Declaration of Independence, that all men were created equal.

To the extent that we are a "model to the nations," that modeling does not flow from our military might nor our technological or economic prowess, but from our commitment to democracy, and, most of all, to liberty. For Greece and Rome, "freedom" meant primarily not being subject to any other government. The notion of individual freedom meant not being a slave. From there, Greek and Roman philosophers developed notions of liberty as not being a slave to one's passions. Jewish, Christian, and Moslem writers suggested that true freedom was in some way being subject only to God. The word "Moslem" means: "servant of Allah."

The American Declaration of Independence was a rejection of the apparently arbitrary laws of a distant King, and an assertion of individual rights, beginning with "life, liberty, and the pursuit of happiness." From Thomas Jefferson, through Abraham Lincoln, to Martin Luther King, Jr., the distinctive American quest has been for individual liberty, of freeing individuals from constraints upon their mobility, their thoughts, their religious beliefs, their economic or political activity. Initially, the constraints on liberty were prohibitions on what could be harmful to others, and we still have lively debates on seat-belt legislation, abortion, euthanasia, and cloning—issues that in one way or another focus on the impact on others of constraints on one's freedom.

Liberty, in its distinctively American formulation, is neither license to do whatever one pleases, which seems to be a form of adolescent rebellion, nor is it independence of responsibility to the larger society. The signers of the Declaration of Independence affirmed: "We mutually pledge to each other our lives, our fortunes, our sacred honor." The Founding Fathers were clearly convinced of this: "I am free to do whatever I please" must always be completed by "within certain limits established by my society."

There is something special about being an American. We share many of our ideas of freedom with other English-speaking countries, which perhaps indicates our common debt to the *Magna Carta*, to English Parliaments, and to a common vision of nationhood as "strong and free." It is the unique events, distinctive political philosophy, and great personages of our American history that do so much to set up apart, and make us a distinctive "model for the nations."

Americans believe that the events of September 11, 2001, were not an attack upon the World Trade Center and the Pentagon, but upon them, as if Freedom itself had been attacked, and Americans everywhere were once again being called upon not only to defend America, but also to defend Freedom. The vocation of America is to be a witness to the world of what Freedom can produce, and of the life, liberties, and happiness that the commitment to Freedom may generate. It may be questionable as to whether or not our vision of democracy is exportable, but certainly the vision of individual liberty in the context of responsibility to others and to humanity is one we are duty-bound to export around the world. It has worked for us; perhaps it is our sacred duty to spread the message of liberty far and wide. True Patriotism means be willing to share the good fortunes of one's own country with the rest of the world.

V-159
Is Patriotism a Virtue?

Philosophy is dialogue, which means talking things through. These brief essays are my attempts to answer the questions posed to me, usually by my friends and associates, sometimes by my students of many years ago, sometimes just by events in the news. They are intended not as monologues, but as implicit dialogues, incitements to thought and inquiry. Philosophy as dialogue is at least as old as Socrates, the father of Socratic inquiry, whom Plato quoted as saying: "It is no small matter we are discussing here, but how we are to live our lives."

An essay of mine on Patriotism drew three remarkable responses. "Claude," an immigrant from Germany via Shanghai, commented that immigrants like him, fleeing Nazi Germany, have a heightened sense of awareness of what America means, in terms of both personal and economic freedom. "Jerry," who fought in World War II, wrote: "Make no mistake about it. There are many democracies. There is no other United States." He went on to quote Lincoln that the American experiment was "Giving liberty not only to the people of this land, but hope to the world for all future time." And George, an immigrant and one of my lifelong philosophical friends, asked if patriotism weren't also a source of great evil.

It seems to me patriotism is a virtue, but in the way that Aristotle speaks of virtues, as reaching a mean between extremes. Saying "My country right or wrong" is not virtuous, nor is it virtuous to be devoid of respect or appreciation for the country of which you are a citizen. It must be a heightened sense of patriotism that makes citizens willing to die for their country. And it must be a form of patriotism that makes an individual want to export to others, the virtues or admirable traits of his or her own country. But it is not patriotism to attempt to impose a particular form of living upon anyone else.

Isaiah Berlin, in his book *The Proper Study of Mankind*, traces the rise of nationalism, and how, in its extreme form, it engendered Italian Fascism, German Nazism, and Soviet Communism. Berlin defines nationalism as: "The elevation of the interests of the unity and self-determination of the nation to the status of the supreme value before which all other considerations must, if need be, yield at all times." Clearly patriotism and nationalism are very different, for nationalism, at least as we have experienced it in the last hundred years, comes across as an attempt to say that my nation or my region, or my race or ethnic group, is an absolute good, and allegiance to it blots out all other allegiances.

Patriotism is very different. The patriot is not establishing hegemony, or claiming absolute dominion over any other nation or race. The patriot is committed to what his or her country stands for, and has a vision of the way that commitment is somehow a benefit to humanity.

The political thought of Socrates, Plato and Aristotle was complemented in the ancient world by the writings of the Stoic philosophers of Greece and Rome, who coined the word "cosmo-politan," which means "citizen of the world." For them, " patriotism" is part of world citizenship, and not a matter of imposing one's own views or way of life upon anyone else. From an American perspective, America does have something to offer the rest of the world, and that is a vision of freedom: individual, political, and economic. It would be a very different world if freedom of speech and freedom of religion were embraced as universal values, but that may be too much to hope for.

When I first heard of the teachings of the Stoics, I knew that I somehow wanted to be a world citizen. Over the years of visiting and living in other countries, I came to realize that being an American, and striving to represent the best of American values, was my best route to world citizenship. When Americans, or the American government, do anything to curtail the freedom of anyone, they are failing to live up to American ideals. As Americans have found out from bitter experience, we cannot impose "the American way of life," nor can we impose American democracy, on any other country. We are much more successful at changing the behavior of other nations, when the good things we do become a pattern that others can modify to fit their needs and circumstances.

Patriotism, in the sense of appropriate love of one's country, and loving one's country as a path to citizenship of the world, is but one of the many virtues necessary to cultivate our humanity. At the end of his treatise on the destructive effects of anger and hatred, the Roman philosopher Seneca wrote: "Soon we shall breathe our last. Meanwhile, while we live among human beings, let us cultivate our humanity." Let us cultivate our humanity by attending to that which is best in us, which includes both love of country, and love of human beings, wherever they may be, and however advanced they may be on the path to greater humanity.

V-160
Philosophy as Conversation

I persistently return to the theme that philosophy is dialogue, some kind of conversation. Clearly it is not discussion about the weather, or which team has the best players. Philosophy is conversation about things that really matter.

Philosophy lost its way in the twentieth century, when it became too professional, too academic, too immured in its own special, technical vocabulary. There are philosophy conferences where the conversations are largely unintelligible to anyone not reading the current literature in that area, although the topics are matters of concern to all of us, including what it really means to be a human being and a moral agent.

There are family gatherings where ordinary people talk about surviving cancer and about enthusiasm for doing things that make life meaningful. Not only does more philosophy go on at such gatherings, but it is also more meaningful. Philosophy, to be faithful to its own nature, has to touch base with real people facing real problems, and that includes the emotions that people have when they try to interpret the meaning of their daily lives.

This challenge has sometimes been called the difference between "thin" and "thick" philosophy. Thin philosophy tends to emphasize logic and the dissection of language. Thick philosophy tends to get into the thick of things, and see things as much as possible from the human point of view, instead of just from the point of view of logic. As such, it attempts to respond to questions like: Why do I want to live? And, How do I impart meaning to my daily round of activities?

Both the academic and the personal are important approaches to the doing of philosophy. To survive and prosper, philosophy needs a steady dose of ordinary people facing ordinary problems and finding solutions to those problems that can be expressed in everyday language.

Would you rather listen to a philosopher expressing the following argument: (1) There is no relevant difference between human beings and robots; (2) Robots are never morally responsible for anything; (3) Therefore, human beings are never morally responsible for anything. Or would you prefer to listen to someone finding a pathway through cancer treatments so that an eleven-year-old boy can have a grandfather around to watch him play baseball and delight in his increasing skills? I think most people would find the second conversation much more rewarding.

Philosophy loses its way when it becomes too academic, too professional, and too far away from the problems that people face in ordinary life. Philosophy should be an attempt to be wise about the business of everyday living. Philosophy occurs in conversations, in the pages of newspapers and magazines, and occasionally, with a little bit of luck, even in the conferences of philosophers.

The very best philosophy never passes into words at all. It is an ineffable perception that life is of great and boundless value, that human beings have responsibilities to each other and to the planet, and that each day of human existence offers an opportunity to do what has never been done before. I think the thick philosophers have it all over philosophers of the thin persuasion. If philosophy isn't the lifeblood of everyday concerns, it has lost its reason for being.

V-161
Ecumenism and its Problems

Years before the Second Vatican Council made "ecumenism" a popular term, the city of Toronto was alive with ecumenical activity. Not only were the various Protestant Denominations in Canada intensely interested in seeing how cooperative they could be in matters both ecclesial and social, but the University of Toronto, with its system of affiliated denominational colleges, offered a lively laboratory for opportunities in ecumenical dialogue.

Outstanding spokespersons for various religious traditions presented their views, and the dialogue soon expanded beyond Christian confines to include Jews, Muslims, Buddhists, and Hindus. Speakers however were not free from the kind of bipolar character of most ecumenical attempts. One individual proclaimed that any attempt at unity was a "sin," because his particular denomination alone held the truth in its divinely revealed splendor. This "my way or the highway" attitude is still very much alive, as a recent poll found that 19% of Christians, and 7% of non-Christians, thought the religion they practiced was the only true religion.

The spirit of the dialogue in Canada was best represented by a Professor from McGill University who said: "I am Catholic with the Catholics, because I want my religion to be universal; I am evangelical with the Protestants, because I want my religion to be based in what God has revealed; I am a Jew with the Jews, because I seek the unity Judaism has proclaimed; and I am a Moslem with the Moslems, because I wish to spend my life in service to the living God."

Over the years of these meetings, various hostilities of course were expressed, as age-old battles still left their scars. The overall impact of the meetings was positive, based in the discovery of shared goals, and an awareness of the importance of religious practice to so many people of vastly different cultures and heritages. The most important outcome was the appreciation of the holiness and sincerity of religiously dedicated people of vastly different theological persuasions.

Religion is often chastised as not so much a solution to our global predicaments, but as the source of innumerable conflicts. The Secular Humanist Society proclaims that a world free of religion would be a much better, safer, more compatible world, free of the absolutism that convinces one group they have God on their side, and that the rest of the world is not only wrong, but also displeasing to God. Religion is certainly subject to being used for doubtful purposes. Abuses conducted in the name of religion have inflicted incredible harm on the human community. But religion at its best makes moral demands upon human beings, opens avenues to the search for meaning, and can create a sense of community based on transcendental values beyond what any political or social organization can provide.

While relatively few maintain that a world without religion would be better, the vision that any one denomination or interpretation contains so absolute a hold on "the truth" that no other vision can be tolerated, can be the source of great mischief. To those who are so set in their own ways, learning to share quiet meditation with Buddhists might be valuable, just as learning from other religious traditions might improve their spirituality

At the time of the Roman Catholic Vatican Council, there was initial enthusiasm in response to the ecumenical vision expressed by some Catholic theologians. That enthusiasm has been somewhat dimmed by a resurgence of Catholic Absolutism. As a Catholic theologian later wrote: "Out of love for the Church, let us reclaim its identity as an intolerant and faithful people." In the eleventh century, a Church Council proclaimed: "Outside the Church, there is no salvation." Some Catholic theologians have suggested that "all who seek truth and pursue justice" belong to the community of the saved, but others have retreated to a much narrower perspective.

True ecumenism requires being devoted to one's traditions, while attempting to appreciate other viewpoints. What the world needs is that kind of ecumenical vision that busies itself with clearing the many different paths to the mountaintop, so that everyone's journey may be expedited. Too long have people been obsessed with taking the stones that paved their own paths, and tossing them at those who were on some other path, thereby hindering everyone's progress. Human community is built with the bricks of tolerance, mortared in place by appreciating that there are

many different paths up the mountain, and that no one gets there more
quickly by demeaning or belittling someone else's chosen path.

V-162
Politics and Philosophy

The most basic principle of "western" logic is non-contradiction:
something cannot both be, and not be, at the same time. We "westerners"
build all our logic, all our metaphysics, all our science, and all our morality,
upon this principle. In Los Angeles, you can visit, among many other
"eastern" religious centers, Paramahansa Yogenanda's Self-Realization
Fellowship Center. You may listen to lectures on "Eastern" logic, where
this principle of non-contradiction is ridiculed.

Western Politics is rooted in the principle of non-contradiction.
President George W. Bush is a typical "western" politician, dedicated not
only to the principle of non-contradiction, but also to other long-standing
western convictions, like the universality of truth, and the omnipresence of
natural law. As he said in a State of the Union speech: "The nonnegotiable
demands of human dignity are the rule of law; limits on the power of the
state; respect for women; private property; free speech; equal justice; and
religious tolerance." These have come to be known as the seven basic
human rights.

Such a list is not only the product of western logic, it is also the
program of western political philosophy since John Locke, anchored
in the conviction that the basic nonnegotiable human rights include the
right to live your life as you see fit, the right to be free from political
oppression, and the right to own property, thereby making your own way
in the economic world.

The so-called "eastern" logic confounds the issue. Not all societies
subscribe to the Lockean notion of basic human freedoms, nor do all
governments agree to the nonnegotiable demands of human dignity. Isaiah
Berlin was a most astute observer of the anomalies of twentieth century
politics, and he persistently referred to the "doctrine of the incompatibility
of ultimate human ends." That means there will be political leaders who
do not feel bound by the "basic" rights of human dignity, nor do they
necessarily subscribe to that very "western" notion of non-contradiction.

Americans tend to listen more favorably to Israeli spokespersons than
to presentations of Palestinian positions. The fact is, Israelis persistently
express a more "western" political philosophy anchored in the principles
of non-contradiction and human rights, whereas a more "eastern"

logic pervades the philosophy and practices of other middle-eastern representatives.

"Western" and "eastern" systems of thinking have less to do with geography than with particular mindsets. Muslim philosophers in the eleventh and twelfth centuries were well aware of the two different "logics," and while the philosophers favored the western approach, the clerics or theologians won out, and Islam still suffers from that victory.

The clash of civilizations will not be resolved unless "western" political philosophy, as exemplified by the basic seven human rights, attains a more widespread acceptance. That will not occur until western logic is universally adopted. That will not happen, as Thomas More says at the end of his "Utopia," "this many a day." But we have identified the roots of the problem, and seen that they are ultimately, like all human problems, deeply philosophical. Politics is rooted in philosophy, and unless you understand the philosophical roots of those with whom you converse, no political progress is possible.

V-163
"Now, What Are We?"

In explaining his commitment to government spending, President Richard Nixon said: "We are all Keynsians now," referring to the work of the British economist John Maynard Keynes, who proposed that governments could in fact spend their way out of economic recessions. Economics is a dismal science, when compared to clear and positive philosophical perception, (well, at least from my point of view.) To about the same extent that economically we are all Keynsians, philosophically we are all Jamesians. William James (1842-1910) has had a great influence on the way Americans think, even those who are unaware of ever having never heard of him.

President, John F. Kennedy identified his political philosophy as pragmatism, "I go with what works." Fifty years earlier, in *Pragmatism*, James wrote: "Truth consists in useful ideas." Neither Kennedy nor James had much time for abstract ideas, for word games, or empty speculation. James wrote: "The pragmatist clings to facts and concreteness, observes truth at its work in particular cases, and generalizes."

Perhaps James' expressions of these ideas helped form the American character. More likely, James' popularity is rooted in the fact that he was simply expressing what has become the American way of doing things. Clearly this combination of interest in what works and the commitment to being empirical, wanting evidence, wanting experience that confirms basic ideas, is a central part of the American approach to business, science, family life, and even to religion.

James was a Harvard Professor of Philosophy and Psychology, and the two interests intersect in his book, *The Varieties of Religious Experience*. James takes mystical experience as the empirical evidence for religious truth, and it leads him to describe God in strikingly original ways, for example, as "the mother sea of consciousness." James' highly pragmatic approach to the study of religion and religious experience has had a lasting effect on the way religion is studied and understood in America. European religious scholars produce biblical or theological tracts, while American scholars tend to do "sociology" of religion, filled with statistics of how many Americans believe which doctrines, or are members of which congregations.

One theme that persists through James' writings is that none of our concepts quite do justice to reality. Reality is more than any of our expressions. An enduring lesson of his pragmatism is this: when something works, don't waste too much time trying to figure out how it works, because it may well be beyond your comprehension, and your time can be better spent making use of it, than in analyzing it. That reality is always more than concepts can convey is integral to his empiricism. This easily carries over to his study of religion, for God is more than any philosophy can hope to express.

If you find that what William James has to say to some degree correlates with your everyday thinking, that's because just about all of us are really Jamesians now, whether we realize it or not. As with all philosophies we unconsciously adopt, it pays to go back to the originators of our big ideas, and study them with care, so that we may understand more clearly what we ourselves are thinking. We may not all be Keynesians, but the odds are most of us live in the universe depicted by William James, and we would stand to benefit by careful readings of *Pragmatism*, *The Varieties of Religious Experience*, and *A Pluralist Universe*.

V-164
But Are We Also Nietzscheans?

To the suggestion that we are all Jamesians, some might want to add that many of us are Nietzscheans. Others might shudder at the thought that Friedrich Nietzsche has had any influence on us at all. The negative reaction is due to the "bad press" Nietzsche has received at the hands of Nazis and other anti-Semites. The Nazis took Nietzsche's use of the word "Superman," and pretended that Nietzsche was predicting the need for some form of Aryan supremacy. Nietzsche was anything but an anti-Semite, but his sister, who became his executor after his death, sure was. To tell the truth, Nietzsche was much more "anti-German," as he not only chose to live much of his life outside Germany, but he also had some very negative things to say about his Teutonic brethren.

There are three ways in which Nietzsche's thought has had an influence on modern philosophy and culture. First of all, Nietzsche was a "perspectivist," asserting that what you see is very much a matter of where you stand. Nietzsche is the first anti-absolutist, first anti-Platonist, and the first one to affirm that there is no "privileged" corner on the market for truth held by any one point of view. While most people retain a conviction that there are absolute truths, most understand that the reason it is difficult to attain consensus, is that so many people have different perspectives, different backgrounds, different angles on things. Nietzsche, like the pragmatists, says the reason for this is that truth cannot be seen as a correspondence between mind and things, for each mind makes up the world that it sees.

Nietzsche, born in 1844 and dying in 1900, wrote at a time when the cultural impact of Darwinism was first being felt, and the pessimism of Schopenhauer's philosophy was pervading European academic circles. Nietzsche feared the kind of nihilism that could be the result of loss of faith in God and the loss of absolute moral standards. Accordingly, in addition to his "perspectivism," the second component of his philosophy is "the transvaluation of all values," the attempt to overcome the "slave" morality of the past---where one did what was commanded by some superior voice---by the assumption of responsibility for one's own choices, with the consequent "enhancement of human life" as the goal. Once again, we are caught between a rock and a hard place: between longing for an absolute morality, even though it is laden with inconsistencies, and the effective morality practiced by those who have different moral visions. Like Nietzsche, we may be concerned at the absence of morality on the part of "anything goes" contemporaries, but we do not yet have a sense of how to embrace the openness of newer moralities, while preserving the best of the old. In the midst of a sensible relativism, we want the preservation of our cherished absolutes.

Lastly, Nietzsche has influenced us all by bringing philosophy into the marketplace. He was himself a professor of philology, with a remarkable knowledge of the Greek classics, but he wanted nothing more than to make philosophy part of everyday conversations. His books, *Beyond Good and Evil, Thus Spake Zarathustra, Human, All Too Human,* can be read by anyone, without any knowledge of the technical terms philosophers hold dear. Nietzsche brought philosophy down to earth, into the give-and-take of everyday concerns, and sought to make important issues part of the fabric of everyday conversation. At least in this sense, we are all Nietzscheans, and we owe a debt of gratitude to this brilliant, often misunderstood, and often abused, great philosophical genius.

Abandoned Monastery, Oaxaca, Mexico

V-165
Holy, Catholic and Modern?

The Catholic Church has come in for some hard times lately. The "renewal" proposed by the Second Vatican Council appears to have been displaced by "restoration" to the absolutist and hierarchical church that seems, at least to Americans, strangely out of keeping with the modern world. No clearer picture emerges of how different the Catholic Church is from the rest of modern society, than the television images of hundreds of male bishops participating in Church conferences. More than half the membership of the Roman Catholic Church is female, but the Church has steadfastly maintained the male hold on priesthood, hierarchy, bureaucracy, and theology, although women theologians are beginning to make their presence felt.

The Roman Catholic Church has come a long way since Pope Pius VI in 1791 rejected "the abominable philosophy of human rights," explicitly rejecting freedom of religion, conscience, and the press, and poking fun at the notion of the equality of all human beings. In the late 19th century, as the pace of modernization accelerated, Pope Pius IX spoke out against railways, gas lighting, the building of suspension bridges, and other similar attempts at breaking away from the safe paths of the medieval world. In the face of developing democracy, he emphasized the absolute primacy of the Pope, demanding that the First Vatican Council accord the Pope the impenetrable shield of infallibility. As a demonstration of his infallibility, he proclaimed that Mary had been conceived in her mother's womb free of original sin. This was a doctrine that had no basis in Scripture or in Catholic tradition, and hence was an excellent vehicle for the Pope to show his absolute and unquestionable authority.

Pope Pius IX had lost temporal power, as the developing nation of Italy took over what had been the Papal State, leaving him only the few square miles of the Vatican. Asserting his absolute spiritual power was a form of occult compensation. Recent texts have painted a dark picture of the pontificate of Pope Pius XII, whose battles against communism and for the preservation of the institutional church, prevented him from speaking out against the evils of Nazism; he excommunicated by papal edict anyone who became a member of the communist party, but never excommunicated Catholics like Hitler, Himmler, Goebels, or Borman. Fr. Martin Rhonheimer presented a more moderate understanding of the perilous pontificate of Pius XII: "Pius was not Hitler's Pope, nor was he ever a friend of the Nazis or of Hitler. He was simply a man who thought as most people did at the time, a man of absolute personal integrity, though with an outlook conditioned by his training as a church diplomat." (*First Things,* August/September 2004, p. 7.)

Pope John XXIII, who called the second Vatican Council in order to promote aggiornamento, coming up to date, had as one of his highest priorities the removal of any trace of anti-Semitism within the Catholic Church, and eagerly sought to make amends for centuries of wrongdoing. Receiving a group of American Jews, he said: "I am Joseph, your brother."

For the benefit of the Catholic Church, I hope that there is waiting in the wings another "papabile" of the stature of Pope John XXIII. There are outstanding Catholic theologians representing both conservative and liberal persuasions. There is a rich spirituality within the Roman Catholic Church that will help see it through difficult times. Is it possible that we will live to see a Bishop's Conference where Catholic women are wearing clerical collars, and have more than "secretarial" duties when great decisions are being made about their lives and their modes of living? Perhaps the Roman Catholic Church can experience a Reformation and Enlightenment that will make it not only Holy and Catholic, but also Modern, and a major contributor to the solution of some of the world's modern dilemmas.

V-166
A Tale of Two Princeton Professors

Nothing proves the existence of academic freedom better than the tenure of two Princeton Professors of diametrically opposed points of view. Robert George is Professor of Jurisprudence at Princeton, and author of, among other books, *The Clash of Orthodoxies*, the title of which plays on Samuel Huntington's book, *The Clash of Civilizations.* George is a proponent of what might be called "Natural Law Orthodoxy," maintaining that our civilization is endangered by the acceptance of all such violations of the natural law as abortion, euthanasia, homosexual and liberal lifestyles, and the practice of capital punishment.

Many religious-minded people will find considerable support for their convictions in the well-argued examples George presents. Some, however, will part company with him when he rejects both divorce, and the practice of contraception, as destructive of the family values he identifies as absolute goods. George finds complete continuity between his philosophical analysis of an ethics based on natural law, and what might be described as traditional, conservative Christian teaching.

George's book might be taken as a commentary on St. Paul's Epistle to the Romans, 2:13-15: "It is not the hearers of the law who are righteous before God, but the doers of the law who will be justified. When the Gentiles who have not the law do by nature what the law requires, they are a law to themselves, even though they do not have the law. They show that what the law requires is written on their hearts, while their conscience also bears witness." (The Hebrew *Torah* actually means "Teaching," and Paul interprets that Teaching as having "laid down the law.")

Peter Singer has been the occupant of an endowed Chair in American Values at Princeton, and the bases of his moral values are diametrically opposed to just about everything that George stands for. Where George supports a rule-based ethics anchored in "natural law," Singer is first and foremost a consequentialist, a kind of utilitarian who claims that we must examine the consequences of our actions, --the total outcomes produced- -to determine what is moral and what is immoral. As George's ethic can be anchored in the quote from St. Paul, so Singer's ethic is summed up by this quote: "Once we admit that Darwin was right when he argued that human ethics evolved from the social instincts that we inherited from our non-human ancestors, we can put aside the hypothesis of a divine origin for ethics."

It should come as no surprise that Singer comes to quite different conclusions than does George with respect to the aforementioned problems of abortion, euthanasia, homosexual and liberal lifestyles. They are, however, in agreement on the limited applicability of capital punishment. Singer asks, what are the consequences to the individuals involved of accepting abortion? Isn't society really better off when there are no unwanted children? With respect to euthanasia, are individuals better off when they know they will be spared useless suffering? And with respect to homosexuality, isn't society, as well as the individuals involved, better off when there are societally accepted arrangements for the expression of sexuality, whatever its particular character?

George occasionally claims to be a consequentialist, in terms at least of foreseeing disastrous consequences to any society accepting the "liberal orthodoxy" Peter Singer espouses. Singer also lays claim to a rule-based ethics, in terms of accepting those rules which society has found, through trial and error, to actually promote the greatest good for the greatest number.

The debate over these extremely divergent ethical positions is not reserved for the faculty club at Princeton. These are the issues, here reduced to their simplest form, that enliven the debates over ethical matters wherever they occur. Both George and Singer offer clear and comprehensible rational analysis of the roots of their respective ethical positions. The arguments presented here serve to document the case that the ethical positions we all adopt, are rooted in our most basic intuitions, our fundamental, pre-reflective, pre-rational convictions about right and wrong. Understanding issues as debated by these two Princeton professors or their various surrogates can only serve to clarify the convictions we all have. Understanding where ethical convictions come from, and appreciating the difficulty people have in changing their most basic intuitions, are the kind of large-scale problems for which Princeton Professors are justly famous. Bringing the issues down in terms we can all understand and work with, is a different kind of challenge, but being exposed to the efforts of great minds like George and Singer cannot but help each of us along the path of understanding.

V-167
Mit Brennender Sorge

The closest things Americans have to papal encyclicals are 9-0 Supreme Court decisions. They come out as authoritative documents with little or no likelihood of being reversed. Now philosophers occasionally find something fascinating in landmark decisions of the Supreme Court, but only rarely find anything of positive interest in decisions of the Catholic Church expressed in papal encyclicals.

Almost all such papal letters are written in Latin. But in 1937, Pope Pius XI was so incensed by what was going on in Hitler's Germany, that he wrote one in German, *Mit Brennender Sorge*, translatable as "With Burning Care," or, "With Passionate Concern." It has become a basic document in the heated debate over the issue of the Catholic Church and the Nazi era of anti-Semitism. It is also of more than passing philosophical interest in terms of religion's role in speaking to moral questions.

Hochuth's play "The Deputy" popularized the perception that Pope Pius XII did little or nothing to come to the aid of persecuted Jews during the Nazi era. Daniel Goldhagen's article in *The New Republic*, "What Would Jesus Have Done? Pope Pius XII, The Catholic Church, and the Holocaust," highlighted many allegations, and painted a very negative picture of the Vatican's response to Nazi anti-Semitism. Ronald Rychlak responded to Goldhagen's article in "Goldhagen vs. Pius XII" (available on the Internet at www. firstthings.com.) Rychlak, going through Vatican archives, documented with great precision what happened when, and why. He provided definitive substantiation of just how active the Vatican was in opposing anti-Semitism, and how much help was extended to Jews by individual Catholics, by priests, by the bishops of Holland, Denmark, France, Hungary, and Germany, and by two Popes.

The basic Catholic teaching on the Nazi era and its anti-Semitism may be found in the encyclical letter of Pope Pius XI. The future Pope Pius XII had been papal nuncio in Germany, and was the principal informant for the Vatican as to what was going on. In *Mit Brennender Sorge*, Pius XI wrote: "Mark well that in the Catholic Mass, Abraham is our Patriarch and forefather. Anti-Semitism is incompatible with the lofty thought, which that fact expresses. It is a movement with which we Christians can have nothing to do. I say to you it is impossible for a Christian to take part in anti-Semitism. It is inadmissible. In Christ and through Christ we are the spiritual progeny of Abraham. Spiritually we are all Semites."

In *Hitler, the War, and the Pope*, Rychlak wrote: "On April 9, 1940, German troops swept across the Danish border. Danes, including King Christian X, Catholic bishops, priests and students, demonstrated solidarity with the Jews by wearing the yellow star in public." Rychlak documented that the Danes smuggled almost the entire Jewish population to safety. This image serves as some small antidote to the indelible images of cattle cars and death camps.

The Holocaust produced by Nazi Germany is one of the darkest events in human history. As Paul Tillich observed, part of the tragedy is that one of the most cultured and refined people in history could have been overcome by such savagery. It is incumbent on us all to keep alive the memory of that dark period, but also to assign blame where it is due, and to relieve the papacy of the dark stains Goldhagen and Hochhuth wished to paint. Anti-Semitism is a wretched aspect of human behavior, as is any form of racism or bigotry. There is some comfort in finding a Pope who could say "We are all spiritually Semites." In a modern, pluralistic universe, there are many ways of being right, but there are still universal wrongs. Anti-Semitism is one of the many ways of being absolutely wrong. It is good to know that a Pope spoke out forcefully against anti-Semitism, and did so "With burning, passionate care."

V-168
"Knowing the difference..."

The Supreme Court decision preventing the execution of mentally retarded criminals referred to a capacity to "*know* the difference between right and wrong." We seem confident that ethics and morality has some knowledge basis. Parents say to wayward children: "You know better than that." The Genesis narrative of Adam and Eve says: "They did eat of the tree of *knowledge* of good and evil."

If ethics is a matter of knowledge, why can't we create a "rational ethics," teach it in elementary schools, and use it as the basis for all the difficult moral decisions people face in the course of their lives? And if ethicians like Socrates can affirm that "virtue is knowledge" or like Kant that each of our actions ought to mirror some easily discovered universal law, why is there so much disagreement about what is ethical, or what we "ought" to do? And why, if morality has a basis in knowledge, is it so difficult to win someone over to what we think is a more reasonable position?

One popular opinion about ethics affirms that reason can tell us very little about morals, for moral judgments resemble differing reactions to works of art. Tradition coerces us to find murder or child abuse repulsive, but nothing in the nature of things really makes such acts morally bad and worthy of contempt. Another very popular opinion affirms that ethics are a contractual matter: if we all began behind a "veil of ignorance," not knowing what our lot in life would be, there would be certain rules we would like to see established, so that we could all have a fair start. If we did not know which piece of birthday cake we might get, we would be sure to cut the cake into very even pieces. This approach says ethics is all about "fairness," and that "reason" can lead us to obtaining equal opportunity for all rational participants.

Not all who think about these issues agree that "reason" is going to get us very far. Skepticism about the capacity to reason to ethical choices was proclaimed by David Hume, who argued that reason had only a very limited role in our choosing what to do. As Hume put it, "Morality is more properly felt than judged of." Hume was skeptical of human reason attaining any truth outside the realm of logic or mathematics, and his most oft-quoted saying is: "You can never derive an ought from an is," meaning that no amount of observation of events justifies any proclamation of what ought to be.

Vigorous response to Hume did not take long. Immanuel Kant affirmed that we all come equipped with something that transcends mere moral sentiment: a longing to do what is right, a will that somehow transcends the phenomena of everyday moral challenges, and leads us to a sense of duty, and an awareness that each of our actions ought to be a model for anyone in that same moral situation. A famous saying of Kant: "Two things fill the mind with ever new and increasing admiration and awe: the starry heavens above me, and the moral law within me."

Hume and Kant represent the polar opposites of modern moral reflection. Hume is the progenitor of the vast sea of moral relativism we see about us, while Kant is the defender, in one way or another, of the ancient tradition that says that somehow, we have a capacity for knowing the difference between right and wrong, and that, because of that knowledge, we are responsible for our moral choices. It is not a matter of reason being a servant of the emotions, nor is it a matter of preferences, like choosing tea or coffee. At the end of the day, the Supreme Court is on the right track: unless you *know* the difference between right and wrong, you do not deserve to be punished, leave along capitally punished, for your bad behavior.

We are not devoid of good moral primers, that is, brief books on ethical theory. Russ Shafer-Landau's *Whatever Happened to Good and Evil,* James Q. Wilson's *The Moral Sense,* and Simon Blackburn's *Being Good,* are all brief, readily available, and inexpensive. Readers of such books have no excuse, for they will *know* the difference between right and wrong....

V-169
A Lively Argument

At an ethics conference, a lively argument developed between a very conservative Catholic moralist, and a disciple of Richard Rorty's. My notes on the argument were incomplete, so here follows a creative reconstruction.

CCM (Conservative Catholic Moralist): Certain crimes deserve capital punishment, and sure, we will execute the innocent some time, but death is not the real issue: God will set things right.

DRR (Disciple of Richard Rorty): That's fine if you believe in immortality. But you are using your religious beliefs as a basis for public policy. You can't use any particular faith that way, especially when not everybody shares that faith.

CCM: I would say to you, what the Catholic Church teaches is true, and except for mysteries of faith like the Trinity and the Incarnation, these truths are available to reason. What's more, Catholic politicians are bound by the teaching of the Church, and that's why you won't find politicians who are good Catholics supporting abortion, contraception, or same-sex marriages.

DRR: I thought President Kennedy and Governor Cuomo made it clear that their duty was to uphold the Constitution, and that their private religious belief did not dictate their public policy, and further, that their beliefs were matters of their own consciences.

CCM: You pick examples of Catholic politicians who simply were not good Catholics. The official teaching of the Church Magisterium is binding on the conscience of Catholics. There is no room for private opinions once the Church has taught something as a matter of faith and morals.

DRR: Wait a minute. I remember Kennedy as a candidate saying American policy would never be dictated by the Vatican, and I remember

Cuomo saying his obligation was to uphold and apply the statutes of the state of New York. Aren't you really saying that a Catholic, with your understanding of what it means to be Catholic, is Catholic first, and American, or a supporter of the Constitution, second?

CCM: Let me say it once more: what the Catholic Church teaches is true. Truth is one, so what the Church teaches is binding on all Catholics. The Church teaches that the existence of God can be demonstrated, that man is immortal, and that to attain salvation, you must do what the Church teaches. Politically, a Catholic politician has a duty to foster what the Church teaches, and he sins grievously if he does not apply Catholic teaching always and everywhere.

DRR: First of all, since Darwin, and the growth of modern science, we have an alternative explanation to everything religion teaches. The existence of God is a matter of faith, and to me at least, such faith has no basis in fact. Human immortality is a nice idea, but it represents pie in the sky when you die. I accept you as a fellow citizen, and I accept your faith, right up to the point where it begins to interfere with what legislatures and courts have accepted as legal practice, including abortion. What I am hearing from you sounds more like "Islamic Catholicism," in which religious conviction supplants and would prevent democratically elected officials passing laws in keeping with the will of the majority.

CCM: We are both citizens of this democracy. You happen to be misguided, and unfortunately you have a public platform that you use to win people over to your erroneous and relativistic views. What the Church teaches is true, and my obligation is to share the truth with whoever will listen.

DRR: Don't you mean, impose your views on everybody else? You represent a kind of close-mindedness that I don't think is representative of what most Catholics believe and practice. What I have heard here today is right out of the dark ages. We have some kind of social hope, some fair degree of tolerance, and s system for debating and deciding social policy. I am alarmed that you seem to oppose these views.

For a book that documents this Catholic conservative point of view, see George Weigel's *The Truth of Catholicism*. For a book that represents a different Catholic point of view, see Hans Kung's *The Catholic Church*. For a book in keeping with the opinions of the second speaker, see Richard Rorty's *Truth and Progress*.

V-170
Jewish Ethics

Buddhism and Judaism have this in common: both place much more emphasis on how to behave, than on what to believe. Judaism is much more concerned with "ortho-praxy," right doing, than with ortho-doxy, right beliefs. Anyone familiar with Judaism knows about Halakhah, a code of norms of Torah-based behavior, and may doubt that any kind of specifically Jewish ethical norms could exist without being subsumed by this code. Conservative Jews view Halakhah as the unchanging expression of God's will on earth, and the last word on ritual, civil and moral law. As such, it would seem to eliminate any need for a separate Jewish ethic.

There is a Yiddish saying that no one has ever died from having an unsolved philosophical problem. Nevertheless, philosophical reflection remains alive and well within Jewish academic communities, and scholars acknowledge four main categories of what can be identified as Jewish ethics: biblical, rabbinic, medieval, and modern.

The Bible does not even have a word for ethics, but there are ethical teachings in the Bible. Six of the so-called 'Ten Commandments' directly relate to ethical matters, such as murder, adultery, theft, deception. What is interesting is the religious context of the ethic prescribed: one worships God through decent, humane, and moral relations with others. This is as clear a statement of a religious ethic as you could hope for: whatever morality is, its basis is in God's will, and doing God's will. Moral actions are not ends in themselves, for they are ways of expressing one's relationship to God.

There is an interesting parallel between the Biblical ethic of the Hebrew authors and Greek ethics as elaborated by Plato. In the Biblical ethic, human beings are created in the image of God, and perfection is a matter of becoming as similar to God as is humanly possible. The Biblical injunctions are to be holy as God is holy, to walk in His ways, and thus to serve the Lord. Socrates in the dialogue *Theaetetus* says: "We ought to fly away and become like God as far as this is possible, and to become holy, just and wise." But the parallels are swallowed up in differences: the Platonic tradition is a flight from things earthly and proposes a kind of contemplative likeness unto the god of your choice, whereas the Jewish tradition implies an imitation of God here on earth, and 'walking in his ways' means to act in a God-like manner so far as this is possible. It is hard to miss the universalistic thrust of the Hebrew Bible, for humanity, not just a few individuals, has been created in the image of God, and the 'imitation of God' is a duty for humanity, not just a prescription for a limited few.

Rabbinic writings of the *Mishnah* are more concerned with piety than with ethics, but the body of law called *Halakhah* (which means 'The Way,') is concerned with how we ought to live our lives so as to make ourselves holy, and thus walk in God's ways. Hillel's 'Golden Rule' is the best-known rabbinic moral teaching: "What you dislike, don't do to others; that's the whole Torah; the rest is commentary."

It is not until the Middle Ages, under the influence of Greek, Moslem and Christian writers, that a Jewish ethical system is explicitly developed. If we are to imitate God, says Moses Maimonides, we must do our best to understand as much as we can of the Divine Nature, and here Maimonides finds help in both the Bible, and texts of Greek Philosophy, especially Aristotle. The God of the Bible is active, doing things in human history, while the God of Aristotle is contemplative, lost in reflection on his own divine essence. Maimonides concludes that the truest perfection involves the imitation of God's loving kindness, justice and righteousness. Maimonides wants, however, to preserve something of that Greek passion for contemplation of the Divine Perfection.

Medieval Jewish literature soon reflected a strong reaction to Maimonides' Hellenic interests, by turning to pietistic and mystical answers to ethical questions, leading to comments like: "the greater the difficulty in performing an action, the more praiseworthy it is." Kabala, a Jewish mystical movement, had no use for philosophical reflections, but produced provocative ideas like this: religious actions can have profound impacts on the very structure of the universe.

With the Napoleonic liberations of Jews in Europe, Jewish ethical reflection became much more "mainstream," and current Jewish writers, exemplified by Abraham Heschel, Emmanuel Levinas and Martin Buber, have shown awareness of the full panoply of modern ethical views, while preserving a distinctively Jewish perspective. Rabbis have testified before congressional committees and presented diametrically opposed positions on abortion, for example. Modernity has generated this kind of fracturing in every moral tradition. As Menachem Kellner, in *Contemporary Jewish Ethics* has observed, "Jews and Judaism are not, of course, unique in this respect. They are like everyone else, only more so."

The enduring impact of Jewish ethics is based in that vision of the purpose of life as response to being created in the image of God. God's creatures are invited to walk in His ways, and be holy as He is holy. No loftier ethical ideal could be elaborated, and Jewish Ethics has taken its place as one of the permanent pillars of meaningful ethical reflection.

V-171
Christian Ethics

One of the unfortunate old saws is that the God of the Hebrew Bible is a God of wrath and fear, while the God of the New Testament is a God of love. The Hebrew Bible was written over a period of a thousand years, and there is not only diversity of opinion, but also considerable development of doctrine over that time. The different names of God are some index of this development. Elohim originally meant "the clouds," El Shaddai means "God of the Mountains," YHWH presumably means "I Am Who I Am," while Adonai means simply "The Lord." The understanding of God in the Hebrew tradition moves from a tribal god trying to carve out a land for his people, who can be brutal and vindictive, to a god who turns out to be everywhere, and finally to a God who turns out to be the only God, not only the Maker of heaven and earth, but a God full of tender loving-kindness for all this creation.

At a scholarly conference, I presented a paper suggesting that both Christianity and Islam were simply Jewish heresies, not really separate religions. My suggestion was not well received, but nonetheless, the similarities and continuities between the three religions are considerable. In terms of basic ethical starting points, Christianity is similar to Judaism, including the vision of a God who watches out for His people, who expects His people to keep His law, and expects atonement for violations of that law. Jesus' basic ethical teaching comes right out of the Torah: "Love the Lord thy God with thy whole heart, and thy neighbor as thyself."

Christian ethics is biblical, but it also centered in the life and teaching of Christ. Jesus radicalizes conventional morality: there is no limit to the forgiveness of injuries; there is no limit as to how much you must be generous to those in need; the motive for an action is more important than the action itself; and trust in God is an absolute, just as rain falling equally on the good and the bad, is a sign of the unconditional love of God.

Jesus shies away from giving precise rulings on ethical issues, rendering to Caesar what is Caesar's and to God what is God's, without specifying which is which. He says nothing about war, capital punishment, sexual equality, slavery, abortion, contraception, or euthanasia. He does say divorce is permissible only on the grounds of *porneia*, a strange Greek word that probably means adultery. It does seem odd that he gives a ruling on only one ethical conundrum. The fourth Gospel uses the Greek word *agape* to describe the love that God has; it is generous, self-giving love. The word is a Greek parallel for the Hebrew hesed, loving-kindness.

Love of neighbor becomes the sign or manifestation of the love of God, demonstrated by a community in which love prevails, a fellowship of repentance, forgiveness, and reconciliation. It is suggested that the ethic of Jesus Christ does not provide a law for either the individual or society, but creates an *atmosphere* that transforms all ethical questions.

St. Paul is sometimes called the second founder of Christianity, and almost half of the Christian biblical canon derives from his writings. Christian writers suggest that his writings are simply a joyful response to the overflowing graciousness of God. St. Paul is the first Christian theologian, both interpreting what the life and death of Jesus is to mean for those baptized into his death, and promoting the marriage of Greek and Roman cultural ideas with the Hebrew tradition.

Three exceptional figures in the Christian tradition produced brief summaries of what distinctively Christian ethics is all about. St. Augustine wrote: "Love, and do what you will." Augustine's point is that if you love God, you will keep His commandments. Thomas Aquinas proposed that the moral life sanctified by the grace of Christ is the avenue to salvation. The point is, actions performed with God's grace have a very different character from actions not so informed. Luther presented a somewhat different take on the moral life: we are saved by faith alone, by grace, not by any action on our part. The moral life is but a paltry indicator of how God's saving grace is being deployed.

Contemporary Christian ethicists have attempted to answer four common criticisms. (1) Christian ethics is intolerant, and breeds intolerance. For centuries, the Roman Catholic position was that "error has no rights," but that has been toned down, and the visions of Locke and Voltaire that tolerance is acceptance of points of view you strongly disagree with, generally prevails. (2) Christian ethics is of dubious moral value, because it is based on Heaven as reward for good behavior, Hell as punishment for evils done. Kant and his successors emphasized that the basis of ethics is doing what is right because it is right, and that vice is in some way its own punishment. Heaven might be a reward for a life well lived, but the passport to heaven, in the Kantian account, is the possession of a "good will." (3) Christian ethics is negative and repressive. Certainly there are caricatures of Christians who have followed the rules but not the spirit of Christianity, and have wound up as psychologically infantile, but that is an aberration and not a norm. Any religion that has "Thou shalt nots" is subject to legalistic and minimalist interpretations but, say the Christian ethicists, this is a failure to see the much larger picture. (4) Christian ethics keeps people at an immature level, complete with superstitious rituals that compensate for evil doing, and a vision of sacraments making up for absence of true growth in character and moral development. Once more, say the ethicists, this is a failure on the part of some Christians, a failure to understand and make use of the channels of God's grace.

Some Christian ethicists wish to distance themselves from the various doctrinal shortcomings of Christian history, and emphasize the positive vision that Christian ethics offers. This vision is anchored in (1) the stress on the dignity of the human person; (2) the intended universality of the community of the church, and (3) a concern for what the church can do to hold humanity together in a pluralistic world. As a statement of the World Council of Churches proposed, what binds Christian communities together is advocacy for the needs of the poor, the downtrodden, and the oppressed. (One might add, what binds Christian communities together must be some belief in the uniqueness of Jesus Christ, and some kind of faith both in his person, and in his teachings.)

Christian ethics is ultimately reducible to the principle that in the end, it is love that really matters. Joseph Fletcher's "Situation Ethics," –do whatever promotes greater love in the world—may have oversimplified the ethic, just as the question, "What would Jesus do? –oversimplifies the issue in another direction. If a simple summary statement of Christian ethics is needed, perhaps the golden rule as expressed by the founder of Christianity will do: "Do unto others as you would have them do unto you." That Rabbi Hillel offered a very similar formula shows the similarity between Judaism and Christianity. Now the question is, Can Judaism and Christianity find a common bond with Islam?

V-172
Islamic Ethics

Everybody knows all about Jewish and Christian Ethics, so brief reminders from time to time is all that is necessary. But relatively few Westerners know much about Islamic Ethics, and some of us, given the visibility of terrorists who claim Islamic roots, are inclined to wonder if there is any such thing.

The study of Islamic Ethics comes in three parts: the Scriptural basis, the Encounter with Greek Philosophy, and Modern Developments. Most Westerners have some familiarity with the Hebrew Bible and the Christian Scriptures, but few have read the Koran, which is unfortunate, because it is a beautiful book. Karen Armstrong relates how, when she was traveling in the Middle East, Arabs with whom she was sharing a taxi grew silent when a reading from the Koran occurred on the radio, and vied with each other to provide her a translation that did justice to its poetic quality.

One might contend that the Koran is as much neglected by Moslems as Jewish and Christian Scriptures are by so many adherents of those faiths. Take for example this rather remarkable passage: "For each community we have granted a Law and a Code of Conduct. If Allah wished, he could have made you one community, but he wishes rather to test you by that which has been given to you. So vie with each other to excel in goodness and moral virtue." (Koran, 5:48). How can any modern terrorist organization claim fidelity to such a text?

It is not only monotheism that binds Judaism, Christianity, and Islam together. All three religions place a heavy emphasis on community. When Rabbis gathered to translate the Hebrew Bible into Greek, they chose the word *"ecclesia"* to translate different Hebrew words that meant "the People of God," or, "God's Chosen People," or, "The People of the Land." *"Ecclesia"* became the Christian word for "Church," and eventually resurfaced as the Arabic word *"Ummah,"* meaning, the Muslim Community, or, those who are the servants of Allah. All three traditions affirm that salvation is a community more than an individual matter, that the way you treat others is a manifestation and extension of your relationship to the Divine, and that Faith is manifested by deeds.

We owe our possession of most of the texts of the great Greek philosophers to Arabic and Byzantine scholars of the seventh and eighth centuries C.E. The writings of Plato and Aristotle had a dramatic impact on the development of Moslem Ethics and Theology more than a thousand years ago. (Later we will deal with the works of Al-Ashari, Al-Farabi, Ibn-Sina, Ibn-Rushd, and Al-Ghazzali. Suffice it here to say that what other scholars did for the development of Jewish and Christian theology, these writers did for Islam, in remarkably parallel ways.) Some Moslem scholars wished to reject all that Greek Philosophy had to offer, as being unnecessary in the light of the Revelation of the Koran, but the "Mutazili" ("intellectuals"), insisted that the Ethics developed by the Greeks could not but help make the Koran more comprehensible to a wider audience.

Within Islam, the fideists (those who believe that faith alone has all the necessary teachings) have generally held the upper hand, and as one scholar wrote: "Acts and obligations were good and evil ultimately because divine commands defined them as such." A "divine command" ethic is simple and convenient, but it can lead to the excesses of Wahabism, which is the version of Islam of Al-Qaida and Usama bin-Laden. Medieval Islam quickly developed a *"Sunna,"* an aggregate of God's commands and prohibitions, which has become *"Sharia,"* or the body of Islamic Sacred

Laws, a kind of sacrosanct Super Constitution that trumps all human legislation.

Modern Islamic ethics differs from the secular ethic that Western democracies follow, in that separation of Church and State is simply inconceivable. As Karen Armstrong put it: "In Islam, it is God and not the people who gives a government legitimacy." Moslem countries that have a "secular" constitution, such as Turkey, Egypt, Iraq, and Algeria, stand in constant danger of alienating religious believers who wish to reestablish theocracy, a government that derives its policies and mandates directly from divine authority. The power of Ayatollah Khomeini in Iran derived from the conviction of the faithful that he spoke in the name of Allah, and his directives were clear expressions of the Divine Will. (An "Islamic Republic" is an inherent contradiction.)

Various attempts have been made to unify Islamic Ethics. Islamic scholars discuss the establishment of "norms" for public and private life, and try to blend cultural, political, social and religious issues into one seamless garment. Current writers in this tradition focus on issues of economic and social justice, and struggle especially with the imbalance of wealth and poverty so visible throughout the Islamic world. Bernard Lewis, one of the best-known western Islamic scholars, has insisted that Islam's central problem is an inability to come to grips with "modernity," seeking refuge in a past that was comfortably agrarian and separatist. Azim Nanji, a Moslem scholar with a considerable following, maintains that, with some help from Western scholars, Islam is "open to the possibilities of and challenges of new ethical and moral discoveries."

It is clearly to the benefit of Westerners to acquire some understanding of the different currents of Islam. It will also be to the benefit of Islam, if Westerners can succeed in convincing Moslems of our common traditions and mutual interests. Perhaps it is the sense of "community," of the interests that we all have in common, that can lead the members of very divergent religious beliefs to adopt an interest in the survival of our common humanity. The Western world can no longer afford indifference to the directions of Moslem cultural, ethical and religious development. Unless a new era of understanding develops, a new form of Mutually Assured Destruction may be on the horizon. Such a vision is ethically unacceptable to Jewish, Christian, or Islamic traditions. A modern Socrates might note that it is no minor matter we are discussing here, but how (and if) we are to continue living our lives at all.

V-173
The Lighter Side

Philosophy is not without its lighter moments. As Dr. Johnson said: "In my youth, I wanted to be a philosopher, but cheerfulness kept breaking in." Philosophers generally have the good sense to know that they do not know all the answers, and some willingness to poke fun at themselves is a component of every serious philosophical conference. Books in philosophy might be more readable, if the authors took time out occasionally to see the humor in what they do.

I once had a paper rejected by a theological journal with the brusque comment: "A strange theological paper that doesn't include a single biblical reference." Since then, when submitting papers to such journals, I cover my tracks by quoting Genesis on the front page: "And God said, Let there be light."

The great irony for me, with a background in History of Philosophy and Ethics, is that the course I taught the longest was "Philosophy of Leisure." I wish I had been more successful, as all about me I see people who recreate, that is, restore themselves, but so seldom go on to practice leisure, to do things for the sake of doing them, activities that ennoble, enrich, inspire, that make the doer better just by doing them, whether productive works of intellect, of art, or of self-giving.

Philosophers have become "public intellectuals," and philosophers like Bertrand Russell, Richard Rorty, Martha Nussbaum, Peter Singer, Gary Wills and John Leo, have been busy trying to influence public opinion and political behavior. While philosophy needs to be practiced in the public marketplace of ideas, philosophy dries up and dies if it does not drink continually from the fountains of its greatest protagonists. Listen to the immortal words of Lucretius:

"Let no one when young delay to study philosophy, nor when old, grow weary of this study. For no one can come too early or too late to secure the health of the soul. And someone who says the time for philosophy has not yet come, or has already passed by, is like someone who says the time for happiness is either future or past, but not now. Whether young or old, you must study philosophy, for as you grow old, you will be young in blessings through the happy recollection of what has been, and that in youth, you will harvest the blessings of age, since you will have no fear of what is to come. The practice of philosophy will encourage you to meditate on the things that make for happiness, both for yourself, and for those in your care."

We all need moments of recreation and leisure, of levity and entertainment. Such escapes prepare us well for the doing of the serious work of philosophy. As Kierkegaard, the master of philosophical irony might well have remarked, "Take yourself seriously, but not too seriously."

Chapter VI.
Taking Ethics Seriously

VI-174
Taking Ethics Seriously

I was a founding member of a Hospital Medical Ethics Committee. Since then, Medical Ethics, or Bioethics, has become a recognized specialty, but at that time, there were few agreed-upon guidelines for medical ethics discussions. There were three very dark clouds visible on the horizon, and clear indications of other, perhaps bigger storms brewing.

The first cloud related to the traditional first principle of the Hippocratic oath: *Primum non nocere*, "above all, do no harm." In our hospital, neonatal care had become a lightning rod for discussion of what "harm" really meant, for it involved keeping alive, premature infants whose chances for a normal life seemed infinitesimal. The problem was soon compounded by several spina-bifida babies, and then an anencephalic infant, a baby born without a brain. Was it a "harm" to strive to keep these infants alive, when the good to them seemed minimal, and the potential harm to the parents and the costs to the hospital seemed considerable? The "harm" of a disproportionate allocation of financial resources became the hottest topic of discussion. If money was allocated to keeping alive infants whose chances for a normal life seemed minimal, money, both in terms of staff time and new medical devices, would have to be taken away from standard care for infants born without such complications.

The deliberations of our committee progressed slowly, in part because of the complexity of the issues, and in part because the neonatal medical professionals were always being called out of our meetings to handle emergencies. The discussions produced heated debates, often between the medical professionals who sought a standard of "Best Medical Practices," and hospital chaplains who endorsed a "sanctity of all life, always and everywhere" standard.

My supposed role in the discussion was to be "a voice of reason," on the presumption that philosophy meant the application of reasoned and unbiased reflection to difficult moral problems. It was clear to me that first of all, cost/benefit analysis was not going to be a very effective way to solve the problems. Economics certainly plays a major role in making medical decisions, but there is some standard behind and beyond the simple formula of how much bang can you get for how many bucks.

The second issue was more complex: we could not resolve our issues based upon any particular religious perspective. The chaplains, whether Catholic, Protestant, or Jewish, differed among themselves as to what religion might dictate in terms of a debate between sanctity of life and quality of life. And the vigorous opposition to religion of one member of the committee made the adoption of formulas from any religious tradition problematic. To the deeply religious members of the committee he would remark: "Get over it. The body is simply an ingenious system of replaceable parts." In the light of what seemed like irreconcilable points of view, my hope was to create a "secular ethic" that would satisfy both the deeply religious, and those who wished to stay more than arms length away from any particular religious point of view.

I soon realized that my project was a very large one, for I would somehow have to synthesize the best insights of ethicians and moralists from over three thousand years of recorded history. Was ethics really something that reason could work out, or is ethics, and morality, simply a matter of custom, habit, and acculturation? Are there any "truths" about ethics that reason can reach, and generate agreement upon, at least among those who will sit around a table in a conference room in a University Hospital? Are there any ethical standards that people can agree upon? Is there any basic common agreement among the religions of the world that might serve as a starting point for discussions of what it means to be ethical?

If I were a participant in those discussions today, I think I could argue my case somewhat more convincingly. Nonetheless, the issues remain just as intractable as they were years ago. Are there any common grounds for making ethical decisions? In ethical matters, is one person's opinion just as valid as anyone else's? Is ethical judgment purely subjective or emotional, or are there "objective" moral truths that should guide our behavior and our decision-making in terms of issues in medical ethics? These topics will be the principal concerns for most of this chapter.

VI-175
Reason, Sweet Reason

Among the famous sayings of Albert Einstein, one is especially applicable to our current concerns: "An explanation should be as simple as possible, but no simpler." Ethical reflections especially should be as simple as possible, but no simpler. Regarding different approaches to doing ethics. I favor the ethics of Aristotle, and his elaboration of what it means to be virtuous. Several commentators, ancient and modern, have said something along the lines of: "To think like Aristotle, and to be reasonable, is the same thing." Natural Law ethics, very popular among certain religious thinkers, has its roots in Aristotle. The Stoics, Hugo Grotius, and Immanuel Kant have each proposed distinctively rational approaches to doing ethics. The Consequentialist or Utilitarian approaches practiced by Bentham, Mill, and Peter Singer offer a very different approach to rational, secular ethics. The Contractarian Ethics espoused notably by John Rawls is especially popular in some circles.

David Hume suggested there was a great gap between fact and value, between observing what is and proclaiming what ought to be. Since that time, reason has been seen as "scientific," able to figure out both how the world is, and how to refashion the world. The pendulum of ethical reflection, ideas of "what ought to be," has meanwhile gone from relativism to nihilism, from "Your opinion is as good as mine," to "You have no right to pass judgment on anyone else's behavior." Every manifestation of relativism, however, has brought about an equal and opposite demand for some assurance of certitude in ethical matters.

Medical ethics and geo-political ethics lend themselves to discussion along the lines of cost-benefit analysis. How much money we should allocate to AIDS research or to searching for a cure for cancer, is formulated in terms of how much benefit can we get for how many dollars. Whether we should oppose tyranny somewhere is phrased in terms of how many American lives will it cost to remove malevolent dictators. What supports cost/benefit analysis, however, is some discussion of right and wrong, of desirable results to be produced, and of acceptable methods for producing those results.

Sometimes it appears that philosophy cannot help us with these issues, for philosophy appears to have lost its way, as well as its audience.

Gene Bammel

Pierre Hadot faults academic philosophers for absenting themselves from the discussion of real issues, getting lost in discussions of the internal coherence of a concept, and not its truth or falsity. Stanley Fish and other postmodernists have worked their spells on philosophy, literature, and humanities departments, convincing various practitioners that all patterns are arbitrary constructions, that truth as well as logic are human inventions, and that all aspects of life are contingent and subject to constant revision. Where pluralism postulated that there are many different approximations to the truth, postmodernism abandoned any hope of attaining anything that could go by the name of truth.

Other philosophers, following the lead of Pierre Hadot, suggested that we had placed too high a premium on the power to demonstrate, and forgotten that philosophy's role is to illumine. We had settled for pragmatism, finding something that worked, without raising the more important question of how do we use things for attaining ever greater goods. The task of philosophy is to stimulate discussion of how we are to use our "resources" wisely, and how we are to go about cultivating and enriching our humanity. The presumption is that there are reasonable and worthwhile answers to the larger questions, and that we can attain those answers.

It should come as no great surprise that "rationalists" would expect that reason could provide directions toward a "good" moral life. That the father of modern empiricism, John Locke, could have so much conviction about reason leading the way to ethical truth is worth quoting: "I doubt not, but from self-evident propositions, by necessary consequences, as incontestable as those in mathematics, the measures of right and wrong might be made out, with as much certainty as in any of the other sciences." It is time to explore whether Locke's optimism about finding and agreeing upon "ethical truth" is justified.

Reduced to its simplest forms, we demand reasons for our own behavior, as well as that of others. We ask ourselves, why should I do this? and we expect a reasonable answer. We have all likely had the experience of hearing a parent ask: "Why did you hit her?" And we have heard the inevitable response: "Because she hit me." Such a common event beggars all our attempts to find good reasons for what we do, and reveals how often our answers are appallingly inadequate!

Oswald Bammel, 80th Birthday

VI-176
"A Good Man Nowadays...."

When Lena Horne sang, "A Good Man Nowadays is Hard to Find," I doubt very much that she had the Aristotelian notion of virtue in mind. Despite the lack of a good theme song, "Virtue Ethics," deriving to some degree from the works of Aristotle, has become very popular among ethicians today. Aristotle is the first 'western' philosopher to write a treatise specifically on Ethics. It begins with the innocuous sentence "Every action is thought to aim at some good," proceeds to an examination of virtues like courage, temperance, justice and prudence, and concludes with a lengthy discourse on why happiness is best found in the life of the mind.

Criticism of "virtue ethics" ranges from "It's just a series of empty phrases," to "An ethical theory based so much on character doesn't really touch the central problems." The greatest current proponent of Virtue Ethics, Alasdair MacIntyre, says that it is the only approach that will hold together the various fragments of conflicting traditions we struggle with. We are, he says, Platonic perfectionists in awarding athletes gold medals; we are utilitarians in applying triage to the wounded in war; we are Lockeans in stressing rights based in property; we are Judeo-Christian in idealizing social justice; and we are followers of Kant and Mill in affirming the importance of duty and personal autonomy.

There are two Greek words that are central to understanding Aristotle's notion of ethics. The first is *endoxa,* impossible to translate, but meaning something like "the wisdom of your contemporaries," or, "the moral practices that have become customary in your community." Aristotle was convinced that long human experience had enabled people to be perceptive about what needs to be done to hold society together. That this is not just an early version of utilitarianism or pragmatism, and not just bowing to custom, is seen in the central position of the second Greek word, "*phronesis.*" This is often translated by the bare word "prudence," and means: "what practical intelligence sees as the proper course of action."

Aristotle makes two odd claims: that you cannot have one virtue unless you have them all, and, your character as a virtuous person is centered in your capacity for "prudence." In every situation, the virtuous person will have "insight" into proper behavior, and this becomes anchored in the "character" of the person who is habituated to acting virtuously. Only the virtuous person, says Aristotle, will live "the good life," and only the virtuous person will be truly happy.

Aristotle notes that happiness comes from living virtuously, and then adds that real happiness comes from exercising well the unique human capacity for thinking. Presumably, Aristotle found great delight in exercising his own considerable intellectual powers, for he concludes: "Thinking philosophical thoughts is clearly the pleasantest of all virtuous activities." (Small wonder that so many philosophers have so much enthusiasm for Aristotle!)

In Buddhism, the Enlightened One comes back to help others along the path to righteous living. Aristotle thought in much the same way, and so do current proponents of virtue ethics. Carol Gilligan says the follower of virtue ethics has "a very strong sense of being responsible to the world." Iris Murdoch, author of *The Sovereignty of Good* and other philosophical classics, is an excellent example. She left her Oxford professorship to write novels so that the "general public" could become familiar with her notions of virtuous living. (Jane Austen's novels are taken as the model of literature discussing the demands of virtue. Occasionally, modern artists will acknowledge the explicitly "moral" intentions of their art.)

The main themes of "virtue ethics" are pretty simple: there is no real happiness apart from virtuous living; the goal of human existence is the development of a virtuous character; and, virtue is a civic enterprise, for you do not become virtuous in isolation, nor is your virtue for your own enjoyment. It should be clear that religious-minded people could find an ally in virtue ethics.

Some critics of virtue ethics have noted that while religious ethics, and any ethics of altruism, may require us to lay down our lives for what we believe in, virtue ethics may be seen as seeking happiness in that prudent behavior that preserves the life and well being of the virtuous person. Proponents of this ethic respond that the virtuous person, like Socrates, may well lay down life for the sake of the apparent good of the community, even when they think the judgment of the community is erroneous. The virtuous person, they say, will see that each of us is a member of the human community, and will want to do what is in the best interests of that community.

Virtue ethics is not complete in itself, and lends itself to supplementation found in other ethical traditions. One of the most influential books on ethics in the twentieth century, John Rawls' *A Theory of Justice*, is a "contractarian" way of completing the vision of what virtue ethics has to offer. Wherever such discussions may take us, we can acknowledge, along with Lena Horne, that a good man nowadays is not easy to find, and perhaps the reason is that, not enough of us have been giving "virtue ethics" its due.

VI-177
Natural Law Ethics?

Is there an unchanging morality, written into the nature of things, that eventually all "right thinking" persons will acknowledge? Such is the basic contention of natural law theorists, along with some endorsers of "natural rights." The big question however is, where does this nature come from, and how do we get to know it?

It was of course the ancient Greek philosophers who first recognized the problem, and once more, two Greek words are the signposts of the dilemma. *Physis*, from which we get our word "physics," means "nature" in Greek, and it signifies "what is written into the heart of things." *Nomos* means something like "custom," or, "the laws that are merely human." That fire burns and is hot is physics, while driving on the right hand side of the road is custom, a law that really could be otherwise.

The *Dialogues of Plato* can be read as so many hymns to an unchanging moral reality, identified in *The Republic* as "The Good," the knowledge of which is best attained by some kind of dialectic or argumentative process that leads to an "intuition" of this eternal and unchanging bedrock of reality. Aristotle in *The Ethics* claimed that clear reasoning would lead to a perception of a justice "that everywhere has the same force, and is not a matter of people thinking this or that."

The Greek and Roman Stoics said human nature is simply one part of the natural order, and hence there is a law of nature applicable to human conduct. As Cicero put it: "True Law is right reason in conformity with nature. It is of universal application, unchanging and everlasting."

Thomas Aquinas is the most influential of all natural law theorists, and his thinking on morals remains the nucleus of Roman Catholic ethical reflection to this day. "Whatever is contrary to the order of reason is contrary to the nature of human beings as such; and what is reasonable is in accordance with human nature as such." In regard to morals, no philosopher has ever been a greater proponent of reason than Aquinas: "The rule and measure of human acts is reason." In our own day, those who would reject relativism or moral skepticism turn with increasing frequency to the apparent certainty offered by natural law and natural law theorists.

Even more popular today, however, are statements of "human rights," and Hugo Grotius, in 1625, wrote that human nature entails human rights, a notion that influenced both the American and French revolutions. In one of the most remarkable of all political statements, Thomas Jefferson wrote: "We hold these truths to be self-evident, that all men are endowed by their Creator with certain inalienable rights." As magnificent as is this idea, philosophers remain puzzled both about how such truths could be self-evident, and how such rights came to be anchored in a human nature. Nevertheless, from Hobbes to Rawls, "contract theories" based in people having rights, have become the bases of most political philosophies.

While natural law theories are appealing in their simplicity, within the community of ethicians, there are more critics than supporters. Modern moralists contend that there are a great many different ways of being human, and that "human nature" is a convenient fiction covering up an underlying diversity. Both utilitarians and rights theorists maintain that morals can be rationally justified, and that there are genuine moral goods. But neither utilitarians nor rights theorists think that reason can support the view of "universal human nature" maintained by the supporters of natural law.

Opponents of natural law theories produce various reductions to absurdity, illustrated by the view that an action is wrong if it is at odds with a relevant biological function. This would eliminate not only contraception and homosexuality, but also kissing (a misuse of the mouth meant for eating) or typing (a misuse of hands meant for hard work). We in fact do violence to "nature" all the time, when we dam rivers, plant fields, prevent mudslides, or kill mosquitoes, which after all are just living in accord with their "nature."

Natural law opponents claim that "human nature" is simply a social construct, and that what we call human nature can be realized in many different ways. As Stephen Buckle, a critic of natural law theories expressed it: "Natural law differs from its competitors by resisting the tendency to accept that human flourishing admits of an immense variety of forms, achievable by equally diverse ways of living."

Few moralists defend either pure relativism or pure skepticism about morals. Natural law theories present one way of rejecting relativism and skepticism, but there may be other, better ways to defend the objectivity of morals. The ethical theories of Kant and Mill may provide more acceptable philosophical support for the moral and ethical standards necessary if individuals are to flourish, and if society is to prosper. Socrates stands as a perpetual reminder of the importance of this project, "for it is no trivial matter we are discussing, but how we are to live our lives."

VI-178
Is Ethics Duty?

"Many people think Kant offers the best possible attempt to find Reasons, and therefore to justify ethics on the basis of reason alone." So wrote Simon Blackburn, author of *Being Good*. Immanuel Kant is not only one of the ten most important of all philosophers; as Plato and Aristotle dominated the philosophy of the ancient world, so does Kant dominate modern philosophy.

By no stretch of the imagination is Kant's philosophy easy to understand. What appears deceptively simple is often simply deceptive. The basic principles of Kant's moral philosophy seem quite elementary: you have free will, and are thus responsible for your actions; there is a Universal Moral Law; the only thing that is good beyond all doubt is a good will; and you should treat others always as ends, and never as means.

Kant philosophized when Newtonian physics was all the rage. His contemporaries were quite taken with the universality of the laws of nature, and the idea was in the air that if you knew the elements of brain physiology, you could predict every action an individual would take. Kant would have none of this; he said even if, at the phenomenal level this were the case, at a deeper, noumenal level, there is free choice, and responsibility for actions.

(A little bit of Kantian terminology: "phenomena" are the appearances of things; "noumena" are things-in-themselves, things perhaps beyond human comprehension.)

Kant thought morality was anchored by this Principle: "Act only according to the Maxim by which you can at the same time will that it should become a universal law." The examples Kant gives are telling the truth, and promise keeping. Suppose you wanted to borrow money, promising to pay it back, but knowing that you would not. Kant says, unless you can count on people always telling the truth, and always intending to keep their promises, not only would the banking system fall apart, so would human society. In the most perplexing example Kant offers, suppose a murderer asks you if his intended victim is in your house; Kant says even here, you must tell the truth, or else the universal maxim falls apart. Kant tries to 'save appearances,' by saying, supposed you lied, the intended victim has actually departed, only to encounter the murderer in the street. In a word, the maxim, once established, permits of no exceptions.

For Kant, the fundamental ethical question is "What ought I to do?" His stock answer is: I ought to do my duty. Not only should I act in the light of what I see as a universal law, but I am most moral when I act simply out of the sense of duty, and not for any hope of reward or fear of punishment. The shopkeeper, who does not cheat for fear of alienating a customer or from fear of losing business, is not really virtuous, but the shopkeeper who is always honest out of a sense of duty, is the truly moral person. (That there is something a little strange here is illustrated by a parent who provides toys not out of a sense of delight but out of a sense of duty, or the lover whose kisses are duty-based, not affection-originated.)

There is a "formalism" in Kant's axiom: "The only thing that is unreservedly good is a good will." Kant wished to emphasize the importance of intention in the moral life, but left it devoid of the human passion, the warmth of emotion, that seems to irradiate the actions of people we identify as acting most morally. Did the passengers who thwarted the hijackers of Flight 93 on September 11, 2001 act out of a sense of duty, simply from a good will, or did they not find some "delight" in the very excellence of their actions? As this illustrates, having a good will, and acting from a sense of duty, is only one aspect of the truly moral life, for such a life is clearly multi-dimensional.

Seeking the broadest possible expression of his Universal Moral Law, Kant wrote: "So act that you use humanity, whether in your own person or the person of any other, always at the same time as an end, never merely as a means." This sense of respect for persons, of not using others as means to our own ends, is the most enduring of all Kant's epigrams. When

Martin Buber wrote: "I only become an I in relation to a Thou," he was revising and enlarging the great Kantian maxim. When John Rawls based his ethics on the constructive principles that would be chosen by genuinely rational agents wanting to make society functional, his indebtedness to Kant remains beyond doubt.

What are we to make of Kant's ethics? It is one of the two great modern attempts to vindicate Universal Moral Principles by the exercise of reason alone apart from any theological framework. If you are convinced that you have free will, that you choose only those actions you are willing to bind everyone else to, and you are willing to make of your life an Ode to Duty, to that extent you are a Kantian. But if you are a truly modern person, I suspect you are also indebted to consequentialism, to which we now turn.

VI-179
Consequentialism, and the Invasion of Iraq

Should we have invaded Iraq? What seems like a straightforward political question is rich in ethical overtones. If you subscribe to a morality of principles, rights, and duties, then, at first blush, since nations are sovereign and no other nation should have any right to interfere with internal politics, such an invasion would appear illegal. If you are a utilitarian and think the ultimate principle of morality is the greatest good for the greatest number, and if you are convinced that Iraq posed a threat to the happiness and well-being of the rest of the world, then you would feel some moral obligation to invade Iraq, for the deaths such an invasion would cause leads to the greater good of a much larger number.

Utilitarianism is an ethical theory developed initially by Jeremy Bentham in the eighteenth century, significantly modified by John Stuart Mill in the nineteenth century, and brought to full flower by such twentieth century moralists as R. M. Hare and Peter Singer. Bentham's initial statement is quite simple: "Nature has placed mankind under the governance of two sovereign masters, pain and pleasure. It is for them alone to point out what we ought to do, as well as to determine what we shall do." In other words, Morality is tailored to the pursuit of what provides pleasure, and what avoids pain. Mill and others established a hierarchy of pleasures, culminating in the catch phrase: "It is better to be a human being dissatisfied, than a pig satisfied; better to be Socrates dissatisfied than a fool satisfied." The question is, can ethics be built on a foundation of what constitutes individual pleasures, however hierarchically arranged?

Is it possible to establish a hierarchy of how many goods for how great a number?

From the beginning, Bentham sought to replace the importance of law or duty with the production of social goods. Bentham and Mill, like Adam Smith, were convinced that if everyone pursued their individual goods, somehow the good of the whole society would be achieved. Some "invisible hand" would produce the common good, out of the pursuit of individual goods. The fact is, if we each desire what is pleasant to ourselves, then nobody desires what is pleasant to others, unless the pleasure of others is somehow an equal object of pleasure to each of us. Simon Blackburn said this would be a world of wonderful universal sympathy, but not quite the world we really live in.

Parents are almost always Kantians at some stage in the moral education of their children. What parent has not said: "*You can't do that. What if everybody did it?*" The categorical imperative of Immanuel Kant comes through in such a universal parental remark. Parents are also consequentialists or utilitarians at some stage in the moral education of their children. Is there any parent who has not said: "*How would you like it if someone did that to you?*" Parenting appears to be very much a matter of educating children into looking at the consequences of their actions.

Modern moral philosophy, as expressed by John Rawls in *A Theory of Justice*, and popularized by T.M. Scanlon in *What We Owe To Each Other*, is more a discussion of justice and rights than an analysis of the consequences of particular moral choices. Nevertheless, the moral analysis found in editorials and popular journals is overwhelmingly consequentialist. A bulletin from Planned Parenthood details the benefits to society of both contraception and abortion. Mixing consequentialism and rights theories, most of the criticism of Islamic societies is based in their rejection of rights to the various "freedoms" long regarded as belonging to every human being under any political regime.

Utilitarianisms' shortcoming is that it requires a moral vision derived from something beyond utility to judge what happiness is, and how it is to be attained. A vision of human excellence, and what must be done to promote that excellence, must be a component of any workable ethic. Notions of duty, obligation, and rights are all important building blocks of any successful ethical vision. Understanding the consequences of behavior is likewise a crucial part of any ethical system that people can actually live by.

Should we have invaded Iraq, and displaced Saddam Hussein? The consequences of not doing so could have been devastating, causing many more deaths than the actual invasion. Does a nation lose its claim to sovereignty when its actions could lead to massive loss of life elsewhere? Does another nation, apart from approval by the United Nations, have a "right" to decide that its own safety is so imperiled by a dictator of dubious morals, that it may initiate massive armed conflict? These are large ethical issues, issues that have in reality been decided very much along the lines of "consequentialist" reasoning. In our everyday moral life, we often mask our consequentialist reasoning with appeals to principles. The strength of consequentialism is that it shows what the elements of good arguments must be, and how the appeal to rights, rules, duties, and principled behavior, is all part of the examination of the consequences of the actions we choose. Object to it how we may, the truth of the matter is, Consequentialism is the leading moral philosophy of our day, even if we do our best to pretend otherwise.

VI-180
A Just War?

Talk about ethics and morals is just talk, until you hit upon puzzling moral issues. An issue that will be with us for some time: does America, the one remaining super-power, have any right to wage war against what are presumably rogue nations? While it is important to understand the differences between Rule-based ethics and the views of consequentialists, or an ethics of duty versus an ethic of results, the issue of "just war" overlaps all the formulas ethicists have proposed.

Philosophers and theologians have elaborated a number of theories as to what justifies war, how a nation might defend itself, how war should be conducted, and whether a deliberately aggressive war is ever justified. Historically, most of those who discussed "the justice of war," presumed some equality between combatants, as if proposing guidelines for battle between two enemies who shared a great community of interests, and who would, after the battles, settle back into happy arrangements of commerce and mutual respect. That warfare seldom has those features has not escaped the notice of modern critics of just war theory.

Writers as diverse as Augustine of Hippo, Thomas Aquinas, Hugo Grotius, and the more recent Michael Walzer, George Weigel, and Stanley Hauerwas have made distinctive contributions to the just war theory. The basic elements of the theory are: the war must have a just cause, it must be declared by the proper authority, it must have a reasonable chance of success, and the means used must be proportional to the end desired. Until the twentieth century, self-defense against physical aggression was taken as the only basis for just cause. Michael Walzer suggested that given nuclear reality, all the traditional arguments for just war went by the wayside.

Pacifists have persistently voiced objections to any talk of just wars. Gandhi said: "An eye for an eye, and pretty soon the whole world is blind." Stanley Hauerwas suggested that war is always and everywhere wrong, and threats of war must be objected to in the most vigorous manner. On the other side, George Weigel rejected pacifism in one simple sentence: "The difference between pacifism and the just war tradition is that the latter recognizes that there are circumstances in which the use of proportionate and discriminate armed force is a moral obligation in pursuit of peace."

Some Consequentialists are disposed to say that if victory is sought, all means should be employed. If your cause is just, use whatever means are necessary. By contrast, Rule-based ethics proclaims that there are rules that govern not only the behavior of sovereign nations, but also a *jus gentium*, a law of and between nations, that establishes absolute limits as to what one nation may do to another nation.

Books like Huntington's *The Clash of Civilizations* and Fukuyama's *The End of History* made the case that we are in a new world order, or perhaps a new world of disorder, and that the old idea of warfare between nations who shared similar moral frameworks no longer applies. We have suddenly discovered that Islam represents a very different context for moral questions than "westerners" expect. Islamic theologians a thousand years ago divided the world into two realms: the Abode of Islam, and the remainder of the world, the Abode of War. Islamic jurists have operated in a much different historical context where the just war theories elaborated by Christian theologians or western philosophers do not apply. (It is important to note that the Just War Theory as elaborated by Thomas Aquinas provided some justification for the Crusades, and for the Inquisition: the elimination of those who imperil your eternal salvation is more important than the removal of thieves or traitors from your midst.) Islamic jurists have for centuries seen themselves as in a battle to the death against the non-Islamic world, so organizations like Al-Qaida should come as no big surprise.

In February of 1998, Osama bin Laden issued a *fatwa* (historically a proclamation by a Caliph in defense of an Islamic country) calling for a *jihad*, a holy war against America: "In compliance with God's order, we issue the following fatwa to all Muslims: the ruling to kill the Americans and their allies--civilians and military--is an individual duty for every Muslim who can do it in any country in which it is possible to do it...."

This proclamation proposed not a new world order, but a new world of disorder, where terror and the killing of non-combatants suspends any vision of combat to right a wrong, or of a battle to fend off an enemy that has invaded your territory. Similarly, the potential for weapons of mass destruction that might be used indiscriminately, goes beyond anything ever considered in traditional "just war" theory.

In terms of a "war" upon Iraq, the western understanding of a just war would appear to apply. It appeared that we had good answers for most of the long agreed upon questions about waging a just war: Is there a just cause for initiating a war? Is there a reasonable chance of success? Have all diplomatic means been exhausted? Can civilian casualties be minimized? Can we use means that are proportionate to the ends we hope to attain?

Cities of the Middle East from Istanbul to Jerusalem retain vivid memories of the bloodshed caused by the Crusades almost a thousand years ago. The battle cries of the western invaders may still echo in some of the region's caves: "Our Cause is just," and, "God wills it." This time, let us hope that justice really has been done, and that the outcome of this "just war" will be the dawn of a new era of peace in the troubled Middle East.

VI-181
Ethics as Contract?

To adapt a joke from Mark Twain: Imagine a Retirement Community, and then imagine a group of people who constantly disagree. Ah, but I repeat myself! (Twain said: Imagine the Congress of the United States. Then imagine a bunch of really ignorant people....). Retirement communities, and Homeowners Associations generally, establish their society through some kind of contract, some agreement as to what is permissible and what forbidden, what behaviors are encouraged, and what community regulations shall be enforced. The big question is, how do you create such a contract, what values do you bring to the table, and how do you insure that the good of the community will prevail over the good of any given individual, without demolishing the liberties of the individuals involved, and without creating perpetual sources of disagreement?

So far, we have looked at ethics as based in the pursuit of virtuous living; we have examined ethics as following the dictates of natural law; we have seen how some ethicians regard duty as the root of all morality, and we have looked at the examination of consequences as the principal basis for ethical reflection.

When you come right down to it, however, practical ethics often seems to be based in some contract, written or implied, about how members of any group retain certain rights, and in return have certain obligations to fulfill. The philosophers who support this point of view are called "contractarians." T.M. Scanlon, for example, says that the "contract" that holds a given group together must be based on reasonable, informed, unforced general agreement as to what goes into that contract. Jurgen Habermas says a contract must have principles "that will provide for the satisfaction of everyone's interests."

But what is the basis for these agreements and principles? John Rawls opened his important book *A Theory of Justice*, with this sentence: "Justice is the first virtue of social institutions." Rawls asked, where do you find these principles of justice that will engender a good society? He suggested we use our imagination, and that, as we envision ourselves creating the contract of our just society (whether it be a Retirement community, a city, or a country), we don't know what social role we will have, we do not know if we will be rich or poor in that society, we do not know if we will be athletically endowed or physically challenged. Since you don't know which piece of the cake you are cutting is going to be yours, it may be in your best interest to make each piece the same size. You will have a vested interest not only in being as fair as possible, but, says Rawls, you should have a special concern for the disadvantaged, since you may be one of them. Such a society is neither capitalist nor communist, but has uppermost in mind the 'welfare' of those who are least likely to care for themselves.

Rawls said all we can bring to the negotiating table are the most basic human concerns, like safety, taking care of human needs, and assurances of self-respect. He thought the contract inspired by these ideals would guarantee a fair distribution of liberties, and those who are most able to be productive would not regret the fair distribution to the less fortunate of some of what they produce. It is no great wonder that, twenty years after the publication of *A Theory of Justice*, Rawls' next major book was entitled: *Political Liberalism*. In fashioning a political philosophy, Rawls has produced clear statements on how some kind of "contract" serves as the charter of rights and duties of the subscribers to the contract. What is still not clear is where the values that are the basis of the contract come from. Suppose the contractarians assert that "capitalism is unfair," or that "women should always be subservient," or that "using preemptive strikes against any potential enemy is desirable." Values in contractarian ethics do not miraculously appear as the contract is being written. As Scanlon observed, "We all believe that some actions are morally wrong. But when we claim that an action is wrong, what kind of judgment are we making?" Where does that ethical conviction come from? Scanlon suggests that those who write contracts should do so with a clear consequentialist orientation, because the contract derives its power from a vision of what consequences the parties to the contract wish to bring about. This seems like a far cry both from the Kantian references to treating all persons as ends and never as means, and the "universal" principles of morality to which Rawls repeatedly refers.

Anyone who is living by a contract--whether in a Home Owners Association, or working in a corporation, is a living exhibit of how ethics are put into practice. No doubt, those who live and work by such contracts must occasionally wonder if there isn't some more secure underpinning for the moral assumptions involved. The experience of all who have entered into such contracts motivates all those who would sit down to the negotiating table, to discover beforehand some fundamental ethical principles. Simon Blackburn concluded: "Ethical principles are those that would be agreed upon in any reasonable cooperative procedure for coming to one mind about our conduct." In civilized society, there must needs be contracts, but there must also be a great deal of moral soul-searching, before, during, and after, the contract, or endless disputations will be the inevitable result.

VI-182
From a Moral Point of View...

The more one reads the theories of the various ethicians, the more applicable the remark of Thomas Aquinas: "When faced with a critical ethical decision, do not consult a moral philosopher, consult a virtuous person." Thomas Aquinas is a major figure for advocates of both the "virtue ethics" position and the "natural law" basis of ethics. Aquinas has been called one of the greatest "rationalists" of all time, so great was his faith in the power of reason. But he is just one of the many philosophers convinced that reason will get you a lot of good answers for your ethical questions. For all such "rationalists," there is a conviction that, if you just reason things through, you will discover universal principles that will guide you through your moral dilemmas. The golden rule, in its various formulations, seems like something most reasonable people should be able to agree to: "Don't do to others what you wouldn't have done to you."

The modern rejection of reason as the basis for ethics begins with David Hume. His summary statement has been widely quoted: "Reason is, and ought only to be, the servant of the passions." ("Passions" was Hume's word for what we would call "emotions.") He says reason will not lead

317

you very far in telling you what you ought to do, but sentiment, feeling, will. Put yourself in the companionship of those who feel deeply, and, says Hume, you will be well treated. In this, Hume has an ancient companion in Confucius, who said *benevolence*, or concern for humanity, was the secure root of all decent human behavior. To put it simply: who would you rather have as a companion: someone who is always looking for good reasons for things, or someone who wishes others well, and has a great sensitivity to what others are feeling?

James Q. Wilson has been a prolific writer on social and political issues. His book on ethics is entitled: *The Moral Sense*, and the opening chapters are entitled: Sympathy, Fairness, and Self-Control. Wilson claimed that moral behavior is rooted in sympathy for fellow-sufferers of the human condition. Being able to put ourselves in someone else's shoes is the beginning of seeing all of the human race as part of our own family, to whom we owe respect and "sympathy," which means "feeling along with."

Ethics in the world of Greek and Roman antiquity was rooted in determining what human "nature" demanded, and seeing how duties and obligations would flow from fidelity to that nature. Modern ethics is not so sure about there being any one human "nature." This results, as Richard Rorty suggests, in trying to figure out what customs, habits and practices will be beneficial to human beings everywhere. Rorty's highest aspiration is that we replace the passion for knowledge with passionate hope for the human future, and that we take the steps necessary to reach that future.

Are there universal and absolute ethical principles that all thinking people should subscribe to, wherever they may be, and however they may be raised? Rationalist philosophers maintain that if people would just sit down and reason things through, eventually agreement on the great ethical principles would be attained. The Parliament of the World's Religions in 1994 created a document of just such proportions, but it has had little effect. Philosophers who seek to combine reason and sentiment fare somewhat better. Those who in the footsteps of Simon Blackburn have distilled what reason and sentiment can agree on: Happiness is preferable to misery, dignity better than humiliation; it is bad that people suffer, and worse if a culture turns a blind eye to their suffering; it is good to promote life, and the attempt to find a common point of view is preferable to a refusal to discuss issues of universal concern.

In matters of morals, there are no easy answers. When faced with great moral questions, it is a mistake to underestimate the value of people who seem to have a sense for what is the right path of conduct. Having the right moral sentiments counts for much, but tempering sentiment with clear-headed rational reflection seems like an even better bet for producing standards for a morally exemplary life, and a society that promotes human well-being.

VI-183
Rawls and Reason

What is the role of reason in ethics? The tradition from David Hume to Richard Rorty maintains that "sentiment" or "feeling" leads you to certain ethical standpoints, and the challenge is to find reasons to justify your point of view. An alternative tradition, stretching from Aristotle to John Rawls, affirms the primacy of reason in establishing a workable ethics, in the expectation that appropriate sentiments will follow.

This is not a trivial issue for individuals hoping to establish their own personal ethics, nor is it trivial in the history of philosophy. Books like John Cooper's *Reason In Aristotle's Ethics* point out ambiguities in Aristotle's account of "how to lead a flourishing life," ambiguities related both to establishing ethical principles, and the process of making personal moral decisions. Aristotle repeatedly refers to the importance of "right upbringing" in the development of moral character, assuming morality is based in something more basic and antecedent to, moral reflection.

Ethicists insist on "seeing the point," as if ethics were not a matter of argument at all, but a matter of "intuition." Beginning with Plato, there is a long and viable tradition that says ethics is based on "seeing" the truth with absolute certainty, quite apart from argument. Husserl said if we do not "see" the truth, there is no point in arguing. G.E. Moore simply gave a withering stare to anyone who did not "see" how "the Good" was something you simply intuited. (How curious the prevalence of visual metaphors in the doing of philosophy!)

John Rawls, who discusses where ethics comes from in his book *Lectures on the History of Moral Philosophy*, refers to "intuitively appealing accounts," "various reasonable and natural assumptions," and finally, "the importance of initial convictions." He admitted, in *Political Liberalism*, that his own ethics was based on "the unsupported assertions of my own political preferences." For a thorough discussion of this issue, see Ch. 3 "Reason and Its Vicissitudes," in John Solomon's book, *The Joy Of Philosophy*.

Allan Gibberd, in *Wise Choices, Apt Feelings*, suggested that the personal ethics each of us lives by is based in a "coherence of preferences." Is it the case that building a personal ethics is a matter of conjoining those principles that get along with each other, and somehow add up to a coherent moral philosophy? Do most of us wind up in the situation of having a variety of moral principles that we earnestly hope will cohere, and add up to something that makes sense? Or, do we begin with some guiding moral principle, and derive lesser corollaries from this one true North Star?

For most people most of the time, it is very difficult to explain where ethical convictions come from, or how they are justified. (Why is it that when you have *done* wrong, you *feel* guilty?) Most of us have ethical convictions, and occasionally try to create a "reasonable" explanation of how we come to have them. It is exceedingly rare that anyone changes ethical convictions as a result of argument. Ethics is rooted in something deeper than reason, so it dwells somewhere beyond the reach of argument.

With respect to reason and feeling, what can we conclude? Only that reason and sentiment are the two intertwined components of our moral lives, and that trying to award primacy to one component is a perilous enterprise. Philosophical reflection on morals may not improve our moral behavior, but it should make us more aware of the seriousness of our moral dilemmas. As Robert Solomon said, "Philosophy is the one academic discipline that tends to naturally emerge in everyone's life, in times of turmoil or traumatic change or simply in quiet moments of reflection." The work of philosophy is to help us make sense of our lives. And ethics, or moral reflection, is the domain of philosophy whose territory we continually occupy, and whose problems remain our most constant companions.

VI-184
Confrontation!

Life is full of confrontations. At work, you may stand by helplessly as unpleasant confrontations occur between employer and employee, or between service workers and customers. In Homeowner's Associations or in civic groups, you may see wrenching effects of dissident groups bringing lawsuits over interpretations of by-laws. At Universities, there may be vibrant confrontations brought about by an impending budget cutback, as decisions are made about which departments or programs will be decimated or terminated, while others receive additional funds.

In the larger world, there are the confrontations brought on by the mismanagement of corporations, resulting in unemployment and financial ruin. The United States, not to mention the United Nations, suffer the consequences of unresolved confrontations around the globe. Different racial, religious, and political groups seem bogged down in endless and irresolvable conflict.

There are, however, at least two different rays of hope. A visitor from Somalia commented that an important part of the British tradition was learning how to argue and work your way through a dispute, "Without taking it personally." Putting that into practice could be universally helpful. "Anger management" and "Resolution through Arbitration" programs seem to be springing up everywhere.

The sad fact of the matter is that life inevitably involves confrontation between opposing points of view. The solution proposed by these programs comes in five steps: (1) listen attentively to the point of view of your opponent. Make sure you are clear about what position is being taken, and try to shed your inclination to read hostility or negativity into what your opponent says. (2) Indicate and express clearly your awareness of whatever good points you can find in your opponent's position. (3) With the least amount of emotional involvement possible, ask your opponent to listen patiently to your point of view. (4) Look for whatever "common grounds" you do have, and see if these provide "building blocks" for a resolution of your dispute. (5) If the dispute seems irresolvable, see if you can agree to disagree on particular issues, while working to resolve other issues. There may be times when you simply have to walk away, leave issues unresolved, and agree to meet at a later date, while striving to maintain civility.

Even with the best will in the world, and great commitment to seeing things from another's point of view, genuine differences of conviction will occur. Some part of maturity, for individuals as for nations, is learning to live with these differences. A variety of western religious, philosophical, and political traditions have maintained throughout the ages that one major goal of all human striving is peace. History demonstrates, however, that there are times when war and open hostility is inevitable. As Aristotle said: "We work that we may have leisure, just as we make war only that we may have peace." There are occasions when peace in any form seems impossible.

Eastern traditions have persistently emphasized that peace, whether personal or global, comes from within. The Dalai Lama said: "Genuine, lasting world peace will only be possible as a result of each of us making an effort internally." And Thich Nhat Hanh, convinced that world peace is only possible when every citizen of the world seeks peace within, wrote: "Continue your daily practice of mindfulness, observing the cypress tree in your own courtyard, with all of your peace, serenity, and presence. The practice is enjoyable. There is no need to waste time or distract ourselves."

The world would be a much more peaceful place if everyone could put into practice of the contemplation of the tree in the courtyard, or pay heed to the biblical admonition: "Do not let the sun go down on your anger."

What better arena for the cultivation of virtue ethics than the establishment of peace, and what better starting place than within our own selves. Perhaps peace itself surpasses all understanding, but without it the world is in danger of becoming an empty and desolate place, devoid not only of human values, but of humanity itself. The end of all confrontation should be resolution, and the goal of all ethics should be the establishment of a peaceful world, where conflicts may be resolved rationally, and every human being can mature as fully as possible, free from the threats of irresolvable confrontations.

VI-185
Religion and Reason

What has Athens to do with Jerusalem? What happens when faith confronts reason? Or what happens when philosophy encounters religious belief? There are three possibilities: (1) belief silences the mind; (2) belief and thinking re-enforce each other; (3) thinking blots out belief, for once you begin thinking, faith becomes impossible.

For belief silencing the mind, Tertullian is the first Christian witness. If it is "faith," wrote Tertullian, it requires a certain "sacrifice of the intellect." If it is "faith," it must be assent to what the human intellect thinks is impossible. Tertullian reflected on what the Christian faith regarded as the two principle revealed mysteries: that the One God was Three Persons in One Nature, and that one of those persons had two natures, one Divine, the other human. Tertullian epitomized what he thought was the appropriate Christian response: "*Credo quia absurdum est,*" "I believe because it is absurd." The Latin adjective *absurdum* means "impossible," or "irrational," or "contradicting reason."

Within Judaism, the gap between faith and reason is summarized by the refrain from Isaiah, "My thoughts are not your thoughts, nor your ways my ways." (*Isaiah,* 55:8.) Judaism has always revered "pious reflection," and the Talmud, like *The Sayings of the Fathers,* is simply "pious reflection on the Word of God." To put it as simply as possible, Judaism is a "practice of the Presence of God," and the Jewish tradition is epitomized well by the request of the Psalmist: "*Taste* and *see* that the Lord is sweet." It is the *experience* of God that matters, not what reason has to say.

Islam has long been aware of the conflict between faith and reason. Some Medieval Moslem philosophers, like Averroes, were disposed to say that the truths religion offered to the uneducated, could be perceived in a deeper way by philosophers. More characteristically, Moslem philosophers from Al-Farabi to Al-Ghazzali claimed that where reason and faith differed, reason was clearly wrong, and had to be put aside. Islam has persistently affirmed that faith means "submission," and the believer prostrates body and mind before the Almighty. While there has always been a strong intellectual tradition within Islam, the mind is not what ultimately matters. What matters, first, last, and always, is Submission to the Will of Allah.

Buddhism would prefer to be silent on the whole issue. "Do not raise these conceptual issues, for they only trouble the mind." The Buddhist tradition consistently affirms that it is not by your concepts that you will be saved or lost, but by your practice. The so-called "Zen Doctrine of No-Mind," simply says, do not let your mind cut you off from the reality of everyday experience.

From a philosophical perspective, there is a long tradition of affirming that belief and thinking re-enforce each other. Generations of Christian writers have reflected on a sentence from the *Letter to the Hebrews*, which reads: "Without faith it is impossible to please God: for anyone who comes to God must believe that He exists, and that He saves those who search for Him." That sentence is not an invitation to leave your intellect at the door, but a demand for thinking about what "belief" means, and how your own intelligence marshals you in the direction of belief or unbelief. It is not very doctrinally demanding: all that's necessary is believing that God exists, and that He saves those who seek for Him...

Among philosophers, the third alternative, that no one who really thinks, can be a believer, has become widespread. Hume suggested that to think all this happened by chance is less an affront to the intellect than to posit an Omniscient Deity as the cause of it all. From the time of Darwin, philosophers have claimed that Evolution presents a compelling explanation for the way things are, and no "God hypothesis" is needed.

In the end, faith remains faith, "an assurance of things hoped for, a certainty of realities we do not see," and the global faith traditions, whether Jewish, Christian, Moslem, Buddhist, or Hindu, offer "pathways to salvation," something quite beyond the ken or capacity of philosophers. Faith offers salvation; the best that philosophy can offer is clarification. One philosopher took great delight in paraphrasing scripture in this way: "Truth, Profundity and Clarity: but the greatest of these is Clarity." It is worth noting that while all the great Scriptural traditions indicate that

323

faith is pleasing to God, none of them make any such claim for clarity or clarification…

Spanish Missionary, Antigua, Guatemala

VI-186
Religion and Ethics

To the question: Why can't the religions of the world get together and agree upon a common ethic? The answer is simple: they can, and they have! The Parliament of the World's Religions met in Chicago in 1993, and produced a remarkable document: *A Global Ethic: The Declaration of the Parliament of the World's Religions.* The document is available from Continuum Press, complete with commentaries by Hans Kung and Karl Kuschel. Its words are powerful and persuasive.

Introduction: "We condemn the abuses of the Earth's Ecosystems. We condemn the poverty that stifles life's potential. We condemn the social disarray of the nations, in particular we condemn aggression and hatred in the name of religion." "We affirm that a common set of core values is found in the teachings of the religions, and that these form the basis of a global ethic." "We affirm that there is an irrevocable, unconditional norm for all areas of life, for families and communities, for races, nations and religions."

"We declare: We are interdependent. We take individual responsibility for all we do. We must treat others as we wish others to treat us. We consider humankind our family. We commit ourselves to a culture of nonviolence, respect, justice and peace. We must strive for a just social and economic order, in which everyone has an equal chance to reach full potential as a human being. Earth cannot be changed for the better unless the consciousness of individuals is changed first."

Two basic principles form the bedrock of the Document: "We each have a responsibility for a better global order," and "Every human being must be treated humanely." The Document cites the most basic of ethical principles, "Do good and avoid evil," and lists various forms of the Golden Rule: "What you do not wish done to yourself, do not do to others."

The Document then lists four irrevocable directives: "Commitment to a culture of nonviolence and respect for life," "Commitment to a culture of solidarity and a just economic order," "Commitment to a culture of tolerance and a life of truthfulness," and "Commitment to a culture of equal rights and partnership between men and women."

It concludes with an exhortation for a transformation of consciousness: "Earth cannot be changed for the better unless the consciousness of individuals is changed. We pledge to work for such transformation, for a conversion of the heart." Then, almost as an afterthought, it adds: "We invite all men and women, whether religious or not, to do the same."

A Global Ethic is a powerful document, deserving of widespread dissemination and reflection. Not everyone will endorse all that the Document proposes, but it is as clear a statement as has ever been made of what the various religions of the world have in common in the ethical sphere. That is a not a bad place to begin reflection on how individuals, families, and nations, can learn to live together in peace, with hope for a peaceful today, and a better tomorrow.

Chapter VII.
Religion, and Other Big Issues

VII-187
Images of God

One of the consequences of ecumenism--the attempt to generate dialogue between members of different religions, -- is that participants often come to understand their own religion much more clearly. Extending the usual reach of ecumenical awareness, ever since 2001, courses in Islam have been very popular on American university campuses. In taking such courses, students have not infrequently come to a clearer understanding of the Jewish and Christian components of the western culture within which they live, and thereby understood more clearly their own religious beliefs or their indifference thereto.

Religions are attempts to affirm Divine Transcendence, usually balancing that with some degree of Divine Immanence. The central fact for most religions is expressing the paradox that the Divinity is somehow far above us, and yet in our midst. What good is a Divinity who is so far removed as to have nothing in common with us, no real contact with us, no way of being represented by us, no way of even being "imagined" by us? Or, what good is a Divinity that is so like us, it has no transcendent powers?

One of the most important verses of the Hebrew Bible is Genesis I: 26: "Let us make man in our image and likeness...So God created man in his own image, in the image of God He created him." This is a crucial text for the understanding of western religions. If man is somehow an image of

God, he does not need a golden calf or a statue to help him imagine what God is like: he needs only to look within himself.

Throughout the Hebrew Bible, the Transcendent God reveals Himself as One Who Acts In History, who leads Israel out of slavery, out of the desert and out of exile, a God who is mysteriously immanent, alternately instructing and punishing Israel. God is both a "hidden" God, and one who can be present on sacred ground, in a bush that burns without consuming, and who, when asked His name, provides the mysterious response of Exodus 3:14: "I will be what I will be." This puzzling phrase sometimes simply translated as: "I am there," or, "I am Who I am." Whatever the correct translation of the Hebrew EHYEH ASHER EHYEH, the point is that the God of the Bible is both near and far, Immanent and Transcendent. His ways tower above His chosen people, but His presence is "imaginable," for His people are made in His image and likeness.

Christianity emphasizes Divine Immanence. "The Word became flesh and dwelt among us." God becoming man is a scandal to other monotheist religions, but one early Christian theologian made the scandal even worse by writing: "He became human, that we might become divine." The created "image" is instructed to become more like to that of which it is the image. Christianity is filled with "images of God," and Christian churches enshrine crucifixes, tabernacles, and statues and paintings and stained glass windows of saints who "imitated" Christ. The enthronements of the Bible and the mysterious icons are all reminders of the Presence of God and his Immanence in the world.

In synagogues, the sanctuary lamp manifests the Presence of God, and the scrolls of the Torah are living symbols of His Presence. When you enter a mosque, however, you enter a different kind of religious sanctuary. The Koran borrows heavily from Hebrew and Christian scriptures, but allusions to man being in the "image and likeness of God" are nowhere to be found. Allah is beyond all imaging, for He is, as one Islamic scholar wrote, "a Transcendent God, beyond all human conceptions." The mosque has no altar, no statues, no imaging at all of this Transcendent God. The mosque is a place for prostration, an expression of total submission to the absolutely sovereign and Transcendent Deity. You may find a pulpit, where an Imam or religious teacher will "recite" the Koran, perhaps commenting upon it, but the Imam is no Rabbi or Priest, not an "intermediary" of any sort between God and man, but simply one who leads the faithful in submission to the Will of Allah.

The special character of Islam is that it is the most "transcendentalist" of the three great monotheistic religions. Its challenge lies in preserving the "Immanence " of God so well maintained by both Judaism and Christianity.

The Koran, like the Hebrew Bible and the Christian Testament, is not without its demands for social justice and equality, as captured in the Surah: "He is not a believer who does not wish for his brother what he wishes for himself." Without some anchor for the Immanence of Allah, His transcendence can obscure what is paramount in Jewish and Christian traditions. In Judaism, it is the community that moves towards salvation, not just the individual. And in Christianity, what you do to someone else is the same as doing it to God. Islam has a vivid sense of the *ummah*, the community of believers, but it would benefit from a greater emphasis on the Divine Presence in the midst of the human community.

When Islam learns to balance God's Transcendence with his Immanence, the world will be a safer place, freer from a potential clash of civilizations, and Jews, Christians, and Moslems, will be able to go about their business as citizens of a heavenly Jerusalem, right here on earth.

Church Painting, God, Oaxaca, Mexico

VII-188
Heart Disease

The re-upholsterers said to Dr. Rosenman: "You guys must be psychiatrists. No other Doctor's office that we have done has all the chairs worn out on the edges. You must have a lot of anxious patients." This came as a surprise to Drs. Rosenman and Friedman, because they were both cardiologists, and had not thought much of the emotional or psychological aspects of heart disease. This led them to years of research, and eventually a book, *Type A Behavior and Your Heart.* The book chronicles the correlation between certain behavioral patterns, and the likelihood of heart disease.

Since heart disease is the number one killer in America, it might be worth reflecting on what the doctors had to say. No one doubts that family history, smoking, a diet high in saturated fats, and a lack of exercise are accurate predictors of the likelihood of heart disease. More recent research has identified anger and "free-floating hostility" as frequent precipitators of heart attacks, but the basic formula developed by Rosenman and Friedman remains intact. They defined "Type A Personality" as "a particular complex of personality traits, including excessive competitive drive, aggressiveness, impatience, and a harrying sense of time urgency." Now the unpleasant fact is, we live in a culture that demands a lot of competitive drive, that rewards aggressiveness, that generates all kinds of situations that try one's patience, and all of us are given more and more things to do, and seem to have less and less time in which to do them.

Fortunately, there are ways to "reengineer" our lives so that Type A-induced heart disease is less likely. We can begin by eliminating events and activities that are of minimal importance. Some people start by canceling the newspapers and magazines they do not need to read, or withdrawing from organizations to which they have already made their contributions. The second step is to spend as much of your day as possible in a milieu that promotes peace. That may seem ridiculous to a harried worker or a mother of five, but there are still "vestibules of peace" that can be established, moments of sanctuary where thoughts can be gathered, good intentions formulated, and some kind of tranquility be found. In this culture of group-think and group-action, we all still need time to be alone, time to take our own pulse, time to be sure we have the creative energies necessary to actually produce benefits for others.

We are all afflicted with sources of hostility, from the unwanted phone that rings during meals, to the undeserved parking ticket, to whatever else that seems to be our own personal demon. Learning not to respond with hostility is a task befitting an advanced stoic philosopher, but there are things we can all do to minimize the impact of an environment that sometimes seems downright hostile. We can avoid some of the people or situations that persistently aggravate us, and we can learn to walk away from situations that have built-in escalation clauses. But most important of all, we can reengineer our responses, so that we tone down the rhetoric, defuse explosive situations, and rise above battles that are not worth our time or own energy.

We live in a society that focuses more on having than on being. Much of our economic activity is centered on increasing our possessions, whether that is a bank account or a garage full of unused athletic equipment. How much healthier we would all be, and how much less busy would cardiologists be, if we could concentrate on being the kind of persons we might most want to become, instead of merely being owners of goods of passing significance. Instead of focusing on increasing possessions, what we really need is a philosophical reorientation, so that we can focus on being rather than having, on doing what is intrinsically worthwhile, rather than on letting time disappear into dark holes. Our minds and bodies benefit from working, and working hard, but our hearts require leisure. Unless we step back and take time to find delight in life, we are in danger of being swallowed up by our own Type A Behavior. We do not want to wind up sitting on the edge of our seats, in some cardiologist's office...

VII-189
The Catholic Crisis

The responses of the American Catholic Bishops to the episodes of child molestation by priests is more of a "canary in the mine shaft" warning signal, than a simple matter of church discipline, or lack thereof. The apparent problem relates to the sexual activity of priests. The more serious problem is much larger, for it involves different understandings of the church, and determining whether it is "teaching handed down from on high," or represents "the voice of the people as the voice of God."

The first problem is clerical celibacy. Permitting priests to marry would not eliminate the problem of pedophilia, which seems to break out periodically among a wide variety of professional groups. But permitting priests to marry, or permitting married men to become priests, might well have a hugely beneficial impact on the Catholic Church. It was a medieval church of celibate men who established the prohibition of a married clergy. In the thirteenth century, the married clergy of the Eastern Church were integrated into the structure of society. The celibate western clergy were totally set apart from the people they were supposed to both serve and lead.

The positive consequence of the discipline of celibacy imposed on the western church in the eleventh century was that church property would not be inherited by a younger generation. The negative consequences were much greater: it separated the clergy and the hierarchy from the people, it promoted the vision that the clergy really were the church, and that "the people" were simply the obedient stewards of the officers of salvation. The role of lay people in the Church quickly became threefold: pay, pray, and obey.

In the intervening thousand years since the imposition of the discipline of priestly celibacy, the church has acknowledged that celibacy is a "gift" for those who can accept it, and not something that is easily practiced. Clearly there have been celibate priests whose lives have been devoted totally to the ministry of the Gospel, free from the demands of raising a family, and free from the demands of financial provision for family members. But the record is also clear of how difficult clerical celibacy is in the modern world. Some might say, all the more important to have the clear witness that spiritual life is more important than physical life. Others prefer to point to evidence of the discipline being too harsh, and perhaps too inhuman a demand, on those who would be priests.

Several studies have been published on the reality of priestly celibacy. Any study of sexuality is bound to have its shortcomings. The Kinsey studies proved nothing in life is more likely to generate deceptive responses than questions about sexual conduct. In one study, Dr. Sipe found that 20% of priests were sexually active with women, another 10% acknowledged the likelihood of future heterosexual activity. While 20% of priests surveyed acknowledged a homosexual orientation, 2% were actively homosexual, while less than 1% admitted to being sexually active with children.

In any realistic analysis, the distance between what is preached and what is practiced has simply become too great, and the church is in danger of no longer being representative of what many Catholics believe, or what perhaps the majority of Catholics prefer to see practiced.

Bishop Vigneron of Detroit says of a married clergy or women priests, that these are not matters of policy, but of doctrine, which cannot be changed, and that "the identity of the priesthood does not include women, married men, or gays," but the overwhelming sentiment of the Catholic people is that it is time for a change. The Boston Archdiocese acknowledged that in the aftermath of the pedophilia scandal, mass attendance was down 20%, and contributions down 25%. When issues become financial, doctrinal matters can suddenly become policy matters, and while doctrine cannot change, policies can.

Episcopal Bishop Kilmer Myers once said that since Christ ordained twelve men to be priests, there was clear biblical precedent for ordaining only men to the priesthood. The good Bishop neglected the further logic involved: Christ also ordained twelve Jews, most of whom were fishermen. Does that mean only Jews and preferably fishermen can be ordained Christian priests?

The real issue is: where does Church power come from? Is the Church a hierarchical organization, with all power descending from above, or is it in some way a democratic organization, with power moving upwards from the people? One Catholic columnist wrote: "New and different forms of community life have been emerging in and out of the Church for years. The rebirth of 'house churches' is likely to strengthen as more and more Catholics distance themselves from the Church they now experience as deceitful." The columnist added: "The heart and soul of all religions always lie far more in the community of believers than it ever does in its priesthood. The priesthood of the people has clearly had enough."

So where is the Catholic Church going, and why is it an issue for the rest of us? The monarchical church, patterned after the Roman Empire with its Absolute Authority, will have a hard time keeping its members in line, in a time of universal education, a widespread spirit of democracy, and a sense of spirituality rising up from the midst of people seeking some form of salvation. A wide assortment of theologians see the Christian Churches as important players in a "new world order," one that sees human beings as having equal rights, one that accepts diversity of cultures, one that sees women as having the same responsibilities as men, one that promotes the peaceful resolution of conflicts, and one that sees spirituality as integral to a harmonious world order. People of faith persistently believe that God is so powerful as to be able to bring good out of evil. Perhaps the scandals among the Catholic clergy, compounded by the authoritarian exercise of episcopal power, may be the source of a Great Awakening within the Catholic community, with widespread implications for the larger human community.

VII-190
Christendom vs. Islamdom?

Just as the Cold War pitted the Soviet Union against the United States, and thereby Communism versus Capitalism, so too it would appear that Islam and Christianity are at loggerheads, the Servants of Allah battling once more against the Followers of Christ. Many who see a coming clash of civilizations along these lines, do not expect that over the next fifty years, Christianity will fare well.

It is clearly a mistake to see Islam as a proxy for backwardness, terror, and religious dictatorship. It is likewise wrong to interpret Christianity as the only source for a vision of world progress. But it is a still larger error to see the world picture as a simple advance of Islam because of conversion and population growth in predominantly Islamic countries, and the demise of Christianity in terms of loss of membership and population declines in nominally Christian countries.

Islam is in the initial stages of its own "Protestant Reformation." Writers like Hashem Aghajari, an Iranian College Professor, are not alone. Much like Martin Luther, Aghajari protested against an Islamic clergy who claimed the sole right to interpret the Koran, and he, like many others, protested against the political power exercised by those whose jurisdiction is spiritual. Much like Luther, he wants to put the Koran in the hands of the believers, and not the imams. To put it in more Lutheran terms, he supports the imamship of all believers! As he said, "Just as people at the dawn of Islam conversed with the Prophet, we have the right to do this today." The clash with western values will be much diminished if Islam follows the path of reform from within, and there are hopeful signs that this will occur.

The science of "demographics" was in its infancy some fifty years ago, but demographers today, while cautioning the accuracy of their results, are much more confident about predicting population growth trends and societal changes. The same demographers that were once worried about the triumph of Islam, now point to the rapid growth of Christianity in Africa and Latin America, and suggest that conversion and population growth in these areas will bring about a resurgent Christianity, and insure some form of Christian dominance for the foreseeable future.

It is difficult to predict population growth, given a variety of social and economic factors, and it is even more difficult to predict social change, given that the winds of politics, economics, and religious conviction blow where they will. Nonetheless, the CIA Factbook estimates that by 2050, the United States will have 330 million Christians, Brazil 195 million, Mexico and the Philippines 145 million each, Nigeria 123 million, and Zaire, 121 million.

Christianity, Phillip Jenkins suggested in his book *The Next Christendom,* will become much more Latin American and African over the next fifty years. There are over one billion Roman Catholics today, but by 2050, there will be a billion and half. While Catholic growth has expanded in Latin America and Africa, Protestant Pentecostalism has grown even faster, and Brazil, Nigeria, and the Congo, will soon have more Pentecostals than Catholics. The Christians of Africa and Latin America are much more serious about their religiousness than many of the nominally Christians of Europe and North America. The political implications are still not clear, but "separation of church and state" is no more likely in such Christian countries than in Moslem countries, and it is not impossible that religious convictions will have beneficial effects on new political arrangements.

Historian Christopher Dawson lauded the Christian Middle Ages as "a glorious time for Christendom." The Egyptian writer Sagyid Qutb assured us that the dawn of a new and glorious age of "Islamdom" was just beginning. One might hope that instead of a clash of these two civilizations, they might wind up benefiting each other, tolerating diverse points of view, and practicing that religion which one biblical writer described as keeping oneself untarnished by the world. Is it possible that some religiously-derived vision of social justice and care for the poor, or some vision of simple justice and fairness, might help overcome both the poverty and the corruption which has characterized the politics of the nations of Latin America and Africa? Might there not be substantial benefits from improved versions of both Christendom and Islamdom?

VII-191
Jews Thinking Like Greeks!

While sweeping generalizations are always suspect, one of the safest among historians of ideas is that just as the ancient Greeks had a genius for the doing of philosophy, the Jews had a remarkable genius for being religious. Greek philosophy expressed itself in various ways, from the "theories of reality" of Plato and Aristotle, to the "philosophy as therapy" of Plutarch and Plotinus. And the Jews had different ways of being religious, including the primacy of worship of the priestly tradition, obedience to the law of the deuteronomists, and the social justice themes of the prophets.

Among historians, the two streams are seen as coming together in figures like Philo of Alexandria and Augustine of Hippo.

Jews of the Diaspora, those who left Israel and Judah for other parts of the world, were among the first syncretists, blenders of the two cultures, practitioners of "both" ways of approaching the world. When Jews arrived in Alexandria in the third century B.C.E., the use of the Greek language was so widespread that the Bible in Hebrew no longer served their religious needs, and some seventy scholars gathered to produce what is called the "Septuagint," the work of the seventy. For these Jews in particular, the bible was not a finished document, and books now called "apocryphal" were soon added, including four books chronicling events related to the revolt of the Maccabees.

The opening verses of the fourth book of Maccabees represent "Jews thinking like Greeks" in its most extreme form. And no matter how carefully you have read the bible, you have probably never seen verses like these:

"Our inquiry is whether reason is sovereign over the emotions. We shall decide just what reason is and what emotion is, how many kinds of emotion there are, and whether reason rules over all these. Now reason is the exercise of the mind that with sound logic prefers the life of wisdom. Wisdom is the knowledge of divine and human matters and the causes of these. This in turn is education in the Law, by which we learn divine matters reverently, and human affairs to our advantage."

The blended vision represented by Fourth Maccabees is desperately needed in the world today. It is a vision of "appropriate syncretism," of not surrendering one's own culture, while striving to adopt what is best in another culture. It also represents an open religious vision, a conviction that the Canon of Revelation is not closed, for everyday experience needs to be understood in the light of a particular tradition, with an openness both to understanding the day's events in the light of that tradition, and of understanding that tradition in the light of what the new day has to offer.

If Jews could learn to think like Greeks, maybe there is hope that Americans will be able to think like Chinese, or like the members of any other culture that seems so distant from us. A State Department official who spent the cold war years in Moscow commented that he harbored the sense that Russians were, deep down, more like us than many of our allies. Is it too much to hope that if the Jews of the Diaspora could learn to think like Greeks, that the cultures of the modern world that have the most difficulty with each other, might eventually be able to reap the benefits of cultural diversity, rather than build enmity over what most keeps them apart? Perhaps we have just begun to tap what the wisdom and practice of the ancient Near East has to offer us....

VII-192
Theory to Therapy

"You are ever on a voyage," said Plotinus, "but the voyage is within you." Plotinus, a philosopher of the third century of the Common Era, represents the culmination of "philosophy as therapy," a movement that occurs whenever philosophy tries to be relevant to current society. In the ancient world, Plato and Aristotle represented the triumph of philosophy as theory, philosophy as the source of abstract reflection about the way things are. Even there, both Plato and Aristotle expected their abstract reflections to have consequences in the way society was organized, and in the way personal ethical behavior affected the lives of the citizens.

Within a century of their deaths, their successors saw the primary question of philosophy as: "How do I live my life?" Philosophy itself was seen as a way of life, and philosophers wore a distinctive garb, and sought to be "public intellectuals," available for discussions of current affairs. A series of philosophers, including Philo Judaeus, Seneca, Cicero, Musonius Rufus, Epictetus, the Emperor Marcus Aurelius, and the biographer Plutarch, proclaimed that philosophy was not some abstract discipline to be practiced by professionals, but that it was everybody's business, and practiced in the public square.

Something parallel is happening to contemporary philosophy, as it recovers from its obsession with logic, and begins to redefine itself as "thinking clearly about issues of everyday concern." Philosophers like John Rawls spent a lifetime asking: "What kind of society do we want to become, and what steps must we take to go down that road?" Iris Murdoch wrote novels so that she could lead readers to reflection about the moral puzzles confronting them in everyday life. A number of significant American philosophers have written that philosophy is primarily thinking carefully about the perennial problems of life, and then doing something about them.

Few people go through life without experiencing some "psychological troubles." While our culture encourages the counseling of professional psychiatrists or psychologists when we experience times of turmoil, it may well be that there is a philosophical dimension to many if not most of the psychological or emotional avalanches that are part of the human condition. I think being "psychologically repaired" often involves seeing the world through new philosophical lenses. At one time or another, we all need the therapy that only "good philosophy" is capable of supplying.

In keeping with "Jews thinking like Greeks," The *Book Of Proverbs* of the Hebrew Bible was written about the time of Philosophy's movement from theory to therapy, hence these verses: "Acquire wisdom, acquire understanding; forsake her not and she will watch over thee; love her, and she will keep thee. Hold wisdom in high esteem, and she will exalt thee. She will bring thee honor, when thou embracest her. Wisdom is more precious than pearls, and all the things you value are not equal to her." The message is clear: to pursue wisdom, is the highest form of therapy. Neither expensive medications, nor costly psychiatrists are necessary. Just the ardent, passionate pursuit of wisdom. Could it be that that is all the therapy most of us really need?

VII-193
Greater Depth Psychology?

When Aristotle discussed virtue, he spoke of "character" as the disposition to act in a certain way. Character is that, but it is also the end result of repeated actions, of the inclinations that emerge from somewhere deep within the individual, as well as the way the individual has come to think of goals, ambitions, relationships, and finding a place in the world.

In other words, what you have done may come back to haunt you. Indian philosophy expresses it as "karma," the fate you have established, by the choices you have made. Freudian therapists would prefer to say your childhood "memories" exert a powerful influence on who you are today, while behavioral therapists seek to change the power of your past decisions. Conversations with therapeutic professionals have made me wonder about how our past influences us. A prison psychologist told me how difficult it was to get even the most favorably disposed malefactor to overcome the indelible marks left by the actions of the past. An art therapist told me of how the power of images deeply carved into the mind rise to the surface and influence the thoughts and actions of those who seek to modify their personality, if not their character. (Personality, this therapist said, in very Aristotelian terms, is the surface expression of the much deeper character.) And a therapist who works with alcoholics and substance abusers, spoke at length of the physical power addictions have over an individual. In terms Aristotle might have used, repeated behavior carves deep channels, and it is difficult to get the ship of character to move in waters that are new, unfamiliar, and have uncertain rewards.

Such concerns apply not just to those who so clearly need therapy, but to the "normal" population as well. What we have done over a long period of time does much to "determine" who we are at present. The behavioral patterns we have established create almost "automatic" responses to the new challenges each day brings.

Apart from our customary actions, there are also deeds that may have surprised us, either by their unaccustomed generosity, or their harshness or unkindness, or simply that they somehow seemed out of keeping with our customary behavior. Psychologists and preachers are disposed to tell us we all have a dark side, an evil demon, and a capacity to 'do wrong' that must be held in check. Sometimes that dark side reveals itself, in a sudden act of bad temper, harsh words, or in some way "getting back" at someone whose actions we feel have wronged us.

At the end of my freshman year in college, the resident advisor in my dormitory apologized to us, and said he had been too harsh. Like him, most of us are aware of times in our lives when we could have been more helpful, more sympathetic, more understanding. And there are doubtless events in our lives we wish we could live over. We presume we have more "character" now, and that we would behave differently. But in reality, we know we suffer from the karma brought on by our actions, and that part of life is making up for past mistakes, and seizing the opportunity to do things right, given a second chance. Depth-psychologist James Hillman said that people are living longer today, because it takes so much longer to develop the character we need to attain before we die. No doubt it takes a long time to erase the ruts of our past mistakes, and build the paths of character that make our daily journeys much more pleasant, and make us much easier to live with….

VII-194
The Primacy of Meditation

I learned to meditate while I was in college, but the practice became much more important to me sitting at a Zendo in Los Angeles. I learned much more under the tutelage of a lawyer/cum Buddhist priest in Morgantown, West Virginia. Wherever you are, there will be opportunities to benefit from experienced meditators. Zen happens to be a particularly useful form of meditation. The concern is misplaced, for those who worry that the practice of Zen Meditation will lead them to some strange Eastern religion. That it developed out of Buddhist practice ties it no more to Buddhism than the vision of social justice that developed out of the

Hebrew tradition ties that to Judaism. Meditation is a major remedy for many of the ills that plague modern people. Most of us are too busy, and have many more things to do, than time in which to do them.

Any time in life is a good time to begin the practice of meditation, but retirement is a particularly good time. Retirement means the opportunity to do the things you never got around to, to read the books you never had time for, or didn't understand the first time around. It means you have the opportunity to be involved in your community in ways never before regarded, but it also means you will spend more time taking care of health matters, perhaps more time taking care of some family problems, and more time managing the financial resources you accumulated over a working life-time.

To the predictable and unpredictable challenges of adult life, there is one universal prescription, and that is, meditation. There is no great trick to it. Begin by setting aside ten minutes a day. Find a place where you will not be distracted, turn off the phone and any other sources of intrusion, assume a comfortable position, and meditate.

Don't try to "produce" anything by your meditation. Try to empty your mind of all thinking, all emotions, and all reflections on your problems. Just as soil benefits from lying fallow, your mind benefits from being emptied. The consequence is, it will have a greater capacity to handle the problems of your everyday existence.

People under stress have different brain wave patterns than people who are in relaxed, positive moods. Control of these brain wave patterns may be attained, and meditation is the best way to do it. Such a capacity for control is especially pertinent now, as we have so much proof that life has become more stressful, the frequency of unpleasant events has increased, and the pace of life has become so much more frantic. Forms of anti-social behavior such as road rage are symptoms of people in general not being able to handle the stressful events that are part and parcel of life in modern America. Analysts of cultures around the world claim the "hurry-sickness" that is characteristic of "time-urgent" Americans has its parallels elsewhere, and is producing similarly erratic behavior.

The violent reactions of a few people at the extremes is indicative of what is happening to us all, as more demands are made on us, and as additional sources of stress exert their influence. Prozac and other palliatives no doubt have their places, but more valuable than medication is meditation. Books like Kabat-Zinn's *Full Catastrophe Living* or Steve Hagen's *Buddhism Plain and Simple*, may be helpful, but nothing, absolutely nothing, works better than setting aside ten minutes, sitting quietly, doing nothing, freeing your mind of all its usual concerns, and calmly permitting the universe to go on about its business. Meditation may not be the only medication you need, but it may be the key to making the medications more effective. It may also be the key to leading a more peaceful life, rising above the stressors that wait to assail you…

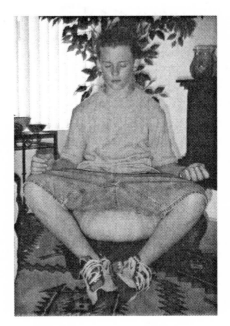

Doyle Boyd, novice meditator

VII-195
"In My Mother's House…."

Philosophy departments are sometimes thought of as hotbeds of atheism, and most philosophy departments do have at least one noteworthy atheist. It is not just that philosophy breeds skepticism, it's more complex than that. Colin Maginn, in *The Making of A Philosopher*, claims the theory of knowledge embraced by modern philosophy is so immersed in "the scientific world view" that it makes religious belief impossible.

What scientists from Galileo to Einstein have made obsolete is not Biblical religion, but the classical worldview of an earth-centered, biologically fixed universe. Oddly enough, just as philosophers like Maginn are claiming science dispels religion, scientists are not only confessing the limits of science, they are claiming scientific support for religious belief.

Particle physicist Stephen Barr, for example, says that belief in God is simply an extension of his scientific conviction of the intelligibility of the world. Attempts to explain the relationship between human reason and the world's remarkable "intelligibility," have been front-burner issues for philosophers from Plato to Kant, and for scientists from Bacon to Einstein, to current Nobel Prize winners.

The hottest area of conflict for contemporary philosophers and scientists is philosophy of mind, or the study of consciousness. Sir Francis Crick claimed we are just "a pack of neurons," but no philosopher or scientist has yet come up with convincing explanations of consciousness, free will, or our awareness of our selves as "selfs." Because of the unsolved puzzlements science has generated, some philosophers regard philosophy as the discipline that works on the puzzles left over when scientists have nothing left to say.

Ancient Greek thinkers assumed the world was eternal, for, as Parmenides said: "nothing comes into being or passes out of being." The authors of the Hebrew Bible affirmed that God, as the author of all that is, created the universe, thus giving it a beginning in time. Modern cosmologists think that the universe is not eternal, but had a beginning in time, in fact started off with a "big bang."

Science was once obsessed with how "mechanical" the universe was, like some giant clock that seldom malfunctioned. Contemporary physicists, like Hermann Weyl, see the beauty of the universe as leading to "a vision of the flawless harmony which is in conformity to sublime reason." Superstring theorists speak of "the incredible consistency and remarkable elegance" of the universe, leading one of them to conclude: "The question of a cosmic designer seems no longer irrelevant, but inescapable."

Much has been written about the "anthropic" principle, the suggestion that so many "coincidences" in nature had to occur to make life possible, that it could not be a matter of chance. To Carl Sagan's suggestion that given billions of planets, life was bound to evolve on at least one of them, statisticians respond with odds against that so great the numbers exceed a single page. If it weren't for the perfect energy levels of the Carbon-12 nucleus, most of the chemical elements in nature necessary for life would have occurred in only infinitesimally minute quantities. Physicist Barr concluded: "The prima facie evidence is in favor of the Biblical idea that the universe was made with life and man in mind."

Scientists and philosophers are so taken with cause-effect relationships as to claim that if you knew all the causes, you would know how determined are all the effects. The ancient Greek Stoics proclaimed the impossibility of free will, given an absolutely determined material universe. The

342

acceptance of quantum theory has come as something of a shock to both physicists and philosophers, but it challenges the absolute determinism some philosophers and some physicists would like to affirm. Physicist Weyl concluded: "The old determinism of Hobbes and Laplace need concern us no longer."

To those who say the mind is just a kind of computer whose neurological workings we do not yet understand, the great mathematician Gödel responded that that was simply "a materialistic prejudice of our time." Oxford philosopher John Lucas concluded: "Gödel's theorem seems to me to prove that mechanism is false, that minds cannot be explained as machines."

In the great play and movie "Raisin In the Sun," a vigorously atheistic and thoroughly secular son returns home to spout his newfound convictions. Overhearing him, his mother says: "Repeat after me: In my mother's house, there is still God." So too, it seems, in the modern houses of physics and biology, and philosophy, there is still room for God...

(Among the innumerable books along these lines, see especially Patrick Glynn, *God: The Evidence*, and Stephen Barr, *Modern Physics and Ancient Faith*.)

VII-196
The Story of Philosophy

If everyone should meditate for ten minutes everyday, so too, as I think, everyone should devote at least a few minutes a day to philosophical reading. I have some suggestions about where to start. While Will Durant's book, *The Story of Philosophy*, reached millions of readers, it is both dated and "opinionated." Durant had a great narrative gift, weaving a story of the gradual development of philosophy from the early Greek search for wisdom to what was, in his eyes, philosophy's grand twentieth century accomplishment. Durant was unduly fond of the skepticism of Voltaire and the pragmatism of John Dewey.

An incomparably better book has been written by a British TV personality with impeccable philosophical credentials, and a willingness to use the same title, *The Story of Philosophy*. Bryan Magee can claim the best of both worlds: he has an Oxford education, and a Yale degree. More to the point, his work is well received both by the general public and by academics, which is no mean achievement.

What makes this book remarkable? Magee not only tells the story of philosophy extremely well, but also his brief summaries are admirably accurate. It is not easy to give thumbnail sketches of the works of great philosophers, but Magee manages to do that for figures as diverse at Plato, Augustine, Maimonides, Aquinas, Kant, Hegel, Mill, and Wittgenstein. This is not just dry textual material: it is a superbly "illustrated" text. Like classroom teachers who use computer technology to provide great images of what they are presenting, Magee fills his pages with splendid reproductions of the famous paintings of philosophers, superb photographs of historical events with philosophical dimensions, and pictures of the contemporary philosophers whose names occasionally make the news, but whose faces are seldom familiar. No text I have encountered is as good as this one as an introduction to philosophy for the general reader.

Why should the general reader be interested in philosophy? And why should anyone want to spend time each day reading philosophy? Philosophy is the attempt to be wise about life. It is not an abstract discipline limited to professionals who have nothing better to do, but an important component of the business of living. The reading and doing of philosophy is not something to be left to vacations and weekends, but should be part of the everyday activity of thoughtful people. In a word, it is too important an activity to be left in the hands of professional philosophers!

Modern philosophers have sometimes retreated into the security and obscurity of playing games with words. Philosophy is not about words; it is about life, and how to live it well. Ancient philosophers took their vocations seriously, exhibiting by their conduct the depth of their convictions. Socrates gave his life rather than violate his philosophical principle of obedience to the laws of his community. Such convictions are not limited to the ancients; Nietzsche said: "A philosopher should be an example," and what a strange example he was!

The philosophical problems that trouble modern people are the same problems that perplexed Socrates: how can you live a just and good life in the midst of a society that does not commit itself to justice? And, how do you live your life in an exemplary manner, in the midst of a society whose notions of what constitutes a good life are contradictory and non-compatible? Magee makes judicious modern applications of the insights of such philosophical geniuses.

There are many excellent introductions to philosophy, but Bryan Magee's book does an especially brilliant job of making philosophical problems come to life. (DK Books, $19.95, available at Amazon, or your local bookstore.) Just as a person who would be religious not only needs to read the sacred text everyday, but also think about it and put the reading into practice, so too the philosophical novice must do some regular reading, and then find a way to put the reading into daily conversation.

World events cry out for philosophical understanding, and they must be seen in some kind of larger context. Reading philosophy on a regular basis can help in that worthwhile project, and Bryan Magee's book is a good place to start.

VII-197
Here I stand...

When you read any philosopher, you should ask, "What does this person really stand for?" Otherwise, somewhere down the road, you may find yourself drawn to certain conclusions you did not anticipate. My goal in doing philosophy is simply to understand and, if possible, make comprehensible to others what great philosophers have to say. As is readily apparent from these essays, I am not offering answers to the great philosophical problems; I am trying to get the reader to understand the questions more clearly, and to see the different sides of debatable issues.

One may ask: "Why Philosophy? Why not simply accept the answers religious faith provides?" The answer is: philosophy is a discipline anyone can exercise, whereas religious faith occurs as a kind of gift. Philosophy has starting points that can be clearly stated, and then discussed, whereas the "starting points" of faith must simply be believed. Jewish faith begins with: "Obey the Lord Your God, whose wonders you have seen." Christian faith starts with: "Believe in the Lord Jesus Christ and you will be saved." And Islam: "Submit to the Will of Allah, as revealed in the Koran." Religions are belief systems, and while beliefs may be presented to someone, actual conversion requires some "inner experience" on the part of the convert, leading to a profession of faith. Philosophy requires assent to first principles, an acceptance of logic, and some insight into how the parts of a given philosophy hang together. While religions do provide moral guidance, that guidance is within the belief structure that may not make sense to the non-believer. It is the inevitable role of philosophy to be engaged in a critical appraisal of every belief system. Philosophy is not necessarily hostile to belief, but it tends to be skeptical, and to keep asking for proof.

In Philosophy, Ethics is where the tire hits the road. Ethics presupposes metaphysics, a doctrine of "the way things really are." And metaphysics presupposes an epistemology: what are the limits of my knowledge, what kind of statements can I make, and, if I can know "the truth," how will I know it when I get there? The components of Philosophy do not stand alone, but ethical reflection is the easiest introduction to doing philosophy,

Gene Bammel

for everyone has experience of moral issues, and almost everyone has some inclination to ask serious moral questions.

Among professional ethicists, some are relativists and some are absolutists. *Relativists* like Nietzsche say that your "perspective" determines the way you see things, and upbringing, cultural background and experiences, will do much to shape "perspective" on things. Accordingly, ethical judgment is "subjective," made up of the way one happens to see things. *Absolutists* prefer to say that since there is a way things really are, and we have a capacity to know these natures, we should know how to treat things and each other, and consequently we are able to have clear and "objective" moral knowledge. If there is one "true" way, then every other way must be either false, or inadequate.

Extreme relativists follow the line of reasoning offered by Jean-Paul Sartre: you choose what you want to be, you choose the moral perspective you wish to follow, and, if it doesn't work out, you are free to move to some other moral perspective. Sartre himself moved from being a communist sympathizer, to a supporter of democracy, to having such a great suspicion of mob rule that he wound up supporting a French-style of authoritarianism. Since, in Sartre's philosophy there are no natures, everyone is "free" to choose what they will become, subject to some inevitable societal rules, but individual free choice is the most "absolute" value.

Real Absolutists come in many varieties. Religious Absolutists often have a "divine command" morality that provides absolute guidance; after all, there is no questioning divine authority! Since God has spoken and God's will on the matter is known, there is no more to be said. As the case of Islam proves, this may be fine for those who share the belief system, but comes to grief when the belief system is not shared by those upon whom you impose God's will. Religious absolutism is sometimes expressed in "natural law" theory, claiming that since God is the author of nature, praiseworthy moral behavior is simply action in accordance with those divinely established natures.

Some absolutists are not quite so sure about things, and are "limited absolutists." From this point of view, while there are absolutes, there are not as many of them as some would like, nor is the knowledge of them as clear-cut or absolute as some would expect. Some actions, like genocide, are always and everywhere wrong, and admit of no exceptions. What we designate as "crimes against humanity" are never permissible. Relativists may acknowledge that "cruelty" in any form is intolerable, but wish to point out that it cannot be absolutely forbidden. They would claim that you might wish to treat a terrorist cruelly, to extract information that would save lives.

346

Relativists begin by looking at the "consequences" of moral actions; absolutists look first at the "principles" or "rules" that govern them. What happens in real life is that the two positions tend to temper each other. Most absolutists take consequences into consideration; most relativists wind up with rules of good conduct. Even those who absolutely condemn lying will lie to prevent a madman from killing someone.

The conviction is widespread that "civilization" does progress, and that cultures come to progressively deeper understandings of what behavior is most appropriate for human beings. It is comforting to know that good arguments can cause people to change their points of view. Philosophy's distinctive contribution is to encourage rational discussion of moral matters. Improving the human condition begins with understanding the reasons for moral convictions, leading to dialogues with those of different moral persuasions. Hope for human betterment rests in such reasoned reflection on the issues that really matter. This works because there are some absolutes to which reason leads us. Wittgenstein acknowledged that occasionally talking nonsense was inevitable; he admonished us to keep an eye on our nonsense. One might add: accept that there are some absolutes, but keep a watchful eye on your absolutes.

VII-198
Got Free Will?

Common sense convinces us that we have free will. We are aware of "making choices," deciding to go left or right, choosing a kind word, or making a critical remark. Common sense also tells us that if we were not "free," it would make no sense to praise someone for good behavior, or to punish someone for doing something bad. When free choice seems so obvious, how can anyone be a "determinist?" Is it even remotely conceivable that the common sense conviction of having free will is an illusion? Or could it be that if we are accurate in assessing our own behavior and that of others, we would establish clear and necessary causal connections between the kind of person we are and the actions we choose?

The philosophic discussion of free will in the west comes in three different stages: *One*: Greek Philosophy: Plato and Aristotle supported the common sense viewpoint that people are responsible for their actions, and the only debate centers around educating people so they will know how to choose what is good. *Two*: Christianity shifts the debate in new directions. Augustine said why, when I know the good I should choose, do I so often choose the evil I know I should avoid? He rejected the Platonic dictum that knowing the good will somehow cause you to pursue it. Augustine said the will is not perfectly free, and this is caused by "original sin," the turning away from good and towards evil by our original parents, an act that darkened our intellects and weakened our wills. A long series of Christian writers, among them Aquinas, Scotus, Luther and Calvin, will struggle with the theological issues of God creating man "free" to choose good or evil, in the light of divine foreknowledge. Since God knows all, and God does not change, how can our choices possibly be free? Calvin agreed with Augustine that "predestination" is a fact, and both of them struggled to find ways to claim that what God knows is known because of our choices, and not that our choices are what they are because of what God knows. Spinoza resolved the debate in a unique fashion by saying: "If the falling stone were conscious, it too would think itself free."

Stage *Three* in the history of the discussion of free will begins with Immanuel Kant and his attempt to reconcile free will with the laws of physics as expressed by Newton. The more "scientific" one becomes, the more one tends to see the world as a great causal chain, each cause having an effect, which becomes a cause, and so on forever. The "determinism" apparently inscribed in The Laws of Physics has led some contemporary brain anatomists to claim that the only possibility for free will would have to come from some application of quantum mechanics, where some degree of indeterminacy would prevail, at least upon rare occasions.

Kant, ever the moralist, wished to defend human freedom and responsibility in the face of the determinism of the physics of his day. He suggested that while nature operates in time and is part of the "appearances" of the world, the human will, which operates "beyond appearances," is outside time, and therefore free from rigid determinism. Kant's empirical successors reject all such talk of what is outside time, and hence beyond human observation, and so have no avenue left with which to reject determinism.

Contemporary philosophers like Dan Dennett do everything in their power, in the light of the work of "science of consciousness" professionals, to defend some form of freedom of the will. Meanwhile, the rest of us go about our business, secure in the knowledge that we really do make choices that could be otherwise. We are convinced that we merit praise for some of our choices, and that we can be blamed for others. We are convinced that we are truly "moral agents," hoping to make ourselves better by the good choices we make, and hoping to build a better world by the influences we have on others. Paradox building upon paradox, we are bound and determined to see ourselves as free. The more determined some scientists are to show us causal explanations for all our actions, the more determined philosophers are, to claim that freedom fundamentally and unequivocally, is what makes us most truly human.

VII-199
Watershed Experiences

At various scholarly conferences, I have been an advocate of "Philosophy" as the mediating discipline between opposing views. Perhaps I am hopelessly misguided in that advocacy. Nonetheless, since Philosophy is all about clear thinking, critiquing assumptions, and logical inference, it seems reasonable to me that Philosophy should play an important role in mediating disputes between opposing points of view.

At Philosophy conferences, this would seem to be the appropriate point of view: Philosophy is discourse, dialogue, open conversation, "argument," an attempt to put things on the table, for honest, open discussion, with the expectation that mistaken convictions can be set aside, superior arguments will win out, and that all participants will reach, if not an agreement, at least greater appreciation of the reasons supporting other points of view.

At academic religious conferences, I have proposed Philosophy as the Arbiter between people of religious persuasions, and those who are agnostic or atheist. At Political meetings, I have suggested Philosophy as Mediator between those supporting vastly different political convictions. A watershed experience for me occurred at a Vail Symposium entitled: "How High the Wall of Separation Between Church and State?" At that conference, I defended the claim that Philosophy can be the "honest broker," establishing areas of agreement between people who see God as Lawgiver, Judge, and Redeemer, and those who claim that human morality and politics are strictly human inventions, with no God to either legislate for, pass judgment upon, nor redeem, human actions. However, I found few people, on either side of the argument, willing to agree with me.

One might propose that theists and atheists can find a common ground for agreement in the "natural law" convictions of most theists, and the vision of *ius gentium,* a "law of nations," that atheistic biologists like E. O. Wilson claim to find evidence for even in the animal kingdom. Wilson claimed that, beginning with ant communities, you can find "laws" that biological organisms follow, in order to facilitate the well-being of the community, and perhaps the well-being of other organisms with whom they develop co-dependency. Rationality, Wilson claimed, should lead us to comparable legal systems enveloping the entire human community.

Religious scholars are generally unwilling to accept such a vision. Let me paraphrase a response I received to my claim that Philosophy could work as an Arbitrator between religious, agnostic, and atheistic points of view: "There is no compatibility between a vision of the goal of human life as having a supernatural end of eternal life in the Presence of God, and a secular, earthly view that the last end of man is simply working to improve the human condition. In terms of morality, if God exists, and humankind was created in God's image, then conformity with God's Will should be the goal of all human striving. With no God in the picture, 'eat, drink, and be merry' is at least as appealing a morality as striving for continued human improvement."

The religious point of view is often stated with great clarity, sincerity, and absoluteness. But I still think it is the role of Philosophy to get proponents of opposing points of view on religious, moral and political issues, to see clearly where and why they disagree, and see if perhaps, there are some workable areas of common ground, where common agendas may be established, and working groups may produce practical benefits. These encounters have been watershed experiences for me, and while they have not changed my convictions, I do see the other point of view more clearly, and I see reasons why the debates are not likely to end any time soon. I continue to see Philosophy as the best Honest Arbitrator between proponents of apparently irreconcilable points of view...

VII-200
Machiavelli

Niccolo Machiavelli was born in Florence in 1469, in 1498 headed the Chancery of the Republic of Florence, in 1502 directed diplomatic missions to Cesare Borgia, was imprisoned in 1512 when the Republic was overthrown, used his imprisonment to write on "How To Succeed in Politics," and he died in 1527. His book, *The Prince*, was published in 1531.

Seldom has a book of a mere eighty pages caused so much controversy, or perhaps been so misunderstood. The Catholic Church banned the book in 1559. To this day to be tagged as "Machiavellian" is almost synonymous with being either underhanded, or evil, or both. Machiavelli's purpose was to explain how someone could obtain and retain power. It was the first handbook of "power politics," and concluded with a passionate "Exhortation to liberate Italy from the barbarians." One sentence can be taken as a summary of the whole book: "It is better to be feared than loved." While such practical maxims pervade the work, there are two key reasons why it caused the uproar it did, and these are the same reasons why the book is still influential today.

It is the first text of the Renaissance that clearly separated the sacred from the secular, the religious from the political. Whatever the Prince may be doing to save his own soul, says Machiavelli, is quite separate from his obligations and activities as a worldly ruler. Rulers, like the leaders of the Roman Republics, keep civil order, engineer the prosperity of their citizens, minimize the threat of enemy invasion, and eliminate the danger of sedition or rebellion. Machiavelli never says: "the end justifies the means," but it is not hard to read that message into the text.

The second reason for Machiavelli's lasting influence is that he is the first real "pluralist' the Western world produced. Western thought, in the aftermath of Plato, persistently proclaimed that there was one perfect answer to the question of how people should live. Machiavelli proposed that there are many different satisfactory answers to the question of how we should live our lives. This is a notion that many still find upsetting, find difficulty accepting, and find philosophically unsatisfying.

Isaiah Berlin, one of the great pluralists of the modern era, wrote: "After Machiavelli, doubt is liable to infect all monistic constructions... this fundamental belief of Western political thought has been shaken." One of the problems of life in America is that while we are perhaps the most "pluralist" society the world has ever known, many Americans, whether for political or religious reasons, harbor the conviction that they have found the one right, true way. This may be harmless, as long as they do not reject the capacity of others to be convinced they have the one right, true vision. But what happens when two irreconcilable absolutists confront each other? This freedom to have differing convictions is both America's greatest strength, and a source of considerable weakness. Contrast this freedom to have and express differing convictions with various "Islamic Republics," which, because they enshrine the one, true way, not only leave no room for alternative visions, but also may wish to blot out pluralism from the world.

The bottom line is, while we retain serious reservations about ends justifying means, we continue to reap the benefits of the pluralistic vision of Machiavelli, hero of the Republic of Florence, and a voice still to be reckoned with. We live in a pluralist democracy, and the vision of Machiavelli almost six centuries ago has had much to do with our good fortune.

Family gathering, Tucson, Arizona

VII-201
Community

Building community is a work in which we all are engaged. As one of my teachers has written: "We grow in community, and the better the community—the more likely we are to grow."

What makes for a good community? Clearly, "openness" is a most important, but easily overlooked, element of every successful community. The American United Methodist Church advertised itself as: "Open Hearts. Open Minds. Open Doors." That is not only a good program for a religious organization, it's a good charter for anyone seeking to build community.

The great Greek philosophers persistently taught that an inherent part of human nature was a sense of public and private responsibility for others. Greek philosophers, including Socrates, Plato, Aristotle and Plotinus, were ardent believers that no one made progress in becoming fully human, apart from a community of those who somehow sought to make things better. John Rist, author of *Real Ethics,* wrote: "The good life is not merely the exercise of our talents, but rather their deployment in an active concern with what we 'ought' to do to make our souls better." The improvement of the soul of which he is speaking is not done in some form of contemplative isolation, but through immersion in the life of a community.

Aristotle is referred to as "the philosopher of the good life," but for him the good life did not mean living luxuriously or opulently, but living a life that not only makes "the soul" better, but does so in the midst of community, and for the sake of the community. He wrote: "He who would live alone must be either a beast or a god." And when he wrote: "Man is a political animal," he meant "a member of the community," not a member of a particular political party.

Modern ethics has emphasized the primacy of autonomy, the "freedom" to make choices by which one expresses one's self. Classical ethics stressed the growth and development of the person in the midst of community. There is something to be said for personal growth and autonomy, and the freedom to develop one's character and personality. But there is much more to be said for the commitment to do what contributes to the building of some community, somewhere, in a manner most appropriate to the particular talents we each have. We are who we are because of our membership in the communities in which we live. "What we owe to each other" is not just the title of a good book, but a good expression of the fact that we live, move, and have our being in the midst of a variety of communities, each of which deserves something from us. Human beings are social animals, and we find our true selves in the process of contributing in some unique way to the communities to which we belong. "We grow in community, and the better the community—the more likely we are to grow."

VII-202
Discourse

Socrates established that the role of the philosopher is to be a gadfly, to "sting" people into awareness, and make them question their assumptions, prejudices, and convictions. The media provide us with daily versions of "Socrates-lite", but few journalists ask us to examine our most basic, most trusted, most long-standing convictions. Real shaking of the foundations is a properly philosophical task, and it takes longer than the one-minute sound bite, or the five minutes of "news-in-depth" the networks offer.

The stimulus to serious philosophical reflection is all around us. It may be accelerated by a sudden illness, by awareness of natural beauty, or by reports of the appalling things human beings do to each other. It may be intensified by exposure to a great work of art, or deepened by reading some great philosopher or sage. Philosophy comes alive by seeing philosophical issues in a contemporary context, and websites are especially good at this. "First Things," www.firstthings.com/, for example, consistently presents articles on some of the most pressing issues of the day, ranging from "Justifying War" to "Defining the Beginning and End of Life."

Commentary magazine, www.commentarymagazine.com, sponsored by the American Jewish Foundation, publishes some of the best articles anywhere on current issues, ranging from "Seeking Good in Radical Islam," to "Presidential Pillars for Action." You cannot open Arts and Letters Daily, www.aldaily.com, without finding some provocative article. These and other similar websites, and the magazines they showcase, have become the Socratic gadflies of the modern world.

Larger problems, like the connection between morality and metaphysics, require spending some time with the books or articles written not only by the great and famous thinkers, but also by contemporary writers. There is no proof that thinking about philosophical problems is "good for you," or that your reading will lead you necessarily to any clearer understanding than you had before. You may feel "enlightened" when you read great philosophers, whether Plato or Nietzsche, because it immerses you in the issues, and is an experience comparable to what the inveterate Bible reader derives from a daily dosage of Isaiah or Matthew.

Iris Murdoch, novelist and philosopher, concludes an essay entitled: "On 'God' and 'Good'," with: "For both the collective and the individual salvation of the human race, art is doubtless more important than philosophy, and literature most important of all. *But there can be no substitute for pure, disciplined professional speculation.* (Italics added.)

In the three-step process of self-improvement, Meditation is step one in clearing the mind for serious work. Speculation is step two, and Enlightenment, step three. But the motivation to it all begins with discourse, a willingness to think and talk things through, usually in the company of other likeminded people, and with the help of great books and now, great websites.

VII-203
Controlling Your Time and Your Life

We all get twenty-four hours a day, but some of us manage to get much more done in those hours, than do others. The classic book on time management is Alan Lakein's *How To Get Control of Your Time and Your Life.* Lakein was a pioneer of "Time Management" programs, and by now everyone knows at least of some of his simple formulas. "Your Time is your Life." "Control Starts with Planning." "Establish Priorities as A's, B's, C's: Do the A Priorities first, and many of the C's will take care of themselves."

"Use the Swiss Cheese Method: make little holes in big projects, as time permits." And also, "Work smarter, not harder." Lakein himself did not own a television set, and he seldom read newspapers or magazines. You may not want to follow him in all his routines, but there are several "time-saving" techniques that may prove helpful to anyone who has a sense of too many things to do, and not enough time in which to do them.

Lakein would have you start by writing down lifetime goals. In the light of those goals, establish daily priorities of those things that move you towards attaining them. He takes list making seriously. At the end the day, sit down and make a list of the things you want to do tomorrow. Then decide which of those are A priorities, and allot your best time and energies to accomplishing them. Arrange to have time in which you are available to others, and time in which you are not to be disturbed, so that you can concentrate totally on what you are doing. He suggests that most people have at least two hours everyday that are not spent as well as they could be, and that with some small re-arranging, this time could be used much more effectively.

Among his suggested ways to save time: Have a place for everything, so you don't waste time looking for stuff. Review your lifetime goals at least once a month. Keep a list of your priority items, so that you are constantly reminded that what you are doing, moves you in that direction. Handle each piece of paper only once. Set deadlines for yourself and others, so that things get done in reasonable time. Focus your attention on the items that will have the best long-term benefits. Plan your day, and set priorities for each day. Have a light lunch, to prevent afternoon sleepiness.

When asked what advice he would give to people who are hopelessly overwhelmed, he said, "Remember the 80/20 rule: 80% of your rewards come from 20% of what is on your agenda." He provides these examples: 80% of sales come from 20% of customers, 80% of phone calls come from 20% of callers.... and 80% of satisfaction probably comes from 20% of what you do. If you concentrate on the 20% that is really important, most of the rest will fall into place.

A good way to exercise our free will lies in choosing how to spend our time. Being clear about lifetime goals is the first and most important step. Establishing priorities, making a schedule, planning on how we will get things done in the course of a day or a week, all this can help us get control of our times and our lives. It may help to keep Lakein's question in mind: "What is the best use of my time right now?" Answering that question can help us get more done each day, help us move towards our life-time goals, and even make us feel good about being productive, time-mastered, life-controlling human beings.

VII-204
Radical Changes?

"Revolution" is not a term to be taken lightly. The astronomer Copernicus used the word to describe the earth's movement around the sun. Because his work radically changed the common perception of the earth as the center of the universe around which the sun "revolved," he was identified as a "revolutionary," and the term has since been applied to any attempt to overthrow the status quo, whether that be a government, a scientific theory, or a form of artistic expression.

Among the many "revolutions" of the twentieth century, none is so misunderstood as the revolution that has taken place in our understanding of "truth." When I taught undergraduate philosophy, I would begin by talking about Socratic Inquiry as the search for truth. I would add that the goal of a philosophy class was not to tell people what the truth was, but to get them to think for themselves. I would note that the progress of modern science has given us an inclination to see scientific theories as provisional, and not as simply adding fact upon fact, until all "truth" was tabulated. One year, a student replied: "But if Philosophy cannot teach us the whole truth, why should we bother with it?" Some other time, a student said: "You really know the answers, you just aren't going to tell us." Both students inhabited the world of an older paradigm, where "knowledge" was static, and "science" was a matter of layering fact upon fact.

The New Paradigm presents a world where "facts" are provisional, where "perspectives" lead to very different ways of viewing the world, and where the "axioms" with which you begin will lead you to very different conclusions that result from the axioms in someone else's world. In keeping with that, Universities went from being fact factories, where the immutable truths of the ages were transferred to young minds, to being places of inquiry, where everything is up for grabs, where everything may be questioned, and where experiment and discovery and the "invention of new knowledge" have displaced the rote memorization of what "authorities" have proclaimed.

Philosophy has been at the heart of this revolution. At various times in its history, Philosophy has been "scholastic," that is, dedicated to the verbatim transmission of the thought of some philosophical "authority," whether Plato, Aristotle, Thomas Aquinas, or Hegel. The various philosophical revolutionaries of the last two hundred years—Kant, Kierkegaard, Nietzsche, Wittgenstein, Dewey, Kuhn—have all been iconoclasts, and all have worked under the banner of: "Dare to think for yourself." The dictum of Karl Marx has influenced them all: "The philosophers have only interpreted the world in various ways. The point is to change it." Modern philosophy, to some degree despairing of certain knowledge, has expressed more interest in action, as if taking its cue from Kierkegaard: "What I really lack is to be clear in my mind what I am to do, not what I am to know...."

The most significant "revolution" of the twentieth century was from a world of absolutes, where knowledge was certain and definite, to a world where knowledge is but a provisional formulation that enables us to go forward in revising provisional formulas. The key question of ethics, "What am I to do?", where certitude is most in demand, became the most unsettled of all. It is in this arena that Philosophy is called upon to make its most important contributions, both by bringing to bear the wisdom of the past, and by applying that wisdom in the world of new paradigms, where perspectives matter, but some perspectives are better than others, and where principle is provisional, but some provisionals produce vastly preferable consequences.

VII-205
Are there Absolutes?

This question could be the central philosophical issue of the twentieth century. An Absolute is permanent, unchanging, forever the same. When Charles Darwin posited "evolution" as the way the human species came to be, evolution soon became more than a biological postulate, it became an axiom about how the world works. "Change" replaced permanence as the basic metaphysical reality. In the light of the primacy of change, Friedrich Nietzsche proclaimed not only the death of God, but also the end of all Absolutes, and the fact of "relativism." There is no "truth", said Nietzsche, for the way you see things, is purely and simply a matter of where you happen to be at the time.

The "Perspectivism" of Nietzsche reached its fullest expression with a series of French "post-modernists," most notably Michel Foucault, Jacques Derrida, Jean Beaudrillard, and Jacques Lacan. Derrida rejected not only the rationalism of the Enlightenment (an age that believed that science would be the great solver of all human problems), but the western tradition of rationality dating back to Plato and Aristotle, a tradition that saw the exercise of reason as a quest for truth, in the service of a political community. Derrida said truth claims are all relative, relative to a certain time and place, a certain vocabulary, a certain agreed upon grammar and syntax.

Scientists—physicists, chemists, and biologists in particular—are uncomfortable with this perspectivism, although scientific theories do displace previously held theories. Physicist Morrison says: "Quantum theory is now a permanent part of our understanding of the way the universe works." But one wonders if Ptolemy, Copernicus, Einstein, and other revolutionary scientists, might not well have said something comparable, regarding the "permanent" axioms of their time.

What goes on in science and the larger society generally, seldom escapes the notice of philosophers for long. Jurgen Habermas wrote a telling critique of perspectivism, relativism, and post-modernism in *The Philosophical Discourse of Modernity*. Habermas' initial concern was political: how can a society survive, unless *rational discourse* can reject defective societal visions, and be the basis of a platform for appropriate political action?

Habermas is the single most vocal proponent of the "restoration" of the ideals of western culture, of the availability of truth, and of the critical importance of the ability to reach agreement through the exercise of reason, on public and political issues. Vaclav Havel, the playwright who became President of the Czech Republic, was among the most influential. For Habermas, Havel, and others of the anti-post-modern mentality, "it's not just a matter of perspective," not just a matter of "your guess is as good as mine," not just a matter of indifference what course of action you pursue, because society ought to be organized according to rational principles, and good arguments should overcome bad ones. Rationality as championed by the Enlightenment and rejected by the "Romantic" and post-modern revolutions, should prevail.

The debate between "rationalists" and "post-modernists" is still very much alive, and neither side has any prospect of demolishing the opposition. But for those who seek some basis for certain "absolutes," writers like Habermas provide both starting point and encouragement. There is a certain odd quality to finding reason used against itself as in the case of Derrida and his associates, and something very comforting to find reason riding, as in the case of Habermas, so valiantly to its own defense. The mandate for reason Aristotle established so long ago may yet prevail. As he said, "Reason, more than anything else, is what constitutes human nature."

VII-206
The Place of Karl Popper

With all the political revolutions of the twentieth century, one might well ask: What were the philosophers doing? Were they just sitting idly by, while Communists, Fascists and other political insanities developed? Were they indifferent when quests for truth and rationality were assailed? Did they sleep while the world went to pieces?

While many philosophers spoke out against the evils of the day, no philosopher was more influential than Karl Popper. He was born in 1902 into a prosperous Viennese family, expressed clear socialist sympathies, but was repulsed by both Nazism and Soviet Communism. He accepted a Professorship in New Zealand in 1937, where he spent the war years, working primarily on the problem of the nature of knowledge. After the war, he moved to the London School of Economics.

The dominant theory of knowledge of the twentieth century maintained that since physical reality is of a radically different order from human cognitive capacities, we have no perfect apprehension of that reality, and so the task is to produce "plausible theories" to explain what is going on. We have a "problem-solving" approach to reality, and we discard a theory when a better one comes along, as was the case with Einsteinian physics replacing Newtonian physics. Popper maintained that it is impossible to "prove" the truth of any scientific theory, but you can "falsify" any particular statement, just by finding one contrary example. If you find one black swan, you disprove the theory that all swans are white. A statement that no observation could falsify cannot be tested, and is therefore not "scientific." Popper agreed with the logical positivists that theology is not a science, because no observations can be made that would falsify theological statements, so while the statement "God exists," may well be true, it is not "scientific."

Popper applied his theory of science to politics. The book that sets forth his political views is *The Open Society and Its Enemies*. Since no one can attain certainty in politics, imposing your views on someone else is never justified. Just as criticism is the way to scientific progress, so too the criticism of political actions that only a democracy permits, proves the need for an "open" society. Popper criticizes Plato's *Republic*, on the basis that since there is no guardian who has a clear vision of the one true way, there can be no "ideal" state, so a government cannot be "close-minded," but must always be open to progress, even if it assumes the form of radical change. The political challenge is to solve society's current problems, and this is a never-ending process. The goal is not the establishment of ideal states or nations, but improving the ones we have. If you were to reduce his political views to one sentence, it would be this: "We do not know how to make people happy, but we can remove avoidable suffering and handicap."

Popper's criticism of Marxism played a role in the overthrow of Communist regimes around the world. In the light of the paroxysms of the twentieth century, Popper's advocacy of democratic openness and tolerance assures him a place in the pantheon of philosophers whose thoughts have had beneficial, real world consequences. If the task of philosophy is to think problems through, and provide some insight for practical people to apply, then Popper's place in history remains secure. History might come to see him as the most important philosopher of the twentieth century!

VII-207
The Motherhood of God

While eating lunch in a Chinese Restaurant, I sat near a mother, father, and daughter. The daughter was very curious and very bright. The father, deep in reading a newspaper, gave her looks that said: "Can't you see I'm busy with something important?" By contrast, the mother devoted full attention to her daughter, answering a series of "Why?" questions, exhibiting great patience and thoughtfulness. Now I know there are fathers who are remarkably attentive and mothers who neglect their children, but all in all, aren't there more mothers than fathers who practice what the Hebrew Bible called *hesed,* loving-kindness? In terms of generous concern for the wellbeing of another, isn't mother love a better model than the love more characteristic of fathers? With good reason, the psychiatrist Erich Fromm spoke of mother-love as "giving," fatherly-love as "authoritative."

At a scholarly conference on "Finding New Terms For Old Ideas," I asked a Biblical scholar why the Bible spoke of the Fatherhood of God, but not Motherhood. She offered two explanations. First of all, she said, the Bible was written to shore up the power of the Patriarchs, at times when masculine, acquisitive, warlike behavior was very much in the ascendancy. Her second reason was even more interesting. She said the Hebrew Bible was written at a time when female goddesses were very popular throughout the Middle East, ranging from Tiamat to Isis to Ashtar, and the masculine metaphors of power and might used in the Bible were meant to obliterate any thought of a feminine deity. By the time the Book of Wisdom was written, this threat was much diminished, so "Wisdom," clearly female, could be clearly characterized as "playing before Him (the male deity) from all eternity."

My question and my concern fit in well with one of the themes of the conference, centered upon a book by Clark Pinnock, *The Openness of God: A Biblical Challenge to the Traditional Understanding of God.* Pinnock thought Judeo-Christian theology was too influenced by Greek Philosophy, and its concept of an omniscient and omnipotent deity, and not dedicated enough to the Biblical God, who "forgets" aspects of the past, does not "remember" the sins of His people (Isaiah 43:25), and seems to be aware of possible alternative futures for his chosen people. Theologians who follow Pinnock walk in the footsteps of A.N. Whitehead, Charles Hartshorne, or Schubert Ogden, and the "Process Theology" they advocated. God is not the static Pure Act of Aristotle, but a God who is in Process, a God for whom the Future is indeed uncertain, a God who participates with His creatures to bring the future into being. These themes found a popular forum in books like *Rescuing the Bible from Fundamentalism,* and *Why Christianity Must Change or Die,* by Bishop Spong.

The Omniscient, Omnipotent God of the monotheistic traditions should be able to prevent the natural disasters that plague His human subjects. The reality of human history is better explained by a God who, like the God of the Bible, works in history, and is limited by the capacities of His creatures. And surely, a God whose motherly concerns leads her to forgive the foibles of Her creatures, and be patient with their mistakes, is more appealing than a God who is so Perfect in His Absoluteness that He cannot be bothered to intervene, even when great evils are at hand? The critics like Spong may be right: it is time to go "Beyond Theism to new God Images." If biblical faith is to survive and be meaningful, the time has come for new metaphors to describe the reality of God. Discussing "The Motherhood of God" might be a good place to start.

VII-208
Socrates' Weight Problem!

Few people know that the Delphic Oracle has taken up residence at the Vapor Caves in Glenwood Springs, Colorado. Much to my surprise, during my recent visit, I found Socrates consulting the Delphic Oracle, on a topic much on the minds of many Americans.

Socrates: I have come to you, because I am at a loss to explain my continuing weight gain. I have tried the various diet plans, Atkins included, but all to no avail. I suspect these dietitians think they know something, when really they are ignorant, and know nothing about weight gain or weight loss, or keeping pounds off once lost!

Oracle: Why are you concerned about your weight, Socrates? Is it merely a vanity issue, that you want to look like you did when you were a young Hoplite, serving in the Athenian Army? Or are there health reasons why you are concerned?

Socrates: O Oracle, you of all should know that I have never worried about my appearance, as I made no response to Aristophanes, when he called me "the ugliest man in all Athens." But I must admit, when I discourse with the young people, I do envy them their slim and youthful appearance.

Oracle: Surely, Socrates, you are aware that all the statues of the gods and goddesses portray them in their youthful appearance, as Apollo and Diana and even Dionysius always appear as if their mid-twenties would never desert them. But Socrates, you of all people should be most aware that beauty of body is fleeting, and beauty of soul is the one thing that matters.

Socrates; I have taken your lesson to heart, O Oracle, for I pursue beauty of soul with all the passion I can muster, striving to make not only myself, but those with whom I hold discussions, as beautiful as possible. But this is the land of the super-sized, and I fear that, instead of listening to weighty discussions, my companions and I are becoming weighted down with meals far heavier than proper nutrition demands. When I served in the Athenian army, and when I walked the streets of Athens in search of those who needed my Socratic questioning, I always burned off far more energy than I took in. But that's not what's happening with the people who gather around me today.

Oracle: Socrates, I have noted that even here in this resort town of Glenwood Springs, the eating establishments put far more food on a plate than anyone needs to consume at one sitting. But in your case, I suggest that you not take in unnecessary food or drink, and that you take the USDA's advice, and "limit treats." When you shop, just don't buy anything that has "high fructose corn syrup" or "partially hydrogenated oils" among the ingredients!

Socrates: At my last Symposium, I stayed and drank everyone under the table, then got up and went about my morning's business; perhaps I should stop doing that. And my fondness for rich desserts has doubtless gotten out of hand. I take your advice to heart, and will reform my errant bodily behavior. I thank you for reminding me that my mission has everything to do with the proper conduct of life, and less to do with the body.

Oracle: Socrates, I have used every device imaginable to spread my message of "Live simply, that others may simply live." But few people pay attention to what oracles have to say. In this land of plenty, it is difficult not to feast every single day, whereas feasts are much more meaningful, when they are rare. What matters, Socrates, is living nobly and well, and attending first to the needs of the soul, and taking due care of the body, as it is the soul's medium of living in the world. When I say: "Lighten up," I mean it much more in the sense of taking all things in stride, and not just losing a few pounds. And I would also say…

----But then the vapors cleared, and I could see and hear no more. I thought the Oracle suggested that "weight" was not the issue, but how one spent one's days and nights, and how one used the body, as an implement of the soul. I came away from Glenwood Springs with a certain lightness of spirit, hoping to return another time, when the Oracle might have such a distinguished visitor as Socrates himself.…

VII-209
The Charm of Descartes

My academic "background" was in the History of Philosophy, a discipline now most often practiced in Departments of "History of Ideas," or "Humanities." While I have sought to stay within the historical discipline, I find myself using the history of philosophy to actually solve philosophical problems, or criticize what goes on today in philosophy, in the light of what the great philosophers had to say.

Rene Descartes (1596-1650) was one of the greatest troublemakers in the history of philosophy. As the "founder" of modern philosophy, he is responsible for leading philosophy into a variety of quick sands from which it has difficulty extricating itself.

The first problem is the very charm of Descartes. It begins with his remarkably enchanting French prose. His *Discourse on Method* and *Meditations* are still read today in the high schools of France, which explains why the French are so familiar with his works. But his charm goes beyond the elegance of his prose: his ability to take large philosophical problems, and produce very comprehensible, simple answers, makes him a happy discovery for anyone looking for brief answers to very large problems.

Descartes was a great mathematical genius. As a young man, he developed an algebraic way of doing geometry, and did it so completely that to this day it is simply called, "Cartesian Geometry." Having dispatched the problems of geometry so expeditiously, Descartes turned to the problems

363

of philosophy, recently brought into doubt by the skepticism of Montaigne. It is as if Descartes had said: "What can I do to build philosophy on truths so certain no one could doubt them? Well, if I am thinking, I cannot doubt that *I am*! What I know for sure, is that I am a mind that thinks."

From this certain beginning, like a good geometrician, Descartes thinks he can reason to the following conclusions: I have within my mind the idea of a Perfect Being. Since nothing in my everyday experience could have put that idea there, a Perfect Being must have placed it there. Therefore, God exists. Am I sure that God exists? Just as surely as a triangle must have three angles, so too existence must be part of an absolutely Perfect Being, hence God exists. (Medieval philosophers had rejected the notion of going from an idea in the mind, to something existent, but the concept of God as an all-perfect being, and since an existent God is more perfect than a non-existent God—the concept still entrances philosophers and logicians to this day.)

Descartes says, the mind should work on clear and distinct ideas: and I have a clear and distinct idea of matter as extension. So my body, being material, has extension, while my mind, not being an extended thing in space, must be a separate substance from my body. Descartes thought of himself as a scientist above all, and wrote a book entitled *Mathematical Physics*, which he thought would be the last word in Physics; alas, thirty years later, Newton published *Mathematical Principles of Natural Philosophy*, and Descartes' Physics was soon forgotten. Unfortunately, Descartes' identification of mind and body as two separate substances is still with us today, and bedevils the study of the science of consciousness, as evidenced by a recent book by a physiologist, Antonio Damasio, entitled: *Descartes' Error*.

Descartes led modern philosophy down the path of beginning with the problem of knowledge. For Descartes, philosophy begins with a quest for certitude, and so the philosopher is asked first to solve the problem of the nature of knowledge. This became the primary philosophical problem for John Locke, David Hume and Immanuel Kant, and for the logical positivists and analytic philosophers of the twentieth century. Philosophers had historically begun with the problem of identifying what was real. For the Pre-Socratic philosophers, the first question of philosophy was: "What is the world made of?" By the time of Socrates, the primary question of philosophy had become a moral one: "How are we to live?" To put the knowledge question first is to do things in the wrong order. First know things, and then ask about the nature of knowledge.

"Science" is a good starting point for doing philosophy: science is an attempt to express "knowledge of the real world." To begin with mathematics, however, can be misleading, for mathematics is an abstraction from the real world, and can enable the philosopher to become so enchanted with axioms and derivatives, that re-entrance into the real world can become difficult, if not impossible.

Descartes is a charmer, both because of the enchantment of his prose, and because of the appeal of his simple, direct explanations of difficult issues. Philosophy is better served by those who look at the real world, ask questions of it, and build their philosophy on some empirical base, which keeps them in the real world, insuring that their philosophy measures up to the demands of everyday, existential, non-geometric, reality. What most annoys me about Descartes, is that he made of philosophy a simple discourse, an essay or treatise or reflection, rather than a "way of life," a way of living in the world. Philosophy as a way of life had been the traditional occupation of the philosopher at least from the time of Socrates. Descartes turned philosophy into an academic discipline, something professors did, instead of something that was everyone's responsibility, and that was his unforgivable sin. As charming as his work is, it is misleading and deceptive. If you want to know the real world, you must begin with that world, come to know something about it, and then ask questions about how you came to obtain that knowledge. It is time for new beginnings in philosophy, new beginnings that harken back to the days when philosophers asked the big questions, like "What is the nature of reality," and, "How are we to live?" It is only after you have worked on these questions, that you are ready to ask questions about the nature of the knowledge you have obtained.

VII-210
Seeking Wisdom Among the Ancients

The work of the historian of philosophy is to apply to present circumstances the words of great thinkers of the past. As each of us face particular problems in life, it is comforting to know that great human beings have faced similar problems, and have had helpful things to say about the problems we all encounter. Take Emperor Marcus Aurelius for example: "Everywhere and at all times it is up to you to rejoice at what is happening in the present moment, and to conduct yourself justly toward the people who are present here and now, and give your whole-hearted attention to what is going on right now...."

These ancient Stoics developed a philosophy of bearing up under challenging circumstances, and taking all things in stride, and that philosophy can serve us well today. These ancient writers were aware that philosophy, as a quest for wisdom, was itself a therapy. Cicero said: "Truly philosophy is the medicine of the soul." Philosophy is not just idle speculation, but practice. Seneca wrote: "Philosophy teaches us how to act, not how to talk."

Epictetus, one of the greatest of the Stoics, said the bottom line of all philosophy lies in encouraging you to get on with the business of living: "A carpenter does not come up to you and say, 'Let me tell you about the art of carpentry,' but he makes a plan for a house and builds it. Do the same thing yourself: eat, drink, get married, have children, take part in the life of your community, learn how to put up with insults, and to tolerate other people."

To anyone about to receive the results of medical tests, the saying of Horace has special significance: "Believe that each day that has dawned will be your last; then you will receive each unexpected hour with gratitude."

The wisdom of the ancient Stoics has exercised a great influence on a number of contemporary philosophers. Pierre Hadot, a Professor at the College de France and author of several books on ancient philosophy, summed up his career by saying: "Such is the lesson of ancient philosophy: an invitation to each human being for self-transformation. Philosophy is a conversion, a transformation of one's way of being and living, and a quest for wisdom." Lest anyone think that conception of philosophy was limited to its ancient practitioners, no less a figure than Immanuel Kant, the very model of a modern academic philosopher, said that the watchword of all enlightenment is: "Dare to think for yourself."

Descartes may have disposed modern philosophers to become obsessed with the question of knowledge. Philosophy, to be meaningful, must always return to its wellsprings, and seek to be wise about life. Stoic philosophers like Marcus Aurelius and Epictetus are among the best guides we could hope for in this quest. "Sooner or later, life makes philosophers of us all." When the challenges of life force us to do philosophy, the great Stoic writers of antiquity may be among our greatest benefactors. "Do not ask, how to become a virtuous person. Become a virtuous person, by the actions you choose." Such is the wisdom of the ancients...

VII-211
Epicurus

No figure of the ancient philosophical world is as misappropriated as Epicurus. He was born on the island of Samos in 341 B.C.E., soon moved to Athens where he spent his life, and died in 270. Shakespeare has one of his characters speak unfavorably of someone else as "mingling with the English Epicures," meaning he sought a life of endless pleasures. Such activity is properly called "hedonism" after the Greek word for pleasure, but such a doctrine did not originate with Epicurus. He is an advocate of such pleasures as can be controlled and enjoyed in moderation, but the pleasures he holds in high regard are friendship, peace, and the appreciation of beauty. Like many of the great Greek philosophers, he anticipated some of the teachings of modern science, as he proposed a theory that might be called "survival of the fittest," to explain why some species survived while others disappeared.

Far from encouraging the all out pursuit of pleasure, Epicurus taught *ataraxia*, a Greek word that defies translation, and means blending tranquility, acceptance, and enjoying the present moment. Epicurus was widely quoted by later Stoic philosophers who thought that his philosophic wisdom required accepting the limits of life, not fearing death, cultivating friends, not desiring what is unnecessary, and not pursuing gratifications that do not enrich the spirit.

Epicurus wrote extensively about being indifferent to one's ailments: "In my sickness my conversation was not about my bodily sufferings, nor did I talk about such subjects to those who visited me; but I continued to discourse on the nature of things as before, keeping to this main point, how the mind, while participating in such movements as go on in the poor flesh, shall be free from disturbances and maintain its proper good. Nor did I give the physicians an opportunity of putting on solemn looks, as if they were doing something great, but my life went on well and happily." And Marcus Aurelius, who saw himself as a disciple of Epicurus, said: "Do the same as he did both in sickness, if you are sick, and in any other circumstances; never desert philosophy in any events that befall you, nor hold trifling talk at parties—this is the principle of all schools of philosophy: remain intent on what you are now doing, and concentrate on doing it well."

So if you wish to become a true disciple of Epicurus, learn to pursue *ataraxia*, to accept what comes your way, to cultivate a peaceful attitude toward those you meet, and to concentrate your attention not on your ailments or those of others, but on what really matters: living your life as well and nobly as you possibly can.

VII-212
Novels and Philosophy

Most novels that identify themselves as "philosophical novels" don't do very well in the marketplace: they tend not to be very good as novels, and not very good in philosophy either. But the eternal themes of love and death are as central to good fiction as they are to philosophy. Novelists can bring abstract problems down to earth, leading the reader to serious philosophical reflection. Novels that deal with legal or political issues, for example, raise innumerable ethical questions, ranging from the morality of the law courts and statehouse or Congress, to the "ethics" of responsibility for actions that have consequences for countless others.

Philosophy tends to get lost in abstractions; novels bring problems back to earth by zeroing in on the particulars of everyday experience. While Dostoevsky may be the greatest of philosophical novelists, novelists in the twentieth century took a serious philosophical turn, beginning with James Joyce. Bloom, the hero of his novel *Ulysses*, is obsessed with his own consciousness, and the novel is mostly the interplay between his serious thoughts and his trivial concerns. The conclusion of the novel is Molly Bloom's "stream of consciousness," showing that thinking is neither logical nor chronological: what matters is "inner experience," not "objective reality." This is a theme many other novels, as well as much of modern philosophy, will belabor.

Virginia Woolf's *To The Lighthouse* suggests there are only a few essential hours in life, a few crucial moments of self-awareness, and that these critical moments form the character of the person, and thus "determine" the rest of life. The theme is simple: it's not events; it's the reaction to them that makes you who you are.

Marcel Proust's *Remembrance of Things Past* has been called the first great modern novel, not only for plumbing the depths of one person's consciousness, but for proclaiming the deep loneliness or isolation that constitutes human life. The characters of Franz Kafka's novels are even more morbid expressions of this dark view: in *The Trial*, Joseph K. is arbitrarily arrested, put on trial, and executed, although he never knows why. Jean-Paul Sartre and Albert Camus continue this grim line of investigation in novels like *Nausea* or *The Stranger*, where anxiety and alienation reach epic proportions.

Iris Murdoch's novels are laden with ethical dilemmas, in which characters search for what is good, in a universe devoid of absolute meaning. In America, we have had no lack of great novelists who have fastened on the ethical and personal dilemmas of life in a capitalist society. Jack London set the stage for all his successors for whom actions, and climactic events, reveal character. Writers as diverse as Theodore Dreiser and James Baldwin focused on the inner life of those struggling with "making a living" in a society of contrasting wealth and poverty. John Grisham spent very little time on the "interior monologue" of his characters, and more on the moral dilemmas in which they find themselves, usually precipitated by oddities in the legal or judicial system. European novels, colored by two disastrous world wars, focused on the dark side of human existence, and the interplay of fate and character. American novels tend to focus on the "actions" of ordinary individuals, and the odd circumstances in which they find themselves. Fiction, from whatever part of the world, proves that philosophy is very much alive, at least within the confines of well-written novels....

VII-213
Avoiding Skepticism

After completing his monumental *History of Philosophy*, B.A.G. Fuller was asked if becoming so familiar with the contradictions of the many philosophers had not left him a skeptic. "I must confess," said he, "even after the Cheshire cat is gone, the grin remains." To some, philosophy remains an endless game of argument and counter-argument, with no expectation of truth prevailing over error, of proper perception canceling out misperception. Wittgenstein once said that his purpose in doing philosophy was "to let the fly out of the fly-bottle," by which he meant, he wished to help people get clear about their own ideas. The goal of doing philosophy after the manner of Socrates is not to promote skepticism, but to get people to think for themselves, to adopt positions because they make sense, not because of prejudice or lack of serious thought.

While Fuller's exposure to the contradictions of the philosophers may have left him forever skeptical, another great historian of philosophy, reviewing the same materials, was led to a quite different conclusion: "Plato's idealism comes first; Aristotle warns everybody that Platonism is heading for skepticism; then Greek skepticism arises, more or less redeemed by the moralism of the Stoics and Epicureans, or by the mysticism of Plotinus. St. Thomas Aquinas restores philosophical knowledge, but Ockham cuts its very root, and ushers in the late Medieval and Renaissance skepticism, itself redeemed by the moralism of the Humanists or by the pseudo-mysticism of Nicholas Cusanus and his successors. Then come Descartes and Locke but their philosophies disintegrate into Berkeley and Hume, with the moralism of Rousseau and Swedenborg as natural reactions. Kant had read Swedenborg, Rousseau and Hume, but his own philosophical restoration ultimately degenerated into the various forms of contemporary agnosticism, with all sorts of moralisms and would-be mysticisms as ready shelters against spiritual despair. The so-called death of philosophy being regularly attended by its revival, some new dogmatism should now be at hand. In short, the first law to be inferred from philosophical experience is: *Philosophy always buries its undertakers."* (Etienne Gilson, *The Unity of Philosophical Experience*, p. 246.) Philosophy, said Gilson, always comes back, because skepticism is both unsatisfying, and self-contradictory. Unsatisfying, because we never give up in the pursuit of truth, and self-contradictory, for the very statement "There is no truth," is being proclaimed as true.

Philosophy is not a pointless discipline, full of arguments that lead only to skepticism. The most important part of philosophy is metaphysics: statements about reality, the mind, substance, and moral responsibility. The greatest critic of metaphysics, Immanuel Kant said: "That the human mind will ever give up metaphysical researches is as little to be expected as that we should give up breathing."

The facts of the matter are, there are various approaches to truth, no one approach can quite get it all, and philosophical dialogue seeks to bring out what is best in each approach. There is no expectation that some knockdown argument will simply demolish every opponent. Some first-principles are better than others, and some "perspectives" produce much more fruitful conclusions than other perspectives. The labor of the historian of philosophy is to make clear the brilliance of the arguments brought forth by various philosophers, leading to a clearer understanding of why some conclusions are vastly preferable to certain other conclusions. The "learned ignorance" of Socrates is not skepticism, but a proper humility in the midst of the quest for truth.

VII-214
Presence of Malice

We say something is "bad" when it is not what it should be. A "bad" day doesn't measure up to our expectations, and a "bad" apple has some serious defect. We use the word "evil" when some element of ill will is involved. A storm is "bad," but someone who willfully puts you in the path of the storm is "evil." The fact that "bad things happen to good people," and the ever-present reality of so much evil in the world, has motivated philosophers and theologians to offer explanations of how existence seems to be an endless battle between the desire for the good and the reality of evil.

Beyond "bad" and "evil," we also have the word "malice." In a court of law, lawyers seeks to prove the "absence of malice" when an event gets out of hand. We are continually made aware of the "presence of malice," in terrorist bombings, in the torture of persons or animals, and when some malefactor admits to causing harm just for the sake of seeing others suffer.

The attack on the World Trade Center was an "evil" act, from our point of view, because it did so much damage, and inflicted physical and psychological harm on so many. We see terrorism as "malicious," because it inflicts its damage indiscriminately. From the point of view of the perpetrator, it is not malicious at all, but an act targeted at achieving some great good: bringing America to its knees, revenging the Crusades, or restoring a particular political or religious group to prominence.

"Malice" is inflicting harm for its own sake. St. Augustine said the wickedest act of his early "sinful" life was shaking down a neighbor's pear tree, not to steal pears, but just for the sake of causing pain. The adolescent mentality is sometimes disposed to play pranks on people—ringing doorbells and fleeing, for example. In the internet age, this kind of behavior has a much larger scope: computer viruses can wipe out someone's labors, financial accounts or social network—for a satisfaction the perpetrator cannot directly enjoy or benefit from.

Police Departments occasionally have to deal with animal mutilations, broken windows or slashed tires on automobiles, the defacing of public property in a manner that is offensive and difficult to repair. Such deliberately malicious acts speak not just of the warped personalities of the perpetrators, but of the dark capacity of human beings to inflict pain on others. C.S. Lewis in *The Problem of Pain* referred to the demonic or diabolical dimension of such actions, while Aldo Leopold spoke of the "still unlovely recesses of the human heart." The main theme of great novels and dramatic presentations is this endless contest between the sovereignty of good, and the presence of evil and malice.

The mass exterminations conducted by Nazi and Communist governments in the darkest years of the twentieth century remain humankind's most monumental expressions of inhumanity. No one has better interpreted the capacity for good to triumph over evil and malice than two death camp survivors, Viktor Frankl, author of *Man's Search for Meaning*, and Primo Levi, an Italian who lived ten months in the Auschwitz death camp, who wrote *Survival in Auschwitz*. For the naked expression of malice, no better example exists than the Concentration Camp Commandant profiled in *Schindler's List*, who randomly shoots prisoners, for no reason at all. To the prayer, "Deliver us from evil," one might append: "And deliver us from the malicious, for they seek to obliterate all that is good, and impose universal darkness upon us all."

Chapter VIII.
A Final Reckoning

VIII-215
Marriage and Divorce

In the last five hundred years, western culture has seen three different models of marriage. A proposed amendment to the U.S. Constitution said: "Marriage in the United States shall consist only of the union of a man and a woman." This is a recent attempt to put into legal form a societal understanding of what marriage is. We may be entering a new stage in the understanding of marriage, as some states, Canada, and some European nations, have moved to legalize homosexual unions, and grant such partners all the legal rights attached to marriage.

There are four perspectives that are part and parcel of our western understanding of marriage. Marriage is first of all a contract requiring the mutual consent of two people to form and to acknowledge publicly what is not only the most important societal relationship, but also the cornerstone of family life. Marriage has been sanctioned by various religions as central not only to the growth and development of the marrying couple, but as an essential component of the community. Thirdly, marriage has generally had certain legal dimensions, with laws of property, inheritance, and clearly defined social obligations within the community. And perhaps most importantly, marriage has been regarded as the pre-eminent natural institution, not only binding two people together, but also insuring the propagation of the race, the care and upbringing of children, and the basis for the mutual care and support without which human life is impossible.

For Jews and Christians, marriage is a religious act, insuring that sexual relations will take place within a socially acceptable context, that children will have parents who are responsible for their nourishment, and that the community will do those things necessary to help the married couple deal with and overcome the various crises that are inevitable parts of adult life. The Roman Catholic Council of Trent in 1563 simply codified what was widely practiced throughout the western world: a marriage required parental consent, the presence of at least two witnesses, some form of public registration, and a religious ceremony of consecration.

The Protestant reformers of that century preferred a social model: marriage was no longer a "sacrament," but a covenantal association of the entire community. What made the marriage was the mutual consent of the couple, not a religious or sacramental consecration. As a social arrangement, marriage was not subject to the church and its religious law, but to the state, and its civil law. With the Protestant Reformation, divorce, in the modern sense, became a possibility. Marriage is not a sacrament with a registry in the church, but a personal, social, civic arrangement, which can be abrogated like any other contract, provided there are good grounds for doing so.

The next stage in the development of the understanding of marriage came as a result of the eighteenth century European Enlightenment. Immanuel Kant wrote: "Have courage to use your own reason: that is the motto of the Enlightenment." Those influenced by the Enlightenment saw marriage as essentially a legal contract, a voluntary bargain struck between two parties, the terms not set by church or state, tradition or community. In the extreme contractarian form, marriage is whatever you want it to be. If Marriage is simply a legal arrangement, it can be whatever the couple, the community, or the state, define it to be. The legitimacy of this interpretation was expressed by Supreme Court Justices Kennedy and Scalia in the 1992 Casey decision: "At the heart of liberty is the right to define one's own concept of meaning, of the universe, and of the mystery of human life."

Thanks to the Enlightenment, western society has come to understand marriage as essentially a contractual matter. All the same, we have sought in some way to retain not only the notion of marriage as societal activity in which the whole community has an interest, but also something of the sacredness of marriage, which the religious traditions established. Nevertheless, we have a great deal of difficulty thinking of a marriage ritual as creating an indelible bond between two people. Marriage is "not lightly to be entered into," but should we think that contracts entered into by people whose brains are not fully formed (anatomists claim that it takes twenty-five years for the brain to complete its development), are to be permanently binding, no matter what changes of character and personality the couple undergo? For those who have happy marriages, the depth of love and affection increases with the years. But why should we condemn to perpetual unhappiness the couples whose marriages have not produced greater depths of affection and understanding?

Several states have initiated mandatory programs in pre-marital counseling, to insure that participants understand the dimensions of the contract they wish to enter. The facts that in the United States, half of all marriages end in divorce, that one fourth of all pregnancies are aborted, that one third of all children are born to single mothers are all strong indications that something is not healthy in this, the most basic of all human institutions. It is time for us re-think our traditions, and come to some realistic understandings of what marriage has to mean in the modern world, and how this, the most important association that we form, can itself become "a more perfect union," better prepared to produce the societal benefits that are the very foundation of human existence.

(I am much indebted to John Witte's book, *From Sacrament to Contract: Marriage, Religion and Law in the Western Tradition.*)

VIII-216
Facing Death with Marcus Aurelius

Dostoevsky commented that facing a firing squad has a remarkable capacity to gain your full attention. The blunt fact of our mortality should be ever before us, but it often takes some life-threatening event to make us fully aware of our fragility. Biblical phrases may come easily to mind: "Remember thy last end and thou shalt never sin," "Death shall come as a thief in the night," and countless others.

Socrates is the first of the great Greek philosophers to proclaim that philosophy is in some manner preparation for death, in two different senses. First of all, philosophy shows that death is natural, a biological fact from which there is no escape. And secondly, philosophy teaches detachment from all material things, and the body is a material thing, no matter how closely we feel attached.

No philosopher in the Greek tradition meditated more steadfastly on death than Marcus Aurelius. Death is a persistent theme of his *Meditations*. Death appears first of all as a hindrance, preventing him from completing his philosophical studies. Death is referred to as a phenomenon of nature no more peculiar than any other. His unique emphasis is on death as liberation from the world where the pursuit of moral virtue is not always seen as the highest good.

For Marcus Aurelius, philosophy consists of three disciplines, the first of which is freeing the mind from the slavery of false judgments of any kind. The second discipline is most truly Stoic: keeping oneself pure from any irritation over what happens to you, or people who seem determined to bother you. This is called a discipline of desire, and it means accepting the portion which "destiny" has prescribed for you. (In Jewish and Christian traditions, this means accepting God's plan for your salvation: "God always wills what is best for me.") The third discipline is action: it is keeping yourself free from choices made frivolously, or without any goal.

The theme of the discipline of action in the face of death recurs throughout *The Meditations:* "Don't act as if you were going to live for ten thousand years. The inevitable hangs over you. As long as you are alive, and as long as it is possible, seek to become a good human being." "Soon, you will have forgotten everything, and everyone will have forgotten you." "He who has seen the now has seen everything." "Toward which goal am I using my soul in this moment?" "Nothing will happen to me which is not in conformity with the Nature of the All. It depends on me to do nothing which is contrary to God and my inner voice." "Carry out each action of your life as if it were your last, and keep yourself far from what is truly frivolous. Think about your last hour. As for the wrong committed by so-and-so, leave it right there." "In some space of time, I will be dead. If I now act as an intelligent human being who places himself in the service of the human community and of God, what more can I ask?"

Marcus Aurelius wrote in the tradition of Socrates, who said: "For a good person, no evil is possible, whether dead or alive." For Socrates and for Marcus Aurelius, the only real evil is moral evil, and we can keep ourselves from doing that. Physical evils befall us all, but they are somehow external to us. Only moral evil can harm the soul.

There is remarkable consonance between the Biblical and the Philosophical traditions in this regard. The Psalmist wrote: "Give me justice, O Lord, for I have lived my life without reproach, and put unfaltering trust in the Lord." Marcus Aurelius wrote: "There is no good for a human being but that which renders him just, temperate, courageous, and free. What art do you practice? That of being good." The wisdom of the Bible can be epitomized with the phrase: "Choose life, that you may live." The wisdom philosophy has to offer may be summarized in this manner: "While you are alive, cultivate your humanity." Marcus Aurelius would be comfortable with either version.

Entrance sign at Dachau

VIII-217
The Roots of Anti-Semitism

The roots of anti-Semitism run deep and wide, but for those scholars who want to pin the blame for modern anti-Semitism on one or another particular group, there is abundant textual evidence to implicate Christians in general, and Catholics in particular. An article in an influential Jesuit journal of 1928 said: "Jews are a danger to the whole world because of their pernicious infiltration, their hidden influence, and their resulting disproportionate power which violates both reason and the common good." In 1933, an Austrian Bishop wrote: "Many of our social and political upheavals are permeated by materialistic and liberal principles stemming primarily from Jews. Every committed Christian has not only the right but the conscientious duty to fight and overcome the pernicious influence of such decadent Judaism."

Are such statements indicative of widespread and "official" anti-Semitism? By no means. Catholic Popes, theologians, priests, and laypeople did speak out vigorously against the rising tide of twentieth century anti-Semitism, including a chaplain who requested that racism be condemned as a heresy and a violation of Christian principles. This is what he wrote to his Bishop in 1933: "No one makes any effective protest against this indescribable German and Christian disgrace. Even priests find their anti-Semitic instincts appeased by this disgraceful behavior. We know that exceptional courage is required today to bear witness to the truth. But we know too that only through such witness can humanity and Christianity be saved." It should not be overlooked that Germany was a predominantly Protestant country. The official Protestant Church failed miserably to protest the rising tide of anti-Semitism. Individual Pastors like the martyred Dietrich Bonhoeffer were outstanding exceptions. There is clear scholarly agreement that while anti-Semitism was never the official "policy" of Protestant or Catholic leaders, most Catholics and Protestants in Germany harbored anti-Semitic convictions.

In 1933, Hitler received an official representative of the German Bishop's Conference, and a transcript records Hitler's remarks, which go far to explain one aspect of anti-Semitism. "I have been attacked because of my handling of the Jewish question. The Catholic Church (Hitler was baptized as a Catholic, but had no use for the Church) considered the Jews pestilent for fifteen hundred years, put them in ghettos, etc., because it recognized the Jews for what they were. In the epoch of liberalism the danger was no longer recognized. I am moving back toward the time in which a fifteen-hundred-year-long tradition was implemented. I do not set race over religion, but I recognize the representatives of this race as pestilent for the state and for the Church, and perhaps I am doing Christianity a great service by pushing them out of schools and public functions." Pushing them into cattle cars and into crematoriums would not occur until a later date.

What are the Christian roots of anti-Semitism? The author of Matthew's Gospel, written for gentiles in Asia Minor and for Jews long dispersed from the holy land, put the blame on those Jewish leaders who feared the man called Jesus might bring down the wrath of the Roman authorities, and with that place severe limitations on Jewish practices. "Then the chief priests and the elders met in the palace of Caiaphas, and conferred together on some scheme to have Jesus arrested by some trick and put to death." Such scriptural quotations formed the nucleus of a religious-based anti-Semitism that persisted over the centuries, reaching fever pitches during the Inquisition and Expulsion, dying down but never dying out. Hans Kung, an ecumenically minded Swiss theologian wrote that Christians and Jews belong together, in a kind of "brotherhood of the book," and that this brotherhood requires the ability to speak openly about past failures and shortcomings. He concluded: "In view of all that Christians have done to Jews in history, it is Christians who should take the lead in the purification of memory and conscience." There is still much work to be done in rooting out anti-Semitism, and it is not only Christians that have work to do along these lines. But Christians have a duty that is both moral and religious to play a major role in rooting out every vestige of anti-Semitism. The "purification of memory and conscience" has only just begun, and no one is exempt from making an appropriate contribution.

VIII-218
Anti-Semitism and "The Passion of the Christ"

The Samaritan woman said: "Sir, I perceive that you are a prophet. Our fathers worshipped on this mountain; but you say Jerusalem is the place where we ought to worship." Jesus responded: "Woman, believe me, the hour is coming when neither on this mountain nor in Jerusalem will you worship the Father. You worship what you do not know; we worship what we know, for salvation is from the Jews." (John 4:19-22)

Betty Edwards, the author of *Drawing on the Right Side of the Brain* said that most of us draw poorly, because we stopped drawing in the fifth grade, and our skills have never progressed. For many of us, knowledge of our religious and cultural heritages has likewise been left at a fifth grade level. This applies especially to people who are otherwise well educated, perhaps as teachers, lawyers, doctors, engineers, business professionals, or politicians.

It would be easy to indict particular Christian fundamentalist preachers who have a penchant for simplifying everything and, in some cases, reducing religious revelation to sentimental slop. But the educational activities of main-line Christian churches have also been at fault, endlessly repeating formulas that have no basis in fact. Hans Urs Von Balthasar, an important and widely read Catholic theologian, managed to repeat the age-old nostrum that the God of the Old Testament is a heartless God of the Law, of revenge, and of punishment, while the God of the New Testament is a God of love, mercy, and forgiveness. This was standard material in catechisms and grade school educational materials years ago, but biblical scholarship in virtually every denomination since then has agreed, "The Jewish God's attitude is one of love. Period." No one can read the Psalms, or the Prophets like Hosea, Jeremiah, and Isaiah, and miss the story of God's love for His people: "I have loved thee with an everlasting love, therefore have I led thee, taking pity on thee."(Jeremiah 31:31) "I will lead her (Israel) into the desert, and I will speak to her heart, and she will respond to me as in the days of her youth."(Hosea 2:12)

The Mel Gibson movie of 2004, "The Passion of the Christ," quoted the passages from the New Testament where "the Jews" are guilty of plotting the Passion and Death of Christ. Biblical scholars have pointed out that, given the time of the writing of the Gospels and Epistles, no one else could

Gene Bammel

have been named as protagonists. There are only two groups of people in the Gospel narratives: Jews and Romans. In the first century, to name "The Romans" as those who put Jesus to death would have been cultural and religious suicide. The Romans held all the cards. All the other players in the drama: Jesus, his mother, his disciples, the scribes, Pharisees, Sadducees, common people, --all were Jews! Pontius Pilate is the key Roman figure in the Gospel narratives, and, in "washing his hands" of the whole business, he figuratively and literally saves the Romans from being the responsible party, which left only "The Jews."

Current Biblical scholarship highlights the political components of the trial and death of Jesus. The Romans could identify Jesus as a political zealot, and the Jewish officials, desirous of throwing off the Roman yoke, did not want to provoke Roman retaliation for a budding revolt they saw as having no chance of success. The mix of religion and politics at that time was even heavier than it is today.

This movie and others like it may dispose viewers to come back and "read the Bible again, for the first time." A new reading, with some perception of what good Biblical scholarship has produced over the years, may lead to a much different understanding of what all was going on. If nothing else, getting Christians to remember that Jesus said: "Salvation is from the Jews," would be a big plus. The celebrated editor of the journal *First Things* Father John Neuhaus has written: "When we Christians do not walk together with Jews, we are in danger of regressing to the paganism from which we emerged." To the question of who is responsible for the death of Jesus, Neuhaus replies: "The Christian answer to the question of who killed Jesus is that we all did." The appropriate Christian theological answer is that all have sinned, all are guilty, and all stand in need of redemption. And Fr. Neuhaus makes the point that Christian teachers bear the chief responsibility for any failure to understand "the Jewish matrix of the story of salvation." If you watch movies like Mel Gibson's "The Passion of the Christ," arm yourself with the biblical quotation: "Salvation is from the Jews." It will put all such films in a much different light.

VIII-219
Jews Conquering Greeks

Paul Tarnas' book, *The Passion of the Western Mind* documents how western culture consists of the two intertwining strands of Hebraic Revelation, and Greek Rationalism. The Hebrew genius taught us about how to believe, how to be religious, while the Greek genius taught us how to be scientific, and how to exercise reason. (Clearly the Hebrews exercised reason, and the Greeks had their gods and religious practices: it is a matter of which approach was dominant). Modern western culture has sometimes been characterized as the "triumph" of the Greek, rationalizing approach, over the believing or religious approach of the Hebraic tradition.

There is, however, one cultural episode where Jews really were victorious over what the Greek traditions of the time proposed. Hanukah is a celebration of that event. The story begins with Alexander the Great conquering the land of Israel in 333 B.C.E. Alexander, something of an ancient pluralist, allowed the Jews to maintain their traditions and their religious and national autonomy. Things went pretty smoothly until 175 B.C.E. when Antiochus IV came to power, and wanted to impose "Greek Culture" on all the lands he ruled. Some Jews were enthusiastic about this, spoke Greek, adopted Greek customs, and were known as "Hellenists." The majority of Jews wanted to maintain their religious traditions and practices, and became known as "Hasidim," or, "the pious ones." It wasn't rejection of Greek Philosophy or Greek rationalism that was involved here. There were certain Greek cultural practices, including infanticide, pedophilia, and prostitution, that were incompatible with Hebrew traditions and beliefs.

Antiochus sought to make Jerusalem a Greek city, and he banned Sabbath observance, circumcision, and the study of the Torah. He put up an altar in the Temple, and insisted that Jews sacrifice to the Greek gods. Within eight years, a Jewish rebellion occurred, led by a priest who killed a Greek soldier sacrificing a pig. The Jews who joined the priest in the rebellion chose as their leader Judah Maccabee, the priest's son. (Maccabee is Hebrew for "he who fights like a hammer.") The Jews fought heroically, and defeated a trained and superior army, liberating Jerusalem in 165 BCE. A festival that lasted eight days celebrated the Purification of the Temple, and the triumph of the Hasidim over their Greek oppressors. Judah Maccabee was killed in battle, but his brother established the Hasmonean Dynasty that ruled Israel for more than a century.

When the Jews sought to re-dedicate the temple, they could find only enough holy lamp oil for one night, but, miraculously, the oil lasted eight nights. Lighting the Menorah during Hanukah is an act of Remembrance and Thanksgiving for this miracle.

The Greek, Western Tradition generally has prided itself for its apparent "triumph" over the Hebraic Traditions. But a well-balanced life, like a well-balanced culture, draws from both its roots. It may be fitting to celebrate this admirable triumph of the best aspects of the Hebrew tradition over the dubious aspects of Greek culture. As Christians try to "bring back Christ to Christmas," it might be appropriate for Christians and Jews, and those who have no religious convictions, to begin lighting Hanukah candles at the appropriate time each year, as a symbolic expression of Remembrance, of Purification, of Re-dedication, to the best values of both Hebraic and Greek culture. It may help to keep alive the hope that the miraculous may erupt into human experience. It might be a good time to recollect the ancient perceptions that good does triumph over evil, that peace is better than war, that love is superior to hatred, that forgiveness is better than holding a grudge, and that doing good for others in difficult circumstances is an important aspect of being human.

VIII-220
Different Paths to the Divine:
Neither Jew nor Greek...

Any comment along the lines of: "Christians and Moslems worship the same God," is bound to draw angry responses from fundamentalists. The Koran says that Abraham "submitted" to God, and so was in some sense the first "Muslim," an Arabic word meaning "servant." Since Jesus Christ identified himself as worshipping the "God of Abraham, Isaac, and Jacob," there's no escaping that the God of the Jews, the God of Christians, and the God of Islam, is the same God.

A tradition at least as old as the monotheism of the Abrahamic religions is that of Vedanta Hinduism, a religion that appears to have no single founder, and is about as "pluralist" as a religion can be. Vedanta persistently proclaims that all religions are different routes to the same end. Karan Singh, a contemporary Hindu sage wrote: "Who are we, denizens of this tiny speck of dust, to say that in the whole cosmos, there is only one path to the divine?"

Buddhism has an "ecumenical" approach, eager to listen to what different traditions have to say, and loathe to proclaim its way as the only way. Shunriyu Suzuki, a master interpreter of Buddhism to western audiences, said: "When you study Buddhism, you should have a general housecleaning of your mind." Suzuki thought that westerners had a passion for absolutism, sometimes in the form of "my way is the only way," that was essentially foreign to the eastern mind. At a time when Greek culture and Greek philosophers assumed that war and rivalry and competition were integral parts of the human condition, Confucius and his followers were emphasizing the virtues of amiability and collaboration. These disparate philosophical convictions seem to have carried over into the respective religious traditions.

At academic conferences in Philosophy and Religion, the point is often made that what we have in common is much more important than what divides us. If that can be true for scholars, who have such vested interests in disseminating their own convictions, why can it not be true for larger communities of political and religious interests? Many are the texts illustrating intercultural identity from Confucian, Platonic, Aristotelian, and Stoic traditions, but none more poetic than a brief saying from a first century Jewish writer, who was also a Christian, and a Roman citizen, Paul of Tarsus: "For there is neither Jew nor Greek, male or female, slave or freeman, for you are all one..." Astronomers have taken to pointing out that we are all "star-stuff," for the carbon base of every human body has its origin in the blazing stars of distant galaxies. Why is it then that both globally and locally, we spend so much time emphasizing what separates us, when what we have in common is so much more important, and serves as the foundation for the distinctively human values of love, understanding, and compassion?

Deep-seated within human nature there is the hope that the future will be better than the past, that we will learn from our mistakes, and that we will "progress" into a bright new day. All the citizens of the world might do well to learn to recite one of the best ecumenical prayers ever uttered: "Where there is hatred, let me sow love, where there is darkness, light, and where there is sadness, joy." In every category of human endeavor, what we have in common is much more important than what divides us, collaboration is preferable to competition, and a vision of "mutually assured assistance" is infinitely preferable to the "mutually assured destruction," which would be the inevitable outcome of the competitive vision of those who think they have cornered the market for truth. "Who are we, denizens of this tiny speck of dust, to say that in the whole cosmos, there is only one path to the divine?"

VIII-221
Limited Relativism

In the search for the first truly modern person, three candidates stand out. Machiavelli deserves mention, for he established the very "modern" idea that personal ethics has little to do with political realities. The Prince does whatever he needs to do to get and retain power. Francis Bacon is a candidate, for his enthusiastic endorsement of the "scientific method" of observation and experiment that set the world on the modern voyage of discovery.

But one might argue, with great justification, that the first truly modern person was the English philosopher John Locke. The ancient and medieval world was characterized by certainty and absolutism. If you have certainty, and can be absolutely sure of your convictions, you can rule and legislate with an iron fist, and no one has any right to oppose you. Into this world of absolutes, Locke proposed that none of our knowledge is absolutely certain, and the best we can hope for is probability. Locke taught that there is no "formula" that contains the whole truth, for all our assertions are but "approximations" of the reality that is out there.

Locke's "probabilism" has had a dramatic effect on ethics, which had been viewed as the terrain of the clearest absolutes: conduct was right or wrong, virtuous or vicious. Explorers of the 17th century had brought back to England tales of other cultures and customs, thereby calling into question the moral absolutism that had prevailed throughout western European society, and providing Locke with some empirical evidence for his questioning of moral absolutes.

This displacement of moral certitude eventually gave rise to "cultural relativism," the belief that morals are relative to different peoples, times and places. Jean-Paul Sartre expressed the extreme of moral relativism: there are no essences or natures, so one is truly "free" to become whatever one wants to become. In America, the Beat Generation and Hippiedom were forms of expressing the absolute freedom of creating essences beyond all constraints and customs.

The probabilism of Locke and the existentialism of Sartre have been transformed today into "limited relativism," a stance that says, while there are exceptions to every rule, rules exist because society has seen they are necessary for human existence and development. In the light of experience, we have come to reject certain behaviors absolutely, such as child molestation, rape, corporate greed, and assertions of racial supremacy, remnants of slavery, and all similar activities regarded as unworthy of human beings, and as simply "wrong."

We may be at the dawn of a new era, where absolutism and relativism will both be passé, and there will be widespread agreement on the issues about which we are absolutely sure, while accepting wide latitude for behaviors that are matters of individual choice. Perhaps a new and enlightened era of limited relativism is about to dawn, where a happy balance of "You can't do that!" and ""Blossom as you please," will survive side-by-side in a new and peaceable kingdom of enlightened moral wisdom. The "probabilism" of Locke has been redeemed by the acceptance of absolutes where absolutes are absolutely necessary, and all other behavior is seen as relative to an individual's time, place, and circumstances. If he had been asked to comment, Wittgenstein might have said, "Let there be limits on your relativism." And even Augustine, the great absolutist, did say: "Do whatever you please, as long as it is in conformity with love, and right reason."

VIII-222
Gay Marriage

When most philosophers disagree with each other, they have a habit of doing so in a nice way, of complimenting those with whom they disagree, and then trying to present "arguments" that are oriented to bringing their opponent around to a new point of view. Moral disagreements, at least among philosophers, can be reduced to two contrasting points of view: (1) There are rules, (perhaps these rules are divine commands), and these rules are written into the heart of things, for they derive from the "natures" that things have, and all moral behavior is a matter of conformity to the natural order; (2) the only source of judgment of moral behavior derives from examining the consequences of particular actions: murder and lying are wrong, because they produce consequences that are destructive of society, but killing in self-defense, and deceiving someone who would use your statements for bad purposes, are praiseworthy.

People who observe rules and see morality as obligations to be fulfilled tend to be "absolutists," with a conviction that what is right behavior can be identified, described, and prescribed not just for a local community but for all the members of the human race. At its core, morality is a matter of natures, and conformity with those natures. The best illustrations of this derive from writers in the "natural law" tradition, who affirm that the natural purpose of marriage is the procreation and raising of children, and that the natural and appropriate use of the sexual organs is for reproduction. (In its most extreme form, a defender of natural law might claim that the only permissible use of drugs to remedy "erectile dysfunction" would be in the case of a husband, hoping to impregnate his wife, but incapable of sustaining an erection.)

That the purpose of marriage was having and raising children was the law in Massachusetts, until the state court set aside that tradition, and ruled that the primary purpose of marriage was companionship. That opened the floodgates of debate about "gay marriage," and the contentious debate over this issue is only in its infancy. The former Dean of the Yale Divinity School wrote that such actions "tempt Christians to adopt a vision of moral and social life that runs counter to the very foundations of Christian thought and practice. And it raises the question of whether we inhabit a moral universe governed by an order we are called upon to understand and to which we are required to conform, or whether that universe is a mere product of preference-pursuing *individuals*, *selves*, and *persons* who create a social world suited to their self-defined goals through an elaborate process of moral bargaining." In a word, no gay marriages, and no gay Bishops, in this or any other universe.

David Brooks expressed the counter-argument quite clearly. He wrote that marriage has become a contingency arrangement of a promise to love, honor, and cherish, until something comes along that makes fulfilling those promises impossible. He claimed marriage should be a contractual agreement to love each other as deeply and enduringly as is possible, and that such a contract can be entered into by gays and lesbians just as well as it can be by the heterosexual population. "Few of us work as hard at the vocation of marriage as we should. But marriage makes us better than we deserve to be. (The couple) may eventually come to the point where they say: 'Love you? I am you.'" In sum, marriage should be a promise and a hope that love will grow and deepen; if that does not happen, then, like any other contractual agreement, it should be subject to cancellation.

Brooks claimed that our society would be better off if we extended such commitment contracts to gays and lesbians who wish to express their desire to spend their lives together. He takes as his model of commitment the biblical promise of Ruth: "Where you go I will go, and where you stay I will stay. Your people will be my people and your God my God. Where you die I will die and there I will be buried." Brooks says this is not at all a matter of liberalism or consequentialism gone wild. It is in fact a genuinely "conservative" move. "The conservative course is not to banish gay people from making such commitments. It is to expect that they make such commitments."

Far from rejecting the natural law basis of human morality, it is better to say that our knowledge of nature and of natural law continues to deepen, and that some of this progressively deeper understanding derives from studying the consequences of our moral choices. To exclude people from making public, contractual celebrations of their lives together seems to be an anachronistic action, more characteristic of a bygone era. Let us examine the consequences of our behavior, and then let us make rules that promote the consequences that are most beneficial. And let us get over the prejudices of a bygone era.

VIII-223
The Bible As Literature

A course called "The Bible As Literature" is bound to attract the attention of state legislative committees charged with reviewing the courses offered by state-supported universities. The "fundamentalists" among the legislators will object to a course that suggests the Bible is merely "literature," and not the revealed word of God. The secularists, always seeking to preserve a clear distinction between church and state, will object to the Bible being a subject within the university curriculum at all.

From the point of view of everyday philosophy, the Bible, while clearly a religious document, is laden with philosophical themes. To the philosophical question, "Why is there something rather than nothing?" the Bible offers an answer no Greek philosopher ever thought of. "In the beginning God created heaven and earth." Greek philosophers assumed the universe was eternal; it always was and always would be. Modern science, with the "Big Bang" theory, seems to agree with the Bible on that issue.

When asked to discuss the meaning and purpose of life, Greek Philosophy proposed that the goal of life was to become a virtuous human being, thereby becoming a "happy" and useful member of society. The Bible's theme is that doing God's will is the source of meaning and purpose in life. St. Augustine summarized the Bible's teaching this way: "Thou hast made us for Thyself, O God, and our hearts are restless until they rest in Thee." While there are parallels between the Greek philosophical vision and the Biblical theme, the biblical literature has a much different take on what it takes to be a successful human being, and that biblical perspective is well worth hearing.

In the debate between determinism and free will, Greek Philosophy tends to side with the determinists. In that eternal universe, there are only so many combinations of atoms and void possible, and somehow "The Fates" rule over what the combinations will be. The Bible, on the other hand, relentlessly teaches, beginning with the story of Adam and Eve, personal responsibility for one's own actions. No matter how forceful the arguments for determinism, it is in our best human interests to keep alive the vision of personal responsibility for our actions, a theme the Bible teaches relentlessly.

The gods of the Greek philosophers have better things to do with their eternity than to bother much with human beings. Aristotle's god contemplates the noblest of all beings: himself. It would be beneath his dignity to think about human beings. The God of the Bible has a never-ending, patient love for his creatures: "I have loved you with an everlasting love, therefore have I led you, taking pity on you." (Jeremiah 31:31) The Biblical God loves the world, forgives His creatures, and persistently attempts to lead them back to Himself. The gods of Greek Philosophy leave man to fend for himself. The Biblical God is providential: not a sparrow falls to earth without His knowledge, and the same God who brought His people out of Egypt, will not let evil triumph over good.

It is not philosophical reflections that convince legislators that "The Bible As Literature" has a place in the University curriculum. It is more likely to be the poetry of the Bible (poetry, after all, is literature!) like *The Song of Songs*, where the poetry is taken as an allegory of God's love for humankind. "Night after night on my bed, I have sought my true love; I have sought him but not found him, I have called him, but he has not answered. When I meet him, I shall seize him, and will not let him go, for I will bring him into the inmost chambers of my heart."

Poetry takes us where prose, especially philosophical prose, has no hope of victory. The Bible is not only literature, but literature that is essential to understanding the passions of the western mind. As such, it deserves a place in the University curriculum. The scholarly, academic reading of the Bible should be no threat to anyone's religious development. It may even facilitate it. Such religious growth is not the University's primary business, but it could be an interesting by-product. The Bible is one of the foundation documents of civilization, and no liberal education is complete without some understanding of the kind of literature the Bible happens to be.

VIII-224
Emil Fackenheim

Because of the professors I had at the University of Toronto, I learned to see philosophy as a way of life, and not just as a dry, academic discipline. Toronto in the twentieth century may have been the best place in the world to study the history of philosophy. Not only were the professors interested in their students, but they reflected in their lives and character the philosophies they professed. On the faculty were famous Platonists like G.M.A. Grube and John Rist, famous Aristotelians like Joseph Owens, famous medievalists like A.C. Pegis, Etienne Gilson and Jacques Maritain, and people who would become famous as interpreters of Anglo-American philosophy.

Among the "modern" philosophers no one was more impressive than Emil Fackenheim (1916-2003). He was born in Halle, Germany, in 1916, became a graduate student in Berlin in 1938, spent three months in the Concentration Camp at Sachsenhausen, was released, ordained a Rabbi, and left Germany for England on May 12, 1939, one week before the Gestapo closed the borders.

He was interned in Canada as "an enemy alien," but pursued doctoral studies at the University of Toronto, and, when the war ended, was accorded "temporary" faculty status, but he soon became a fixture in Toronto's philosophical firmament. He was interested in medieval Jewish and Arabic philosophy but his specialty was German Idealism, -- Kant, Fichte, Shelling and Hegel.

As a refugee from Nazi Germany, he sought to understand the Holocaust, and how anti-Semitism could have reached such a fever pitch in what should have been a highly civilized society. He said philosophers believed too much in "eternal rational verities," whereas the Holocaust was "a truth within History" that defied rational analysis. In 1984, he moved to Israel, which he saw as the logical conclusion of a life-long journey of understanding. He wrote: "Talking with survivors is vital if we're to test the validity of our philosophical thought against their witness."

Emil Fackenheim died in Jerusalem in October 2003. He left behind many great books, first among them *Jewish Philosophers and Jewish Philosophy*. His even greater legacy was his impact upon his students: he was a great man, who lived his philosophy. He belongs to the pantheon of great teachers, who expressed in their lives the philosophy to which they were deeply committed. His autobiography, *An Epitaph for German Judaism: from Halle to Jerusalem*, records his philosophical and personal development. This great man, so deeply committed to seeing the truth within history, somehow stood above it, as a witness to the eternal verities of goodness, justice, and the passionate pursuit of truth.

VIII-225
"The Pope and St. Emil"

If the Pope had known Emil Fackenheim, my imagination leads me to believe he might try to canonize him, identifying Emil, a philosopher and Jewish Rabbi, as a saint. The dialogue between the Pope and the Cardinal in charge of proposing saints might go something like this: "But Your Holiness, this man not only rejected Catholic teachings, he enjoyed making jokes about priests." The Pope replies: "Don't forget that the word 'saint' simply means 'holy person,' and over the years, we have canonized a lot of saints whose beliefs weren't exactly main stream. Sts. Ambrose and Augustine said and did a lot of things not in keeping with Christian doctrine. And St. Thomas Aquinas, whom my predecessors named the 'official' theologian of the Church, wrote: 'If there is a heretic in your midst, admonish him twice, and, if he does not recant, turn him over to the secular authorities for immediate execution, lest he corrupt the faithful.' It may seem quaint and amusing now, but it hardly seems in keeping with Christian charity."

The Cardinal pays no attention, and says: "But with so many eminent Catholic philosophers and theologians, why would you canonize this unbeliever?" "Ah," replied the Pope, "precisely my point! While philosophers and theologians were arguing fine points of dogma, Fackenheim was out there practicing the love of God and His creatures. I can think of no better way to remind the faithful that being pleasing to God is a matter of what you do, not a matter of how you define your doctrines."

Exasperated, the Cardinal says: "But why do you want to proclaim this particular man a saint?" And the Pope responds: "Once more, you seem to miss the point of what it means to be a saint. A saint is a model for others to follow, and this man led a holy and exemplary life that was surely pleasing to God. As the Sacred Scriptures say, 'How can someone claim to love the unseen God, and not love the brother whom is seen.' From the evidence of his friends and family and students, this was a man who simply exuded love: love for learning, love for the truth, and patience with everyone he met, even forgiveness for his captors. Perhaps it will disturb some people, but I have to say, this man was truly a saint!"

"But what about those jokes of his?" And the Pope responds, "He exercised the ironic humor I enjoy. His favorite story, after the American President Kennedy had gone to Berlin and said, 'I am a Berliner,' was to ask, what if the Pope had gone to Berlin in 1933, and said: 'Ich bin Jude, I am a Jew?' It might have stalled Hitler in his tracks." "But Your Holiness, what about those jokes at the expense of our priests?" "Ah yes, that too. Apparently he never tired of telling the story of how a priest and a minister, at the end of World War II, were preparing to go back to the states, and the priest said: 'Well, we return to our respective parishes, you to serve God in your way, and I to serve Him in His.' That's actually very funny, even if it is painful to think of how arrogant we have been sometimes. The Papacy in the last fifty years has been all about ecumenical dialogue, about establishing better relations with other communities of faith. I need to do more along those lines. I am reminded that Rabbi Abraham Heschel said: 'God is a pluralist.' On your way out, my dear Cardinal, would you pick up the files we have on Rabbi Heschel? After we identify the saintliness of a philosopher like Emil Fackenheim, I think we need to take a serious look at Rabbi Heschel." Exasperated, the Cardinal quietly whispers, "Holy St. Emil, pray for us." Once a Pope's mind is made up, there really isn't much you can do about it.

VIII-226
True Ecumenism

In Samuel Huntington's influential book, *The Clash of Civilizations,* the point is made that while language and religion are the central elements of every culture, it is "religion" that motivates and mobilizes people. While philosophers tend to emphasize the importance of philosophy, there can be no doubt that the influence of religion is immeasurably greater. More than thirty million people will read some text of Aristotle this year. More than three billion people will read from some sacred text. Of the world's six billion people, two billion are Christians, one billion are Moslems, and a billion are Hindus or Buddhists. Of the additional billion who identify with some religion, fifteen million are Jews. Of the remaining billion, less than half are totally non-religious.

Early in the twentieth century, "ecumenical" movements occurred, attempts initially to get Christians to overcome their differences and work on doctrinal agreements and social action programs. The "World Council of Churches" played an influential role in promoting inter-denominational discussion and developing "inter-faith" charitable programs. One of the reasons Pope John XXIII gave for calling the Second Vatican Council was the promotion of Church Unity, under the Biblical injunction, "That all may be one." In America in particular, theologians, pastors, and members of various Christian congregations engaged in friendly discussion, emphasizing the "truths" they held in common. Around the world, religious-minded people of various persuasions enjoyed a brief "honeymoon" of discovering that members of other communities did not have horns, were not engaged in devil-worship, and sought to lead exemplary lives.

Ecumenical dialogue seldom runs smoothly, however, and eventually practitioners of different faiths began to zero in on the reasons why they were separate, why they worshipped in different ways, and why they sometimes had conflicts with others. After the initial euphoria of saying: "We are all believers," the reality set in: "But we are on very different paths." A document published in 1994, "Evangelicals and Catholics Together" was a major milestone towards "convergence and cooperation," highlighting the crucial different visions of "Scripture and Tradition" among the participants.

In 2000, some two hundred Jewish scholars issued *Dabru Emet*, "To Speak the Truth," offering a Jewish understanding of Christianity, as a response to the many Christian understandings of Judaism. While *Dabru Emet*'s purpose was to advance theological understanding, the basic premise is that Christians and Jews will live together "in greater security and mutual respect" if they understand one another as participants in a covenant seeking to be faithful to the God of Israel.

The ecumenical movements of the recent past have had some remarkable successes, but they have been marked by outstanding failures. The first great success lay in disposing members to examine their own traditions and convictions, thereby coming up with a clearer understanding of why they believed and practiced as they did. The second successful dimension has been in the dialogues that have promoted an appreciation, and in some cases an acceptance, of other traditions, as "acceptable" ways of being religious. The failures might be summarized by the lack of answers to two abiding questions: "What kind of unity is really possible?" and, "Can we be satisfied with Unity in Diversity?"

The distinctive challenge of the twenty-first century will be the encounter with Islam. The ecumenical movements of the twentieth century happened because various Jewish and Christian communities recognized their need to understand themselves and to talk with each other. Important components of the Islamic community have not yet reached the stage where they are prepared to engage in meaningful dialogue. When philosophers cannot get along, the consequences are usually minor, and the problems remain the concern of the philosophers involved. When religions do not agree, the consequences are culture-wide, and we all have a stake in the outcome. That is why Jews, Moslems and Christians, Hindus and Buddhists, believers and non-believers, theologians and philosophers, all have a vested interest in the continuation and enlargement of these various ecumenical dialogues. It may well be that the survival of the human race is at stake. It is in the best interest of us all that we prevent clashes of civilizations, and that we generate a new and safer world order. This cannot happen without some great advances in all forms of ecumenical dialogue. Philosophers may have some small role to play in this, but the real action will be among the world's five billion religious believers.

VIII-227
Patient Patients

While the vast majority of people over 65 have no serious disability, most people, by the time they reach that age, have the experience of being a "patient." The word comes from the Latin *patiens,* which means, "one who is suffering." People suffer different maladies, and bear their sufferings with different degrees of success. Most people of mature years will at some time experience at least one of three very challenging problems: coronary artery problems, cancer, or arthritis. Heart disease may require major surgery; cancer may require surgery, radiation, or chemotherapy, while arthritis may lead to some form of joint replacement.

There are three coping strategies that one should become expert in long before problems present themselves. Jon Kabat-Zinn has suggested that the best strategy is Meditation. Meditation requires setting aside a block of time each day—15 minutes is a good start—to simply empty the mind of all that assails it. Meditation is not an attempt to "focus" on some particular problem or response; it is an exercise rather of heightened awareness and acceptance.

At a sesshin, a form of Buddhist retreat, a woman wept uncontrollably throughout the meditation sessions. Afterwards, she offered various explanations for her weeping, then rejected them all, saying: "I was weeping just to be weeping." In a similar vein, Meditation is attentiveness to attentiveness. If you practice Meditation for 15 minutes everyday, when disturbing events come your way, as come they must, you will have a mechanism for coping with them and transcending them. Do not practice Meditation to accomplish anything. Meditate simply to meditate, and the benefits will appear.

The second strategy is the development of a positive attitude. Whatever the diagnosis and prognosis, patients with a positive attitude fare better than those who focus on the negativities of their circumstances. Support groups are especially good at fostering positive attitudes. The leaders of such groups are often members who have experienced the full brunt of a disease, and have mastered a challenging situation. Serious diseases often bring about some degree of depression, and support groups are especially effective at overcoming the depressing dimensions of diagnosis and treatment.

The third coping mechanism is exercise. The amount and form of exercise varies from patient to patient, but forms of physical activity, whether easy stretching, yoga, walking, or games of some kind, are available to everyone. Exercising, much like Meditation, produces its benefits simply by the doing of it. As one eminent physician said: "The best prescription I can write is one for regular exercise."

Meditation, a Positive Attitude, Exercise—may not cure all the ills that wait to assail us, but they will help us cope with the predictable and unpredictable challenges of adult life. We need to learn to be patient patients, not only that we may recover as well as possible, but also that we may make the best of each day that comes our way. Each day provides its distinctive wonders—that's why we only get them one day at a time. Meditation, a Positive Attitude, Exercise—these are the secrets of being a successful patient. Practice them, so that when and if the time comes, you will be ready.

VIII-228
"Shame" As A Moral Touchstone

In a series of articles for the New York Times on the "War of Ideas," Tom Friedman pointed out that we have been engaged in such wars for some time, most notably with Fascism, with Soviet Communism, and now with Militant Islam. The Nazis used German military might in the attempt to impose the reign of the perfect race. Marxists used the Soviet Union to impose the reign of the classless society. And now, some religious totalitarians are using terror tactics to impose the reign of the perfect faith, Islam.

While we overcame Nazism with our own military might, Soviet Communism collapsed because we ultimately shared certain basic bedrock rules of civilization. They loved life, more than they hated us. With suicide bombers, things are different now. The sad fact is, with the Islamist militant groups, we face people who hate us more than they love life.

What Friedman and other journalists are searching for is an ethical common ground. Why did Soviet Communism break down? Because ultimately, we and the Soviets agreed on what is shameful. Here we may have found the rock-bottom nucleus of an ethical common ground. Shame, more than any laws or police, is how a family, a village, a society, or a culture expresses approval or disapproval and applies restraints. There is no culture that does not have the ethical equivalent of "Shame on you." In public discourse, it is customary to think of sexual misconduct as the clearest source of shame, but there are other shameful acts of which we can readily find politicians, business people, those who drive while under the influence, and those who practice a motley list of other misbehaviors, guilty.

We must not overlook shame in our search for moral bedrock. We find it "shameful" that mothers abandon their babies, that adults would abuse children, and that politicians or business people might think themselves above the law in their activities. It is the absence of shame that makes corporate greed so despicable, and the absence of shame or remorse that makes those who have done wrong seem guilty of more than just their offense. Most significantly, it is some capacity to agree on what is shameful that binds us into a moral community. In singling out shame, we have found a very important touchstone of morality, and an important basis for distinguishing the moral from the immoral. Shame on the moralists for not noticing it sooner...

VIII-229
"Asceticism."

The Greek word "askesis" means exercise or training, implying both discipline and self-denial. We clearly live in the midst of a self-indulgent culture, where discipline and self-denial are looked upon as quaint and slightly peculiar. The formulas of self-indulgence can be heard on every corner: "I will deny myself nothing pleasurable." "If it feels good, do it." "Don't knock it until you have tried it." The evidence of the consequences of such thinking--taken to extremes--is apparent in the skid rows of every major city, in the various detention centers around the country, and perhaps even on the empty faces of the semi-sated pleasure seekers at various entertainment venues.

We are paying the penalty for our cultural forgetfulness of asceticism. From the TV ads for gambling casinos you would think all the participants were ecstatic at the pleasure of instant gratification produced by slot machines that cascade coins into overflowing receptacles. Walk through any casino, however, and the visual experience is much different. The majority of players seem anything but ecstatic, and some seem downright desperate. While sociologists insist that gambling is addictive for only a small percent of casino goers, economists are sounding alarms about how much money is wagered, how many hours of otherwise productive activity are squandered, and how the gambling industry fails to generate any new real wealth.

Americans spend more than $70 Billion gambling each year, more than twice the amount spent on car insurance, and almost three times as much as is spent on books. Casinos do not appear to be places where human beings advance the horizons of what is meant to be human, or as places where people are making the best possible use of their time. What a distance we have traveled from the ascetic vision of disciplining oneself, so that human nature is perfected by its activity, and not demeaned by it.

TV specials frequently profile the diet industry in America, highlighting the various popular programs like Weight-Watchers, and medical approaches like gastric by-pass surgery. Science has documented that being overweight is a genetic matter for some people, for some people have a gene programmed for obesity. But for many people, becoming overweight is simply the result of the absence of discipline in their lives. In a land where fast and fattening food is available on every corner, it is difficult not to give in to the satisfactions of the taste buds, especially when the pressures of daily life are not compensated for by vigorous physical activity. Those on successful weight-loss programs acquire a discipline, an askesis, a regimen that enables them to control their appetites, and take charge of their daily eating routines.

As a culture, we seem to have lost all real sense of discipline and self-control. For every Lance Armstrong we have hundreds of people who live by ever searching out new sources of satisfaction, and less-demanding ways of doing things. The time has come to pay attention to the wise ones of the ancient world. Marcus Aurelius, for example, said: "I seek simplicity in my way of living, far removed from the habits of the rich. I desire only a plank bed and simple clothes, and all that goes with Greek asceticism." One of the great preachers of the ancient world wrote: "I discipline my body and bring it into subjection, lest, when I have preached to others, I should myself become a reprobate." In a culture of immediate gratification, there is something to be said for moderation, discipline, restraint, and a renewed and proper sense of asceticism...

VIII-230
Novels About Early Christianity

My objections to most novels written about early Christianity are philosophical, historical, and literary. Generally they are poorly told tales. Ancient Greek critics rejected dramas that were solved by a *deus ex machina*, usually a basket lowered down at the end, when a god intervened to solve an otherwise insoluble dilemma. For some reason, most novels in this genre have thinly drawn characters, unlikely events, and improbable resolutions. Dan Brown's *The DaVinci Code* was no exception to this general rule.

Christian history is usually the first casualty in these novels. Recently, attempts to restore "the sacred feminine" have become the second historical casualty. The true record of ancient Christian history is not easy to establish, given the vested interests of parties ancient and modern to widely divergent interpretations of what actually happened. Understanding "the sacred feminine" is comparatively easy. Many ancient religions had male and female deities. Babylonian religions have Marduk creating the cosmos out of the body of his female counterpart, Tiamat. Egyptian religion has tales of how Isis works to restore the body of her deceased beloved Osiris. Fertility cults the world over play off the sexual union as symbolic of planting seed in the earth, a union of heaven and earth leading to perpetual renewal.

The God of the Abrahamic religions interrupts this dualism of male and female deities, for He is the creator and sole ruler of the universe. The masculine imagery of the Biblical narratives is an attempt to smother any resurgent interest in a consort for the deity, but oddly enough, in the Book of Wisdom, "Wisdom is from all eternity, playing before him at all times," as if Wisdom is somehow co-eternal with the Creator-God. Modern novels purport to set the record straight, by establishing some kind of divine or quasi-divine role for female protagonists. The Hebrew Bible has Eve, Sarah, Esther, and a number of other leading ladies, all of them clearly human. The Christian testament gives Mary, the mother of Jesus, a very central role, and women play important roles in the Gospel narratives, as is the case with Mary Magdalene, whom popular novels would like to identify as not just a disciple of Jesus and the author of a separate gospel, but as his wife or consort.

Most of the popular novels allude to some conspiracy to keep "Gnostic" texts and other early "gospels" from making it into the Canon of the New Testament. It took two centuries to determine what were to become the official and accepted texts, and there were many early documents lost to the sands of history. The primary controversy for most of the early writers centered around the nature of Christ: was he a human especially favored by God, was he God appearing in human form, or was he both God and man. This controversy is still very much alive in Christian circles today.

It may be tantalizing to think of Christ facing his Last Temptation, as in the novel by Kazantzakis, or to think in terms of Christ marrying and having a family, but to claim that there are any ancient documents to support such stories is the wildest of fantasies. Of *The DaVinci Code*, Sandra Miesel wrote: "In the end, Dan Brown has penned a poorly written, atrociously researched mess. How many lay readers will see the blazing inaccuracies put forward as buried truths?"

It is inevitable that novels will continue to be written about the characters of early Christianity, and in particular about the person of Jesus Christ. The European theologian Romano Guardini wrote: "Christ is the central figure of human history." While many would be inclined to give Christ a less exalted status than that, the figures of the New Testament lend themselves to endless re-interpretations, and imaginative reconstructions of early Christian history are inevitable. One might hope that some of them will do greater justice to the Biblical narratives, and to history, sacred, feminine, and as true as possible to interpreting "what really happened."

VIII-231
Consciousness Decoded

The liveliest debate in today's philosophical arena has to do with the nature of Consciousness. We know about consciousness from the inside, and we are aware that it seems to be incremental: as we move from sleep, to a dream stage, to half-wakefulness, to full consciousness, we know that some kind of continuum characterizes our experience. We use the word "unconscious" for the absence of awareness, although Freud insisted that, below the level of our conscious mind, memories we would rather forget slumbered, and perhaps could be coaxed to a level of awareness. If consciousness among humans is a continuum, what is the continuum of consciousness between "lower" animals and the human animal?

Consciousness Studies developed rapidly with the practice of Anesthesia, as doctors sought to explain how a patient could be put into such a deep sleep that no "awareness" of procedures was possible. The bizarre fact that one in a thousand patients does not totally lose awareness motivated neurobiologists to examine what all went on in the brain to produce conscious states, so that, for the benefit of those undergoing anesthesia, the elimination of Consciousness could be more accurately practiced.

With the advance of neurophysiology, much greater understanding developed of which areas of the brain were involved in visual perception, sensory analysis, and logical or artistic activity. This progress encouraged philosophers to ask questions about philosophy of mind and philosophy of human nature, and led to an ongoing and fruitful dialogue between scientists and philosophers. Congresses for "The Science of Consciousness" meet regularly and produce lively debates between and among scientists and philosophers.

Three basic points of view dominate these discussions. Group One is Reductionist, claiming that Consciousness is an entirely biological phenomenon. Given enough time, we will have a brain-based analysis of what Consciousness is, and how it works. Some reductionists maintain that human beings are incredibly complex machines, and that artificial intelligence will some day be able to duplicate all that human beings do, and do it better.

Group Two will have none of this. According to them, Consciousness is simply not reducible. It is one of the basic facts of reality, much like time, space, or gravity. For the religious-minded members of this group, Consciousness is what sets us apart from the rest of creation, and is perhaps the unique phenomenon that makes us Images of God.

Group Three says study it how we will, and examine it from whatever perspective, Consciousness is and will always remain, an impenetrable Mystery. We will never unlock the secrets of Consciousness. Just as using a microscope to study microscopes doesn't work, you cannot use Consciousness to study itself. Whether Consciousness is "an emergent property of matter," or an activity irradiated by immateriality, we can never hope to understand this quasi-miraculous event of Awareness, the mind-boggling activity of being fully conscious.

The conversation between these three Groups will continue and intensify. With every new discovery about how the brain works, Reductionists feel they are closer to a final explanation. As every new explanation reaches a dead end, those who claim that Consciousness is irreducible, and those who claim it is an impenetrable mystery, feel victory for their camps. Meanwhile, experiments in Consciousness continue, not just among scientists and philosophers, but also among the rest of us who exercise and analyze the contents of our consciousness on a daily basis. It is not just scientists in laboratories and philosophers in libraries who can make contributions to the understanding of Consciousness. We each do it everyday, just by being conscious, and reflecting on and exercising what clearly is one of the greatest mysteries in the entire universe, the wonderment of experience that is conscious of itself…

VIII-232
"Confusionism"

Among the many debates in Europe in the nineteenth century, none was more interesting than between those who favored monarchical absolutism and those who espoused more liberal, democratic views. It was during the time of Queen Victoria, an absolute monarch if ever there were one, that John Stuart Mill published *On Liberty,* defending the freedom of the individual from social or political control. The traditional absolutist vision appeared to be in open conflict with notions of individual freedom of thought and expression. Philosophers following Mill coined the term "pluralism" to suggest that perhaps there were many different ways of being a good citizen, a good neighbor, or a good human being.

Some philosophers are absolutists: they are convinced they have cornered the market for truth, and that with them philosophical history has come to an end. Georg Friedrich Hegel is the most absolutist of the absolutists, for he was convinced that with his system, philosophy had reached its zenith, and all that was necessary for philosophers in the future was to read and understand his work. That his absolutism was unsuccessful is evidenced by the absolute, but very different, rejections of his thought by both Kierkegaard and Marx.

The Pluralism of William James and the Perspectivism of Friedrich Nietzsche have dominated modern philosophy. No one has captured this better than anthropologist Richard Schweder, who confesses that he is a pluralist of "confusionist" persuasion. As he says, "A confusionist believes that the knowable world is incomplete if seen from any one point of view, incoherent if seen from all points of view at once, and empty if seen from 'nowhere in particular'."

Schweder rejects the radical relativists, for whom "everything is interesting but nothing is true." He also rejects the "uniformitarians" who wish to reject everyone else's vision but their own. This is the kernel of his pluralist vision: there are universally binding values, like justice, equality, beneficence, autonomy, sacrifice, liberty, loyalty, sanctity, duty. He is a pluralist because he believes there are many different ways of realizing these values, and that some cultures will place greater value on one of them than on some other one, as best exemplified by the conflict between liberty and equality.

At the conclusion of an ecumenical meeting, one participant said: "Not only have I understood other traditions better because of this conference, I have understood my own tradition much more clearly. I thought my path to the mountaintop was the only one. I now understand that there are many different paths, and that we can help each other on our different paths." The "absolutists" present were not favorably disposed to her conclusion, but for most of the participants, the pluralist vision made sense. There are universally binding values, but they are realized in different ways, according to a variety of needs and capacities. It is curious that pluralists make room at the table for absolutists, even if absolutists would like to push the pluralists away. That's what makes for an interesting, pluralist world, one in which there are bound to be serious and unresolved conflicts. To our vocabulary of useful words for cultural understanding, we might do well to add the term "Confusionism." It may be help to explain our current situation.

(Schweder's Essay, "Moral Maps," occurs in *Culture Matters,* Harrison & Huntington, editors, Basic Books, 2000.)

VIII-233
The Problem of Evil

My academic background was in the history of philosophy. My intention in this pursuit was not just to understand how one philosopher led to another, but to do philosophy, with the hope of solving philosophical problems. When I turned to teaching the history of philosophy, students would occasionally say: "I just want to understand a problem like free will, why do I need to understand what different philosophers had to say about it?" The fact is, you cannot "do" philosophy without doing the history of philosophy. You can sit down and think about the paradoxes of free will and determinism, or any other great philosophical problem, but why not do so while reaping the benefits of what the great minds of the past and present have to say about the problem?

Some historians of philosophy simply want to know what Plato or Kant said. That is a good starting point, but it is even more important to know what Plato or Kant *meant.* The guiding principle is: "it is not who has said it that matters, but the truth of what has been said." And while it

Gallows at Dachau

is important to be accurate in understanding precisely what philosophers have thought, it is even more important to see how successful they have been in solving the great problems philosophy poses.

The discipline of approaching a philosophical problem historically has served Susan Neiman extremely well. Her book, *Evil in Modern Thought: An Alternative History of Philosophy* is a masterful treatment of the problem of evil. The modern approach to the problem began with Leibniz, who said: "Everything happens for the best, in this, the best of all possible worlds." But in 1755, an earthquake struck Lisbon on a Sunday morning, killing thousands of people. How could this be the best of all possible worlds? Philosophers responded to Leibniz' theodicy by saying, since evil of this magnitude exists, either God is not benevolent, or He is not omnipotent. In the twentieth century, with the unspeakable evil of Auschwitz and the Holocaust, the prevalent alternative explanation became, that God does not exist.

Given the decidedly theological turn of the arguments, it became the provenance of theologians to discuss the issues. Theological reflection moved in three different directions: (1) God does not exist, and humans have invented stories of gods and goddesses to help make it through life; (2) God exists, but He is a God who is in process, who suffers along with us; (3) God is inscrutable: "My ways are not your ways, my thoughts are not your thoughts."

Historians, this time historians of theology, have done their best to state the problems as clearly as possible, in spite of all the complexities. For those with a passion for scholarship and an interest in the development of Christian doctrine, Jaroslav Pelikan's *The Christian Tradition*, in four volumes, is a good place to start. Writing from within the Jewish tradition, Abraham Joshua Heschel's *God In Search of Man: A Philosophy of Judaism* is brief and to the point. For a detailed analysis of the pagan and Christian roots of the evil of anti-Semitism, see James Carroll's *Constantine's Sword: The Church and the Jews.* The American-Spanish philosopher Santayana said: "Those who are ignorant of history are condemned to repeat it." Reading books may not do much to diminish the total amount of evil in the world. But reading one or more of the aforementioned books might provide some understanding of the evils that have been among the worst plagues of human history. The problem of evil is among the knottiest of philosophical problems, one that inevitably leads to theological discussion. It is a problem for which everyone needs to find a personal, albeit provisional, solution. And reading what great thinkers have said about the problem cannot help but assist us in finding our own provisional solutions.

VIII-234
Where Were the Philosophers?

Philosophy, the "quest for wisdom," should presumably make its practitioners "wise people." Where then, were the philosophers, and what were they doing, when darkness spread over Europe during the Nazi era? The greatest German philosopher of the twentieth century, Martin Heidegger, not only endorsed Hitler and Nazism, he could never quite bring himself to repent his pro-Nazi statements, nor did he apologize for his mistakes. As Rector of Freiburg University, on November 3, 1933, he addressed his students as follows: "The Fuhrer himself and he alone is German reality and its law, today and henceforth. Learn to realize ever more deeply: from now on each thing demands decision, and every action, accountability." Heidegger would eventually disappear into the crowd, would produce brilliant analyses of "the loss of the sense for Being that characterizes our generation," and would, before his death in 1976, begin introducing specifically religious concerns into his philosophy. His failure to revisit whatever it was that led him to support the Nazi regime condemns him to some degree of "inauthenticity," his own word for moral failure.

Heidegger was not alone in his support of the Nazi regime; Daniel Goldhagen's book, *Hitler's Willing Executioners,* profiles how so many "ordinary" Germans were swept along in the currents of racism and mass murder that characterized the Nazi years. In 1919, Hitler had written: "Rational anti-Semitism must be directed toward a methodical legal struggle. The final aim must be the deliberate removal of the Jews as a whole." The persistent question in books about the Holocaust is: How could a cultured and well-educated nation become captivated by Hitler's madness? Distinguished analysts of the Holocaust like Emil Fackenheim responded: "Without Jew-hatred in Christianity itself, Auschwitz, in the heart of Christian Europe, would have been impossible."

But what about philosophy and philosophers? Was there no one who stood up against the Nazi regime? Students in Munich, led by philosophy professor Kurt Huber, began distributing anti-Nazi pamphlets in 1943. They knew their action was futile; they knew they would be caught and brutally murdered, but they did it anyway. When Kurt Huber appeared in court before the *Volksgericht,* he said he acted out of responsibility for all Germany, that his action was not illegal, but a restoration of legality, and that this was so "because there were unwritten as well as written laws." Huber's story is told in *Die Weisse Rose,* "The White Rose," the code name for the group. A more complete documentation occurs in Inge Scholl's book, *Students Against Tyranny.*

Moralists are either Absolutists or Consequentialists, --absolutists claiming there are moral principals that always and everywhere must be adhered to, consequentialists claiming that the only criterion of morality remains the consequences of the action. Both groups can find support in Huber's actions. The consequences included torture and death, but the actions were performed in order to witness to the deeper truth of the categorical imperative, of always treating humanity as an end in itself and never as a mere means. The real consequences of the actions were that someone in Germany stood up for truth and decency.

Where were the philosophers? Heidegger may have been lost at the crossroads of his abstractions and racism, but Kurt Huber put his life, and the life of his students, on the line, for the sake of a moral absolute: you cannot be silent against the evils of your time, even if it costs your life. Hegel, the most influential of the nineteenth century German philosophers, had said: "The owl of Minerva (doing philosophy) spreads its wings only with the falling of the dusk." In the dusk of Nazism, Kurt Huber's actions offered a token of redemption for the shortcomings of other philosophers.

Dusk fell, and there were few to shine a beacon in the darkness, but that some did, redounds to the eternal credit of philosophy, as the passionate pursuit of truth.

VIII-235
Secularism and Religion

The dominant voices at philosophy conferences these days are not only secular, but also frequently dismissive of religious perspectives. A keynote speaker at a conference began by saying: "No one believes in any of that theological hokum anymore." A general summary of the situation might read as follows: "Most modern analytic philosophers are liberal, tolerant, agnostic, slightly left-wing, and rather tender-minded."

In terms of ethical foundations, one might propose that we need to establish a rational, "secular" ethic, so that all might agree on acceptable ethical practices, however or from wheresoever they drew their principles or motivations. This could furnish a basis for decision making in the arena of medical ethics, while also working in the "Public Square," where political decisions are made that involve all the members of a political community, whatever their religious beliefs or practices.

One may find the roots of a modern, secular ethic in the Enlightenment philosophers of the 18th and 19th centuries, figures as diverse as David Hume, Immanuel Kant, and John Stuart Mill. One of the most outspoken advocates of a secular ethic, however, was Dietrich Bonhoeffer, the Lutheran Pastor and theologian who was executed in 1945 by the Nazis for his involvement in the plot on Hitler's life.

Bonhoeffer began by saying that ethics is not some neat package of rules one may discover in a textbook, nor is the ethician someone who knows all the answers. "An ethic cannot be a book in which there is set out how everything in the world ought to be but unfortunately is not, and an ethicist cannot be someone who always knows better than others what is to be done and how it is to be done."

The puzzling question is this: Will the person with a secular ethic behave exactly like the person with religious convictions? Bonhoeffer hoped so, for he thought reason was the basis for the choice of right actions, as exemplified by his action against Hitler. The difference, said Bonhoeffer, is a matter of intention. Think of this text in the context of Nazi Germany, 1944: "Man is challenged to participate in the sufferings of God at the hands of a godless world. He must plunge himself into the life of the godless world, without attempting to gloss over its ungodliness with a veneer of religion. He must live a 'worldly' life, and so participate in the suffering of God. He may live a worldly life as one emancipated from all false religions and obligations. To be a Christian does not mean to be religious in a particular way, but to be truly human. It is not some religious act which makes a Christian what he is, but participation in the suffering of God in the life of the world."

Martin Buber and Emmanuel Levinas spoke in terms of human moral behavior as response to the call of a Transcendent God. H. Richard Niebuhr saw a religious ethic as an expression of responsibility: "Responsibility affirms—God is acting in all actions upon you. So respond to all actions upon you as to respond to his action."

Where does this leave us in the matter of secularism and religion? Will an agnostic or atheist philosopher respond in exactly the same way to a given moral dilemma as will someone who sees every moral choice as a response to the action of God? And will a secular, "reasonable" ethic really support exactly the same behavior that a person with religious motivations will pursue? Because the jurors are clearly at loggerheads on this issue, I put the ball in your court. One of the great moralists of the ancient world said: "Think on these things." It would be convenient if secular and religious moralists could agree on what constitutes praiseworthy moral behavior, but the issues on which secular moralists and religious-minded people disagree—issues such as abortion and homosexuality—show that such a harmonious situation is not likely to happen anytime soon. And there are very clear examples of how, given the same situation, the choice made by a secularist would be radically different from the choice made by a religious believer.

VIII-236
A Secular Response

The word "secular" has become very popular. The word means "of this time," and is often contrasted with what is "sacred," or religious. We are called a secular society, because we seem more concerned with what is going on here and now than with issues of eternal significance. The so-called "wall of separation between church and state" is taken by some as a commitment to a secular society, by others as an impediment to imparting religious truth. Politicians with enthusiasm for "faith-based initiatives" have sought to increase the influence of religious belief and practice in public life. On the other hand, theologians like Harvey Cox have claimed: "Secularization is an authentic consequence of biblical faith." A secular society permits a variety of religious practices, while insuring that those with no religious beliefs will not be disadvantaged. The Biblical injunction: "Render to Caesar what is Caesar's, and to God what is God's," is regarded as the charter for the separation of church and state. Geo-political issues, particularly those centered in the Middle East, have lent additional weight to the conviction that the political sphere itself should be "secular," and not controlled by religious convictions.

Can there be a wall of separation between church and state? Can we have a secular society, when most of the population has deeply held religious beliefs? Can a government be "secular" when religious denominations claim the right to tell their members how they must believe and vote on particular issues? Is there some benefit to being a secular society, or is that a model with built-in contradictions? It is in the realm of ethics that the divisions become most apparent.

John Rist's book *Real Ethics* is an excellent example of a theistic ethic. As Rist expressed it, "...for morality to function God must function both as final and (at least in great part) as efficient cause of our moral life" (257). Peter Singer's book *Practical Ethics* is an equally clear expression of a secular ethic. His book can be summarized in one line: "Actions are not wrong in themselves but only in terms of their results." Like most one-line reviews, that epitomizes Singer's consequentialism, but misses the larger context. The guiding principle of the book is that "ethics is not relative or subjective." Singer has his absolutes: what is good is always good, what is just is always just. Singer assumes we have some basic insights into right and wrong, and that in every moral decision, there is a rational basis for making the right choice. "The consequences of an action vary according to the circumstances in which it is performed. Hence a utilitarian can never be properly accused of a lack of realism, or of a rigid adherence to ideals in defiance of practical experience. The utilitarian will judge lying bad in some circumstances, and good in others, depending on its consequences"(3). The "absolute" is that good is to be done, evil avoided.

In the circumstance of being asked where your children are by someone intent on murdering them, the right thing to do is to deceive. The moral onus here lies in being able to determine what circumstances justify deception. So too in every other circumstance: the moral absolute is "to do the right thing," which may not produce results beneficial to the agent. I cannot lie just to get myself out of a jam; I cannot claim innocence when I know I am guilty. "Consequentialism" does not mean producing consequences temporarily favorable to the doer, but consequences that are beneficial to society in the long term.

Secularism and consequentialism appear to go hand in hand, and to be in opposition to the sacred absolutes offered by religious perspectives. But just as the presumed wall of separation between church and state has many openings, the secular and the sacred are not necessarily in opposition to each other. The principled consequentialism of ethicists like Peter Singer may have greater moral depth, and a better hold on some moral absolutes, than his opponents would suspect. Just as there can be harmony between faith and reason, there can be considerable harmony between the ethical visions of secular consequentialists and religious true believers, and the benefits of being a "secular" society clearly outweigh the disadvantages.

VIII-237
Ethics, The Tax Code, And Cheating

Usually while sitting in a restaurant conversations at other tables are an annoyance, but a conversation about income taxes may well be hard to ignore. Imagine hearing something like: "My brokerage sent me wrong numbers on a stock I sold last year, and I wound up declaring a loss. I never thought about it until I was cleaning my files yesterday, and I found that instead of a $3,000 loss, I had gained that much. My taxes were all filed, nobody would ever know, and if I'm ever audited, I got the brokerage account to back me up." If you were there, you might respond: "You can't do that. What if everybody mocked the system like that? We'd become as corrupt as countries where tax collection is a joke." The repartee would continue: "What if everybody did it? Everybody does do it. The tax system is so complicated, even when you ask tax lawyers, or the IRS, they come up with different answers. Besides, think of all the big companies who have fudged their accounts. Why should I inconvenience myself for what was an honest mistake, when the big players get loopholes passed especially for them by their Congressmen?"

Cheating on income tax is just the tip of the iceberg. Surveys find that 75% of high school students have cheated on a test within the past year. All kinds of "reasons" are given for cheating in high school: Everybody does it; it's only the G.P.A. that matters, it doesn't matter how you got it; all the sources of information you need are out there on the internet, so you really don't have to remember anything anymore, etc. The bottom line seems to be that dishonesty is so widely practiced, being honest would place you irreparably behind the legions of the dishonest that would finish ahead of you in every category.

Ethicists are either "absolutists" or "consequentialists." The absolutists say there are moral rules which must be obeyed if people are to become virtuous, society is to survive, commerce practiced, and order prevail. The problem with Absolutism is apparent inflexibility. Consequentialists say having rules is all well and good, but it is the results of your actions that determine their real moral character, not some abstract system of rules. The problem with consequentialism is the danger of shortsightedness. One whose ethical horizon is limited to immediate consequences is in danger of missing the larger picture.

The world of cheating students and corrupt business people is an example of consequentialism gone astray. The real long term consequences of cheating on taxes, on exams, and anywhere anyone can get away with it, is not only the destruction of personal integrity, but with it the collapse of society, government, and the hope for preserving law and order. "Absolutism" may not be very popular because of the very "absoluteness" with which rules are proclaimed. Fanatics of every sort have absolutes they wish to impose on everyone else. Consequentialism appropriately practiced leads to an establishment of "rules" or "contracts" that are necessary if society is to flourish. It is not just that "honesty is the best policy" is a comfortable and familiar formula, but the fact that honesty makes society possible, and makes the life of the individual practitioner of honesty more coherent. The poet had it right when he said: "Oh what a tangled web we weave, when we first practice to deceive."

Whether dealing with the tax code, or with students who seem to have good reasons for cheating, it is clear that some kind of code of ethics must be established. The fact of the matter is, Absolutists must come to see that, as important as rules are, there may be exceptions to every rule. Consequentialists must accept that, if society is to flourish, the true consequences of actions must be understood—which inevitably leads to the establishment and observance of appropriate rules. So it comes down to this: if you should happen to overhear a restaurant conversation about taxes, or hear students discuss the benefits of cheating, what kind of counsel will you offer, and on what basis?

VIII-238
Women, and Philosophy

Why are there no famous women philosophers? Whether it is Socrates in Greece, Immanuel Kant in Germany, or John Dewey in America, the doing of philosophy appears to have been a male prerogative. A male philosopher, John Stuart Mill, with his 1869 essay *The Subjection of Women*, played a significant role in the feminine revolution. Mill wrote: "The legal subordination of one sex to the other is wrong in itself, and now one of the chief hindrances to human improvement...it ought to be replaced by a principle of perfect equality." While a number of women took up various feminist causes, best exemplified by those who sought the right to vote, no one was more influential philosophically than Simone de Beauvoir. Her 1949 book *The Second Sex* may be one of the most significant books of the twentieth century. Her initial philosophical problem is the nature of self-knowledge, and the importance of "the other" for anyone's self-knowledge. She begins her critique of historical male dominance with the observation that "woman is man's Other, and the self-understanding of both depends on it." Much of the feminist literature of the mid-twentieth century was derivative from or dependent upon the charter for feminism that Simone de Beauvoir established.

A variety of women philosophers have flourished within the academy over the last fifty years. Carole Gilligan's *In A Different Voice* suggested that philosophy would benefit from the activity of female philosophers, because women who do philosophy would have distinctly different concerns. Philosophy as practiced by women would be more personal, more humane, more centered in the nature and nurture of human relationships. Medical ethics has, accordingly, benefited from the contributions of women philosophers.

As women's voices have been heard more frequently in the academy, and as women make up a progressively larger share of the university professoriate, their voices and their distinctive issues are heard ever more clearly. Nevertheless, philosophical indices continue to list male philosophers more frequently, and anthologies of modern philosophy hardly ever include female authors.

It is puzzling that Iris Murdoch, philosopher and novelist, does not have greater popularity. She did not see herself as a woman doing philosophy, but regarded herself simply as a philosopher who happened to be a woman. She did not go out of her way to espouse particularly feminine issues, for she regarded such matters as subsets of the larger philosophical problems of human relationships. She was born in 1919, read "Classics" at Oxford, held important British and United Nation's Relief Organization positions during and after the war, and became a "fellow" at Oxford in 1948. After years of publishing noteworthy philosophical papers, she turned to writing novels, in the hope of presenting her philosophical ideas to a larger audience. By the time of her death in 1999, she had published twenty-five novels, several plays, and two extremely important philosophical texts. Her novel *The Philosopher's* Pupil shows how artfully she could blend the literary genius of the novelist with the traditional concerns of the philosopher. Her works in philosophy are much more readable than almost any other modern British philosopher. *Metaphysics as a Guide to Morals* was published in 1992. Her 1971 book *The Sovereignty of Good* is a masterpiece of philosophical reflection.

Four tantalizing quotes from that book should be enough to showcase her importance. She wrote: "...few artists achieve a vision of the real." She turned to writing novels because she thought she could convey more "reality" in novels than she could in philosophical essays. Sidestepping the subjectivism of the post-modernists, she sought to anchor her realism in the objectivity of knowledge and the authenticity of her artistic vision. "For both the collective and individual salvation of the human race, art is doubtless more important than philosophy, and literature most important of all." From her studies in Greek literature, she was aware that far more people have read Homer than have read Aristotle. She was convinced that a philosophical spirit pervaded every great work of art, and that self-knowledge was at the root of both good philosophy and great art. "To do philosophy is to explore one's own temperament, and yet at the same time to attempt to discover the truth." Lastly, she saw moral issues as the real heart of philosophy, and it was not without some feminist irony that she asked: "What is a good man like? How can we make ourselves morally better? These are questions the philosopher should try to answer. We realize on reflection that we know little about good men." She was capable of great Socratic irony, and made distinctively subtle plugs for feminist philosophy.

Women in philosophy? With philosophers of the caliber of Simone de Beauvoir and Iris Murdoch, the subjection of women, at least in philosophy, is clearly over.

VIII-239
Ayn Rand, Iris Murdoch, and Truth

Ayn Rand is regarded as an American version of the very British Iris Murdoch, and indeed they do have similarities. Both had clear philosophical convictions, and both wrote novels in order to convey their ideas to a wider public. Both called themselves "realists" or "objectivists," both were atheists, and both regarded the discussion of moral matters as the primary task of philosophy. Their differences however, leave them not just a continent apart, but worlds apart.

While *Atlas Shrugged* is Rand's most popular novel, her most important book is *The Virtue of Selfishness: A New Concept of Egoism.* In it, she offers a passionate plea for ethics: "Ethics is not a mystic fantasy—nor a social convention—nor a dispensable, subjective luxury, to be switched or discarded in any emergency. Ethics is an *objective, metaphysical necessity of man's survival*—not by the grace of the supernatural nor of your neighbors nor of your whims, but by the grace of reality and the nature of life." (From "The Objectivist Ethics," p. 23.) Rand has a unique vision of what a virtue ethics might be: it is whatever contributes to one's self-realization, and altruism has no place in this pursuit. She is "libertarian," in the sense that she sees the sole legitimate role of government as maximizing the liberty of citizens. There will be an invisible hand that will control society's affairs, and one has no need to rush to the aid of others unless it contributes to one's own self-development. In *The Virtue of Selfishness* she wrote: "The proper method of judging when or whether one should help another person is by reference to one's own rational self-interest and one's own hierarchy of values: the time, money or effort one gives or the risks one takes should be proportionate to the value of the person in relation to one's own happiness." (p.45).

In terms of political philosophy, she agrees with John Stuart Mill that there are severe limits to what government should do. "The only proper, *moral* purpose of a government is to protect man's rights, which means: to protect him from physical violence—to protect his right to his own life, to his own liberty, to his own *property* and to the pursuit of his own happiness. Without property rights, no other rights are possible." (p. 33, "The Objectivist Ethics.") From the capitalist vision of making a profit, she derives the foundation of her objectivist ethics: "The principle of *trade* is the only rational ethical principle for all human relationships, personal and social, private and public, spiritual and material. It is the principle of *justice,"* (*Ibid*, p. 31.) In her vision, you form relationships based on the expectation of mutual gain. Friendship becomes a kind of business relationship, in which both partners expect to make some profit. The two pillars of Ayn Rand's philosophy are: unregulated capitalism, and the pursuit of rational self-interest.

Iris Murdoch wrote, in *The Sovereignty of Good,* "I assume that human beings are naturally selfish and that human life has no external point or goal." But there, any similarity she has to Ayn Rand abruptly stops. In the absence of God, she still sought some objective, transcendent standard for human behavior. She interpreted life as the pursuit of a mysterious goodness that pervades reality. This "goodness" is elusive, and the perception of it resembles the comment of the Supreme Court Justice with respect to obscenity: "I know it when I see it." Murdoch wrote: "Good is indefinable…because of the infinite difficulty of the task of apprehending a magnetic but inexhaustible reality."

While the works of Ayn Rand are very appealing, there is a depth to the writings of Iris Murdoch that is inexhaustible. *The Sovereignty of Good* is available in an inexpensive paperback, as is Ayn Rand's *Atlas Shrugged.* Both writers have something to teach us, both provided high quality examples of women doing philosophy. Their works have a place among the classics of modern literature. Plato was the first philosopher to exhibit literary skills equal to his philosophy. Rand and Murdoch are among the most recent. If one begins the study of philosophy with some reading of Plato, one would do well to embellish and make current one's philosophical readings with the reading of Rand and Murdoch. And how thoroughly Platonic is this summary statement from *The Sovereignty of Good*: "Love…is the unmistakable sign that we are spiritual creatures, attracted by excellence and made for the Good. It is a reflection of the warmth and light of the sun."(100).

Epilogue

IX-240
From a Philosophical Point of View

As we approach the end of this "doing philosophy as if philosophy mattered," or, "the kinds of philosophical thoughts appropriate for everyday life," some form of summary statement is appropriate. We begin by using a form that Wittgenstein used in *Philosophical Investigations*.

For philosophers, all problems are philosophical problems. And for philosophers, a logical form of argument that appears almost mathematical is the norm. This is how a summary expression in such form might look.

1. All problems are ultimately philosophical problems.

1.1 Philosophical problems admit to at least these four different forms of resolution:

1.1.2 Wittgenstein: no serious problem should be talked about, for it cannot be solved.

1.1.3 Heidegger: Since we dwell poetically upon the earth, we must let Being speak, but we should not expect clear answers.

1.1.4 John Rist: Apart from acceptance of a moral and transcendental realism, all discussions about politics and morality are simply catalogues of personal preferences.

1.1.5 Karl Marx: the philosopher's role is not knowledge of the world, but agitation for societal progress. "The important thing is not to know the world: the important thing is to change it."

2. Whatsoever form of resolution you follow, *the nature of morality* and *the structure of society* are the key philosophical problems.

2.1 Pure Relativism: if it works for you, that's fine. Don't impose your convictions on others.

2.2 The "Sentimentalism" of Hume: There are "moral sentiments" that are quite successful at getting most people to do what they should.

2.3 The "Rationalism" of Kant: Reason is the ultimate arbiter of morality and how society should be structured. There are categorical imperatives (statements about how everyone should act) that are best summarized as: "Treat all other humans as ends-in-themselves, never as mere means."

2.4 The "Contractualism" of Hobbes: Every society is a "social contract," wherein contractors agree upon a common good, and what needs to be done to reach that common good. This contract designates rights and duties.

2.5 The "Utilitarianism" of Bentham: Society-whether local or global- is a matter of establishing "the greatest good for the greatest number," and the execution of this should be the primary work of some organization like a United Nations.

3. There is no escaping the fact that *culture matters*, and the values with which you are raised will do much to determine your moral and political convictions.

3.1 On the one hand, Richard Schweder's proclamation should be taken seriously: "I am a pluralist, and I believe in universalism without conformity: I believe there are universally binding values—but they are diverse, heterogeneous, irreducible to any one common denominator."

3.2 On the other hand, the admonition of Samuel P. Huntington should be kept in mind: Multiculturalism or pluralism will not work. America, unless it forswears pluralism and finds its cultural core (of morally absolute values) will not endure as a coherent society. Worldwide, a clash of civilizations is inevitable unless one cultural model—that of the west—prevails.

4. Do not overlook the insight of Mahatma Gandhi: There are many paths to the mountaintop. Such an assertion does not deny the existence of the mountaintop, nor the importance of getting there. Climbing on one route should not hinder the success of climbers on some other route. Climbers who stick to one route may get there most readily. All climbers will be successful, but some paths may be better than others.

4.1 If today, prosperity, democracy and social justice remain out of reach for a substantial majority of the world's people, that is a call to action, not a cause for pessimism.

4.2 The Greek word *oikumene* means "the inhabited world." Political discourse must become "ecumenical," in the sense not only of dealing

416

with all the world's inhabitants but also in the sense of seeking to make all human beings citizens of one world, and giving them a sense of being "at home" in that world, and a neighbor to every other world citizen. We should learn to become "cosmopolitan,"--that is, citizens of the one world.

5. Philosophy must become common language, and part of the everyday discourse of everyday people. It loses its way, and loses its proper audience, when it becomes distant, artificial, and merely academic. Philosophy is not an abstraction, but a way of life.

IX-241
A Map of the Ancient Philosophical World

Pre-Socratics: **Atomists:**
    Protagoras   **SOCRATES**   **Democritus**
    Heraclitus   **PLATO**   **Leucippus**
    Parmenides

ARISTOTLE

Stoics and Skeptics: **Neoplatonists:**
    Lucretius, Epicurus   **Philo Judaeus**
    Marcus Aurelius   **Plotinus**
    Epictetus   **Augustine**

Philosophy began as a separately identifiable discipline somewhere in the Mediterranean world about the time of Thales, about 585 Before the Common Era. The word may have been coined by Pythagoras, in the same century, meaning "the love of wisdom." Protagoras is taken as the model "sophist," meaning one who sought the appearance of wisdom, not necessarily wisdom itself. Socrates becomes the model for doing philosophy: ask questions until you either reach a satisfactory answer, or have disproved all the commonly accepted answers. The *Dialogues of Plato* are the first archetypal philosophical documents, purportedly conversations in which bad arguments are revealed while better and more convincing arguments are proposed. Aristotle was a pupil of Plato's for twenty years, and developed a philosophical system with answers to the major philosophical problems Plato had posed, some of those answers espousing points of view quite opposite to what Plato had taught. Aristotle wrote texts on Logic, Rhetoric, Poetics, Ethics, Politics, Physics, and Metaphysics.

In the following centuries, different philosophical schools developed, most notably the Stoicism which was very popular in the Roman Empire, and the revised versions of Platonism characteristic of the last great pagan philosopher, Plotinus, and the first great Christian philosopher, Augustine.

The ancient world set the agenda for the doing of philosophy. It is difficult, if not impossible, to "do" philosophy, absent familiarity with the great thinkers of classical antiquity.

IX-242
A Map of the Medieval Philosophical World

Boethius
John Scotus Erigena
Anselm
Peter Abelard

> **Al-Ghazzal**
> **Avicenna**
> **Averroes**

> > **Ibn Gabirol**
> > **Moses Maimonides**

> > > **Albertus Magnus**
> > > **Thomas Aquinas**
> > > **Bonaventure**
> > > **John Duns Scotus**

> > > > **William of Ockham**
> > > > **Meister Eckhart**
> > > > **Nicholas Cusanus**
> > > > **Marsilio Ficino**

There was a presumption that the years between the death of Augustine and the rise of Descartes were devoid of genuine philosophical speculation, so dominant were the religious convictions of the medieval writers. The truth is, modern philosophy owes many of its problems to the philosophical reflections of the medieval theologians. The nature and existence of God, free will and moral responsibility, and the logic necessary to think through such problems, were persistent problems for Jewish, Moslem, and Christian writers throughout the Middle Ages. Boethius (480-524) wrote *The Consolation of Philosophy* while he was in prison, and in the book he highlighted what would be the persistent problems of medieval thought: what is the purpose of the universe, how do you find happiness, the compatibility of human freedom with God's foreknowledge, how to understand the goodness of God, and the contrast between time and eternity. Boethius was a channel of Greek thought to the Christian Middle Ages, but Syrian and Arabic writers, who wished to make use of Plato and Aristotle to help understand their Moslem faith, were much more important. Al-Ghazzal, Avicenna, and Averroes were very important Moslem writers, seeking to reconcile the truths revealed in the Koran, with the wisdom of the philosophers. A number of Jewish writers, most notably Ibn Gabirol and Moses Maimonides, created remarkable syntheses of Biblical Revelation and the insights of the philosophers.

While Anselm and Abelard reflected on the nature of God and the exercise of reason, the golden age of Christian Scholasticism began with Albertus Magnus, Bonaventure, and Thomas Aquinas, whose *Summa Theologiae* is a veritable summary or encyclopedia of the philosophical and theological wisdom of the time.

With William of Ockham and Meister Eckhart, faith in reason was replaced by faith in faith and skepticism about the capacity of reason to help one understand faith. The decline of philosophical speculation was in full force. Modern Philosophy began when skepticism was rampant, and Descartes' labors were regarded as "a great blockade-lifting task," attempting to restore reason to its rightful eminence.

IX-243
A Map of the Modern Philosophical World

Rationalists		Empiricists
Descartes		**Locke**
Spinoza	**Hobbes**	**Berkeley**
Leibniz		**Hume**

KANT

IDEALISM	POSITIVISM	PRAGMATISM	EXISTENTIALISM
Fichte	Moore	Pierce	Kierkegaard
Hegel	Russell	James	Nietzsche
Marx	Wittgenstein	Dewey	Sartre
	Ayer	Rorty	Camus
			Heidegger
			Buber

(The Post-modern Philosophical World)

Kuhn-Foucault-Lyotard-Derrida

"Reality is a social construct"
"There is nothing outside the text."
"There is nothing good or bad, but thinking makes it so."
"There is no truth, only play: the play of words and meaning."
"When I use a word, it means what I want it to mean, that's all."

"Modern" philosophy begins with the rationalism of Descartes. "I think, therefore I am" is one truth of which Descartes can be absolutely certain, and, proceeding like proofs in geometry, an entire philosophy is developed, based on ideas that are "clear and distinct," and beyond all doubt. Leibniz and Spinoza build similar, quasi-mathematical philosophies, while British thinkers like Locke and Hume seek down to earth, empirical evidence for every truth to which they will give assent.

The battle between rationalists and empiricists is mediated by the central figure of modern philosophy, Immanuel Kant. If there is truth, it must be because the mind brings certain categories to things, and what we know, is really what we have made up. Fichte and Hegel develop the "idealist" response to Kant, and the antitheses to Hegel take many forms. The positivism of Moore and Russell and Ayer becomes a dominant form for philosophy in the twentieth century. The typically American response is pragmatism, where the "cash value" of a statement is the consequences it produces in the real world. The theme common to the existentialist response is that you are what you make of yourself; since existence precedes essence, you are condemned to the freedom of choosing what you will be. For Sartre, since there is no God, there are no divine ideas, and hence no natures or essences that determine the way things have to be. In response, the religious existentialism of Martin Buber maintains that at all times, you know in your heart that you need God more than anything, and that human existence only has meaning in the light of the Divine Existence. Modern philosophy is practiced in dialogue form, an unending dialogue of diverse points of view, diverse starting points, and diverse, and often irreconcilable, conclusions.

Post-modernism is one inevitable consequence of the Kantian revolution. If truth is a construct of the mind, there is no "reality" that determines truth or falsity, only the subjective judgments of individual perceivers. In the attempt to overcome post-modernism, contemporary philosophy looks for new ways of re-interpreting the traditions, and searches for the untapped mother lode in those traditions. The laboratory of philosophy is its history, and every philosopher mentioned here leaves behind a treasure trove of rich ores that can be helpful in finding new ways out of old philosophical dilemmas. Philosophy always buries its undertakers, and every generation must discover for itself its own distinctive philosophical problems, and its own distinctive solutions. History, however, provides both guidance and direction.

This book is both summary and prologue: summary of the author's life-long philosophical reflections, and prologue to the reading of the great masterpieces of philosophy. There is no substitute for reading the great works of philosophy, from *The Dialogues of Plato* to the *Philosophical Investigations* of Wittgenstein. The Bibliography cites contemporary works that the author has found helpful in understanding the great works of philosophy. It is my hope that, after reading the classics and the commentators, the reader will appreciate that the quest for wisdom is a lifelong experience, with innumerable rewards along the way. This book is simply a dipping of one toe in the great ocean of wisdom. As with every ocean voyage, the horizons are infinite, and each day brings its distinctive rewards.

Bibliography

History of Philosophy

Gilson, E. *The Unity of Philosophical Experience.* Ignatius Press, 1999.
Kenny, A. *A Brief History of Western Philosophy,* Blackwell, 1998.
Kolak, D. *Lovers of Wisdom,* Wadsworth, 1997.
Magee, B. *The Story of Philosophy,* DK Books, 2001
Tarnas, R. *The Passion of the Western Mind,* Ballantine, 1993.

Ethics

Blackburn, S. *Being Good,* Oxford, 2001.
LaFolette, H. (ed.) *The Blackwell Guide to Ethical Theory,* Blackwell, 2003.
Rist, J. *Real Ethics: Rethinking the Foundations of Morality,* Cambridge, 2002.
Shafer-Landau, R. *Whatever Happened to Good and Evil?,* Oxford, 2004.
Singer, P. *Rethinking Life and Death,* St. Martin's, 1994.
Singer, P. (ed.) *A Companion to Ethics,* Blackwell, 1997.
Sterba, J. (ed.) *Ethics: The Big Questions,* Blackwell, 1999.

Theology

Armstrong, K. *A History of God,* Ballantine, 1994.
Buber, M. *I and Thou,* Touchstone, 1996.
Buber, M. *Eclipse of God,* Harper and Row, 1957.
Kenny, A. *The God of the Philosophers,* Oxford, 2001.
Kenny, A. *The Unknown God,* Continuum, 2004.

Philosophy
Hadot, P. *Philosophy as a Way of Life,* Blackwell, 1998.
Sample, R., Mills, C., & Sterba, J. (eds.) *Philosophy: The Big Questions,* Blackwell, 2004
Bammel, G. Website for New Philosophical Review: http://home.earthlink.net/~ebammel/philosophy

Buddhism
Hagen, S. *Buddhism, Plain and Simple,* Broadway, 1997.
Hahn, Thich Nhat, *Peace is Every Step,* Bantam, 1992.

Other
Bammel, G. & Burrus-Bammel, LeiLane, *Leisure and Human Behavior,* Brown & Benchmark, 3rd Edition, 1996.
Fackenheim, E. *To Mend the World: Foundations of Post-Holocaust Jewish Thought,* Schocken, 1989.
Harrison, L & Huntington, S., Eds. *Culture Matters: How Values Shape Human Progress.* Basic Books, 2000.
Neiman, S. *Evil in Modern Thought,* Princeton, 2002.
Murdoch, I. *The Sovereignty of Good,* Routledge, 2001.
Murdoch, I., *Metaphysics As A Guide to Morals,* Penguin, 1992.